10688100

INVENTING PERSONALITY

PERSONALITY

Gordon Allport and the Science of Selfhood

INVENTING PERSONALITY

Gordon Allport and the Science of Selfhood

Ian A. M. Nicholson

American Psychological Association • Washington, DC

YEARY LIBRARY
LAREDO COMM. COLLEGE
LAREDO, TEXAS

Copyright © 2003 by the American Psychological Association. All rights reserved.
Except as permitted under the United States Copyright Act of 1976, no part of this
publication may be reproduced or distributed in any form or by any means, or stored in a
database or retrieval system, without the prior written permission of the publisher.

Published by
American Psychological Association
750 First Street, NE
Washington, DC 20002
www.apa.org

To order
APA Order Department
P.O. Box 92984
Washington, DC 20090-2984

Tel: (800) 374-2721; Direct: (202) 336-5510
Fax: (202) 336-5502; TDD/TTY: (202) 336-6123
On-line: www.apa.org/books/
E-mail: order@apa.org

In the U.K., Europe, Africa, and the Middle East, copies may be ordered from
American Psychological Association
3 Henrietta Street
Covent Garden, London
WC2E 8LU England

Typeset in Goudy by EPS Group Inc., Easton, MD

Printer: Data Reproductions, Auburn Hills, MI
Cover Designer: Naylor Design, Washington, DC
Technical/Production Editor: Rosemary Moulton

The opinions and statements published are the responsibility of the authors, and such
opinions and statements do not necessarily represent the policies of the American Psychological Association.

Library of Congress Cataloging-in-Publication Data
Nicholson, Ian A. M.
    Inventing personality: Gordon Allport and the science of selfhood / Ian A. M.
Nicholson
      p. cm.
    Includes bibliographical references and index.
    ISBN 1-55798-929-x
      1. Allport, Gordon W. (Gordon Willard), 1897–1967.   2. Psychologists—United
States—Biography.   3. Personality   I. Title.
    BF109.A54 N53 2003
    155.2′092—dc21

                                                                        2002033217

British Library Cataloguing-in-Publication Data
A CIP record is available from the British Library.

Printed in the United States of America
First Edition

BF
109
'A54
N53
2003

APR 0 5 2004

CONTENTS

ILLUSTRATIONS

ACKNOWLEDGMENTS

Writing this book has given me an added appreciation for something that I learned in my first contact with the history of psychology: The production of knowledge—scientific or historical—is a social process. My initial interest in Gordon Allport and the history of personality psychology was nurtured in the stimulating intellectual environment of York University's History and Theory of Psychology Program. I would like to thank my advisor Raymond Fancher for his friendly counsel and strong support. I am also grateful to Kurt Danziger and Michael Lamphier for their astute advice. While at York, I derived a great deal of support and inspiration from the graduate students who participated in York's Graduate Colloquia in the History of Psychology. I would like to extend special thanks to Paul Ballantyne, Adrian Brock, Geoff Bunn, Gail Donaldson, Jennifer Macdonald, Rachel Rosner, Alexandra Rutherford, and Peter Shermer.

My work on Allport was also aided by a number of people outside the York community. I am grateful to Nicole Barenbaum for her sage advice, scholarly generosity, and careful reading of many drafts. I would also like to thank Fran Cherry, Ben Harris, Henry Minton, Sam Parknovick, Wade Pickren, and Andrew Winston for their thoughtful commentary and encouragement over the years. Friends and colleagues at the University of Prince Edward Island were an unflagging source of inspiration in the long process of transforming a manuscript into a book. I am grateful to Irene Gammel, Scott Lee, Neb Kujundnzic, Nicole Neatby, Henry Srebnik, and Mark Yaniszewski. I am particularly indebted to my friend J. Paul Boudreau, who spent countless hours discussing all things psychological with me and who consistently promoted a message of research in a context of heavy teaching responsibilities. My colleagues in the Department of Psychology at St. Thomas University have helped see the manuscript through the final stages. My thanks to Del Brodie, Kim Fenwick, Tom Fish, Ian Fraser, John

Gillis, Nancy Higgins, Doug McKenzie-Mohr, and Doug Vipond for their interest and support. I would also like to express my appreciation of the editorial staff at APA Books. I am particularly grateful to Susan Reynolds for her input into the stages of the manuscript and to Anne Woodworth, Jennifer Macomber, and Rosemary Moulton for their attentiveness, hard work, and editorial acumen. Writing this book would have been impossible without the cooperation of Robert and Ardys Allport. The Allports graciously answered my many questions, and they generously shared with me a number of important unpublished documents about Allport's early life. To the Allport family, I would like to extend my sincerest thanks.

My research was made a good deal easier by a doctoral fellowship from the Social Science and Research Council of Canada and by a faculty research grant from the University of Prince Edward Island Research. These funds enabled me to make use of a number of excellent archives. I would like to thank the archival staffs of the American Philosophical Society, the History of American Psychology Archives at the University of Akron, Dartmouth College, Harvard University, and the State Historical Society of Wisconsin.

Throughout this project, my family has been a source of support and inspiration. I give thanks to my father John, my brother Andrew, and Brian and Margaret Prior for their encouragement and interest. My biggest debt and warmest thanks go to my partner, Suzanne Prior. Suzanne has lived with this project from the outset, and her love and support have helped me through those difficult moments that confront most authors. Over the years she has taken valuable time away from her own academic career to bring her editorial savvy and scholarly insight into innumerable drafts. Suzanne also helped me deal with the untimely loss of my mother, Margaret Rose Nicholson, which occurred as the manuscript was nearing completion. My mother was not an academic person, but she was a person of character, and her love and faith helped me immeasurably. This book is dedicated to her memory.

INVENTING
PERSONALITY

Gordon Allport and the Science of Selfhood

1

INTRODUCTION

One of the outstanding events in psychology of the present century has been the discovery of personality.

—Gordon Allport, 1938[1]

The psychologist's own personality, his training and his particular interests and dispositions are unwittingly reflected in all that he does, and have to be taken into account in evaluating his contributions to psychology.

—Philip Vernon, 1933[2]

In 1919, physician Richard Clarke Cabot commented on the poor state of "personality study." Addressing a group of psychiatric social workers, Cabot told his audience that the field was in its infancy. "The social worker is liable to disappointment when she tries to find textbooks on personality study," he remarked. "The study of personality does not exist, either as a science or an art, written down."[3] Although his remarks pertained to psychiatry, Cabot could have made a similar comment about "personality" psychology. Between 1880 and 1920, personality was not regarded as a basic psychological category that warranted special attention. None of the first generation of American psychologists identified themselves as personality psychologists, nor was it discussed at the annual meetings of the American Psychological Association (APA). In E. G. Boring's 1920 study of the research interests of APA members, personality was not included as a scholarly category, nor was it included in Fernberger's 1928 study.[4] On those occasions when personality was discussed, it was usually in the context of bizarre clinical phenomena. In *The Principles of Psychology*, William James devoted several pages to a discussion of the "alternating personality."[5] Morton Prince's 1905 book, *The Dissociation of Personality*, continued the trend into the 20th century.

Unable to register much of an academic pulse in 1919, the field of personality came to life in the 1920s and 1930s. With surprising suddenness, the category became salient in contexts that extended well beyond the domains of abnormal psychology and psychiatry. Psychologists working in the fields of education, personnel selection, applied psychology, and criminology began to view personality as central to their work, and numerous calls were issued to "bend our efforts to making a scientific analysis of personality and to developing tests for the social and dynamic traits."[6] A number of scholars responded to these appeals, and by the early 1930s interest in personality was so extensive that it threatened to eclipse more traditional psychological categories: "Could anyone have predicted, even as late as a decade ago," psychologist A. A. Roback wondered in 1932, "the avalanche which bids fair to sweep away from the foreground nearly all interests in American psychology, to the exclusion of personality measurement?"[7]

Roback's fears proved to be unfounded, but enthusiasm for personality remained high, and by the early 1930s psychologists began to develop an academic infrastructure to sustain their interest.[8] In 1932, the first psychological journal specializing in personality research was launched, and in 1934 *Psychological Abstracts* began to index a separate category for personality. Undergraduate courses on personality began to appear in the 1920s, and by 1938, 31% of 157 American universities and colleges surveyed offered at least one course in personality. Introductory psychology textbooks followed this example; a 1939 study showed that 10 of 11 leading texts had at least one chapter devoted to the topic of personality. By the late 1930s, the field of personality had come of age and was generally recognized as having a "respectable house of its own on a main thoroughfare of psychology."[9]

Of the many American psychologists who experienced the fascination of personality in the early 20th century, Gordon Allport was the most influential. Known as the "patron saint" of personality, he did more than any other scholar to establish personality as a category of mainstream psychological research.[10] His 1921 literature review on the topic was the first of its kind, and his 1922 dissertation is widely viewed as the first psychology dissertation on personality.[11] He taught one of the first psychology courses on personality in 1924, and his 1937 textbook, *Personality: A Psychological Interpretation*, was a pioneering work and a key marker of the field's legitimacy.[12] Prolific and persuasive, Allport was elected president of APA in 1939—the first personality psychologist so honored. A 1951 survey by APA's Division of Clinical and Abnormal psychology placed him second only to Freud as a personality theorist of direct value to clinical work.[13]

Standing at the center of one of American psychology's major categories, Allport did much to establish the language of American psychology. This book explores his rise to prominence and examines the history of the personality category he championed. Although Allport's early career is examined in considerable detail, this book is not the full-length biography that he richly deserves. I have focused on the first half of his career, from his birth in 1897 to his election as president of the APA in 1939. This time frame does not completely contain the theoretical issues under consideration, but it does represent a significant period in the history of American psychology. It is within this time period that America gradually moved from a language of "character" to a language of personality—a move paralleled by the emergence of a new field of personality psychology.

The principal argument of this book is that the scientific project of personality with which Allport was so intimately connected was itself closely linked to a broad change in the way late 19th- and early 20th-century Americans talked about themselves. For much of the 19th century, character, rather than personality, was the category of choice for discussions of human experience. A thriving discourse grew up around character, and bestselling writers like Orison Marden spoke for many when he described character as the "greatest thing in the world."[14] Programs of character building were established, self-help books were published on the topic, and innumerable papers were published on the theme of character as a fundamental element of political progress.[15] The hallmark of character was its moral flavor; Emerson described it as "moral order seen through the medium of individual nature."[16]

The language of character continued to exert an important hold on the American imagination well into the 1920s. By the late 19th century, however, character's salience began to wane, and Americans found themselves drawn to new categories and new visions of what it meant to be a person. At the center of this discursive shift was the category that now seems so intrinsic to American psychology: personality. The term *personality* has a long history of English usage, but before the mid-19th century it was used infrequently, often in specialized discussions of religion and ethics.[17] By the 1910s, however, personality had emerged as an important term in American vocabulary. The category became a part of everyday conversation, and with increasing frequency Americans began to weigh their own life experience in its terms. "I have neglected one of the most important duties of the modern high school girl," one young student wrote in a 1915 yearbook: "the development of an attractive personality."[18] As Americans began to envision themselves in terms of personality, an enormous literature flourished on the promise of improving personality, and by the 1920s a "tidal wave" of popular interest in the topic had developed.[19]

The gradual shift from a language of character to personality was much more than a change in linguistic fashion. Personality's emergence signaled a gradual change in values; it was an alteration in the way Americans made sense of each other and themselves. Although this change was a complicated and subtle process involving a multitude of complex meanings, a discernible distinction can be found in their respective points of emphasis. The self of character was communally based, and it drew on the language of duty, service, and shared moral understanding. In contrast, personality was a self for an industrialized and urbanized age: expressive, adaptable, and morally unencumbered. The language of personality gauged not morality, but individual distinctiveness. To be a personality, one contemporary remarked, was to be a "somebody."[20]

Allport's career embodies the transformation from character to personality, and it reveals ways in which that change was incorporated into the sciences of human nature. At the same time, Allport's experience provides an intriguing variation on the standard historical accounts of America's shifting discursive landscape. Far from reflecting a smooth and seamless transition, his career highlights the complexities and contradictions that these discourses involved. On the one hand, Allport was a scientist and a modernist: a champion of what one of his contemporaries described as the "culture of personality."[21] On the other hand, he was also a romantic, a religionist and, most decidedly, a "man of character." He had been reared on the language of character, but he came of age intellectually in the 1910s, when the personality ideal was emerging. Captivated by this discourse, Allport was simultaneously opposed to many of its central precepts. Indeed, in this book I argue that much of his scientific work as a personality psychologist may be viewed as an attempt to breathe new life into discredited Victorian notions of selfhood. His experience reveals the cultural plasticity of psychology and the remarkable range of cultural projects to which it has been directed. In turn, I suggest that the complexities of his experience reveal the limitations of the ways in which character and personality are typically theorized in the historical literature.

Part biography and part intellectual history, the book may be viewed as part of a body of scholarship that explores the various ways in which human nature is constructed in language and the contributions that the human sciences make to this process. Often referred to as *critical historiography*, this body of scholarship is distinguished from other accounts of psychology's past by its attention to the complex ways in which psychologists create what they study. Instead of portraying psychologists as disinterested scientists who discover naturally occurring processes, critical historians characterize the field in terms of "knowledge production."[22] The field invents products—intelligence, personality, motivation—in concert with a complex network of cultural, commercial, educational, and military interests. Critical historians search out these connections and, in the process, endeavor to show the politically and culturally contingent nature of that which seems essential to human experience.

THE CULTURAL POLITICS OF PERSONALITY

This book brings the critical historiographic spirit into the domain of personality psychology. I argue that the categories of personality and character are fluid entities imbued with a diverse and often contradictory range of meanings. In the case of personality, the term was frequently used in everyday speech in the early 20th century to refer to qualities of individual distinctiveness and vivaciousness; however, the word also featured prominently in medical literature of the day to refer to an objective, measurable essence.[23] Religious theorists were partial to the category as well, and they often used the term to refer to that which distinguished persons from objects. Intriguingly, social workers used the term in a contradictory manner to advance the idea that it was possible to have an objective understanding of a person while appreciating his or her spiritual uniqueness.

In chronicling this range of meanings, the historical task is not to determine which definition is "correct," but rather to explore what philosopher James Farr called the "political constitution" of psychological language. According to Farr, language does not typically function as a politically neutral vessel for relating ideas or describing things. "Most of language," he argued, is "politically constituted by the ends to which it is intentionally put or by the consequences which it is subsequently seen to entail."[24] Within this framework, categories like character and personality are viewed not as natural objects to be apprehended, but as political ideals to be mobilized, defended, or abandoned as circumstances dictate. One of the tasks of this book is to survey the political and cultural issues at stake in psychology's embrace of the category of personality.

Coming to terms with the political constitution of psychological language involves recognizing ways in which discursive systems *naturalize* certain kinds of understandings. This process refers to the movement of socially negotiated understandings into the realm of the "taken for granted." Once there, categories are often shorn of their social origins; they come to be viewed as timeless facts of nature.[25] Gail Bederman's insightful history of the terms *manliness* and *masculinity* is a useful illustration of this process.[26] Like personality and character, categories like manliness harbored a wide range of ideas about what it meant to be a person. According to Bederman, the power of those categories lay not simply in the ideological load they could carry, but in the way they could camouflage contradictions and "obscure the fact that gender is dynamic and always changing." In this book, I advance a similar claim about the category of personality. I argue that personality's emergence as a research category in American psychology lay in its ability to house and obscure contradictory messages about human experience. Personality reflected the stress that modernity placed on flexibility, self-presentation, and social effectiveness, but the term could also be used to assuage deeply felt concerns about the dehumanizing effects of rapid industrialization and urbanization. To talk of personality in this context was to speak of a self of mystery, dignity, and timeless authenticity. The category of personality thus allowed psychologists to position the individual within the new reality of industrial America without completely surrendering romantic ideals of spirituality and distinctiveness.

AMERICAN PSYCHOLOGY AS A MORAL TECHNOLOGY

Historically, the discipline of psychology has not been particularly interested in the historical analysis of its language and methods. Kurt Danziger argued that many psychologists can be thought of as "naive naturalists" with respect to how they understand their topics of study: "They tend to proceed as though everyday psychological categories represented natural kinds, as though the distinctions expressed in their basic categories accurately reflected the natural divisions among psychological phenomena."[27] Although philosophical reasons underlie this position, I argue that psychology's approach to language is also related to the social function the discipline performs. That function involves more than the development of theories, data, and the institutional apparatuses to sustain them. American psychology's social function has an explicitly moral dimension. As Graham Richards noted, the field's task is "to supply a culturally authoritative foundation for conventional morality in a society which is constitutionally pluralistic in terms of religion and ideology."[28]

Psychological discourse helps define the ethical parameters of American life; through its categories, Americans are schooled in how to structure their experience. The way in which psychology carries out this task is particularly relevant to the present study. Instead of portraying its categories and theories as normative—as one of several possibilities—psychological discourse is naturalized. As I have already noted, the categories in many discursive systems take on an aura of inevitability. What makes psychology's categories particularly potent in this regard is the scientific machinery that surrounds them.[29] Experimentation, data collection, and statistical analysis all serve to divest psychological categories of their social origins. Thus, the pronouncements of psychologists appear to be much more than a set of ethical opinions. Rather, they come to be viewed as the "scientifically confirmed normal outcome of psychological development."[30]

Nowhere in psychology is the discipline's "moral project" more evident than in the field of personality. One of the major reasons for proposing the category was its apparent objectivity. It was thought to provide psychologists with a morally neutral way for talking about the totality of human experience. Beneath the rhetoric of objectivity, however, lay a rich and often contradictory cluster of values about what it meant to be a person. Allport's experience with the category of personality is a particularly compelling illustration of this process. Throughout his early career, he repeatedly insisted on the "objectivity" of both personality and his theories about its workings. His objectivity, however, always carried a heavy cultural cargo, and his psychological notions of personality should be viewed as part of a process whereby science came to underwrite America's ethical norms.

Psychology's moral project may be linked to what Nikolas Rose described as the discipline's "technological" orientation. In Rose's analysis, psychology is portrayed as an administrative science. The field's task is to generate categories and techniques that can accommodate human nature to varied needs of industrial democracy. The field is an "ensemble of arts and skills entailing the linking of thoughts, affects, forces, artifacts, and techniques that do not simply manufacture and manipulate, but which more fundamentally, order being, frame it, produce it, make it thinkable as a certain mode of existence that must be addressed in a particular way."[31] Thus, for Rose psychology's task is technological as well as moral; the field produces politically and economically useful renderings of human nature, and those renderings in turn become a kind of ethical standard for judging experience. In this book, I explore how the technology of personality opened up human experience to new forms of scrutiny. At the same time, however, I explore a theme that is often understated in the historiography of psychology: the paradoxical pursuit of bureaucratic regulation and spiritual transcendence. I suggest that psychology's power to fascinate lay not just in its ability to discipline human difference. What appealed to Americans like Allport was the extraordinary way in which psychological language could accommodate people to the social order while delivering them from anonymity. The discipline harbored the paradoxical promise of calculability and freedom: Through psychology's categories, human nature could be scrutinized for the sake of administrative efficiency and safeguarded from those same homogenizing pressures.

THE PROFESSIONAL CONTEXTS OF PERSONALITY

Although much of this study is devoted to the task of positioning the psychological category of personality within a broad cultural context, the disciplinary context figures prominently in the discussion. Like most academic disciplines, psychologists constructed a kind of metalanguage that served to maintain some semblance of cohesion within the field. Psychology's metalanguage was largely methodological in nature, and it revolved around a vision of the discipline as a natural science.[32] Proponents of personality, like Allport, were obliged to come to terms with these disciplinary pressures. By the time personality was institutionalized as a legitimate category of psychological research, it had accommodated itself to the idiom of natural science.

The priorities of academic psychologists were not the only professional influences on the development of new psychological categories; there are other academic disciplines to consider. Biology, psychiatry, sociology, and social work all border on psychology, and their categories and claims play a role in shaping the discipline's language. Rivalry between disciplines often occurs when psychologists wish to extend or defend their professional borders. Danziger provided a clear illustration of this process in his discussion of social attitudes. Through some theoretical repackaging, he observed, psychologists "were able to lay claim to an area of popular concern that had previously been the concern of sociologists."[33] Allport's engagement with personality reveals a similar history of moving borders, professional rivalries and, in some cases, professional cooperation.

In exploring Allport's role in the "invention" of personality as a scientific category, this book traverses relatively uncharted terrain. Despite his prominence in the history of American psychology, no biography of Allport's career has been published.[34] A sizable periodical literature on various aspects of his work exists, but the bulk of this scholarship is devoted to the theoretical task of understanding Allport's contributions to the discipline of psychology.[35] The relationship between his personality psychology and American culture is a topic that is seldom broached. Historian Katherine Pandora's recent examination of Allport and Gardner Murphy and Lois Murphy is one notable exception. Characterizing Allport as a "rebel within the ranks of academic science," Pandora examined the connection between dissenting science and democratic politics in the 1930s.[36] Thoroughly researched and carefully argued, her work brought much-needed attention to the cultural and political sources of personality and social psychology. By embracing the rhetoric of rebellion that Allport used to describe his own work, however, Pandora placed sharp limits on the sorts of conclusions she could draw. The "Allport as rebel" construction led to a heroic conclusion, with Allport emerging as the "Franklin Roosevelt" of psychology: a partisan of rationality, freedom, diversity, and all things progressive.[37]

What is left out of Pandora's analysis are the strong currents of scientific and cultural ambivalence that ran throughout Allport's work. Scientifically, Allport was both an incorrigible rebel and a champion of positivist progress. He did present a forceful challenge to the positivist orthodoxies of his day, and he repeatedly insisted that personality could never be known in any ultimate sense. However, Allport's eloquent statements concerning the limits of the scientific reach must be viewed alongside his psychometric inventories and his argument that personality consisted of objective, knowable units. His work helped render human nature into a graspable idiom of measurement and exactitude while lamenting this very process. This professional–scientific incongruity paralleled an equally pronounced cultural–religious ambivalence. Educated amid the secularizing currents of American consumer culture, Allport sought glory as an agent of "progress," and he was enamored of the professional trappings of scientific life at the nation's most prestigious university. He moved rapidly up the ladder of scientific success, but all the while he continued to glance back longingly at the spiritual certainties of a premodern world. The medieval aesthetic and mystical suggestiveness of Anglo-Catholicism fascinated him, and he was convinced that science needed to somehow supplement and not replace time-honored spiritual categories of meaning and purpose.

In this book, I argue that Allport's science of personality was less an expression of rebellion than an ambivalent and broadly based search for accommodation. By championing personality, Allport hoped to finesse cultural tensions between the sacred and the secular; progress and tradition; and the individual and society. His was an antimodernist project, and it reflected not a single, secular, political vision, but a complex blend of nostalgic romanticism, ongoing spiritual desire, ethical mindedness, and middle-class ambitiousness.

2

"FINE CHARACTER AND SPLENDID IDEALS": ALLPORT'S EARLY YEARS (1897–1915)

It has been my earnest prayer that God would raise up a spiritual people here who would go on to know him in all his fullness.

—Nellie Allport, 1896[1]

Hear, my child, your father's instruction,
and do not reject your mother's teaching;
for they are a fair garland for your head,
and pendants for your neck.

—Proverbs 1:8–9

In an 1896 diary entry, Gordon Allport's mother Nellie wrote of the hopes she harbored for her newborn son's future:

Many important things have come to my life of which the most important is the life of another precious boy to train for God.... This event stirred my soul more than tongue can express with the great responsibility of three precious souls to train for him. I have no thought to train them for worldly praise, fame, or honor. One thought surpasses all others—to train them to be for Christ and His [sic] work. As this little one was given me I had one wish, one desire, that he would be worthy to be called to labor for him in dark heathen lands.[2]

Nellie's choice of missionary as a vocation for her son reveals a great deal about the moral landscape in which Gordon Allport grew up. In the late-19th-century mind, missionaries were the consummate characters. They had sacrificed all the comforts of Western civilization to save "heathen" souls. Moreover, by venturing into inhospitable climes, they demonstrated their bravery and piety, and in so doing they deflected charges of effeminacy that were sometimes leveled against American-based churchmen. Kind, brave, pious, and self-sacrificing, the missionary embodied all the virtues that Nellie endeavored to instill in her young sons.

13

In a strict sense, Nellie's late Victorian missionary aspirations went unrealized. Her sons did not devote their careers to laboring in "dark, heathen lands." A more figurative reading of Gordon Allport's career, however, reveals several distinct points of connection between the missionary character for whom Nellie prayed and the personality psychologist that Allport became.

BUILDING CHARACTER IN AN AMERICAN BOY

Born in Montezuma, Indiana, in 1897, Gordon Willard Allport was the youngest of four sons of physician John Allport and Nellie Wise.[3] Allport remarked in an interview that he had been named after Charles George Gordon, the British general famous in Victorian America for his philanthropic work with poor boys, his devotion to the Bible, and his defense of Khartoum against Muslim fundamentalists.[4] Although General Gordon's righteousness and dash would have almost certainly made him an esteemed figure in the Allport's Methodist household, a close scrutiny of Nellie Allport's journal reveals that Allport's name has a less romantic, though no less religious, etymology. In actual fact, Gordon Willard Allport was named after Dr. A. B. Gordon and Frances Willard, a leading advocate of higher education for women, and a national president of the Women's Christian Temperance Union (WCTU). Willard had been particularly active in the temperance crusade in Ohio, and Nellie clearly saw her as a figure worthy of emulation. "May the mantle of these *devoted* people rest on him," Nellie noted earnestly.[5]

The Allports had a clear idea of the kind of men they hoped their young sons would grow up to be. At the heart of their vision was the quality of *character*.[6] Character was one of the key words of the late Victorian age and a crucial concept in the vocabulary of American selfhood. It figured prominently in the political and religious discourse of the day, and it was a recurring theme in popular magazines and youth-oriented literature. Most Americans believed that character was human nature at its very best. Popular writer Samuel Smiles described character as the "crown and glory of life" and the "noblest possession of man."[7] Henry Drummond called it the "greatest thing in the world," and the progressive politician Robert LaFollette thought of the man of character as "the embodiment of moral force and moral enthusiasm."[8]

Opinion about the exact essence of character varied widely, but there was considerable agreement over the general qualities that made someone a "man of character."[9] Theodore Roosevelt mentioned a number of these attributes in a 1913 address, "Character and Civilization": "resolution, courage, energy, self-control, fearlessness, taking the initiative, assumption of responsibility, just regard for the rights of others, and common sense."[10]

Other qualities that were frequently mentioned in discussions of character included duty, honor, manliness, service, reputation, and integrity. What united all of these elements was their moral orientation and their emphasis on the transpersonal. In the discourse of character, one became a self by subordinating one's own selfish impulses to higher moral ideals. To have character, Samuel Smiles maintained, is to have "moral order embodied in the individual."[11]

As historian Craig Cunningham noted, the late-19th- and early-20th-century fascination with character reflected the growing secularization and diversity of American culture. Successive waves of immigration and urbanization undermined the religious consensus of early American society, and educators and moralists cast about for an idiom that could affirm a moral subject without inflaming denominational antagonisms. Character emerged as the discourse of choice. The term had a moral resonance, but unlike *soul* it lacked explicitly religious connotations. As an ostensibly secular category, character could also be studied objectively without reference to any particular faith tradition. This subtle blending of objectivity, neutrality, and morality enabled educators to finesse the religious and cultural divisions in America without breaking awkwardly with the past. Cunningham wrote, "If educators could not use explicitly Christian narratives and curricula, then they could frame their educational agendas in the seemingly secular language of character which is inherently evaluative without being overly sectarian."[12]

John and Nellie Allport were very much a part of the culture of character, and they endeavored to raise sons in the spirit of service, duty, and "playing the game fairly." Both parents were committed Methodists, and they put a distinctive denominational gloss on the values associated with character. The responsibility for cultivating the appropriate spiritual atmosphere in the home was primarily Nellie's, reflecting a conventional division of labor in the typical 19th-century Methodist household, one that rested on both a "scientific" and a historical foundation. The science of the day maintained that women had a natural inclination toward spirituality and were thus better equipped to oversee their children's religious formation. Women have "no interest or concern in civil and political affairs," according to one contemporary authority, but "in matters pertaining to the education of their children, in the selection and support of a clergyman, in all benevolent enterprises, and in all questions relating to morals or manners, they have a superior influence."[13]

Nellie Allport was raised with the Methodist ideals of female decorum and spiritual duty firmly in view. Born on December 6, 1862, in Fulton, New York, Nellie had grown up in one of the more stridently ascetic Methodist families in the "Burned Over District" of upstate New York, an area famous for its religious fervor.[14] Of his maternal grandparents, Allport remarked that "there was scarcely ever any more strictly religious principled family."[15] Nellie's religious instruction came mainly from her mother, Mary Ann Wise, who was a member of a Methodist splinter group known as Free Methodism. This austere sect believed that the Methodist church had been corrupted by a worldly concern for respectability and material success. To regain the proper perspective, Free Methodists called for a more vigorous application of what they regarded as the apostolic essence of Methodism. This approach involved an increased emphasis on spiritual matters, plainer patterns of religious service, and a stricter code of moral conduct.[16]

In his thoughtful discussion of the language of character in the lives of 19th-century university presidents, Burton Bledstein commented on the unrelenting seriousness of the Victorian man of character. The discourse of character, he argued, was a language of earnestness, solemnity, and judgment. Through the concept of character,

> the smallest feature about a person's behavior now related to a higher meaning, to an ulterior purpose, to a potential basis for approval or condemnation of his innermost character. Mid-Victorians dismissed no utterance or act as a trifle, unrevealing about a person's character; and too often they eliminated those human tolerances that saved a life from misery.[17]

The Allports' Methodism imparted their family with the kind of intense seriousness of which Bledstein spoke. Allport's maternal grandmother, Mary Ann Wise, was particularly important in establishing the family's moral tone. Wise had helped found a Free Methodist Church in Fulton, New York, in 1869 after becoming disillusioned with the spiritual laxity of the local Methodist Episcopal Church. She became a leading lay member of the "Free" church and was widely known in the community for her "mighty sense of rightness." Impromptu sermons at Free Methodist services cemented her reputation as a spiritual force. She had, to use the jargon of the day, a "tongue of fire" that attracted spiritually minded people from all around the area. Locals frequently spoke of going "to the meeting tonight . . . [to] hear Mary Wise get the power."[18] In her own family, Mary's "boiling hot" religious enthusiasm made her a commanding presence.[19] She set the spiritual tone for her husband and daughter and, later, for her grandchildren. Her influence on the young Gordon Allport was particularly strong during the last 3 years of her life, 1903 to 1906, when she moved into the Allport home. Though physically infirm, Mary Ann quickly assumed a position of spiritual leadership. Allport recalled that his grandmother "ruled the roost" and with "austerity patterned the family life—right up until her dying day." One incident stood out in Allport's mind as being particularly indicative of his grandmother's severe manner and dominant standing. He remembered an occasion when his great-aunt Nellie, after whom his mother was named, somehow irritated Mary Ann, whose response was as swift as it was severe: "The trouble with you, Nellie, is that you lack the grace of God in your heart."[20]

Before and after Mary Ann's stay with the Allport's, the family's religious life was determined by Nellie Wise Allport. Nellie had not developed into as commanding a spiritual force as her mother, but she was heavily influenced by Mary Ann Wise's Free Methodist convictions. As a student at Falley Seminary in Fulton, she was well known for her "self chosen path of personal service to a religious ideal." Some years later, Nellie recalled an example of the religious dedication of her youth: "The other girls in the class suggested that I wave [sic] my convictions and wear a stylish dress for once; and I remember my stand, *if it be right at all, it is right for always*" [italics added].[21] This principled sensibility followed Nellie into early adulthood and marriage. Allport recalled that his mother was "on the severe side with a strong sense of right and wrong and quite strict in her moral ideals."[22]

Nellie set a morally severe tone for her family, and when Allport was a young child, Free Methodism's ascetic code was carefully followed. Ostentation in the form of jewelry, bright colors, and distinctive clothing was avoided. Allport later recalled that his mother refused to wear a wedding ring because it was a sinful form of jewelry.[23] Smoking, drinking, dancing, and card playing were also prohibited. Some sense of the importance Free Methodists attached to these restrictions can be gleaned from the reaction to an incident that occurred when Nellie was a student at Falley Seminary. She decided to follow the fashion set by some of her classmates by getting her ears pierced. This seemingly innocent act apparently met with a censorious reaction from Mary Ann Wise and the members of the Free Methodist Church. Allport remarked that his mother "bore the scars in her ears with shame . . . for years."[24] (See insert, Figure 1.)

Piety pervaded the Allport household, and John Allport worked hard to maintain the spiritual tempo. Born on April 12, 1863, in Scriba, New York, John grew up in a world of poverty, brutality, and limited opportunities. His father, Smith Allport, was a hardworking but inefficient farmer who struggled to provide for his family. John later recalled that his father never took the time "stop and organize . . . [so] it was always nip and tuck to make ends meet."[25] Smith's shortcomings as a farmer were also evident in his approach to fatherhood. He put little thought into his relationships with his children, and he simply beat them in order to maintain control. "My dad had about an average of one whipping a day laid up for me and my brother Elmer," John recalled. "We always got whipped at the same time. . . . If there was nothing very much to whip us for, we would get one for something we were sure to do soon."[26] With no money and little direction from Smith, the family depended largely on the do-it-yourself resourcefulness of John's mother, Mariah, for staples such as clothing, soap, and supplies for the winter. A tireless worker, Mariah fashioned almost everything in the family home from scratch in addition to helping out in the fields:

Every carpet we ever had was made by her. . . . Every stocking or mitten we had was made by her from the spinning of the wool to the knitting. . . . The gloves that we wore, the woolen blankets on our beds were all made from sheep which she helped to raise. . . . Our house was lighted with candles which were made from tallow which she prepared. . . . Every time we got our hands and ears scrubbed it was with the soap that she made.[27]

Tragically, Mariah died in 1876 while giving birth to her eighth child, but her extraordinarily industrious spirit lived on in 13-year-old John. Smith found it difficult to cope on his own with six children under age 16, so John helped take care of his younger brothers and sisters for a year, and then at age 14 he left school for a job in Syracuse. Over the next 6 years, John traveled widely, working as hotel clerk and in sales in Milwaukee, Kansas City, and El Paso before finally ending up in Fulton as the local representative of the Wheeler & Wilson Sewing Machine Company. It was in Fulton that John met Nellie, whom he later described as the "most divine thing I had ever met." Driven by a combination of ambitiousness and what he described as "wanderlust," John relocated to Milwaukee, where he accepted a position as area manager of sales for Wheeler & Wilson. He maintained a correspondence with Nellie, and after a long courtship the two were married on April 12, 1887.[28] (See insert, Figure 2.)

After their marriage, John continued to work in sales in the Milwaukee office of Wheeler & Wilson. It was here that the Allports had their first son, Harold, who was born on January 19, 1889, and was followed by Floyd on August 22, 1890. With a growing family to feed, John worked all the harder, and after 4 years he had increased sales from 300 machines per year to more than 6,000. Sensing a lucrative sales opportunity in St. Louis, he relocated again only to conclude that a life of sales was not especially fulfilling. Although he now had a third son, Fayette (born January 25, 1893), to care for, John abandoned steady work in sales to study medicine at Beaumont Medical College in St. Louis. His career as a medical student proceeded fitfully and was interspersed with a series of unsuccessful, small-time business ventures in such varied fields as lime kilns, butter and eggs, laundry, and money lending. After relocating to Baltimore, John finally obtained his medical degree from the Baltimore Medical College in 1897. "I now bade good-bye to the sewing machine business forever."[29] A medical degree in hand, he initially joined a medical practice with a friend in Montezuma, Indiana, where John and Nellie's fourth son, Gordon, was born. After a year, John moved once more, to the small town of Streetsboro, Ohio. "Within a few weeks my family joined me and within a year we built a new large home and barn." The medical practice flourished, and John "formed a strong attachment for country folk and country life."[30]

THE CITY ON A HILL

The austere intensity of Free Methodism was embedded in an agrarian world of limited opportunities and cultural homogeneity. It was a world that John and Nellie knew well; however, like many late-19th-century Americans, the Allports began to glimpse new possibilities in rapidly industrializing urban spaces. City living promised greater educational opportunities, a significant consideration for a family with four young sons.[31] Economic considerations also loomed large as the Allports contemplated their future. John Allport had been able to find steady employment as a doctor in small Ohio towns, such as Streetsboro and Hudson, but like many rural physicians of the 19th century, he found the conditions onerous and the pay modest. Reflecting on his father's career, Gordon Allport recalled that "the life of the country doctor was heavy in those days, and night calls at great distances with Old John slogging through mud and snow were a strain."[32] Sensing the potential of a "bigger theater of operations," the Allports moved to Glennville, Ohio, an attractive suburb of Cleveland.[33]

At the turn of the century, Cleveland was a bustling city of 380,000. Strategically situated at the mouth of the Cuyahoga River and Lake Erie, the city had been a pastoral mercantile town. In 1850, its population was a scant 17,000, and numerous farms were close to the town center. In the late 19th century, however, industrialization brought steel production and oil refining to Cleveland, and the city's landscape underwent a dramatic transformation.[34] An observer in 1880 commented on the "copper smelting, iron rolling, and iron manufacturing works, lumber yards, paper mills, breweries, flour mills, nail works, pork-packing establishments, and the multitudinous industries of a great manufacturing city." By the 1890s, industrial development in Cleveland was even more intense. In 1892, a *Times of London* correspondent took note of the numerous "black hives bordering the [Cuyahoga] river, where the grimy yet profitable business is conducted that has done so much toward making Cleveland progressive and wealthy."[35]

Cleveland's prosperity attracted thousands from the countryside and huge numbers of immigrants from southern and eastern Europe. Between 1890 and 1900, the city's population grew by 46%, and Cleveland experienced an equally dramatic expansion of its population in the decade from 1900 to 1910. In joining this surge to the Cleveland area, the Allports came into contact with a dynamic and increasingly diverse urbanism. John established a practice in an old store on 105th Street in Glenville, a location that provided him with a particularly revealing window into the growing diversity of urban America. Allport recalled that his father had a "cosmopolitan practice" that included large numbers of "Germans, Poles, [and] Jews."[36] The city's complexity and promise gradually dulled the sharp edges of the family faith. Free Methodism and its prohibitions on dancing, card playing, and ornamentation slowly gave way, and the family joined the emotionally lighter and socially more accommodating Methodist Episcopal Church.[37]

THE CALL TO SERVICE

Abandoning Free Methodism's outlandish austerities, the Allports remained an earnest family committed to the values of character and the ideal of service. For the Allports and, indeed, for many of their contemporaries, service was a principle of some importance, and it had significant implications for the question of character.[38] The power of service lay in its use as a gauge of character. Through service, Americans could manifest such intangible values as charity, honesty, thrift, and courage and thereby prove that they possessed character. The prominent American theologian Lymon Abbot put the matter succinctly in a 1910 paper. "The end of education," Abbot argued, "is the development of character [and] the test of character is the capacity for service."[39]

The dynamic economy of the Cleveland area provided plenty of opportunities for an energetic physician to test his character. At the turn of the century, the city was struggling to come to terms with the social dislocations wrought by rapid industrialization and urbanization. A new generation of reformers entered municipal politics led by the "gas-and-water" socialist Tom Johnson, who was elected mayor in 1901. Inspired by a belief that cities would be the dominant force in the 20th century, the Johnson-led city council undertook an ambitious program to combat privilege by promoting the public ownership of the street railway, electric, gas, and telephone utilities. Freely mixing politics and religion, Cleveland reformers spoke a revivalist idiom that invested religiously charged phrases such as "seeing the light," "getting religion," and "rebirth" with a political meaning.[40] Their political skill matched their progressive idealism, and under Johnson's leadership Cleveland developed a reputation as the "best governed city in the United States."[41]

The religiously tinged idiom of Progressivism resonated strongly with John Allport, and he quickly glimpsed the extraordinary medical possibilities that lay in the rapidly expanding city. For most of the 19th century, medical services in American towns and cities were limited in scope and institutional infrastructure. Care of the sick was typically viewed as a family responsibility, and hospitals were regarded as charitable institutions for the destitute and the insane. With the dramatic growth of cities and the increase in scientific knowledge, medical care gradually moved from the household into the marketplace. Professional authority was consolidated, certification standards were stiffened, and hospitals shed their earlier moralistic focus and emerged as centers of expert medical intervention.[42] Arriving in the Cleveland area at the turn of the century, John Allport soon became part of a broad initiative to modernize medicine in Ohio. He converted an old Methodist Church into a home for his family and used the adjacent land to build a small hospital. Located at 653 East 105th Street, the hospital initially consisted of five consulting rooms on the ground floor and five rooms for patients upstairs. Two years later, John built an annex, and by 1918 the "Glenville Hospital" had cared for more than 16,000 people.[43] Impressive in its own right, the hospital was soon followed by a training school for nursing staff; a drug cooperative for area doctors; and a string of commercial ventures, including a cinema and a restaurant.[44] (See insert, Figures 3 and 4.)

Intoxicated by the idea of unlimited opportunity, John mapped out an exhaustive schedule for himself, and he proudly boasted of never taking a vacation. His mother Mariah was his inspiration, and he would contrast his own work as a physician and businessman with the back-breaking labor of rural farm life. "I suppose that we think that we have hard times now," John remarked in a letter to his sister Bessie, "but in reality we do not know anything of work compared to her [Mariah]."[45] With the memory of his mother firmly in mind, John's plans and workload grew ever more expansive, and he became involved in hospital construction in a number of towns and cities across the Midwest. Business associates were impressed by his enormous energy and organizational efficiency. "From a point of view of saving money," one admiring hospital board member wrote of John Allport, "I don't believe any man living could handle a [hospital] proposition like ours more economically than it has been handled."[46] (See insert, Figure 5.)

Caught up in the rough-and-tumble of competitive business, John Allport also made his share of enemies; at one point, he was accused of ethical impropriety for selling fraudulent medicine to alcoholics. The details of the case are murky, but financial gain does not seem to have been the motivating factor behind all this frenetic activity. John Allport's definition of success was embedded in a moral context not unlike that found in the popular novels of Horatio Alger.[47] For John Allport, as for Alger, success was more a matter of character than finance. He took great pride in self-control, and he bragged of being a "life long bitter enemy" of smoking and drinking.[48] Proud of his own character, John Allport delighted in opportunities to build it in others. As a physician, he often combined medical ministrations with character-building messages. A former patient recalled that "at each visit he [John Allport] said a sentence or two that I clung to and thought on until the next call."[49] Morally minded and highly ambitious, John Allport did derive some satisfaction from his ability to draw on large amounts of capital to finance his numerous projects. In discussing these large capital ventures, however, he was careful to link money to a wider public good. His restaurant was established because his "patients . . . wanted a place to eat [and] . . . there were no places to eat for miles."[50]

The $125,000 medical supply business he founded was run on a cooperative rather than a for-profit basis. The activities that occupied the bulk of John Allport's time—hospital administration and construction—were also embedded in a moral context. "All of my hospital work was for the love of the work," he remarked. "It never yielded me one cent."[51]

Nellie Allport shared her husband's devotion to service and hard, "serious" work. She assisted him in some of his business activities in addition to looking after her four children, her physically ailing parents, and some of the patients from John Allport's medical practice. Somewhere amid this hectic schedule, Nellie also found the time to pursue her "natural" female interest in benevolent activity, and she was a good illustration of what historian Estelle Freedman has described as the "female reform tradition."[52] This tradition mobilized the language of motherhood and brought it into the public sphere through an extensive network of voluntary organizations that provided social services to the poor and political support for morally uplifting projects. Nellie became a prominent local leader of the female reform tradition and helped organize and administer a number of voluntary philanthropic organizations, including the Woman's Foreign Missionary Committee, the Mother's Club, and the WCTU.[53]

Local newspaper summaries of Nellie's social meetings provide a good indication of the extent and tone of her philanthropic activities. One article reported on a meeting of the "Mother's Club" at the home of its president and founder, Nellie Wise Allport. "Fifty fathers and mothers enjoyed the discussions and music by the young people," the reporter noted. The program for the meeting included musical performances by the Allport boys and discussions on education and character building. John Allport presented a paper titled, "What Equipment Do Our Boys and Girls Need to Make a Success of Life?" Another article reported on a meeting of the "Hudson Home Circle." On this occasion, Nellie Allport occupied center stage with what the reporter described as "an excellent paper on 'The hidden forces in the development of children' dwelling on the responsibilities of the parents of the children."[54] (See insert, Figures 6, 7, and 8.)

For the Allport children, the hectic lives of John and Nellie made service seem like both a virtue and a necessity. However, John and Nellie did not leave this important lesson to chance. The Allport children were given "useful" work of their own to perform as soon as they were old enough. Gordon Allport's working life began at age 6. His father had him look after the office, wash bottles, deal with patients, and deliver medicine. When he was a bit older, Allport was required to administer the weekly expenses incurred by his father's medical practice.[55] Allport's range of working experiences grew with his father's business interests. As an adolescent, he was put to work on a mimeographing machine that his father purchased for the practice. Allport recalled that his father encouraged him to use the machine to set up "a little [printing] business of my own from the time I was eleven till about fifteen."[56] A few years later, Allport was brought in as a part-time waiter and cashier in his father's restaurant. The call to service was unrelenting, and although Allport cooperated, he sometimes resented his father's obsession with work and his insistence that all the members of the family cultivate a similar devotion to duty. "He kept us working pretty hard," Allport recalled. "He couldn't see why we should rest because he didn't."

CHARACTER, PERSONALITY, AND MASCULINITY

Urban living had generated new business opportunities for John Allport, and it had extended the range of Nellie Allport's philanthropic activities. Enmeshed in the dynamism of a cosmopolitan city, the Allports cast aside their premodern asceticism and adopted the mores and idiom of an increasingly affluent middle class. Their approach to child rearing underwent a particularly significant transformation. While struggling to make ends meet in Milwaukee, John Allport had regularly beat his sons, just as he himself had been routinely whipped by his own father. As the family's fortunes improved, however, the brutality subsided, and by the time Allport was a boy his father approached the discipline of his children in a spirit of benevolent progressivism: "What children need is proper teaching and instructing—not beatings," John Allport remarked earnestly. "They are intelligent beings and need intelligent instruction. Most of the faults and delinquencies of children are due to ignorance or poor management of parents."[57] (See insert, Figure 9.)

Observing and, in some cases, initiating changes within the family, the Allport children were themselves obliged to come to terms with the challenges urbanization posed to American boyhood. For most of the 19th century, young boys of up to age 5 were typically thought to be part of a feminine, domestic sphere. Frequently monitored by their mothers and often clad in feminine clothing of loose-fitting gowns, young boys had a feminine identity and were expected to behave like girls. The tender affection and stern morality of this early, feminine phase of a boy's life were widely believed to be crucial in the development of good character and powerful "manhood."

As we have seen, Allport's mother and maternal grandmother took a keen interest in building character, and they were careful to supply the Allport boys with a feminine identity. A photograph of Allport at age 5 provides a revealing visual record of their feminine influence. In the photo, the young Allport is clothed in a flamboyant suit heavily adorned with frills and a girlish bow. His long red hair has been carefully washed and curled, and he has been fitted out in decorative high-heeled shoes. To further enhance the connection to femininity, Allport has been strategically positioned alongside customary emblems of feminine domesticity: beautiful flowers and a pretty tablecloth. The effect is striking, but like most Victorian Americans, the Allports saw no contradiction in connecting this early feminine identity with adult "manliness." (See insert, Figures 10 and 11.)

What sustained the practice of feminizing boys was a set of related beliefs about the nature of boyhood and the goal of manly character. Boys were widely viewed as essentially brutal and barbaric. Leading authorities of the day described boys as "primitive savages" who were "wild" and "careless." Henry Coit, the first headmaster of St. Paul's School in New Hampshire, argued that boys were "possessed, in a greater or lesser degree, by the devil."[58] The barbarism of boyhood stood in contrast to the self-discipline, honor, and high-mindedness of the man of character. A man with character had complete control over his impulses, and it was this self-restraint that gave him authority over women and the lower classes. By giving young boys a form of feminine identity, Victorian Americans believed that they were preparing the foundation of a conscience that would, in turn, bridge the divide between the natural savagery of boyhood and the "civilization" of manhood.

The interplay of gender and its link to manly character were crucial themes in the Allport home. Like many of his contemporaries, John Allport believed that as a man he had an intrinsically savage nature that had been tempered into a finely controlled force through the timely intervention of virtuous women. He described his own mother, Mariah, as a "kind, even tempered, wonderful woman" who balanced his violent, boyish exuberance with a measure of "orderliness and a knowledge."[59] Viewing his wife in similar terms, John Allport contrasted his own "baseness" with Nellie's "high ideals, ... moral attainments and absolute purity."[60] Thus, for the elder Allport, the "baseness of the [male] creature" was focused and spiritualized through the purity of true womanhood.

As a boy, Gordon Allport came to view his mother in similar terms, and like other boys, he was obliged to contend with the sharp dichotomy that existed between the early feminine phase of boyhood and the "boy culture" that most young males entered at age 5 or 6. The subculture of boys existed alongside the larger culture, and boys routinely shuttled back and forth between the civilized, feminine world of the domestic interior and the "savage" exterior world of streets, back alleys, and sandlots. Boy culture existed in opposition to feminine culture, and it celebrated the very themes and characteristics that motherly civilization tried to suppress: self-assertion, energy, dirt, noise, violence, physical activity, brutality, spontaneity, and independence. Jealous of its domain, boy culture dealt harshly with boys who did not pay appropriate homage to its transgressive creed. Sensitive, well-mannered boys were branded as a "mama's boy," "girl-boy," or "Tom Apronstring."[61] Such taunts helped solidify the ethic of boy culture, and they provided a powerful counterbalance to maternal influence.

Allport's older brothers relished the transgressive vigor of American boy culture, and like many American men, they defined themselves in opposition to the feminine world of morality and domesticity while adhering to its general precepts. In an unpublished interview, Allport recalled that his eldest brother, Harold, was "an extremely masculine person" and that the third brother, Fayette, was "a lady killer" and "troublesome to father."[62] Both brothers were football players, and physically and emotionally they patterned themselves more after their father than their mother. Photographs from the period show them modeling John Allport's posture and expression, and in their behavior they displayed the gendered assumptions that had structured their father's world. Allport admired his father's tremendous energy and initiative, but his relationship to boy culture differed markedly from that of his brothers. A slim and sensitive youth, Allport was disgusted by his father's "crudeness," and he was repelled by the violent and competitive creed of boy culture. "I suffered agonies on the playground because I wasn't up to it," he later recalled. His dismal performance in the physical world of boyhood struggle introduced a distinct psychological gulf between himself and his more hard-nosed brothers. "I never really got on with my brothers," he recalled. "They didn't like me and they weren't kind and I couldn't possibly compete with them. They were all a little more masculine in type that I was."[63] (See insert, Figure 12.)

Psychologically distinct from his older brothers, Allport and his brand of boyhood were not always appreciated by his father. Indeed, with his busy schedule and manly way, John Allport had a difficult time differentiating among any of his sons, and he left the emotional subtleties of child rearing to Nellie. "You remember Dad's ability to mix us all up," Allport remarked in a letter to his brothers some years later. "We were all 'stimulus equivalents' for him."[64] Distanced from his father and unwilling or unable to measure up to the wilderness existence of boy culture, Allport cultivated a space for himself closer to the feminine world of civilization. He studiously avoided the "football crowd" and "fights and competition" and found solace and affirmation not in the friendly rivalries and companionship of other boys, but in the supportive feminine world of the home and school.[65] (See insert, Figures 13 and 14.) Nellie was a source of some support, and Allport recalled that he used to love to "nurse" his mother whenever she was ill. A woman named B provided Allport with another link to the tenderness and sensitivity of domesticity. "Dear old B" was a nurse employed by John and Nellie to assist in running their large and busy household. Over the years, she became especially close to Allport, sometimes rivaling Nellie in his affections. The depth of the bond did not go unnoticed, and B was frequently asked by those who knew her, "Why do you make that baby love you so? You will make him love you more than his parents."[66] B was unperturbed by these queries, and for his part, Allport found her a welcome relief from the aggressive boy culture of his brothers and the solicitude of his mother. Recalling B, Allport thought of "those early years and our five o'clock kitchen suppers. While I sat at the square oak table and told her about the events of the day, she [B] fussed around the black range assembling our meal." She was "my confidant and comforter," Allport noted. She "never moralized and I was able to tell her things that I could never discuss with my parents."[67] (See insert, Figure 15.)

Allport was certainly not the first male to have ever been ostracized from boy culture, but the social dislocations of the late 19th century gradually changed the meaning of the unboyish boy. Previous generations of sensitive boys found consolation in the moral superiority of their feminized maleness. They were the "good" boys, and their virtue brought them approval from adult society. This understanding of a good boy was still in place when Allport was born, but a gradual shift in meaning was clearly discernable. Virtue was slowly being eclipsed by vigor in the definition of the good boy. Discussions of boyhood started celebrating the transgressive, violent themes of boy culture while condemning the civilized boy.[68] Psychologist G. Stanley Hall was perhaps the most famous critic of the overcivilized boy. Like most other Americans, he was convinced that boys had an intrinsically barbarous nature. "Boys are naturally robbers," he wrote. "They are bandits and fighters by nature." But while many of his predecessors had condemned this nature, Hall regarded it as an important asset that was to be nurtured:

> Unless you want to make a selfish, knock-kneed weakling of him, teach him to double up his fist and strike back. . . . Physical courage is the foundation for moral courage later in life. One is to the child and the savage what the other is to the grown and cultured man.[69]

Hall's condemnation of the "weakling" boy signaled a broad shift in the meaning of American manhood. Morality and self-control—the hallmarks of character—gradually gave way before assertiveness, aggression, and vigor as the true markers of manhood. The sensitive, contemplative man was put on the defensive, and his very identity as a male was implicitly questioned. Theodore Roosevelt even went so far as to suggest that sensitive men were responsible for national decline:

> The timid man, the lazy man, the man who distrusts his country, the overcivilized man, and the man who has lost the great fighting spirit, masterful virtues, the ignorant man, and the man of dull mind, whose soul is incapable of feeling the mighty lift that thrills "stern men with empires in their brains"—all these . . . shrink from seeing the nation undertake its new duties. . . . These are the men who fear the strenuous life, who fear the only national life worth leading. They believe in that

cloistered life which saps the hardy virtues in a nation, as it saps them in the individual.[70]

Allport's identification with the feminine world of civilization had led him to the sort of "cloistered life" that "strenuous" types like Roosevelt so despised. "Keenly aware" of his need to avoid the "football crowd," he fashioned a social world of dances and academically oriented extracurricular activities with other sensitive souls that he "could do business with."[71] A 1914 newspaper story from the *Cleveland Plain Dealer* is typical of the temper of Allport's high school times. The item concerned an exhibit staged by the Glenville High Latin class to "demonstrate [how] the study of Latin bears an important relation to everyday life."[72] In the photographs accompanying the story, Allport is featured in a contemplative pose, accompanied by a dignified-looking young woman. Both are wearing period costumes and are surrounded by the icons of classical civilization. Comfortable in these civilized spheres, Allport emerged as one of the academic leaders of his school. By the time he graduated in 1915, he was second in a class of 100, editor of the student newspaper, and the faculty choice to read the commencement address. According to H. H. Cully, the principal of Glenville High, Allport had a "quiet and masterly way of managing things" and was "highly esteemed by every teacher."[73] Despite his many successes, however, the new masculine imperative ate away at his self-esteem. He emerged from high school with a "great inferiority feeling" and "sensitivity," and a certain diffidence was to be a permanent feature of his character.[74] (See insert, Figures 16 and 17.)

Allport's confidence problems may have been further exacerbated by his relationship with his brother Floyd. Second in the birth order, Floyd seemed to skate effortlessly over the tension between tenderness and toughness that troubled Allport. As a young man, Floyd felt that he "mixed the wild, adventurous spirit of youth" with a "sober, scientific propensity."[75] From Allport's vantage point, Floyd seemed quite masculine: He had his father's large frame and chiseled features. At the same time, however, Floyd was not part of the football crowd, and he maintained a more intimate communion with his femininity than Harold and Fayette did. Allport recalled that Floyd was "well groomed" and that he "wrote poetry and music" and was "much the most gifted in intelligence."[76] Floyd had graduated from Harvard in 1913 and taught at Glenville High School for a year while Allport was still a student. His combination of academic accomplishment and masculine aura impressed Allport immensely, and he later described his brother as a "truly amazing person."[77] Floyd's example had a strong influence on Allport as he contemplated his future after graduating high school. His father suggested that he attend business school. Allport "rather liked the idea," but after talking the matter over with Floyd decided to follow his "amazing" brother and enroll at Harvard.[78] Thus, in September of 1915 Allport began what would be a lifelong association with the famous university. (See insert, Figure 18.)

CONCLUSION

In his authoritative work on American industrialization and urbanization, historian Robert Wiebe suggested that late-19th-century America was undergoing a "search for order." In a manner that eludes precise explanation," he continued, "countless citizens in towns and cities across the land sensed that something fundamental was happening to their lives, something they had not willed and did not want."[79] The Allports were among those "countless citizens" who recognized the dramatic changes sweeping the nation, and they strove to meet those challenges while preserving the moral universe of small-town America. Moving to Cleveland from rural Ohio, the family emerged as a shining example of the prosperity the new industrial order promised. Prosperity brought change, however, and throughout Allport's youth his parents were obliged to rethink their small-town convictions and temper their enthusiasm. By the time Allport graduated from high school, the family stood close to the center of American middle-class respectability: professional, prosperous, sober, and earnest without being overbearing.

Allport was carefully schooled in the parental idiom, but he felt a special kinship with the categories and concerns long associated with femininity. Books, poetry, dancing, and refined discussion of big ideas were among his favorite pursuits. Allport was thus a youthful illustration of what James had described as "tender-minded," and he experienced the strain of a culture that was undergoing a searching reexamination of what it meant to be a man.[80] Older values associated with the idea of manly character were beginning to come undone. In their place emerged a new emphasis on aggression, activity, and physicality—qualities reflected in the new category of masculinity.

3

A NEW WORLD:
HARVARD (1915–1919)

When the young men shall see visions, the dreams of old men will
come true.
  —A. Lawrence Lowell, inaugural address, Harvard University, 1909

On or about December 1910, human character changed.
                              —Virginia Woolf, 1924[1]

In the late 19th century, the American university president was the
archetypal "man of character," and he typically envisioned university education in character-building terms.[2] Charles Eliot of Harvard was perhaps
the most distinguished illustration of the character ideal in the American
university. Born a Unitarian, Eliot's term of office ran from 1869 to 1909;
throughout this time he preached the values of character with a certainty
that many of his more intellectually minded contemporaries found off-
putting. George Santayana thought of Eliot as an "awful cloud" that hung
over Harvard, and Ralph Barton Perry thought he "had something of that
shallowness which seems to be the penalty of health." Shallow or not,
Eliot worked hard to put character at the center of Harvard life. The
"growth of human character," he told the incoming class in 1906, "is what
we are all in the world for. . . . [We are] men who in freedom through trial
win character."[3]

Eliot's approach to character stressed the values of individualism, hard
work, service, and freedom. The man of character was a robust individual,
not swayed by the emotionalism of religion or the passing enthusiasms of
fashion. High-minded and aware of his responsibilities, such a man conducted his life with a level-headed seriousness of purpose and an unrelenting sense of duty. A man of character "cannot be a lazy, shiftless, self-
indulgent person," Eliot wrote. "He must be a worker, an organizer, and a

disinterested laborer in the service of others."[4] In considering the question of character, Eliot placed a great deal of emphasis on the relationship between the individual and the group. The man of character was able to maintain a creative and moral tension between these two polarities. His actions were those of an independent and free-thinking individual, but they were thoughtfully applied to a larger moral order.

Like many of his contemporaries, Eliot was convinced that the nation's future depended on such men, and he undertook a series of institutional initiatives on the basis of this conviction. He openly discouraged participation in fraternities, and he studiously avoided paternalistic intervention in student affairs. Although Eliot was not indifferent to scientific research, his administrative emphasis lay in developing character among undergraduates. In 1904, he remarked that "neither the serviceableness nor the prestige of the University is determined by the work of the Graduate School in Arts and Sciences." Eliot's most controversial policy was the introduction of the elective system in undergraduate education. Like most of Eliot's policies, the system was designed to foster the sort of individuality and reasoned decision making that were part of good character.

Eliot's successor at Harvard was A. Lawrence Lowell, who took office in 1909. A political scientist by training, Lowell was, in many respects, quite different from his predecessor. He had been propelled into office by supporters who were convinced that Eliot's individualism had gone too far. Under Eliot, Van Wyck Brooks remarked in 1908, "the Harvard man is left to himself and is given every opportunity, and even every encouragement to develop a personality harshly individual."[5] Although Lowell was circumspect in his criticism, his appointment was viewed as a reaction against Eliot's individualistic emphasis. Lowell believed that Eliot's policies had cost Harvard some of its collegial atmosphere, and he was determined to recapture a spirit of social cohesion. "The task before us," he wrote in 1909, "is to frame a system which, without sacrificing individual variation too much, or neglecting the pursuit of different scholarly interests, shall produce an intellectual and social cohesion."[6]

Lowell brought a different emphasis to Harvard, but he drew on the same idiom of character to articulate his vision. The language of character is clearly evident in his address titled "The Duty of Scholarship," which he delivered in 1912. In this paper, Lowell invited his audience to think of scholarship in broad, character-building terms. Scholarship was not strictly a matter of technical proficiency or personal prosperity. It was also a process of cultivating the appropriate "mental habits" that reflected on the "welfare of the community." The sort of mental habits Lowell had in mind were those long associated with character: "hard work, self-sacrifice, renunciation of facile indolence and of many a fleeting pleasure."[7]

Convinced of the importance of these values, Lowell wanted to cultivate an atmosphere in which students would regard scholarly endeavor not as an option or a requirement, but as a duty. His model was the Samurai, who Lowell believed had "acquired the conviction that an obligation lay upon every member of their class to be not only a warrior and a gentleman but also a scholar." Manly, genteel, and learned, the Samurai possessed character in abundance, and Lowell hoped to spread that spirit to "the whole people." Dismissing suggestions that this ideal was no longer practicable, he boldly asserted that the young men of 1912 were crying out to have their characters built: "The normal young man, the man worthy of college life, craves—even if not himself aware of it—a chance to use his power for a noble end; and if the end fires his imagination, he is not deterred by the discomforts in his path."[8]

Lowell signaled his commitment to this socially minded conception of character in his 1909 inauguration speech, and he maintained it throughout his tenure as president. Throughout his term of office, he emphasized undergraduate instruction over graduate instruction, urbanity over technical proficiency, and cohesion over specialization. At the undergraduate level, Lowell knew just what this system would entail. Harvard College was to be remade in the image of Oxford and Cambridge. Students were to be housed in college residences, and a tutorial system was to be established to encourage intellectual and cultural development.

Lowell's conviction that American youth were in search of "noble ends" may have been exaggerated, but in 1915 many Americans thought in similar terms. The Allport family was among this constituency, and the son they sent off to Harvard in the fall of 1915 was a paradigmatic example of the sort of idealistic youth of which Lowell had spoken. Between 1915 and 1919, Allport came to embody the ideals Lowell had described, and as Harvard's president had prophesied, he was "not deterred by the discomforts in his path."

THE MAKING OF A HARVARD CHARACTER

When Allport entered Harvard in 1915, he already knew a great deal about the institution. Floyd had given him an insider's knowledge of the university, its reputation, and its various customs and personalities. Floyd's insights, however, did not make the transition between high school and university any easier. In his first semester, Allport struggled academically, receiving "an array of D's and C's."[9] To make matters worse, Harvard of 1915 was in the midst of what fellow classmate Malcolm Cowley described as "an ineffably snobbish period."[10] Student life was then dominated by a system of social clubs that served to replicate the social gradations of New England society. Membership in these clubs was not so much a matter of individual ability as it was a matter of background. An "old" bloodline, membership in high society, and graduation from one of the "right" sort of high schools—usually a New England preparatory school, such as Groton, Exeter, or Andover Academy—were the usual prerequisites. The spirit of exclusivity that suffused club life may be sensed in a short poem that Allport pasted into his undergraduate scrapbook:

> O, I come from the town of Boston,
> The home of the bean and the cod
> Where the Lowells speak only to Cabots,
> And the Cabots speak only to God.[11]

Students who aspired to membership in these elite societies were subject to intense scrutiny during their freshman year. They were expected to "say, do, [and] wear the right thing, avoid the company of ineligibles, and above all, eschew originality."[12]

Allport's midwestern background excluded him from the ranks of the aristocratically minded. The tradition of Harvard individualism, however, made it possible to cultivate a sense of connection without belonging to the fashionable set. Reflecting on student life at Harvard in 1910, John Reed remarked that

> all sorts of strange characters, of every race and mind, poets, philosophers, cranks of every twist, were in our class. . . . So many fine men were outside the charmed circle [of aristocrats] that, unlike most colleges, there was no disgrace in not being a "club man." . . . No matter what you were or what you did—at Harvard you could find your kind.[13]

Reed's experience was consistent with that of Allport, but it took the young Clevelander a while to "find his kind." He was "lonely as heck," and initially his shyness prevented him from venturing much beyond the confines of his classes and dorm room.[14] Most of his free time was spent with his roommate Paul Berryman.[15] Some sense of the depth of Allport's isolation may be gleaned from a short paper he wrote in 1917 for an essay contest sponsored by the Council of North American Student Movements. Titled "Harvard's Best Tradition," it is a story of a freshman socially isolated by a lack of athletic talent and social grace. The student grows depressed "listening to his classmates call their favorites to come and join a happy crowd" without ever hearing them call his name. In desperation, he goes outside the dormitory and calls out his own name just to hear how it sounded. An observant classmate "witnessed this scene, and associating with it the remembrance of certain timid advances and wistful looks, divined the secret." The classmate proceeded to tell his friends about what he had seen, and from then on the lonely student was invited to "come and join in all excursions."[16] It is not clear whether Allport resorted to such desperate measures himself, but by the end of his first year he had successfully overcome most of his difficulties. His academic standing had returned to the A range, and socially his contacts became much more diverse. (See insert, Figure 19.)

Allport's high school career had been a testament to the virtues of character, and in his high school yearbook he underscored his earnestness with the following quotation: "He who knows most grieves most for wasted time."[17] At Harvard, Allport continued along in much the same vein, mapping out an exhaustive program of work for himself that literally stretched from sunrise to sunset. Each half-hour period was dutifully planned and executed, including slots for rest, socializing, and philanthropy.[18] It was a program of which President Lowell himself would have undoubtedly approved, and it spoke to a broad, religious sense of social responsibility shared by many of Allport's contemporaries. Harvard student Winthrop Hamlin's 1913 article in the *Harvard Illustrated Magazine* captured the ethic of responsibility and uplift. Drawing heavily on the idiom of character, Hamlin described the "spirit of human brotherhood" and the "social aims and ideals" of Harvard students.[19] Arguing that social service was a "natural trait of high character," he drew attention to a development that would feature prominently in Allport's undergraduate experience: the professionalization of social service. Hamlin maintained that the spirit of human brotherhood could potentially suffuse all manner of activities, but he noted that social service was also taking a more focused, institutionalized form. The most visible manifestation of this trend at Harvard was the Department of Social Ethics.

Harvard's Department of Social Ethics had been founded by theologian Francis Peabody in 1906 in an effort to bring together the 19th-century denominational college's traditional concern for religion and ethics with the emerging scientific ideal of pure inductive scholarship.[20] By uniting moral philosophy with the scientific method, Peabody thought that his new department could overcome a debilitating materialism and "summon the young men who have been imbued with the principles of political economy and of philosophy to the practical applications of those studies."[21] Peabody had retired by the time Allport enrolled as a social ethics student in 1915, but the elder scholar's interest in mobilizing social science in support of Christian character was taken up by his successors Robert Foerster and James Ford.

Allport had little contact with Foerster, but he came to know Ford quite well through course work and field placements. Ford had been a student of Peabody's, and although he tended to be more technically minded, he also envisioned social ethics as a kind of morally earnest, applied sociology. In Ford's view, social ethicists directed the insights of modern social science into social programs designed to realize an "ultimate ideal of human perfection." They endeavored "to determine what constitutes goodness" and to study the "adoption of social method to the achievement of moral purpose."[22] Again like Peabody, Ford placed great emphasis on the direct application of social ethics research. All of his students were encouraged to undertake extensive programs of "social service" with a variety of government and philanthropic organizations in the Boston area. Convinced that social change went hand in hand with personal growth, Ford insisted that participation in service would speed up "social progress" at the same time that it contributed to the "informing and stabilizing [of] a man's character."[23]

As a young man of "high character," Allport identified strongly with Ford's assessment of the merits of social service. As an undergraduate, he undertook an extensive program of social work that included stints at the Boston Juvenile Court, the Bureau of Industrial Housing and Transportation, and the Cambridge, Massachusetts, YMCA. He also wrote the 1916–1917 report of the Social Service Committee of Harvard's Philips Brooks House, and he helped acclimatize foreign students as a member of the Harvard Cosmopolitan Club. It was a demanding program, but one that Allport greatly enjoyed. "I got a tremendous kick out of doing good," he recalled, "and that always was a close second to my studies."[24]

THE PROFESSIONALIZATION OF BENEVOLENCE

The themes of self-sacrifice, duty, morality, and character figured prominently in the discourse of social ethics, just as they did in the moral universe that Allport had inhabited since his youth. As an undergraduate, however, Allport became aware that the future of moral endeavor in America was not simply a matter of recapitulating the past. The nation was changing rapidly, and America was moving from a predominantly agrarian economy to one that was dominated by heavy industry. The new industrial economy ushered in a host of changes that were to have a profound impact on American life.[25] One of the most significant developments was population distribution. With the onset of industrialization, people left the countryside to work in the expanding urban centers; by the time Allport enrolled at Harvard, the percentage of people living in cities was nearly equal to those living in the country. The shift to the cities initiated important changes in the lifestyle Americans had come to know. In the 19th century, the life of the average American was structured by nature and the traditional institutions of family and church. People worked extremely long hours—from sunup to sundown—although they usually controlled the pace of the work. The necessities of life were relatively few in number, and most were either homemade or obtained locally. Opportunities for socializing were relatively limited. In most rural communities, social life was focused on the church, general store and, on special occasions, evangelical revivals and summer fairs.

All this changed with the shift from a rural to an industrial economy. The move to the city gave rise to a new kind of neighborhood society, which was dominated not by the village store and the church, but by saloons, department stores, street corners, and commercial amusements. People began to spend less time with their families and more time with peers. The enormous number of goods generated by industrial innovations helped shift the focus of American life from production to consumption. This shift reoriented American attitudes toward material wants and leisure time. Luxuries became necessities, and amusements developed into regular, highly organized activities.

These changes had not gone unnoticed by the social ethicists and social workers that Allport encountered at Harvard. A number of scholars spoke of the need to rethink the means by which the ideals of social service were implemented. In the past, high-minded Americans had set out to "build character" by exposing wayward citizens to the influence of educated, virtuous volunteers.[26] Sometimes known as "benevolent" volunteerism, this model of social work enjoyed widespread support in philanthropic circles throughout the late 19th and early 20th centuries. Drawing heavily on a gendered language of maternal nurture and responsibility, support for benevolent social work began to wane during the early part of the 20th century, and it evaporated in the 1920s. Social work theorists such as Richard Cabot, Mary Jarrett, and Mary Richmond argued that industrialization had rendered religiously based philanthropy obsolete. Contemporary social problems overwhelmed the ability of amateurs: Modern circumstances required professional attention. The issue for professional social workers like Jarrett and Richmond was not simply the amount of time one spent working in the field. The crucial point was the way one went about tackling social problems. Professionalism required a new ethic and a new way of conceptualizing the social field.

As a Harvard social ethics student, Allport had an opportunity to view the transformation in American social work close up. The principal hallmark of the "new" social work was a commitment to a scientific idiom. Social workers in the past had construed social problems, such as illegitimacy and alcoholism, as moral problems to be solved by the benevolent understanding and example of an evangelical volunteer. By 1917, social work theorists had begun a wide-ranging campaign to reconfigure the field's language and methods. Moral problems were redefined as scientific questions that were treatable by scientific methods. Part of the trend of social work professionalization involved establishing a specialized body of knowledge that could be applied to special problems. Between 1915 and 1920, American social workers constructed a specialized knowledge around the concept of *casework*. It would be difficult to exaggerate the centrality of casework in the thought of the professionally ambitious social workers to whom Allport was exposed. As social work historian Roy Lubove noted, casework "formed the basis of a professional identity."[27] Like many professional code words, casework was a broad and generic term. For most of its proponents, however, the term conveyed three ideas that were central to the practice of modern social work.

First, casework involved detailed record keeping. By encoding the lives of their clients in writing, social work theorists believed that they would be better able to accurately diagnose problems and to develop practicable solutions.[28] Second, the proponents of a casework model of social work were committed to the principle of "differential diagnosis." Sometimes stated in terms of "individual differences," differential diagnosis called attention to what professional social workers believed was one of the principal limitations of the older form of benevolent social work: its inattention to the nuances of each case. For the professional social workers, human diversity was the salient theme of industrial life, and it sustained an ongoing commitment to individualized treatment and diagnosis. "Treat unequal things unequally," counseled Mary Richmond, for "social workers have the great fact of ineradicable individual differences in human beings to face."[29]

The final component of the casework orientation was its reflexive regard for science and sentimentality. Professional social workers were convinced of the necessity and efficacy of scientific thinking. At the same time, however, they were not indifferent to the human element in their craft. Theorists acknowledged that social workers traversed a domain of lived experience and that to approach that realm with the steely detachment of the natural scientist would not be appropriate. Social workers must avoid "cold, sterilized, depersonalized ideas," cautioned sociologist Arthur Todd. In his book *The Scientific Spirit and Social Work*, Todd presented the emerging professional ideal. The modern social worker would "steer between" an extreme form of scientific indifference and the "warm, saccharine, oily, oozy, intoxicating, overpersonalized sentimentalism" long associated with benevolent volunteerism.[30]

THE CULTURE OF PERSONALITY

From Allport's perspective, one aspect of this ongoing dialogue between science and sentimentality was to assume particular importance. To achieve the necessary balance between science and sentimentality, social workers began to scrutinize their concepts in light of current social conditions. Part of this process involved reexamining the concept of character as a designation for a person's nature. As we have seen, character had been a dominant part of the cultural landscape of Victorian America. With its emphasis on hard work over leisure, courage over popularity, self-sacrifice over self-aggrandizement, and moral conviction over intellectual ability, character reflected the circumstances of a morally stable, predominantly agrarian, production-oriented society. With the onset of rapid industrialization and urbanization, however, the logic of character began to lose its coherence. As historian E. P. Thompson noted, industrialization "entailed a severe restructuring of working habits—new disciplines, new incentives, and a new human nature upon which these incentives could bite effectively."[31]

The "new human nature" that Thompson referred to was symbolized in the United States by the term *personality*. The difference between the language of personality and that of character is evident in their strategic foci. In the language of character, selfhood was achieved through surrender to a "higher" moral standard. In the new discourse of personality, selfhood was achieved through the realization of the self's own abilities. The true self of personality was not one of duty, honor, and self-sacrifice—terms that referred to a framework outside the self. A personality was instead embedded in a language that reflected back on the self—"fascinating, stunning, attractive, magnetic, glowing, masterful, creative, dominant, forceful."[32] The self-focused dimension of personality is apparent in the work of Orison Marden, a popular writer of self-help books. In 1921, Marden published a book entitled *Masterful Personality*. Marden's self is considerably different from the man of character. Concerns about ideals, morality, and duty were largely eclipsed by an interest in self-expression and self-fulfillment. Marden devoted much attention to "personal charm" and "fascination."[33] He urged his readers to pay close attention to the subtleties of manners, clothes, and conversation: "You can compel people to like you," he remarked, if you attend to the rules governing "life efficiency."[34]

As with character, personality reflected the culture of the day. The overriding concern of popular works on personality was how to develop a self capable of functioning in an increasingly impersonal and morally fluid world. The strategy that began to emerge at the turn of the century involved shifting attention away from the permanent inner self that had been emphasized in character and toward the outer self. Americans were encouraged to concentrate on their behavior, their manner, and the immediate impression they made on people. The new values were celebrated in popular periodicals such as *Personality Magazine*, published in Boston beginning in 1910. Consisting of a loosely organized collection of inspirational stories and poems, the magazine's publisher, Arthur Fisher, encouraged his readers to "come into the woodshed" for a "verbal spanking" and psychological pick-me-up. By developing their personalities, Fisher maintained, Americans could be transformed from workaday "ocean liners ... plodding between known and monotonous ports" into exciting "tramp ships ... trafficking for new and uncharted seas."[35] (See insert, Figure 20.)

The priorities of personality populists like Fisher were also reflected in works of well-known intellectuals, such as Herbert Croly and Randolph Bourne, who are, in this respect, quite typical. In *The Promise of American Life*, Croly explained that "success in any ... pursuit demands that an individual make some sort of personal impression."[36] Bourne echoed this theme in his well-known book *Youth and Life*. He argued that nothing was as important as a "most glowing personality." The development of self "becomes almost a duty, if one wants to be effective towards the great end (the regeneration of the social order)."[37]

As a youth, Allport caught fragments of the new idiom as his parents struggled to come to terms with the complexities of the new industrial order. Their discourse was, in fact, an amalgam of small-town virtue and big-city possibility, and it drew on a wide variety of sources. Nellie Allport had an encyclopedic knowledge of the Bible, and she could recite long passages of scripture from memory.[38] At the same time, Nellie sensed the spirit of change that urbanism had initiated, and in her spare time she consulted a wide range of increasingly secular sources for assistance with life's problems, including William James's *Principles of Psychology* and Edward Griggs's *The New Humanism*.[39] Griggs's work is of particular interest insofar as it made palpable the subtle transition that the Allports were themselves experiencing.[40] Theorizing that history had eclipsed both the Christian emphasis on self-abnegation and the Greek emphasis on self-culture, Griggs called for a new language that would synthesize the social and the individual, the past and the present, and the spiritual and the material. Personality was the capstone of this new discourse, and in Nellie Allport, the new idiom found an attentive audience. In her notebook she observed that "this age [is] one of personality."[41] In a long chapter on the "evolution of personality," Griggs sketched out the hallmarks of the new ethic. To be a personality was to feel liberated from tradition and the "control of external forces."[42] Modern "personalities" were fascinated by their subjective experience, and they possessed a heightened awareness of their own transformative potential. Griggs claimed that "the life of the human spirit is a process of perpetual becoming, an unstable equilibrium, —it is life only while it is growth in life."[43] Enamored of the possibility of self-development and growth, Griggs also stressed the social outcome of personality development. The "emancipation of the individual," he argued, would be "accompanied by a deepening of the content of personal life." In the fully developed personality, "primitive existence ... brute reactions ... and the blind impulse of sex" were transformed into "forms which embody the higher human experience."[44]

PERSONALITY AS A PROFESSIONAL OBJECT

American social workers sensed that a new discourse was needed to come to terms with the pronounced changes that industrialization and urbanization had brought to the American experience. By the time Allport encountered social work, many in the field concluded that character was beginning to lose whatever morally compelling edge it once had. Talk of character started to sound curiously antiquated; it conjured up images of moralistic amateurs preaching to the unenlightened. Professional social workers wanted to go beyond the amateurism of this earlier age. Rather than try to purge character of its moral connotations, social work theorists encouraged their readers to abandon the term in favor of the newly emerging category of personality. Indeed, in the late teens and early 1920s, personality became the primary target of social casework. Mary Richmond put the matter succinctly in her authoritative *What is Social Case Work?*:

> Let me … make the broadest generalization about social case work that I can. Its theories, its aims, its best intensive practice all seem to have been converging of late years toward one central idea: namely, toward the *development of personality* [italics added].[45]

What made personality so appealing to social workers like Richmond was the category's freshness and flexibility. As historian Warren Susman noted, personality had a decidedly modern resonance, and it enjoyed increasingly wide usage as the century wore on. Its popular appeal lay in the lightness of its moral load. In contrast to the Victorian category of character, which carried the full weight of Christian ethics, personality referred largely to the traits of self-presentation. For social workers, however, personality's attractiveness lay not only in its popularity but also in its ambiguity. For all its modernist charm, personality was an extraordinarily broad term. In scientific circles, the term was often used to refer to the "objective" self—a summary statement of the individual when viewed apart from a moral context. In literary and religious circles, commentators frequently used the term in a very different sense. In discussions of ethics and art, personality referred to that aspect of human nature that made a person distinctively human. For most religious theorists, this entailed a religiously motivated engagement with the social world.[46]

The footnotes of Richmond's definitive book on casework provide ample testimony to the wide range of interests that personality was able to tie together. Richmond quoted scholars from literary criticism, religion, psychology, pedagogy, biology, and social science; each theorist used the term in a different way. For the behaviorist psychologist John Watson, personality was an objective term that referred to the "'reaction mass' as a whole."[47] In contrast, the literary critic Bliss Perry used personality to refer to the distinctively human element within each individual:

> If the revelation of personality unites men, the stress upon mere individuality separates them, and there are countless poets of the day who glory in their eccentric individualism without remembering that it is only through a richly developed personality that poetry gains any universal values.[48]

For a profession struggling to navigate a course between science and sentimentality, the ambiguity of personality was not a liability, but a resource to be exploited. The category had a scientific cachet, and it enabled social workers to forge alliances with professional communities in psychiatry and psychology who were interested in personality. At the same time, however, personality was not without its ethical suggestiveness. By orienting their professional project around personality, social workers could be both scientific and ethical. As an undergraduate, Allport did not yet grasp the full significance of these discursive shifts, but the spirit of modern social inquiry was something of which he felt very much a part. He described sociology as his favorite subject, and like many progressives, his imagination was fired by the idea that humanity was at last on the cusp of alleviating all of its social ills.[49] Although this youthful idealism was soon tempered, Allport never completely abandoned the language and logic of social ethics. He was convinced that social improvement depended on the development of personality, which was in turn both an ethical vision to be realized and an objective reality to be scrutinized.

AN INTRODUCTION TO PSYCHOLOGY

Inspired by the fusion of science and morality in the social ethics field, Allport was intrigued by another field with moral potential: psychology. Several scholars had a hand in nurturing this interest, including Edwin Holt, Leonard Troland, Walter Dearborn, Ernest Southard, and Robert Yerkes.[50] Allport recalled that his initial interest in the field was sparked in his freshman year by his first psychology professor, Hugo Münsterberg, who was a truly impressive figure in both style and substance. In appearance, he was a kind of 19th-century professorial archetype: He had a waxed Prussian mustache, a large physique, and an imposing air. Allport later recalled that Münsterberg looked like the mythical German figure Wotan.[51] Known as the "chief" by his graduate students, Münsterberg's mannerisms conformed to his stereotypically Teutonic appearance. He spoke with a strong German accent, and he possessed a self-confidence that "amazed" Allport and a good many others besides.[52] As philosopher Josiah Royce's wife quipped, "Münsterberg is our God."[53]

Münsterberg's scholarly credentials were just as impressive as his carefully cultivated professorial image. In 1892, William James had described him as the "ablest experimental psychologist in Germany."[54] When Allport enrolled in his class in 1915, Münsterberg was the senior psychologist at Harvard and widely recognized for having "profoundly altered the course of American psychology."[55] His position and influence were based on a scholarly output that was impressive in its size, breadth, and originality. Between 1906 and 1916, he published an average of two books a year on topics as diverse as general psychology, value theory, Japanese art, psychotherapy, the cinema, and applied psychology. Among these works was a recently published textbook that Allport used in his first psychology course: *Psychology: General and Applied.*[56] The book summarized what were for Münsterberg the two major standpoints in psychology. The most "natural" standpoint, in his view, was *purposive psychology.* The goal of this branch of the field was to develop an understanding of mental life. Purposive psychologists endeavored to "enter into [a subject's] thought" in order to render "his whole inner experience ... clear to us." To achieve this goal, it was necessary to develop a certain sympathetic identification with the subject. The psychologist had to "think [him- or herself] into his mind." Once there, Münsterberg believed that the psychologist would be in a position to elucidate the "system of purposes" in the subject's mind.[57]

Münsterberg attached a great deal of importance to the systematic consideration of the purposeful side of human nature. Like a number of other late-19th-century German psychologists, he saw it as a necessary component in the development of a "complete psychology."[58] Unlike many of his German contemporaries, however, Münsterberg subverted his own carefully laid-out defense of purposive psychology. Two aspects of his discussion are of particular importance. Methodologically, Münsterberg undertook a vigorous defense of the scholarly character of the purposive approach. He argued that nothing was mysterious or fanciful about systematically investigating the purposes of others. "Purposive psychology is not controlled by faith or imagination or intuition, but depends upon a thorough study and analysis of actual facts." The problem with Münsterberg's argument was the relative absence of supporting evidence. No "factual" examples of purposive psychology were cited. The best he could offer was an apology: "At present it would be a vain undertaking to present even in outline the facts of purposive psychology."[59]

A more serious challenge to the viability of purposive psychology was Münsterberg's formulation of the other half of psychology: *causal psychology.* Causal investigations did not attempt to cultivate the sympathy necessary in order to "enter into" a subject's sphere of meaning. Causal psychologists maintained an air of studied objectivity, and they looked "upon the content of the mind with the neutrality equal to that of the astronomer." The goal of this branch of the discipline was to "explain mental life" by seeking out the causes of "thoughts and feelings."[60] The place to look for these causes, Münsterberg believed, was in physiology. Basing his psychology on a philosophical doctrine known as *psychophysical parallelism*, Münsterberg argued that every mental state was paralleled by a physical process: "There is no shadow of an idea," he wrote, "no fringe of a feeling, no suggestion of a desire which does not correspond to definite processes in the brain." The key issue for Münsterberg was not simply that mental events corresponded to bodily events. What mattered was that mental events *followed* physical events. He argued that mental states should be "understood as accompaniments of brain processes [and that] they are completely linked with the bodily life of the organism and through it with the whole psychophysical development." This materialist view led Münsterberg to discount attempts to explain action by referring to a mental state. A proper scientific explanation in psychology was one that showed the "true physical causes" of our "emotions or ideas or volitions."[61]

The duality of Münsterberg's thought reflected the scope of psychology's social ambitions in the early 20th century. Industrialization, urbanization, and immigration had generated a multitude of social dislocations and a climate for a language and technology that could bring order to a rapidly changing America. Causal psychology played off desires for control, and its idiom of *scientific* measurement and exactitude suggested *social* order and human predictability. Inspired by what historian David Bakan described as the "vaulting urge towards the mastery of other human beings," psychologists were also attentive to another desire modernity had created: an urge to be rescued from impersonality and alienation.[62] Americans feared the homogenizing forces of mass culture, and many believed that big-city comforts and scientific advances had somehow rendered life less authentic and meaningful. Moralist Hamilton Wright Mabie's cautionary remarks typified widely shared concerns about the dangers civilization posed to the spirit:

> In our slippered ease, protected by orderly government, by written constitutions, by a police who are always in evidence, we sometimes forget of what perilous stuff we are made, and how unseparable from human life are those elements of tragedy which from time to time startle us in our repose.... A stable world is essential to progress, but a world without the element of peril would comfort the body and destroy the soul.[63]

For writers like Mabie, technology, order, and predictability added up to a prefabricated experience and a diminished sense of one's own self. Münsterberg's purposive psychology acknowledged this sentiment, and his system attempted to finesse the tension between social control and personal authenticity. Like his colleagues in social work, Münsterberg used the category of personality to bridge those ambitious and somewhat contradictory goals.

Münsterberg devoted an entire chapter of *Psychology: General and Applied* to personality, and he used the term to link the themes of determinism and control to the ideals of meaning and personal significance. Grouping personality in his section on causal psychology, he argued that personality was a scientific category that referred to the unification of disparate elements of experience into a functioning whole. "The cell mechanism furnishes the explanation [of] this unity [of which personality] is then nothing but the interconnection of causally connected parts."[64] Insisting that personality was a natural object, Münsterberg also maintained that personality transcended the boundaries of natural science and the physical body. "We demand an enlargement of the personality idea," he argued. "We have to acknowledge in the personality a oneness which is incomparable with that of the objects of nature."[65]

Convinced that personality was both an object of natural science and a transcendental human quality, Münsterberg struggled to find a coherent way of connecting subjectivity to objectivity. Fellow German William Stern observed that there were "two souls in Münsterberg which were never completely harmonized."[66] In the minds of many of Münsterberg's American readers, the explanatory powers of causal psychology made purposive psychology redundant. Why study something that has no influence on human action? Veteran psychologists had a difficult time formulating an answer to this question. If Allport's experience was any indication, undergraduate students found the question impossible to answer. As a first-year student, he did his best to assimilate Münsterberg's complex disciplinary division, but having the book's author as course instructor did not make the job of understanding the material any easier. Münsterberg proved to be a "terrible teacher" because of his "very heavy German accent" and "vague" lectures.[67] Allport recalled that Münsterberg "spent most of the term ... discussing whether the pillar *was* there or whether the pillar *was not* there."[68] By the end of term, Allport recalled feeling "completely mystified." He did not understand the philosophical subtleties of the system, but the possibility of applying natural science to human nature did register, and Münsterberg's chapter on personality provided another measure of the category's scientific and social significance.[69]

Allport's criticism of Münsterberg makes one wonder why he did not follow the path of his future colleague Henry Murray, who had enrolled in Münsterberg's introductory psychology course 2 years earlier. Murray recalled that a "bud of interest in psychology was nipped by the chill of Professor Münsterberg's approach. In the middle of his second lecture I began looking for the nearest exit."[70] Allport had felt Münsterberg's "chill," but he decided to continue with the course despite the difficulties. He later attributed his decision to stay to a curiosity about the very vagueness he had complained about. "I'm quite sure one of the major reasons that I went into psychology was to find out what Münsterberg was talking about."[71]

There may have been some truth in this explanation, but the fact that Allport continued in psychology after such a disagreeable introduction was probably due more to the personal influence of Münsterberg's assistant: Floyd Allport.[72] Floyd had received his A.B. from Harvard in 1913, and he returned to Harvard 2 years later as "one of those unspeakable fossils known as 'graduate students.'"[73] Enrolled as a PhD candidate under the direction of Münsterberg, Floyd quickly proved himself to be an able psychologist.[74] A year after enrolling in graduate studies, his knowledge of experimental procedures enabled him to collaborate with Harvard psychologist Herbert Langfeld in the production of a laboratory manual.[75] In 1919, Floyd was awarded the PhD for his dissertation on the "effect of the group upon individual and mental processes."[76] Allport had always admired his brother's "well-groomed" style and facility in poetry and music, and as the young understudy of his accomplished brother, he continued to look upon Floyd as a mentor.[77] "Between times and out of hours," he later recalled in his autobiography, "I gained much from my brother's more mature reflections on the problems and methods of psychology."[78] The psychology Allport received from his brother differed sharply from that of Münsterberg, especially with regard to the value of philosophy and the nature of human experience. Münsterberg had argued that a dimension of personality transcended nature, and he suggested that this purposive domain could be productively engaged through a more philosophically oriented psychology. Floyd was unmoved by Münsterberg's elaborate arguments, and in his autobiography he recalled that his advisor's ideas were "uncongenial to my line of thinking since they seemed to me to lack a suitable criterion and basis in physical reality."[79]

Enamored of the idea of natural science, Floyd inveighed against Münsterberg's "rationalism." Philosophical discussions "can never take the place of observation" he insisted, even when considering the intangible world of consciousness, purpose, and personality.[80] In place of the chanting of "mystics," Floyd called for the reworking of psychological categories "in terms of the behavior complex."[81] Gordon Allport did not record his undergraduate reactions to Floyd's materialist vision of psychology. His reference to Floyd's "mature reflections" suggests a degree of sympathy, but his subsequent intellectual and personal meanderings indicate a feeling of disquiet with this new vocabulary of selfhood.

THE ANTIMODERNIST IMPULSE

The language of character was a world of conviction, and Allport had grown up surrounded by moral certainties and eternal truths. Suburban living had softened the sharp edges of his parents' Methodism, and his experience at Harvard provided a further challenge to the earnest sensibility of his youth. "Almost overnight," he later wrote in his autobiography, "my world was remade" by a new "horizon of intellect and culture."[82] Allport's world may have been "remade," but as a Harvard student he still had a healthy appetite for the kind of order, meaning, and sense of destiny that the culture of character provided. Although psychology and social ethics were compelling subjects with a persuasive vocabulary, they could not completely satiate this hunger.

Still very much the son of Nellie Wise, Allport set off in search of spiritual fulfillment, and he pondered the big questions of life's meaning. A thoughtful and sensitive young man, he had become dissatisfied with the flamboyant emotionalism of Methodism while in high school, and at Harvard he began to explore a variety of religious alternatives then available in the Boston area. Allport attended services of the Episcopalians and the Unitarians in addition to exploring what Mary Baker Eddy described as Boston's "spiritual underground": Christian Science and spiritualism.[83] Ultimately, he found a spiritual home in the Anglican Episcopal Church, but as an undergraduate, it was the Unitarian faith that seemed most congenial to him. "Here surely was a free and unfettered faith, requiring just enough belief to focus the mind and not enough to hamper the operations of the intellect."[84]

Allport's hunger for spiritual sustenance amid the lavish scientific fare of Harvard was no idiosyncratic aberration. Many of his contemporaries felt the same peculiar tension between a desire to break free from the rigidity and literalism of an evangelical upbringing and a yearning for the intense depth of feeling that revival culture had offered. Affluent and educated, they had been exposed to the liberalizing currents of Darwinian theory, biblical hermeneutics, and social science and could no longer accept the ideas of eternal damnation and a personified devil that had figured so prominently in their youth. Shorn of these beliefs, many late-Victorian Americans sallied forth with confidence in the redeeming power of science and a nagging sense of loss. Life somehow seemed less interesting and meaningful with the devil reinterpreted as a shadowy abstraction and hell "relegated to the far off corners of the Christian mind." Historian T. J. Jackson Lears described this condition as one of "weightlessness"—a feeling of being emotionally adrift on a sea of empty principles, values, and standards.[85] In a weightless world, everything was up in the air, cut free, Reverend Theodore Munger remarked, by a doubt that "envelops all things in its puzzle—God, immortality, the value of life, the rewards of virtue, and the operation of conscience. It puts quicksand under every step."[86]

Weightlessness provoked a multiplicity of responses that Lears collectively referred to as *antimodernism*. The antimodernist impulse involved a complex mixture of accommodation and opposition to the growing rationalization and mechanization of American life. More of a sensibility than a coherent intellectual movement, antimodernism involved a critique of the superficiality and emotional impoverishment of modern life and a search of the intellectual and cultural wreckage of medieval society, premodern religion, Eastern civilizations, and the wilderness for signs of "authentic" experience and meaning. Their quest was not one of escapism, but adjustment. Antimodernists did not wish to flee modern America; their struggle involved a journey to the past, the primitive, or the wild to somehow find meaning and authenticity amid the fleeting frenzy of commercial culture.

Allport's plunge into the religious life of Boston brought him into this larger antimodernist current. Although he found some temporary solace in Unitarianism, its spiritual efficacy was less than satisfactory. He described himself as a Unitarian on college forms, but he never established an "official relationship" with the church.[87] Moreover, Allport maintained more than a passing interest in Christian issues and organizations. Two years into his studies, in 1917, he attended the annual Conference of Eastern College Men on the Christian Ministry at Union Theological Seminary, New York, New York, where he heard the well-known minister Harry Emerson Fosdick deliver the speech "Personal Religious Needs of Men" and the equally famous minister Harry F. Ward deliver "The Minister's Opportunity."[88] That same year, Allport was elected secretary of the Harvard Christian Association. His Harvard scrapbook also testifies to an ongoing spiritual hunger. The book contains several newspaper cuttings on Billy Sunday, a former baseball player turned evangelical revivalist who made a widely publicized visit to Boston during Allport's time as an undergraduate.[89] In one article, Sunday was quoted as saying:

> I know there are thousands of young men at Harvard who would come into the Kingdom of God if the professors would only give them a little bit of encouragement. But more than half of the instructors ... in our colleges today themselves think it is smart to look with superiority on religion. God himself would have an awful job converting some of those Harvard professors.

Allport did not comment on the story in his scrapbook, but his interest in Sunday's crude emotionalism is a measure of his antimodernist temper. He yearned for the intensity and conviction that Sunday represented while chaffing at its intellectual shallowness.

Inspired in these activities by a sense of religious uncertainty, Allport remained unsatisfied with the teachings of organized Christianity. Formal religious doctrines seemed unable to stand up to the withering scrutiny of modern scholarship. Hungry for a theological "hitching post for my slight spirit and slighter intelligence," Allport later lamented that as an undergraduate, he seemed unable to "throw down his rationalistic tendencies and thereby get a true perspective on them and on his other (submerged) tendencies."[90] Despite these concerns, the psychological reality of spiritual feeling seemed undeniable. Allport recalled that while an undergraduate, a "few convincing mystical experiences came to me—usually in the morning when I arose before my roommates and took a walk by the river."[91] Mindful of his brother Floyd's strident materialism, Allport had tried to explain these experiences naturalistically, "in terms of [his] digestive processes."[92] However, these scientific explanations could not dislodge an intuitive conviction that he had experienced a real spiritual connection with some sort of transcendental other. "There was something remarkably direct and vivid about these contacts between myself and Something [sic] infinitely bigger than myself."

Convinced of the psychological reality of religious experience, Allport could look to a large body of American religious and philosophical thought for support. As historian Robert Fuller noted, American religious thinking took an increasingly psychological turn over the course of the 19th century.[93] Inspired by the work of German scholars such as Schelling, Kant, Hegel, and Schleiermacher, American theologians began to rely less on the Bible and more on a prerational mode of thinking and feeling when searching for evidence of religious truth. Arguments about the existence of a special kind of spiritual consciousness beyond the physical senses were put forward, and Americans were encouraged to look inward for proof of God's existence. Religious authorities did not usually articulate specific psychological mechanisms to account for knowledge of the divine, but most were convinced that a knowledge of consciousness would provide the support for religious faith that theology was no longer able to offer. According to theologian Lyman Abbot, the "foundation of spiritual faith is neither in the church nor in the Bible, but in the spiritual consciousness of man."[94]

Allport's knowledge of this theological literature is uncertain; however, as an undergraduate he was familiar with the work of William James, the scholar most strongly identified with psychological religiousness. James's influence on Allport has been the subject of a number of discussions in recent years. Katherine Pandora described Allport as a "second generation Jamesian psychologist," and Richard High and Bill Woodward argued that Allport's career "signaled the beginning of a reintegration of the two Jamesian themes [humanistic and scientific].[95] David Leary stated the connection even more forcefully by arguing that Allport was "perhaps the most 'Jamesian' psychologist of his generation."[96]

Clearly, a wealth of important parallels can be drawn between James and Allport, and their scholarly pairing in the historiography of psychology is apt. However, what is often obscured in this literature and, indeed, what is seldom considered in larger discussions of psychology's past is the religious source of James's appeal.[97] Many Americans turned to James because he legitimized a spiritual impulse that they themselves felt but had difficulty articulating. James provided an intellectually respectable vocabulary to engage the world beyond the senses—a trend that infuriated many of his positivistically minded colleagues in psychology. In 1920, for example, James's former student G. Stanley Hall noted sharply that the "'medium-mad' Bostonians ... all point to James and say with him that there is a germ of truth in all this bosh and dross [psychic phenomena and spiritualism]. It is James who laid the foundation of all this credulity."[98]

As an undergraduate, Allport was among the many spiritually restless Bostonians who turned to James for guidance. Like James, Allport had a deep hunger for the divine and an uneasiness with modernity's homogenizing power. Dissatisfied with the faith of his forebears, Allport was looking for new language to describe his spirituality and to affirm his place in a larger metaphysical order. James's pragmatism and his phenomenological frame of reference known as *radical empiricism* helped Allport speak to both of these ambitions. In *Pragmatism*, James outlined a spiritual dilemma that perfectly paralleled Allport's experience. Identifying the empirical temper of the times, James still sensed a deeply felt desire for a world in which ideals did not "appear as inert by-products of physiology" and where "what is higher is [not] explained by what is lower and treated forever as a case of 'nothing but.'"[99] He noted that many Americans were searching for language that would enable them to experience meaning and transcendence, but having been schooled in scientific materialism, they were intellectually wary of dogmatic theology and uninspired by the compromising tone of liberal Protestantism. Some sort of synthesis seemed to be the order of the day:

> You want a system that will combine both things, the scientific loyalty to facts and willingness to take account of them, the spirit of adaptation and accommodation, in short, but also the old confidence in human values and the resultant spontaneity, whether of the religious or the romantic type.[100]

James offered pragmatism as a "philosophy that can satisfy both kind of demands."[101]

In James's hands, the pragmatic method linked the truth of an idea to its "practical cash-value ... within the stream of your experience."[102] Ideas were true insofar as they made a positive and practical difference in the lives of people that held them. Whatever one might say about religious experience, James argued that it had an undeniable effect and that it was, in this pragmatist sense, real:

> [Pragmatism's] only test of probable truth is what works best in the way of leading us, what fits every part of life best and combines with the collectivity of experience's demands, nothing being omitted. If theological ideas should do this, if the notion of God, in particular, should prove to do it, how could pragmatism possibly deny God's existence? She [Pragmatism] could see no meaning in treating as "not true" a notion that was pragmatically so successful. What other kind of truth could there be, for her, than all this agreement with concrete reality.[103]

James's pragmatist philosophy was closely linked to his interest in the nature of experience, a focus that he termed "radical empiricism." The overarching goal of Jamesian empiricism was to somehow do justice to the complexity and multifacetedness of the world that was actually experienced. James was convinced that many scholars practiced a kind of "halfway empiricism" that distorted, denied, and compartmentalized experience for the sake of precision and order.[104] "Philosophers have always aimed at cleaning up the litter with which the world apparently is filled," he argued. "They have substituted economical and orderly conceptions for the first sensible tangle; and whether these were morally elevated or only intellectually neat, they were at any rate always aesthetically pure and definite, and aimed at ascribing to the world something clean and intellectual in the way of inner structure."[105] Convinced of the partiality of existing philosophical and scientific categories, James hoped to develop a framework that would bring the totality and fluid complexity of experience into its orbit. Radical empiricism would "neither admit into its constructions any element that is not directly experienced, nor exclude from them any element that is directly experienced."[106]

Among the many elements that radical empiricism freely admitted were individuality and religious experiences. James thought it was crucial to acknowledge individuality as a scientific as well as a cultural ideal. In an essay on the "importance of individuals," he condemned "talk of the contemporary sociological school about averages and general laws and predetermined tendencies, with its obligatory undervaluing of the importance of individual differences."[107] Unlike later generations of American psychologists, however, James was not especially interested in surveying individual differences across a broad range of psychological measures; his passion with respect to individuality had a distinctively spiritual and antimodernist dimension. What fired his imagination was the transcendental quality of individual experience. James was convinced that no amount of experimentation or quantification could ever completely capture the felt sense of individuality. Each person had within him or her a quality of spiritual uniqueness that could be intuitively experienced, but never fully known in any comprehensive sense. "In every concrete individual, there is a uniqueness that defies all formulation," he wrote. "We can feel the touch of it and recognize its taste, so to speak ... but we can give no ultimate account of it, and we have in the end simply to admire the Creator."[108]

James's reverence for individuality reflected a theory about the nature of human experience. Motivated in part by his own sense of spiritual uncertainty, James was convinced that levels of experience existed that extended well beyond ordinary awareness. "May not we ourselves form the margin of some really central self in things which is co-conscious with the whole of us? May not you and I be confluent in a higher consciousness, and confluently active there?"[109] Mindful of the need to find scientific-sounding terminology in an increasingly secular age, he used the concept of the *subconscious self* to refer to these extrasensory modes of experience. The subconscious self was a "well accredited psychological entity," he argued, and he enthusiastically quoted Myers's work on "subliminal consciousness" to support his views:

Each of us is in reality an abiding psychical entity far more extensive than he knows—an individuality which can never express itself completely through any corporeal manifestation. The self manifests through the organism; but there is always some part of the Self unmanifested; and always as it seems, some power of organic expression in abeyance or reserve.[110]

As an undergraduate, Allport needed no convincing as to the reality of mystical experiences or the legitimacy of the religious quest. What James provided for Allport was not so much a novel set of spiritual propositions as an intellectual charter for a highly personal, emotional spirituality that he had learned as a child and never wholly disavowed. Through James, Allport could look at traditional Methodist themes, such as the emphasis on personal experience with God, alternative modes of awareness (i.e., the conversion experience), and sanctification (i.e., Christian perfection) through a new and philosophically up-to-date lens.[111] As Allport entered adulthood, his religious consciousness continued to develop, and he became more conventionally theistic than James ever was. However, in Allport's subsequent career as a personality psychologist, he drew heavily on James's understanding of the multilayered, indeterminate quality of human experience. Like James, he spent much of his career questioning the extent to which individual experience could be satisfactorily captured by natural science. And like James, Allport often struggled between a desire to venerate the unknowable, spiritual complexity of individual experience and a practical wish to roll up his sleeves and provide serviceable language that practitioners of scientific benevolence could use to bring modern salvation to those in need. As we shall see, Allport found the category of personality useful in mediating among all of these issues.

"THE LONG BOMBARDMENT"

While searching for God and goodness, thoughts of war were seldom far from Allport's mind. Although the United States did not officially enter World War I until April 1917, the roar of the guns resounded in Boston's newspapers and in the imagination of Harvard's faculty and students. The war dominated discussions large and small, and from the outset of the conflict support for the British and French was strong. A number of prominent Harvard faculty used their position to mobilize public opinion against Germany, and according to historian Bruce Kuklick, they "were little less than propagandists for the British."[112] Harvard philosophers Josiah Royce, George Santayana, Ralph Barton Perry, and Ernest Hocking were among those who put their intellectual weight behind the British cause—convinced, as Perry noted, that Germany had been consumed by a "pride that claims the world in the name of those spiritual powers which are man's prerogatives."[113]

As an undergraduate, Allport was witness to this jingoistic clamor, and the presence of Hugo Münsterberg on the faculty gave the conflict a personal dimension. A proud German, Münsterberg tried to counter the groundswell of pro-British feeling in America. Between 1914 and 1916, he wrote three books on the war and America's relationship to it. Not surprisingly, Münsterberg presented the German cause in a sympathetic light, and he encouraged Americans to stay out of the war. It was a plausible argument, but in pro-British New England, Münsterberg's Teutonic sympathies made him an unpopular figure. One disgruntled Harvard graduate threatened to withhold a $10 million dollar bequest unless Münsterberg was fired.[114] President Lowell did not succumb to the threat, but he criticized Münsterberg for "indulgence in popular writing and speech making [and] for self-advertisement."[115] Many of Münsterberg's colleagues in the Department of Philosophy and Psychology openly broke with him, and former Harvard president Eliot accused him of immorality and insanity because of his pro-German views. Evidently, the strain became too much for Münsterberg, and he died dramatically in 1916, toppling from the podium while delivering a lecture at Radcliffe.[116]

The Harvard community was unmoved by Münsterberg's dramatic death, and political sentiment on campus assumed an increasingly strident, warlike tone. Allport followed these developments closely, and when American preparations for war began in earnest in early 1917, he decided to enlist in the Student Army Training Corps (SATC). A reluctant soldier, Allport said to his parents in February 1917:

> I do not expect to get into war, nor favor war ... still I can conceive of cases where it may be an absolute necessity to use military knowledge. I sincerely believe that it is the solemn duty of college men to be able to take as high a rank as possible, and for this purpose get the superior training offered them at this time. Nearly all Harvard has taken this attitude, and, in consequence, next September you will find two thousand, or so, able second lieutenants ready for service in the reserves.[117]

Quickly adapting to the rigors of military discipline, Allport was spared the horrors of trench warfare. He served in the Harvard SATC throughout the war, but the conflict was not without its personal dimension. His brothers had all enlisted and been shipped to France: Fay had a desk job, but Harold and Floyd both saw action. Commissioned in the infantry, Harold served in the trenches, where he was gassed in a German attack. Floyd served in the field artillery and was decorated for bravery while serving in France.[118] Alive to the significance of the moment, Floyd put his experience into words, and his poetry gave Allport a personal, albeit unrealistic, sense of the drama. Floyd's 1918 war poem *Behind the Soldier* is a case in point:

> The long bombardment now is fired,
> Our guns have played their game;
> I lean across my table, tired,
> And watch the candle's flame.
>
> And groping shadows stretch from me
> Athwart my shelter bare,
> I yearning turn and seem to see
> My mother praying there.
>
> For holiness of truth and right
> The noblest ideals of the free
> The very things for which we fight
> I learned them at her knee.[119] (See insert,
> Figure 21.)

Fueled by such sentimental verse and secure within the gates of Harvard Yard, Allport's youthful idealism emerged from the war largely unscathed. He maintained his scholarly interests throughout the conflict, and with the support of Herbert Langfeld, he even produced "reports on psychological aspects of rifle practice."[120] On Armistice Day—November 11, 1918, his 21st birthday—Allport marched smartly into Boston with the rest of the Harvard SATC past a sea of patriotic banners and a jubilant crowd of 500,000 people. Allport's personal reminiscence of the day, written in barracks on November 12, 1918, resounded with hope for the future and happiness at the war's end.

> When we came home from the parade, we had a fall out for five minutes behind the houses on Beacon Street. Two ladies came out with huge smiles and similar baskets of apples. Everyone gave and took with gratitude and the selfishness of the human animal receded to absolute ebb.[121] (See insert, Figure 22.)

CONCLUSION

Allport described his undergraduate education as a world-making experience, with social ethics and psychology having a particularly large impact on his thought.[122] Through these disciplines, he learned to question the religious and ethical certainties of his youth and to venerate professionalism, objectivity, and scientific prowess. The change in outlook was pronounced, yet his conversion to an increasingly ambitious scientific materialism was not so complete as to affect a total breach between past and present. The values of character continued to structure Allport's life, and he graduated from Harvard with the kind of dutiful, earnest sensibility that President Lowell hoped to foster in every student. Allport's professional interests also bore the stamp of his earnest upbringing. As a boy, he had had extensive exposure to the female reform tradition, and he had come to identify with its emphasis on uplift, social welfare, and personalized social service. At Harvard, he came to recognize the limitations of this voluntarist tradition, and in social ethics and psychology he found a new, objective-sounding, masculine vocabulary for expressing his reformist interests. Personality was one of the key words of this new discourse, and it provided the conceptual link that connected the older tradition of female, sentimental voluntarism with the new ideal of objective science.

Floyd Allport was emboldened by the new scientific idiom, and he embraced a materialist approach to psychology with the same fervor that he had once proclaimed his ambition to become a Methodist preacher. His younger brother's conversion to the new faith was nowhere near as pronounced. Ambivalence and confusion characterized Allport's outlook, and like many other antimodernists, he mined both traditional religious categories and scientific discourse in his search for meaning and certainty. He was drawn toward the ideal of a science of human nature, yet he retained a strong sense of spiritual freedom and enchanted otherworldliness. Unsure of how to articulate and integrate these seemingly disparate interests, Allport toured the intellectual and spiritual landscape of Boston widely, and in James he found philosophical guidance. Pragmatism and radical empiricism helped legitimate the religious quest while linking it to a scientific vocabulary of psychological processes.

4

THE MISSIONARY LIFE:
ROBERT COLLEGE, CONSTANTINOPLE
(1919–1920)

Great God, I'd rather be a pagan,
suckled in a creed outworn,
So might I standing in this pleasant lee,
have glimpses that would make me less forlorn.
—Quoted in the diary of Gordon Allport, 1919[1]

The conscious person is continuous with a wider self through which
saving experiences come.

—William James, 1902[2]

Allport graduated from Harvard in June 1919 along with his brother
Floyd, who received his PhD. It was a proud day—the first graduation
ceremony since the end of the war—and at the commencement address
future U.S. president Calvin Coolidge struck an appropriately inspirational
note. Observing that the "salaries of college professors are much less than
like training and ability in the commercial world," Coolidge argued that
"we have lost our reverence for the profession of teaching and bestowed it
upon the profession of acquiring." What was needed, he told the class of
1919, was a commitment to the "cause of education ... with a soul."[3]
Allport's 4 years of hard study at Harvard had given him an appreciation
of the value of a soulful education, and as he looked out upon a world
devastated by war, the cause of education seemed as worthy as any other.
The numerous As on Allport's undergraduate transcript certainly made
such a career possible. His self-confidence, however, did not match his
academic ability or the optimism that he had for humanity. Despite his
many social and scholarly successes at Harvard, he later recalled that he
had a "generalized inferiority feeling" that made him doubt his potential
as a university professor.[4] (See insert, Figure 23.)
Allport's sense of uncertainty in his youth was a negative reflection

of the confident swagger of his older, more masculine brothers. Although Harvard had exposed Allport to a much wider variety of social types, he continued to feel the strain of familial expectation and the pressure to become the sort of man he knew he was not. If anything, the events of 1917 and 1918 only served to widen the gulf between Allport and his brothers—especially his eldest brother, Harold.

Allport knew that his brothers viewed him as a somewhat effeminate character, and he had hoped that military training might change their perception. In a letter to his mother, he noted sarcastically that his brother Harold would undoubtedly approve of his enlistment because "six months military training *might* make a man of me."[5] As events unfolded, the masculine Harold continued to regard Allport's sensitive brand of manhood suspiciously, and as noted in chapter 3, World War I did not provide the youngest Allport with any opportunities to find masculinity on the field of battle.[6]

In search of perspective on himself and his future, Allport decided that upon graduation, he would undertake his own foreign expedition. However, instead of traveling overseas in the masculine role of soldier, Allport ventured forth in the gentler and more civilized role of teacher and missionary. In June 1919 he accepted a 3-year appointment at Robert College, an American-sponsored religious college in Constantinople, Turkey. (See insert, Figure 24.)

A MISSIONARY HERITAGE

The missionary life was something with which Allport was closely acquainted. His mother had been a founding member of the local Committee of Women's Foreign Missionary Committee, and she had served as its corresponding secretary for many years. As was the case with most religious issues that Nellie considered, the missionary movement did not remain on the level of the abstract within the Allport household. Allport's three older brothers were named after American missionaries, and Nellie gave her sons a direct education in the merits of missionary endeavor by inviting visiting missionaries to stay with her family and minister to her children. One telling episode, Allport later recalled, occurred when he was 6. He had contracted a serious illness and was asleep in bed: "I must have been delirious but I can remember coming to and finding one of mother's missionaries praying by my bed. He was a member of the alliance she was mixed up with and I can remember this fervent prayer for my life going on." The normality of the missionary presence in the family home is evident in the young Allport's reaction to this incident. He did not recall feeling surprised or upset by the missionary's prayers: "I think I just took it as a matter of course."[7]

Regarding missionaries as a "matter of course" was something that Allport continued to do even after he began questioning the family faith. As an undergraduate, he took up his mother's interest in overseas missions by joining the Harvard Mission Committee. At Robert College, he served as the Harvard Mission Committee's "representative in the foreign field."[8] Allport was directed to "keep in close touch with the mission and inform the Committee of any opportunities for either reconstruction or missionary work."[9]

On one level, Allport's decision to accept the position at Robert College was a continuation of a long-standing tradition of American missionary endeavor. His approach to the question of becoming a missionary, however, also betrayed an antimodern sensibility that many of his 19th-century predecessors would have found difficult to grasp. The missionaries that he had known as a child had cared deeply about the place of Christianity in the world, and they were inspired by a desire to redeem as many "heathen" souls as possible. Allport was not indifferent to the spiritual well-being of his Turkish students, but his reason for going to Robert College had more to do with his own sense of spiritual unease than with any larger concerns about saving humanity for Christ. He ventured into the world of missions to find a sense of personal conviction, rather than to proselytize from an already entrenched spiritual foundation. Just before departing for Turkey, he noted that "the final analysis of my purpose in going to take the teaching position in Robert College reveals this desire for securing a sense of proportion at the base." This elusive sense that Allport sought was a "theory of value ... is this or that thing of significance." Evidently, Allport was still caught in a welter of doubt, and like many of his contemporaries, he hoped to find personal value and significance by stepping out of the mainstream of American life and immersing himself in an exotic world.[10]

This decision did not sit well with Allport's family, despite their earlier missionary enthusiasm. He was criticized by his mother and his brother Floyd for not pursuing a more conventional professional path, and the pressure continued right up until the day he departed. Convinced of the importance of his spiritual venture, Allport was still torn by feelings of ambivalence, and he felt the pull of his family's appeals to rejoin the mainstream. While making his farewells, he finally relented and "practically promised to return within a year to take additional graduate work at Harvard."[11] This promise put Allport on a moral precipice. His term with Robert College was for 3 years, but professional expedience seemed to require a much shorter term. Principled and professionally ambitious, the young Allport was not entirely sure what to do, and the uncertainty gnawed at him throughout his stay at Robert College.

A CHARACTER IN CONSTANTINOPLE

The first few weeks that Allport spent at Robert College did little to alleviate the ambivalence he felt about the bold venture he had undertaken. Constantinople was exotic almost beyond description: "My impression of Constantinople has been ever since arriving that chiefly of utter cosmopolitanism." The city was a multicultural kaleidoscope of "fezes [sic], turbans, helmets, sashes, cowls, and embroidered capes" fascinating both in their variety and the nature of the social problems they suggested.[12] Robert College was perched impressively amid this dynamic display of humanity, but despite its aesthetic charm and exotic location, Allport frequently doubted the wisdom of his decision. "There is no doubt about my work [at Robert College] being practically valuable since planning and managing five English courses is a pedagogical feat, but I often long for a more scholarly atmosphere, specifically, Harvard."[13]

Robert College was a different world from Harvard, and Allport quickly realized that few opportunities would arise for weighty intellectual and spiritual discussions. The College had been founded in the 1850s, at a time when thousands of Americans were traveling to China, India, Africa, and the Middle East in an effort to win "possession of the world" for Christianity.[14] The early history of Robert College is in keeping with the sense of spiritual imperialism that informed many American missionary efforts in the middle to late 19th century. The College's founders went to Constantinople convinced that "the mosques and pagodas were about to tumble down."[15] Western, and particularly American, standards of education, taste, and moral propriety were boldly put forward as the most well-developed expression of Christian ideals. The missionary spirit is evident in the 1860 constitution of Robert College:

> [Robert College] is to be founded and administered on the principles
> of the Bible: it is hereby declared and ordained that, while it is to be
> a scientific and literary institution, God and his word shall be distinctly
> acknowledged and honored therein: the Scriptures . . . being read and
> prayers offered at least once each day . . . at which services the Faculty
> are expected to be present, and all the students shall attend.[16]

When Allport arrived in 1919, the college had lost much of its Christian single-mindedness and world-conquering enthusiasm. In a letter to the Harvard mission, Allport reported that he had not met "a single person who has come from sentimental reasons. This college at least is completely free from 'missionary zeal.'"[17] Modern commerce and communication, Darwinism, hermeneutics, and comparative religion had eroded the 19th-century zeal of which Allport spoke. What remained was a humbler commitment to Christianity, broadly defined in terms of world peace, tolerance, general education, science, and social service.[18] The shift was familiar to

Allport because it paralleled a broad change within mainstream American Protestantism. In the late 19th century, a liberal theology had emerged that linked the salvation of the individual soul to the social elevation of society as a whole. Protestants were encouraged to lay aside older forms of individualized religious exhortation and attend instead to politics, social organization, sociology, psychology, and the techniques of business administration. Philips Brooks House, the organization that sponsored Allport in Turkey, is a revealing case in point. The House was committed to "spiritual activity, benevolent action, [and] religious aspiration," but it took pride in its "practical efficiency" and "business-like appearance of the office."[19]

The self-consciously practical college that Allport encountered may have been devoid of arrogant zeal, but the missionary spirit had not been completely dispelled. American tutors were recruited using standards that virtually guaranteed an atmosphere of moral earnestness:

> The candidate should be a man ... of a fervent symmetrical piety, combined with a missionary spirit, a willingness to do hard work, the ability to work harmoniously with others and one who is not unyielding, stiff, or one who would be conscientiously obstinate ... ; in short a man who wants to live a Christian life and do a Christian teacher's work, desiring to do good to the souls of his pupils as well as to improve their understanding.[20]

The records of Allport's stay at Robert College suggest that he was a nearly paradigmatic example of an ideal candidate. In a letter of recommendation, the treasurer of the Harvard Mission Fund described him as a man of "very fine character and splendid ideals," an endorsement that Allport did his best to live up to.[21] His primary responsibility was to teach English to five classes of approximately 20 students each.[22] But taking a page from his parent's notebook, Allport quickly extended his responsibilities into other areas of philanthropic endeavor. He organized a boys club "according to Brooks House Principles," and he assumed the chairmanship of the social service committee of the local YMCA.[23] To round out an already busy schedule, Allport agreed to teach an additional course in sociology on top of his regular teaching load.

The hearty appetite that Allport displayed for service was one indication of the depth of his character. His journal provides additional glimpses into the kind of man he had become. Particularly striking are the aesthetic considerations that he frequently referred to. Implicitly following the lead of Harvard President Lowell, Allport displayed a strong preference for the refined, the dignified, and the tasteful. The idiom and posture of the "gentleman" impressed him, and he endeavored to cultivate those qualities in himself. On the voyage over to Robert College, Allport commented favorably on the refined nature of a contingent of college faculty that had accompanied him on the trip. "There is one quality which pervades them all," he remarked, "a sort of gentility which makes everyone likeable or at least entirely tolerable."[24] On arriving in Constantinople, Allport continued to speak highly of those well-mannered and socially accomplished European and American gentlemen whom he met, who occupied various educational, military, and government posts. The dignity and bearing of the English officials were especially appealing to the young American. After dining with an English colonel, Allport spoke approvingly of the "finest [qualities] of English life" that had been displayed in such abundance:

> The appointments of an English better class family dinner deserve praise in comparison to American family dinners of the same class in society. There is an exquisite service and taste in the English meals which the Americans certainly don't get. Our own people, for example, could never learn how to enhance a meal by wines and liqueurs. . . . I can see also the famous fortitude and uncomplaining character of the British in the face of their extreme war sufferings. Americans commercialize their sufferings.[25]

Clearly visible in these observations is precisely the sort of refined, high-minded gentleman that Lowell had envisioned. However, Allport's admiration for the genteel existed alongside a fascination with the vulgar. He was intrigued by the failure of so many to cultivate the kind of purposeful, dignified life that had presented itself so persuasively to him. "As I write," he commented on the voyage to Constantinople, "I hear the steerage [class] howling and shrieking below our bepalmed writing conservatory. 'Countless dirty lads and wenches in many thousand stinking stenches.' . . . They appear to be an undesirable assortment, but I like to watch them writhe about in their enforced proximity."[26]

During his tenure at Robert College, Allport had additional opportunities to watch the multitudes "writhe about," and in keeping with the best traditions of American benevolence, he pondered the inability of the masses to become men of character. After visiting the Grand Bazaar one day, he noted that most people lacked that sense of definition, purpose, and dignity that he had been taught to revere. "The thousands of faces which passed us on the bridge revealed no ambition or happiness," he remarked glumly. "The greater majority were distinctly miserable. Ignorance, pain, shame, anaesthesia, [and] indifference were plainly stamped on nearly every visage."[27] By this juncture, Allport had read enough sociology to interpret this condition in social terms. But after considering economic deprivations and "personal inefficiency or lusts," he found himself drifting back to the notion of individual will that was so central to character: "The fault, I am inclined to believe, lies in the failure of the masses to adopt any reason for living—[and to] shape their lives consistently by it." This notion of a failure of will may have satisfied previous generations of benevolent workers, but as a student of the new social work,

Allport hoped to probe still further. Why did some people fail to develop a reason for living while others developed into sterling, purposeful characters? After 4 years of psychology and social ethics at Harvard, he did not yet have an answer to this question, but he was convinced of the gravity of the issue. The person who solved the question, Allport noted optimistically, could "alleviate all the ills of mankind."[28]

A TENDER SOUL

The trip to Constantinople had been conceived as a spiritual odyssey, and through his travels in Turkey and beyond, Allport attained a breadth of perspective on his distinctively tender, unmasculine brand of maleness. It soon became apparent to him that Robert College was a place where the tender-minded could thrive, and indeed, most of the male faculty had the same sort of refined, sensitive disposition as he. Allport felt an immediate kinship with these sensitive souls, and he developed an especially strong friendship with Edwin Powers and Pete Dodge, two young Robert College faculty members. Like Allport, Powers and Dodge were recent college graduates fascinated by beauty, gentility, and big ideas.[29] When not teaching, the three men would often tour around Constantinople together in search of aesthetic splendor and mystical wonder. "It is an unrestrained pleasure to go with them on such rambles," Allport noted fondly. "They are chaps of real appreciation and [are] personally very attractive."[30]

Dodge was a particularly compelling figure, and he had a fascination with beauty and refinement that was notable even by Robert College standards. In his diary, Allport commented on his friend's aesthetic sense and charismatic personality. "Pete has a passionate love for the beautiful and it is a pleasure to walk with him" he observed. "His sense of humor saves him from despondency over the routine of the task ahead."[31] Some years later, acquaintances of Dodge speculated that he was gay, and his friendship with Allport contained some sexually suggestive elements. The two men would often seek out beautiful secluded spots for vigorous rowing; "lusty" singing; and deep, soulful conversations.[32] "There is something positively invigorating about the stream," Allport noted in his diary. "Whenever we [himself and Pete] get out upon it we feel refreshed and joyous. Our best times have been the free, pleasant conversations and songs that we indulge in as soon as the kayik [sic] shoves off."[33] These enchanting boat trips would sometimes turn into moonlight swims, and in his diary Allport wrote lavish descriptions of trips with Dodge that were replete with romantic imagery:

> At night sweet Pete and I took our favorite old boatman and rowed to Kur–fez for a starlight swim. This spot is paradise itself; sheltered, unvisited save by us, with a fig tree within reach of our pier, water

lapping its phosphorescent tongues about the piles. O, the sweet relief from care and heat in the crystal stream! The joy of bare bodies churning the limpid waters into a glow within the shadow of sparkling minarets signaling the end of Ramadan.[34]

The emotional intensity and sexual imagery of Allport's friendship with Dodge are unmistakable, but the meaning of these passages is not as straightforward as it might initially appear. As historian Jeffrey Richards argued, "changes in language and modes of expression render statements of affection from previous ages highly complex and ambiguous matters."[35] The complexities of interpretation are particularly apparent in cases involving intense male friendship, like that of Allport and Dodge. As Richards notes, since Freud many scholars have "found it impossible to dissociate close male friendship from homosexuality." This axiom of modern interpretation does not stand up to sustained historical scrutiny, however. A number of scholars have noted that in the late 19th and early 20th century, homosexuality was typically differentiated from "manly love"—an intense, nonsexual form of male friendship. Tying together ideals of service, sacrifice, and brotherhood, manly love was celebrated as the highest form of friendship, but it was never considered to be a substitute for the love of a woman. "The difference [between manly love and heterosexual love] lies essentially in the fact that the love of a woman is sexual and therefore inferior; the love of a man for a man is spiritual, transcendent and free from base desire."[36]

Allport's relationship with Dodge is a good illustration of manly love. The two shared strong feelings for each which were—at least in the case of Allport—more spiritual than physical. There is no explicit reference to homosexuality in Allport's diary, and the romantic topics that were mentioned assumed a conventional heterosexual form. At one point, he observed that Dodge "fell for" a "vamp-like" woman in a vaudeville act,[37] and in a 1920 poem that Allport wrote about his friendship with Powers and Dodge, "affairs of heart were ... discussed" in the context of "who'd be the first to wed."[37] Unfortunately, Allport's journal and correspondence contain no further clues on the matter, but in later life Allport did not identify as a gay man and lived a conventionally heterosexual lifestyle. Nevertheless, his close friendship with Dodge and Powers was important insofar as it gave Allport confidence in his own "tender" self-definition. Affirmed by their support and example, Allport felt ready to stand more decisively against the pressure of his older and ever masculine brother Harold. Using the heavily gendered language of business, Allport wrote to Harold while in Constantinople and frankly admitted his "deficiency": "When I think of my un-businesslike propensities, of my counter-commercialism I blush with shame." Allport quickly added, however, that the posture of the hard-nosed businessman was simply alien to him and it would be foolish to pretend otherwise. "But honestly, Harold, I can never make any money, and what is disastrous is that I don't care to."[38] (See insert, Figure 25.)

PROFESSIONAL DEVELOPMENT AND THE DEATH OF IDEALISM

Allport may have been inspired to travel to Constantinople by a spiritual desire for proportion, but he was quick to recognize the practical value of his experience. Robert College gave him an opportunity to polish his teaching skills, something that would be invaluable if he were to continue with graduate work at Harvard. Before his trip to Turkey, Allport had little experience as a classroom instructor, and he harbored grave doubts about his potential as a lecturer. He was particularly concerned about the sociology course he had agreed to teach. The students in the course were not the generally compliant boys that he had in his English classes, but young men—"seniors and engineers"—most of whom were in their 20s. At 23, Allport was, in fact, younger than most of the students in his course. The class's maturity raised an alarming question in Allport's mind: Would they be "skeptical of my ability to teach the subject?"[39]

This question weighed heavily on Allport as he entered the class on the first day of the course. He had prepared careful notes for his lecture, but as the hour approached, feelings of inadequacy came to the surface. "When the last pupil had arrived and the door was shut, I felt like Daniel just delivered to the lions." For an instant, Allport's self-doubt got the better of him. He had a "momentary experience of paralysis," but he quickly recovered, and as the "morning progressed ... I warmed up and discoursed volubly on the relation of the various social sciences, the task of social ethics, illustrating social problems with the story of the Kallikak family."[40] Throughout the lecture, Allport was relieved to see no sign of skepticism in the faces of his students. "On the whole," he wrote in his journal, "they listened with gratifying attention and respect." Allport was understandably pleased to have come through his first true lecture in such fine form. However, the pleasure he felt at having given a successful lecture was tinged with a recognition that he was not a not a natural platform speaker. To avoid "embarrassment" he had to be "well prepared." Even when he had a thorough grasp on his material, teaching "fatigued [him] almost to exhaustion."[41]

If the added work and responsibility of the sociology course dampened Allport's enthusiasm for missionary life, he did not show it. In a letter to Philips Brooks House, he admitted that he had "a program of work exceeding the average schedule for a single teacher" but quickly added that he was "glad to do all I can for such a good purpose."[42] Years later, Allport would have occasion to question the "goodness" of that purpose. In a 1931 letter to a Robert College official, he admitted that he had been "unquestionably guilty" of displaying a "patronizing" attitude toward the "natives."[43] But in 1919 his efforts were interpreted as expressions of hard work and fine character, and they soon earned him the respect of College officials. The College's vice president said that he had done "exceedingly good work for a first year man," and a year after Allport left Turkey, the College's president wrote to Philips Brooks House asking for a "worthy successor to Mr. Allport who has left behind only good memories."[44]

Allport had traveled to Constantinople imbued with a mixture of spiritual uncertainty and progressive idealism. His search for proportion remained an ongoing concern, but 8 months of living in Turkey blunted the keen edge of his idealism. Recalling his undergraduate experience, Allport noted that he had been a "thoroughgoing idealist, hopeful about every good project, fired with zeal to participate, to reform and to increase human happiness." Although he experienced some modest success in his service activities while in Turkey, the net effect of his efforts had been to "disillusion the hopeful enthusiast and to quench idealism":

> Frankly said, in Turkey, I have grown skeptical concerning the possibilities for human betterment. People here are so hopelessly dishonest, indifferent and fatalistic, that all endeavors seem wasted. Why should one waste his life in addition to the lives of the wretches who will perish ignominiously in spite of all efforts for their improvement.[45]

Glimpsing the limitations of social reform, Allport found himself checking his spiritual bearings as well as his moral sentiments. Coming from a relatively prosperous family, he had viewed poverty and ignorance as objects of exotic fascination. Squalor had its own kind of peculiar romance, and its novelty and intensity helped satiate his antimodernist desire for authentic experience. As an undergraduate he had felt a "thrill and stimulation . . . from the primitive condition of the immigrants to the U.S." Mired in the turmoil and misery of Constantinople, Allport began to rethink his personal relationship with the poverty of others. The sheer banality of squalor in Turkey made it less enticing as a source of spiritual validation. To his consternation, Allport observed that the "thrill" of poverty had been transformed into "nausea at the almost animal existence of the natives here."[46]

THE RELIGION OF BEAUTY

Deprived of yet another source of authenticity and spiritual sustenance, Allport found a measure of solace in a familiar antimodernist motif: religious aestheticism. For many late-Victorian Americans, spiritual weightlessness provoked an intense desire to recapture the form and feeling of premodern religiosity. Abjuring the artistic minimalism of their Protestant past, spiritually hungry Americans developed an intense interest in the aesthetic legacy of medieval Catholicism. European cathedrals and abbeys became places of pilgrimage, and Catholic art, ritual, and Gothic architecture enjoyed a wide following.[47] Allport had sensed this impulse while in Boston, but the antiquity of Constantinople dramatically underscored the spiritual power of ancient forms.

The Church of St. Sophia made a particularly dramatic impression on him. Built by order of the Emperor Justinian in 537 A.D., St. Sophia was conceived as a massive monument to Christianity. It had been converted into a mosque when Constantinople fell to the Turks in 1453, and it was still in use as a Muslim holy site when Allport visited one evening in 1920. Strolling up and the down the galleries, he sensed "the whole romance of religion for fifteen centuries." In the basilica, he paused to observe a "sea of ten thousand Moslems, swaying in unison to their simple prayer." Dazzled by the building's antiquity and by the spiritual energy of the faithful, Allport struggled to capture the intensity of the moment. "It was too impressive for words," he remarked, "to think of the religious force which has exercised itself in this edifice; a thousand years the center of Christendom and six hundred years the center of Islam."[48]

Although Allport appreciated the intensity of Islam, the increasingly aesthetic tenor of his own spirituality lent a critical edge to an otherwise ecumenical sensibility. At St. Sophia, he noted with dismay that "Mohammad's name blazed from the space between the minarets and huge plaques with Koran inscriptions everywhere hid the Christian images." For Allport, the spiritual vigor behind these symbols was less important than the vulgarity involved in merging two distinctive religious aesthetics: "One thought only of the imposition, of the sacrilege of using an obvious Christian masterpiece for the service of a weak, incomparably inferior religion."[49] A trip to the "whirling dervishes" saw Allport in a more charitable frame of mind, but here again he was drawn to the religious aesthetic of the sect as much as he was to its spiritual energy. "This sect [the dervishes] is more dignified and aesthetic than the gruesome howlers," he noted approvingly. "The mosque itself is very artistic, being a perfect hexagon with an open space in the center with [a] perfect floor for the barefooted whirlers."[50]

The dramatic displays of religious antiquity had a profound impact on Allport, and the ancient forms brought him a measure of spiritual gravity. A trip through the heart of Europe in the summer of 1920 gave him still more opportunities to indulge his religious aestheticism. He was dazzled by the antiquity of Rome and noted breathlessly that the city's "ornamental features surpass all imagination."[51] Dutifully surveying the city's famous attractions, Allport recorded their aesthetic and historical significance in his diary. "The galleries of the Vatican and the Cathedral's are overpowering," he wrote, and at every turn he could feel the "beauty and profound significance of this city."[52] Allport was similarly moved by the splendor of Florence and Milan, and his gaze carefully registered the spiritual significance of what lay before him. "I was impressed especially with the eastern door of the Baptistry which Michael Angelo himself said was suited to be the door to paradise."[53]

Having glimpsed the door to paradise, Allport was not inclined to let it slip from his sight. Meaning, significance, and authenticity seemed to lie in the timeless beauty of premodern Christian forms. In the coming years, what had begun as a vaguely felt sense would crystallize into a firmly held conviction. Taking his spiritual bearings for the present using aesthetic reference points from the past, he set off down a path that would eventually lead him to a community of Americans who found an imagined premodern sensibility a useful counterweight to the spiritual emptiness of an industrialized, commercialized existence. Intriguingly, Allport's path would also intersect with that most modern of sensibilities—the psychological—and it was to this voice that he responded in the spring of 1920.

RETURN TO THE PSYCHOLOGICAL

Allport's voyage to the exotic world of Robert College had been propelled by a kind of spiritual uncertainty, and his immersion in the antiquity of Constantinople and Europe intensified the vague antimodernist feeling he had sensed as an undergraduate. Living amid the "undisturbed venerableness" of a historic city and nurtured by sublime friendships, he felt increasingly distant from the frenzied rationality and shallow optimism of modern America. Constantinople made the charms of a quieter and more spiritually fulfilling contemplative life easier to see, and Allport found himself becoming "discouragingly subjective." He was moved by the "sensuous beauty of the [Turkish] evening," and he felt torn between the spiritual intensity of aesthetic contemplation and the active, interventionist ethic he had learned at Harvard. "Why must individuals be always passive objects, enjoying the impressions of nature, or else blind men, fighting with it and invariably losing?" he wondered. Unfortunately for Allport, an answer to this question was not forthcoming. "It seems, however, that one must be either a passive lover of nature's creations, leaving man to himself, or else he must be a rank biologist." It was a stark polarity, and at Robert College and, indeed, for much of his career as a personality psychologist, Allport felt himself oscillating between these extremes. "Sometimes I feel myself one [an aesthete]; sometimes the other [a biologist]."[54]

In 1920, Floyd Allport provided a temporary solution to this dilemma by encouraging his brother to return to the grounded world of scientific investigation. Floyd did not share his brother's antimodernist temper, but he remained an influential figure in Allport's life. Having completed his

PhD in 1919, Floyd's academic career had gone from strength to strength. In the fall of 1919 he accepted an instructorship at Harvard, and the following year he was made a coeditor of the *Journal of Abnormal and Social Psychology*.[55] Aware of his growing professional stature, Floyd urged his younger brother to follow his example and return to the United States to pursue graduate work in psychology at Harvard. Lest Allport have any concerns about finances, Floyd assured him that the prospects for a scholarship were good. Accommodation would not be a problem either: Allport could live in Floyd's apartment.[56] The thought of becoming a psychologist and perhaps becoming more like his successful brother appealed to Allport, despite his growing antimodernist fascination with antiquity. He took Floyd's advice, and in February 1920 applied for the Henry Bromfield Rogers Memorial Fellowship. If successful, Allport would begin graduate studies in the fall of 1920, a full 2 years before he was due to leave Robert College.

Allport was awarded the Rogers Fellowship in March 1920. Shortly after applying for the fellowship, however, he began to question the wisdom of his decision. Robert College was a rewarding place to work. What it lacked in intellectual sophistication it more than made up for in cosmopolitan charm, "sensuous beauty," and spiritual depth. By mid-April, Allport found himself in "one of those nerve racking moral quandaries." He very much wanted to take Floyd up on his offer, but at the same time felt a growing sense of distance from the busy, ordered world of American academia. Allport wrestled with the merits of each option and finally decided to stay "unless a cable from Floyd says that I don't stand a good chance for the award another year."[57]

Confident in his decision, Allport conveyed the news to Robert Foerster, his social ethics teacher, from his undergraduate studies. Allport noted that he had "become quite tied down by my work here" to the point where "it would be extremely difficult to leave just now."[58] He also pointed out that he had been asked to participate in a "social survey of Constantinople" that was being undertaken by a group of philanthropic organizations. "This activity interests me," he wrote, "and I am anxious for the experience it will offer." Anxious or not, Allport was quick to clarify his professional priorities. He told Foerster that he would prefer to remain in Turkey for one more year, if it were possible to "secure a postponement" of the award. If no such assurance was forthcoming, he would "make every effort to cancel my work here rather than lose *permanently* my chance at Harvard for a fellowship."[59]

Unfortunately for Allport, the Rogers Fellowship could not be deferred. Shortly after receiving Allport's request, Foerster informed Floyd Allport that "it would be necessary for [Gordon Allport] to give up the award for this next year and to take his chances with the other applicants the following year."[60] Allport may have anticipated this answer, for he began to experience misgivings the same day that he made his request to

Foerster. He spent the evening in a state of "acute misery" and "nervous destruction." The following morning, Allport concluded that he could no longer live with the "soul-destroying suspense."[61] A concrete and irrefutable decision was needed. "Without any doubt of my course I proceeded to inform the strategic people and to send a reply cable" to Floyd accepting the offer.[62] Floyd was clearly delighted by the news. In a letter to Foerster, Floyd wrote that he felt "very glad of his [brother's] decision, since graduate work in psychology and social science will probably be of greater value to him in preparation for a career at this time than work in the field in the near east."[63]

"DOCTOR PROFESSOR FREUD"

Unsettled by the calculating careerism that had surrounded his departure from Robert College, Allport sought out a distinctively modern benediction for his new psychological undertaking. Who better to provide such a blessing than the Viennese scholar who was rapidly emerging as the spiritual leader of the psychological world: Sigmund Freud. Allport had stopped off in Vienna on his way back to Cambridge, Massachusetts, to visit his brother Fayette, who was then serving on the U.S. Trade Commission.[64] While in the Austrian capital, he decided to round out his trip by visiting Freud at his famous home, 19 Berggasse.

Allport's undergraduate education was the most likely source of his interest in Freud. Like most universities, Harvard did not formally recognize psychoanalysis, and there were no psychoanalysts on the faculty. However, psychoanalytic ideas were routinely discussed in the Department of Philosophy and Psychology, and not always in disparaging terms. Indeed, shortly before his death in 1910, William James told the American psychoanalyst Ernest Jones that "the future of psychology belongs to your work."[65] James's interest in psychoanalytic thought was subsequently developed at Harvard by his student Edwin Holt. In 1915, Holt published a sympathetic discussion of Freud's work titled *The Freudian Wish and Its Place in Ethics*.[66] Allport took Holt's course in social psychology in 1917 to 1918, and although he did not explicitly mention reading *The Freudian Wish*, it seems likely that the basic axioms of Freud's position were reviewed at some point in the course.[67] Allport later recalled that his "solid undergraduate training" had made Freud's work "fairly well known to me."[68]

Having decided to undertake professional training in psychology, Allport thought it would be interesting to meet the scholar who had generated such "frantic worship."[69] With the "callow forwardness characteristic of age twenty-two," he sent Freud a note asking for an appointment. A short time later, he "received a kind reply in his own handwriting inviting me to come to his office at a certain time."[70] On July 28, 1920, Allport "called upon Dr. Prof. Freud."[71] The meeting began well enough. Allport later recalled that Freud appeared "promptly at the appointed time" and "ushered me into the inner office with a friendly and attentive welcome in English."[72] At that point, however, what Allport had undoubtedly hoped would be a confidence-boosting consultation with a "man of genius" took a turn for the worse.[73] In his "youthful naiveté," he had not thought to map out a plausible pretext to justify the interview.[74] Thus, after Freud showed him into his office, Allport was momentarily at a loss for words. There was an "awkward pause" while Freud "sat at his desk waiting for me to state the reason for my coming."[75]

Social proprieties of this sort were something in which Allport was well versed. At Robert College, he commented repeatedly on displays of grace and tact, and he himself moved through formal dinners, dances, and meetings with well-mannered ease. When confronted with a psychoanalytic world in which social conventions masked sexual and aggressive wishes, however, Allport was suddenly less sure of himself. Freud's predictable query left him scrambling for something to say. In the heat of the moment, Allport decided to showcase his psychological sophistication by telling Freud about something he had seen on the tram: "A small boy about four years of age had displayed a conspicuous dirt phobia. He kept saying to his mother, 'I don't want to sit there ... don't let that dirty man sit beside me.' To him everything was schmutzig."[76] Allport's intention in telling the story was to provide Freud with some case material to comment on. Since the boy's mother on the tram was a "well-starched Hausfrau" with a "dominant and purposive" look, Allport expected Freud to make a connection between the mother's manner and the boy's phobia.[77] Freud did respond to the story, but he did so in a manner that took Allport completely off guard. Instead of treating the anecdote in the spirit the young American had intended, Freud interpreted the story as an expression of Allport's own character. "When I finished my story," Allport later recalled, "Freud fixed his kindly therapeutic eyes upon me and said, 'And was that little boy you?'"[78]

Allport was "flabbergasted," by Freud's response, and he later insisted that the psychoanalyst had completely missed the mark with his pointed interpretation.[79] However, as several scholars have since noted, Freud's observation was not as wildly speculative as Allport would later claim.[80] In 1920, Allport may have had a measure of psychoanalytic sophistication, but as his brief tenure at Robert College made clear, he was still very much the son of John and Nellie. He was a man of character, and his "habits of the heart" were those of the evangelical Midwest: duty, respectability, good works, and cleanliness of mind and body.[81] Freud knew nothing of Allport's personal background when he made his comment, but he was familiar enough with American middle-class sensibilities to spot their telltale signs. He often spoke derisively of "prudish" and "virtuous" America, and he frequently condemned "the strictness of American chastity."[82] For Freud, Allport's brief anecdote must have seemed predictably American.

Freud was too polite to pursue this analysis, and Allport too embarrassed. The young American "contrived to change the subject."[83] Looking for validation for his decision to study psychology, Allport told Freud of his plans to return to Harvard and he asked if there were any good American-based analysts that he might consult with. Freud listened patiently while Allport developed his questions. The famous psychoanalyst gave his visitor the impression of being a "kindly man, approachable and sympathetic." However, the answers he provided to Allport's questions made it equally clear that he was also a "jealous man." In his journal entry describing the visit, Allport noted that Freud was "quite unwilling to recognize any psychoanalyst in America except Brill."[84] What was perhaps even more disturbing to Allport were the doubts Freud raised about his plans to pursue graduate study at Harvard. "Freud failed to see why I should waste time at Harvard when no adequate representative of his school is present."[85]

Allport did not dwell on any of these concerns in his journal, nor was he particularly unsettled by Freud's probing analysis of the boy on the tram. Viewing the meeting as a rather routine affair, Allport did not even mention the story of the boy, and he concluded his journal account of the discussion by casually mentioning that he and Freud "discussed also repressions and their mechanisms. To understand psychoanalysis one must, according to him, read German."[86]

Meeting Freud may not have had a great impact on the initial development of Allport's thought, but their discussion was to figure prominently in his subsequent career as a personality psychologist. Later in life, Allport described his meeting with Freud as "an event of pungent significance."[87] Freud's apparently hasty interpretation "started a deep train of thought" that led to the conclusion that "depth psychology, for all its merits, may plunge too deep, and that psychologists would do well to give full recognition to manifest motives before probing the unconscious." As a professional psychologist, Allport developed this idea more fully, and he became well-known as a critic of what he termed "psychoanalytic excesses."[88]

CONCLUSION

Historians in search of the origins of American psychology are unlikely to descend on Constantinople, yet the one year that Allport spent in the Near East made a lasting impression on his career as personality psychologist. Allport had traveled to Robert College in pursuit of meaning, and although he did not come away with any definitive answers, the Old

World's squalid despair and sublime antiquity provided some welcome clarity. Unrelenting displays of wretchedness exploded Progressive visions that Allport had harbored of a world redeemed through enlightened science. No amount of professionalized benevolence could eliminate anguish, nor could the eradication of squalor serve as a center of personal meaning. Convinced of poverty's permanence, Allport now saw anguish as being ugly, rather than uplifting, and without completely surrendering the ideals of social reform, he drifted further into the antimodernist currents he had entered as an undergraduate.

Those currents took Allport into an ancient idiom of spiritual devotion. The time-honored majesty of St. Sophia and Rome satisfied his spiritual uneasiness in a way that the scientific catechism he had learned at Harvard never had. Allport internalized these venerable forms, but in keeping with the flow of American antimodernism, his experience involved a complex blending of dissent and accommodation.[89] Reverence for the ancient and mystical went hand in hand with a strong desire for more science, more rationality, and a bigger stake in shaping the new order. Aware of the incongruity of his vision, Allport struggled to work these competing impulses into a coherent vision. Freud did not provide any answers to this spiritually challenging task, and Allport returned to the United States to begin his graduate studies in an ambivalent frame of mind. He was now convinced that meaning, in the fullest and most profound sense of the term, could never be found solely through progress, rationality, or anything else self-consciously "modern." The door to paradise lay where it always had: in the religious idiom and iconography of the past. Yet, as Allport noted in his diary, "the undisturbed venerableness of this old world is about to face alterations," and no amount of spiritual feeling could alter that fact. Modernity had to be confronted, and by going into psychology while embracing antiquity, Allport hoped to somehow find a spiritually fulfilling way forward.

5

A SCIENCE OF PERSONALITY:
GRADUATE SCHOOL (1920–1922)

The development of a complete and sensitive instrument of individual measurement for personality as well as for intelligence is a distant but perhaps not an unattainable goal.
— Floyd Allport and Gordon Allport, 1921[1]

Allport was scheduled to sail to New York in September 1920. Having toured many of Europe's ancient splendors, shortly before sailing he decided to visit the site of a modern catastrophe: the devastated landscape of Flanders. Although the war had been over for 21 months, the Belgian battlefields were still a horrific spectacle. On the Ypres salient, Allport found a "desolated waste of shell holes and morass. Not a living tree can be seen for miles. Formerly picturesque Flemish towns are now totally unrecognizable piles of bricks." Moving across the Belgian killing fields, Allport was mesmerized by the scale of devastation and depth of human suffering. "It was pathetic to see peasants everywhere digging in old ruins to salvage a bit of a utensil or piece of furniture from their former home." Looking every bit like hell on earth, Flanders was a museum of modernity's darker creations, and Allport gingerly walked through a landscape strewn with "dug-outs, barbed wire, shells, tanks, trenches, [and] bodies."[2]

As historian Modris Eksteins noted, meaning was one of the major casualties of the Great War. Old customs and justifications were blown apart, "and as the external world collapsed in ruins, the only redoubt of integrity became the individual personality."[3] As a student in the Harvard Student Army Training Corps, Allport had not lived the horror, but as he crisscrossed the scarred landscape as a tourist, the hope and idealism that had seemed so alive in 1917 and 1918 were noticeably absent. His mind was stirred not by ethics and politics, but by the battlefield's brutal aesthetic. Unfettered by meaning, Allport simply absorbed the awesome spectacle and registered its extraordinary depth and drama. "To walk around the shell-holes and pick up bits of metal and significant bullets was fascinating. It is extremely dangerous however to handle grenades and shells which lie everywhere on the hills."[4]

The trip to Flanders had been a memorable experience, but the sight of European devastation did not alter his antimodernist faith in the spiritual power of Old World forms. Indeed, imagining an American future with an eye on his newly acquired experience of Europe's past, Allport felt somewhat dismayed. He sensed a spiritual kinship with the antiquity and dignity of the Old World, and he felt strangely alienated when he overheard fellow American passengers boasting of America's superiority to Europe. American tourists were "poor narrow souls," he observed, who were incapable of appreciating America "in the true sense for their scale of evaluation was never put to the acid test of living in Europe." What dismayed Allport most was not the breezy superiority of American travelers, but their blatant disregard for the values that he learned to revere. "The average American ... neglects to consider the art of Europe, its dignity and history, its philosophy of life and infirmities," he wrote despairingly. Sounding a familiar antimodernist refrain, Allport lamented the nation's complacent celebration of progress and its fascination with the newer, the bigger, and the better. The typical American "is blinded by the crushing progress of the States," he noted dejectedly. "The Juggernaut car drags him along, and poor simpleton, he thinks himself blessed if it cuts him down in its mad rush toward 'progress.'"[5]

Alienated by the spiritual emptiness of modern America, Allport questioned his future in a culture that equated "progress" with ever more spectacular displays of technological prowess. "I fear I am the soul-stunted individual who will go down to the vile dust, unwept, unhonored and unsung; for I can't summon much of the fervor which the native land is supposed to elicit from the wanderer."[6] Unable to conjure up an optimistic vision of the future, Allport's thoughts drifted back to Constantinople's exoticism and premodern allure. "I would prefer to be in Turkey this very day (September 15, 1920) officiating at the opening of the Hamlin Hall dining room."[7] The sentiment was sincere, but impractical, and Allport did not allow memories of Constantinople to weigh down his professional ambitions. In keeping with the plans carefully developed in concert with Floyd, he registered as a graduate student at Harvard in the fall of 1920. Still interested in the professionalization of benevolence, he enrolled as a student in psychology and social ethics and submitted his dissertation to both departments.[8]

As we shall see, Allport's dissertation was cast in the upbeat idiom of positivist science, but his graduate work was as much a self-conscious performance as it was a statement of belief. Allport knew that success as a psychology graduate student involved enacting certain ideals that the discipline held sacred. He had to live natural science, measurement, classification, and prediction, and he had to affirm the idea that human nature was a natural object. Always a keen student, Allport could articulate those beliefs as well as anyone, but his words lacked the conviction of the true believer. Immersed in a new world of "science, SCIENCE, SCIENCE!!!! [sic]," Allport felt himself "valiantly swimming the whirlpool—competing, repressing, stealing the march, stretching my talents, losing my romance and mourning sadly":

> Would you believe it if I told you that for eight hours to-day I have actually been administering monotonous intelligence tests to Portugese, Lithuanian, Negro, and other miscellaneous children in a public school ...? I felt between a drained out school-marm and a relentless scientist who classifies, indexes ever, uses a microscope and tweezers. But that I did, and shall continue for moons to come.[9]

Professionally active but personally disposed to doubt, Allport viewed his scientific training more as a matter of posture and endurance than as a source of personal deliverance. Real meaning was to be found in the contemplation of spiritualized beauty and the companionship of like-minded souls. "The happiest moments of my life," he remarked to his Robert College friend Edwin Powers, "were the flashes of paradise which one or all of you led me to experience in Baltaliman rambles, moonlight rows, coffee house languor, intimate and friendly conversation, and above all the moments of intense, utterly spiritual sympathy."[10] Bereft of these spiritual outlets and "friends of my heart," Allport worried that his "finer sentiments [were] being squashed—like the Riva bed-bugs—by the indignation of my thesis":[11]

> Must I go on with the necessary sham [of graduate school]? Is it necessary? I can do it, putting on intellectuality and pseudo-intellectuality; and finally I can attain the goal. But what will become of the true spark of my inner nature?[12]

Unsure of the answer, Allport pressed ahead with his scientific training while seeking to preserve his "sensuous, groping soul."[13]

PSYCHOLOGY AT HARVARD: 1918–1922

Allport may have enrolled in both psychology and social ethics, but as a graduate student most of his attention was devoted to the questions and methodological procedures of psychology. The graduate program in psychology that Allport entered was an illustrious one. The program had been instituted in the 1870s by William James, who supervised the first

American PhD in psychology: G. Stanley Hall in 1878.[14] Hugo Münsterberg succeeded James as head of the Harvard Psychological Laboratory in 1895, and for the next 20 years his numerous scholarly contributions and lofty reputation kept Harvard at the forefront of American psychology. In 1910, however, the fortunes of psychology at Harvard began to wane. James died, and concerns had started to emerge over the nature of Münsterberg's publications. Most of his scholarly work after he arrived in the United States had been in the field of applied psychology, efforts that earned him a large readership among the general public. Münsterberg's American colleagues were not averse to the application of psychology, nor were they opposed to public discussions of the subject. What they disliked was the crudely sensationalistic way in which Münsterberg sometimes presented psychology to the public. Harvard University President A. Lawrence Lowell expressed the view of the American academic establishment as a whole when he told Münsterberg that "your high standing as a scholar would be more appreciated if you never allowed your name to appear in the press."[15]

Münsterberg chose to ignore Lowell's advice, and at his death in 1916 his scholarly reputation had undergone a marked decline. His demise was a setback for psychology at Harvard, and in 1917 Harvard philosopher Ralph Barton Perry noted, "[O]ur prestige in psychology is at the lowest ebb in our history" [italics added].[16] To revive the field, the university needed to recruit a well-known psychologist and promote some of the existing faculty. Perry, among others, made this case to President Lowell. A political scientist by training, Lowell was a strong and capable administrator who had been in office since 1909. His interests were broad, but somewhat out of step with the emerging academic culture of the 20th century. The new university ethos was oriented toward professionalism and specialization. As historian Bruce Kuklick noted, "the order of the day was technical specialized research published for technically competent audiences in technical journals, with popularizations in all areas of speculation frequently relegated to hacks, incompetents, and has-beens."[17] As we have seen, Lowell's vision was rooted in the language of character, and he struggled throughout his term of office to reconcile his cultural and moral ideals with the increasingly specialized, technical turn of modern scholarship.

Nowhere was Lowell's dilemma more apparent than in graduate studies. He had inherited a university that was, in most fields, a national leader. Lowell valued scholarship, and he was committed to maintaining Harvard's reputation for excellence; the problem was how to go about preserving that reputation without sacrificing the ideals of character. Lowell's solution was to appoint faculty members who possessed both character and technical ability, but in the emerging academic culture of the 20th century, this was easier said than done. Academic disciplines were becoming increasingly professionalized and specialized. The scholars who were beginning to dominate those fields were not cut from the genteel cloth that Lowell so admired. Their cultural backgrounds were more diverse; their interests were narrower; and their scholarship was more technically involved. Whatever allegiance they had to the culture of character was usually subordinate to the ideal of "pure research."[18]

Lowell was aware of the professionalizing currents that were sweeping through American universities, but he continued to insist on the viability of the gentleman–scholar. Frederick Keppel, head of the Carnegie Corporation, put the matter succinctly in a 1933 report:[19] "[President] Lowell is quite frankly more interested in the urbane scholar of the British type, who will charm and stimulate the undergraduate, than in the authority of the multiple-footnote variety, who might prove more useful to the candidate for the doctorate."[20] Lowell's academic preferences complicated efforts to rebuild psychology at Harvard after Münsterberg's death. The structuralist psychologist Edward Titchener was considered as a possible replacement for Münsterberg, but he declined the invitation. The department then proposed James McKeen Cattell. One of the best known psychologists in America, Cattell would have given Harvard psychology an immediate legitimacy.[21] Lowell knew of Cattell's academic reputation, but he was not moved. Cattell was too independent for Lowell, and he lacked that combination of scholarly ability, character, and genteel polish.[22]

In the short term, Lowell's policy with respect to psychology was to simply make do with short-term appointments until a "suitable" replacement became available. Responsibility for running the psychology laboratory was given to two junior members of the faculty: Herbert Langfeld (1879–1958), an assistant professor with a 1909 PhD from Berlin, and Leonard Troland (1889–1932), an instructor who had been a student of Münsterberg. In 1920, the recently graduated Floyd Allport was appointed to an instructorship in the newly emerging field of social psychology.[23] That same year, Lowell found his "suitable" replacement—William McDougall (1871–1938). McDougall was an Oxford-based, British psychologist with unusually eclectic tastes.[24] He had published extensively in the fields of social psychology, philosophy, anthropology, experimental psychology, psychicalism, and eugenics. Morally committed, broad-minded, and internationally known, he was a "man of character"—the embodiment of Lowell's gentleman–scholar.

Unfortunately for the future of psychology at Harvard, McDougall's views and demeanor won him few friends, and he often found himself at the center of controversy. His views on eugenics generated a particularly rancorous debate. In his widely publicized 1921 book *Is America Safe for Democracy?*, McDougall linked American national prosperity to the future of the White race and urged White America to adopt an aggressive program of eugenic policies before it was too late: "As I watch the American nation speeding gaily, with invincible optimism down the road to destruction, I seem to be contemplating the greatest tragedy in the history of mankind."[25] Although McDougall was hardly alone in such views, his high-profile position at Harvard and his "outwardly cold and arrogant" manner drew national attention, and he was vilified in the liberal press.[26] To make matters worse, McDougall's other psychological interests were also badly out of step with the dominant trends in American psychology. His concept of the "group mind" was regarded with suspicion, his emphasis on instincts was seen as dated, and his interest in psychic phenomena was nothing short of scandalous. His datedness is clearly evident in his book *Character and the Conduct of Life*, a humorless, sermonlike text published for a popular audience in 1927. In the book, McDougall reasserted an earlier vision of selfhood, one that was based on the "durable" and morally contingent qualities of will, effort, and responsibility: "I, for one, would rather define that final purpose and chief aim [of life] as the production of nobility of character."[27]

Increasingly enamored of the idiom of natural science, American psychologists came to view McDougall as a kind of psychological dinosaur. The perception was not lost on the British psychologist, and in his auto-biography he noted despairingly that American psychology students and faculty alike regarded him and his theories as "back-numbers, relics of a bygone and superseded age."[28] Dismissed as an antiquarian, McDougall did little to rebuild Harvard's reputation in psychology, and he may have weak-ened it. The task of restoring the department to its former glory thus fell to Langfeld and Troland, who had remained on the faculty. Both scholars were competent, but neither possessed the necessary experience or ability. Floyd Allport was a promising appointee, but his major contributions were still years away. All in all, the department that Gordon Allport entered in 1920 stood at the same low point that Ralph Barton Perry had noted in 1917.

The Academic Culture of Personality

In later years, Allport would become an important player in the cam-paign to rebuild psychology at Harvard. As a graduate student, the de-partment's weakened condition gave him license to cultivate a measure of scholarly independence. Following the pattern he had established as an undergraduate, Allport looked past the department's leading intellectual light. He took McDougall's graduate course in social psychology, but he got little out of the experience.[29] In his autobiography, he recalled that he "harbored all the prevailing anti-McDougall prejudices. I deplored his doc-trine of instinct, interactionism, and the group mind."[30] The depth of All-port's antipathy to McDougall is apparent in a 1921 letter:

Tonight is McDougall's [seminar], tomorrow night it is my loathed duty

to pilot said gentleman to the Graduate Schools Society meeting where
he will speak to a small handful of men—while I dissolve into chagrin
—why do I always get lassoed?[31]

Indifferent to McDougall's brand of psychology, for his dissertation
Allport worked instead with Herbert Langfeld. A former diplomat, Lanfeld
was known for his "trim, erect, well-groomed" appearance and dignified,
friendly manner.[32] He received his PhD in 1909 from the University of
Berlin, and he began teaching at Harvard in 1910. A specialist in the
psychology of aesthetics, Langfeld was also interested in emotion and sensory processes. Allport found him to be a congenial mentor, and he privately referred to his advisor as "Daddy Langfeld."[33] Although Allport respected Langfeld, Floyd Allport was the most influential figure in his
graduate training. The two worked closely together, and Allport often
turned to his brother for clarification on the controversial psychological
issues of the day: "After the seminar I had a two hour mental gymnastic
period with Floyd on 'Instincts,'" Allport noted in December 1920. "It was
fascinating and of great clarifying value to my own conviction in the
matter."[34] Floyd's influence also extended into his younger brother's personal life. Floyd played the role of realist, and he kept a watchful eye over
his brother's romantic aestheticism and burgeoning spirituality:

> After visualizing my room as I'd love to have it . . . I discovered that
> I had myself seated in a morris [sic] chair amidst luxurious flowers and
> lamps reading literature and writing leisurely "impressions." It would
> be bliss to spend a slow sweet college year of intellectual and literary
> dabble. As I said, however, Floyd crashed me to earth with a few
> pointed observations (he knows my vulnerable points).[35]

Ever attentive to his brother's advice, Allport later recalled that it
was Floyd who "suggested that I go to work on personality."[36] The younger
Allport again followed his brother's lead and developed a program of research that culminated in a PhD dissertation on the "traits of personality."
Floyd's interest in personality reflected a growing scholarly fascination with
both the category and the ways in which it could measured and mobilized.
As we have seen, social workers had come to regard personality as one of
the conceptual cornerstones in a larger project to professionalize benevolence. In the 1910s, American psychiatrists had also begun to reexamine
their language and professional priorities, and by 1920 personality had
emerged as one of the field's key categories. According to psychiatrist
Aaron Rosanoff, personality was a subject of "fundamental importance"
that had generated a "good deal of interest."[37] Psychiatric interest in personality had been heavily influenced by the work of 19th-century French
physicians studying psychopathology.[38] Eschewing earlier theological and
philosophical meanings, French doctors began to construct personality as
an embodied entity prone to disease. This medicalization of personality was

consolidated in Ribot's authoritative 1885 text *The Diseases of Personality* and was disseminated in the United States by Morton Prince through his investigations of multiple personality.

As historian Elizabeth Lunbeck noted, personality appealed to psychiatrists for much the same reason that it appealed to the social workers that Allport had studied as an undergraduate.[39] Personality carried a lighter moral load and an aura of modernity suitable for an ambitious science. Moreover, personality enabled psychiatrists to widen their professional vision. Character, in contrast, was a gendered category for the morally well-to-do. Limited primarily to men, character suggested a measure of respectability, participation, and influence that comparatively few could attain. Personality, however, was something that everybody had, and psychiatrists insisted that everyone could now be implicitly placed onto a single psychiatric continuum from "normal" to pathological. The new language thus allowed psychiatrists to construct a multitude of previously "borderland" spaces where the normal and the abnormal merged together. No longer confined to the starkly differentiated categories of the 19th century, the new language of personality brought the everyday world into the psychiatric imagination.

The academic appeal of personality extended beyond the fields of psychiatry and social work. As historian Nicole Barenbaum noted, sociologists also began to focus their attention on personality.[40] In the late 1910s and early 1920s, calls were issued for the development of a "sociology of personality," and many scholars within the field responded.[41] Inspired in large measure by the work of W. I. Thomas, a number of sociologists began to investigate personality using life histories and social case materials. The growing interest in personality was soon reflected in the system used by the *American Journal of Sociology* for classifying abstracts of recent literature. The framework's first category was "Personality: The Individual and the Person."[42]

Legal scholars were also fascinated by personality. Beginning in the late 19th century, attempts were made to construct personality into a legal right, and a number of scholars spoke of the "increased regard for human personality."[43] The legal meaning of personality hinged largely on the idea of equality before the law. Personality was a fundamental capacity to acquire or hold legal rights, and it transcended the social categories of status, social class, marital status, and citizenship. It was in this sense that University of Chicago law professor Ernst Freund spoke of a "right of personality," which he linked to the "abrogation of personal slavery and serfdom, ... the disappearance of legal·class distinctions, ... the recognition of the legal rights of aliens, . . . [and] the emancipation from domestic subjection."[44] In addition to its use in discussions of equality and freedom, personality was also mobilized in legal discussions of privacy. In their influential article on the right to privacy, Samuel Warren and Louis Brandeis argued that individuals possessed an "inviolable personality" that they likened to the "impregnability" of property rights. The law recognized the right to safeguard one's property, and Warren Brandeis argued that the law should also allow an individual to protect his personality from "idle or prurient curiosity."[45]

A Behavioral Unit

Although Floyd Allport was aware of the broad scholarly interest in personality, his own fascination with the topic was inspired more by developments in his own field. The radical behaviorism of John B. Watson was a particularly important influence. A comparative psychologist by training, Watson had developed into a leading figure in the campaign to transform the discipline into a science that was both objective and practical.[46] The way forward, in Watson's view, was to refashion psychology in the image of biology, and rigorous application of the evolutionary principle of adaptation was the conceptual key. Watson believed that by studying the adjustment of the organism's biological equipment in relation to the demands of the environment, the "educator, the physician, the jurist and the business man could utilize our data in a practical way."[47]

The biologically oriented psychology that Watson advocated entailed a marked physicalist reductionism. Complex processes were reduced down to their "simplest terms," which in Watson's view were the stimulus and response.[48] The *stimulus* was what called an organism to action. Watson thought that organisms were always animated by something that was either environmental—"external to the body"—or biological—"the movements of . . . muscles and the secretions of glands." The *response* was the behavior that an organism carried out in an attempt to adjust itself to the demands of the stimulus. It was at this point that personality entered Watson's theoretical formulation. Watson argued that a proper understanding of an organism's adaptation required a detailed consideration of a broad range of responses and a thorough scrutiny of the way in which those responses related to one another. *Personality* was the term Watson used to signify this higher level of analysis. The term referred to an "individual's total assets (actual and potential) and liabilities (actual and potential) on the reaction side."[49]

The appeal of radical behaviorism has been discussed extensively, but as Franz Samelson noted, historians have often overlooked the holistic promise of Watson's message. "Contrary to the conventional categorizing [of behaviorism] as elementaristic and atomistic, Watson was occasionally praised, in the early years, for his novel emphasis on the whole organism and its integrated functioning."[50] At Harvard, Floyd Allport and Walter Dearborn were among those who were enamored of Watson's holistic vision, and they passed on their enthusiasm to Allport. In the preface of his dissertation, Allport credited Dearborn with having taught him "the importance and value of behavioristic thinking in relation to genetic problems, such as the one represented by the traits of personality."[51] Had he wished, Allport could have said much the same thing about Floyd. The elder Allport's psychological sympathies had always rested with the "causal," physicalist side of Münsterberg's two-part model of psychology.[52] When Watson's book appeared in 1919, Floyd Allport's behaviorism became even more pronounced. His 1919 article "Behavior and Experiment in Social Psychology" was strongly influenced by Watson's reductionism and his natural science orientation.[53]

Historians of psychology have been careful to note the impact of behaviorism on Floyd Allport, but the influence of radical behaviorism on the thinking of Gordon Allport has gone largely unacknowledged.[54] The oversight is understandable; in his later career Allport was a prominent critic of behaviorism and its idiom of prediction and control. Nevertheless, as a graduate student Allport drew heavily on Watson, and the shadow of the famous behaviorist looms large in almost every chapter of his dissertation. At one point, Allport described Watson's emphasis on the "integrations and total activities of the individual" as a welcome addition to psychology and a convincing demonstration of "how barren all other approaches have been."[55] The most immediately obvious manifestation of Watson's influence was the model of selfhood, or personhood, that Allport advanced. Like Watson, Allport constructed a self that directly reflected the fluidity, impersonality, and competitiveness of the urban–industrial world. Indeed, in good behaviorist fashion, Allport refused to speak scientifically of an "inner life or selfhood." He argued that the "inner life" was too subjective to pass the scientific muster of psychology. If one wished to get personality admitted to the house of science, Allport maintained, a different formulation was needed. Psychologists would have to stop thinking about personality as a mysterious inner essence and start conceiving of it in terms of visible, calculable behavior. "The psychological problem [of personality] is strictly objective," he wrote, and "entirely consistent with the needs of laboratory procedure."[56]

To explain what he meant by an objective approach to personality, Allport again turned to Watson. Allport began with the view that personality was essentially a product of the interaction between the demands of the environment and a set of simple reflexes rooted in the "innate systems of nervous organization." Initially the child responds to the environment instinctively, but within a few weeks the child adjusts to the environment, and a number of "simple habits" develop. As the child grows, "the learning process widens to embrace a broad range of stimuli, and unique adaptive responses are called forth by the special sets of stimuli which the child is subjected to." Over time, these responses become extremely complex, and eventually the network of simple habits "become[s] grouped into dynamic sets of behavior" that Allport termed *traits*. Despite this increasing complexity, Allport was convinced that even the most intricate behavior that differentiates one person from another was ultimately nothing more than the "operation of reaction systems gradually evolved through the integration of simpler reflexes."[57]

One of the tasks that Allport set himself in his dissertation was to formulate a means of measuring these "reaction systems." Measuring simple habits was easy enough. "As regards simple motor habits the speed and accuracy of response alone need to be measured." The measurement of the more complex "systems of habits," or traits, was an altogether different affair. How was one to identify these traits? More important, perhaps, by what standard were they to be measured? Allport admitted that these were difficult questions, but he believed in the power of the psychological laboratory to overcome such technical difficulties. J. B. Watson again provided Allport with the necessary inspiration: "During the next few years," Allport quoted Watson as saying, "the laboratory should make such further progress that it will be capable of making by *actual tests*, serviceable and comprehensive surveys of *personality*" [italics added].[58] An *Experimental Study of the Traits of Personality* was Allport's attempt to realize Watson's prediction.

A Masculine Science

The imprimatur of so vigorous and respected a figure as Watson was important, for Allport was up against deeply entrenched disciplinary prejudices. Not only was the topic of personality suspiciously reminiscent of New Thought, Mind Cure, and other forms of popular psychology, it also skated dangerously close to a carefully policed divide in mainstream psychology between the masculine and the feminine. As historian Laurel Furomoto noted, early American psychology was a largely male preserve.[59] The vast majority of the faculty at the nation's leading graduate schools were male, and more important, they tended to construct scientific psychology in decidedly masculine terms. Science, like the idealized male psyche, was considered objective, detached, rigorous, and hard-nosed. It celebrated a vigorous ethic of action and viewed with suspicion, if not outright scorn, the "feminine" categories of contemplation, sensitivity, intuition, and sentimentality. In 1920, personality occupied an uncertain position on this gender continuum, but its strong ties to social work and the female reform tradition raised doubts as to its scientific suitability in the male minds of many of the more stridently scientific. The tentative status of personality is clearly evident in David Shakow's recollections of Allport's dissertation. A Harvard undergraduate with strong interests in psychopathology, Shakow recalled that it was "highly encouraging" to hear in 1922 of Allport dissertation work on personality: "At least fields *related* to clinical were not taboo and those interested in personality *could* receive recognition."[60]

As a graduate student, Allport came face to face with psychology's masculine ethic at the annual meeting of the Society of Experimental Psychologists. Dominated by its flamboyant founder and undisputed leader, Edward Titchener, the society is perhaps the clearest example of the gendered character of early American psychology.[61] Although Titchener trained large numbers of female graduate students, he viewed scientific psychology as a male domain and envisioned scientific practice through an idiom of male affiliation. "For many years," he remarked, "I wanted an experimental club—no officers, the men moving about and handling [apparatus], the visited lab to do the work, no women, smoking allowed, plenty of frank criticism and discussions, the whole atmosphere experimental, the youngsters taken in on an equality with the men who have arrived."[62] In the succeeding years, Titchener was largely successful in realizing his dream. The society developed into an organization of tough, hearty, cigar-smoking men in pursuit of "tough-and-hearty" topics and methods. It was into this "purely masculine assembly" that the young Allport ventured under the tutelage of "Daddy" Langfeld in April 1921.[63] The manly, scientific banter was incessant, as was the cigar smoking, and in a letter Allport sarcastically noted, "McDougall smokes body–mind cigars—more body than mind" and added that Titchener was "wooley [sic] faced" with "cigars [that] are very black."[64] Titchener was in the habit of allocating a small amount of time for graduate students to present their work and to thereby receive his "manly" benediction. Unfortunately for Allport, what was supposed to a rite of passage into the brave company of psychology's men turned into a humiliating repudiation of his work and, by extension, his masculinity. After summarizing the results of a recent study he had undertaken on the "traits of personality," Allport later recalled that "one of the greatest silences you can imagine fell over the group. [Titchener] looked right through me and said, 'As I was saying, the brightness of metals....'"[65] (See insert, Figure 26.)

Allport was shocked by Titchener's cavalier dismissal of his work, and the sting of rejection from this group raised doubts in his mind about his suitability for a career in so virile a field. He had realized long ago that he was not a masculine type, and he had at least partially come to terms with his tender, feminine-style disposition. At first glance, psychology appeared to be a space where a tender-minded male ought to prosper, but like a number of aspiring female psychology students during this period, Allport began to realize that academic psychology was not especially receptive to the values and talents typically encoded as feminine.[66] "Psychology is evidently nothing but sensation," he noted bitterly after his rejection by Titchener. "I prefer it with philosocial [sic] dressing!"[67] Alienated by what he perceived as the disciplinary mainstream in psychology, Allport began to "suffer from vocational misgivings [believing that he] had no giftedness in natural science, mathematics, mechanics [laboratory manipulations], nor in biological or medical specialties."[68] Titchener's rebuke thus confirmed a suspicion that been building in Allport's mind: Perhaps he was not scientific enough (i.e., "man enough") to be a psychologist.

The dynamics within Allport's own family helped amplify his professional concerns. As noted in chapter 2, Allport had grown up on the periphery of a group of manly brothers, and despite years of education and travel, he was still viewed as a pleasant but rather inconsequential figure. Aware of his standing, Allport was given a reminder of his status on a trip to Cleveland in September 1921. Walking into the family home unannounced, he approached his eldest brother, Harold, who was busy brushing his shoes.

> I quietly asked him to brush them well. He looked up for an instant, said "For Christ's sake, I'll be damned," and after shaking hands went on brushing—no more from H[arold]. Floyd asked him if I'd changed in the past two year[s] (This while I was not around). H merely replied, "No, except he has a little more 'ah' in his 'can't'!"[69]

Harold's quip may have been meant in jest, but for Allport it was a frustrating reminder of the difficulty he had experienced throughout his life in garnering recognition or status within the family. As a youth, he had tended to withdraw in the face of fraternal challenges, but as a well-traveled Harvard graduate, Allport was finally in a position to offer some resistance. During his visit to Cleveland, all four brothers went on a moonlight fishing trip on Lake Erie. Gradually, the calm beauty of the lake "release[ed] all inhibitions," and each brother spoke out on "what they think of life in general." In times past, Allport would have concurred with the pronouncements of his manly brothers, but no more. "The suppressed youngest calls the older two _ _ _ _, _ ah! [sic]." Exactly what Allport said to his brothers is unknown, but it was "good for the soul" and "vilification to an express elevator from the sub-cellar of passivity to the roof-garden of ascendency."[70]

Fortunately for Allport, the growing confidence he felt in relation to his family also extended into his professional life. Titchener's rebuke stung, but he remained alive to the possibility of a career in psychology. Langfeld played an important supportive role in this regard, and he reassured Allport that the psychological world extended beyond the smoky confines and back-slapping banter of Titchener's men's club. Buoyed by this encouragement, Allport remained mindful of the disciplinary mainstream's masculine ethic, and his dissertation was cast in the idiom of positivist science. Evidently, his tender-minded disposition did not preclude a degree of tough-minded posturing in order to advance his career.

PERSONALITY AND INTELLIGENCE TESTING

Behaviorism helped render personality into a suitably masculine form, and the field of intelligence testing expedited the process. The first intelligence tests had been designed by British scholar Francis Galton in 1884.[71] However, the first extensive use of mental tests did not occur until World War I, when they were administered to just under 2 million U.S. Army recruits. The tests suffered from a variety of problems that limited their effectiveness, and the U.S. Army discontinued the testing program immediately after the war. For all its problems, however, the Army testing program did put psychology "on the map of the United States."[72] As one of the testers noted some years later, "Before the World War, the average intelligent layman probably had little confidence in the value or the use of mental tests. After the War, he believed that psychologists had devised a simple and relatively perfect method of measuring intelligence."[73] The public relations capital that psychology had gained from the war was spent in the postwar period on promoting the use of intelligence tests in a number of applied settings.[74] Education was regarded as a particularly promising consumer. Educational administrators needed information that would allow them to make or, in some cases, justify decisions in a growing and increasingly complicated school system.[75] Psychologists had begun to respond to this need before the war. In its aftermath, the trend continued at an accelerated pace.

Administrators were initially excited by the prospect of having an "efficient" administrative device at their disposal, but they quickly became skeptical as to the value of the tests. Educators pointed to the low correlations between test scores and success in schools. Prison psychologists argued that tests of intelligence left unexamined a number of dimensions that were important in understanding criminal behavior. A person's "own responsibilities," their "attitude toward society," and their capacity to perform in the "industrial situation of the present day" were "neglected in the studies that have been made to the present date," criminologist Edith Spaulding wrote in 1921.[76] A similar complaint about the tests' limited utility was registered by a number of psychiatrists. Psychiatrist Guy Fernald asked the following:

> What of the part of personality which acts or resists, that which is closely associated with and dependent upon conation, volition, impulses, instincts and other innate or acquired dispositions or forces which eventuate in or modify behavior? The latter mental factors or processes ... are not susceptible of correct demonstration in any intelligence age level presentation for they are in a different category and are not closely related to intelligence.[77]

What was needed, these critics agreed, were measures of self that did not involve intellectual capacity. As psychologist Goodwin Watson noted, "much of the dissatisfaction that has arisen ... has expressed itself in a demand for tests of something more important than the [intellectual] abilities thus far measured."[78] Psychologists reasoned that tests that measured facets of personality or character would yield more practical information than measures of intellectual performance. In an educational and social reform setting, personality tests could provide a knowledge of "the sore spots of a person's personality."[79] Armed with this information, educators and social workers could develop programs of instruction that would facilitate the growth of the most desirable "social and dynamic qualities."[80] In an industrial setting, tests of nonintellectual traits would enable administrators to handle personnel more efficiently. Managers would be spared the inaccuracies of their own judgment and the wastefulness of trial-and-error decision making. A scientific measure of personality would allow the manager to better match personalities to appropriate jobs.

Allport perceived his dissertation to be a response to calls for a more practical measure of self. In the dissertation's preface, he noted that "the recent development of mental tests has served to accentuate the need for methods for the measurement of personality, for it is recognized that this aspect of a man's nature, even more than his intelligence, determines the success of his adjustments to his environment."[81] The practical aim of the dissertation was reflected in the categories Allport selected for empirical study. In one set of experiments, Allport examined the traits of "ascendance–submission," and in another he explored the traits of "introversion–extroversion." Both sets of tests purported to measure important types of "adjustment" to modern American life.

The terms *ascendance–submission* referred to the forms of adjustment that characterized social interactions. Allport reasoned that "every social relation" could be understood as a conflict of personalities. When two people come together, regardless of the circumstances, "one individual will dominate and be the 'victor,' and the other will yield and become the 'vanquished.'"[82] Allport believed that there was a certain degree of variability in this process. In certain circumstances and with certain people, one may be the victor of the interaction, and in others one may be the vanquished. In the majority of circumstances, however, Allport thought that the outcome was the same. A person who dominated in one context would tend to dominate in another: "It may be safely said ... that in dealing with the aggregate of responses, most individuals *habitually* assume one of the two roles."[83] For his study of extroversion–introversion, Allport relied heavily on the conceptual work of Carl Jung, whose definitions of extroversion–introversion were incorporated directly into the study. A person was an extrovert "when he gives his fundamental interest to the outer or objective world, and attributes an all important and essential value to it." In the introverted condition, "the objective world suffers a sort of depreciation, or want of consideration, for the sake of the exaltation of the individual himself, who then monopolizes all the interest, [and] grows to believe no one but himself worthy of consideration."[84]

The Individual in an Industrial Age

Allport's choice of categories reflected the new realities of American mass culture. His tests helped answer the questions of the prospective employer or social service worker. These questions did not involve the qualities associated with character: duty, honor, and self-sacrifice. Administrators were more interested in the categories associated with personality: magnetism, glow, masterfulness, dominance, and forcefulness.[85] Officials wanted to know how successful the individual would be in competition with others. Was this person a go-getter? Did he have the masterful personality necessary to succeed in a changing and increasingly competitive world?

Allport was not coy about speaking to these practical concerns. In the dissertation's abstract, he noted that a "psychological study of the traits of personality has immediate practical value. In all spheres of personnel work the analysis and valuation of the personal equipment of the individual is urgently required."[86] Improving administrative efficiency was thus an important theme in Allport's study. However, like many social scientists of the day, Allport did not view administration as an end in itself. The real significance of the tests was to be found in the ethical precepts on which they were based, and for Allport, the value at issue was individuality. While traveling in Europe, he had been struck by a class-based indifference to individual worth. The less affluent were commonly assimilated into social categories such as "maid and manservant," and the "personality of each servant [was] disregarded."[87] Back in the United States, Allport noticed a similar process at work. Modern bureaucracy obliged the administrator to handle the person not as an individual, but as a type. As Harvard social ethicist Richard Cabot noted, in modern society the individual "must be paid as 'a hand,' must be enrolled in school as 'a pupil,' must be treated at the dispensary as 'a patient,' [and] summoned before the court as 'a prisoner.'"[88] The problem, for both Cabot and Allport, was the "danger of dehumanization": Would the individual vanish in the rush to bureaucratic efficiency? Quoting Cabot, Allport wrote that "there is always the danger [in modern society] that the individual traits ... will be lost sight of."[89]

In expressing concern over the disappearance of the individual, Allport was sounding a theme familiar to many Progressive Era Americans.[90] Urban living and an industrial company had stripped many people of control of their working lives.[91] The self-made man so revered in American life seemed to be a thing of the past. In its place was a homogenized mass identity. Floyd Allport's dissertation on "social influence" is one of the most compelling illustrations of Progressive Era anxiety over individuality. In the introduction, Floyd used the example of a crowd at a football game to illustrate the ease with which individuality can be submerged by the group:

> Every human soul is carried aloft by the mighty power of the sound [of the crowd]. Every being is exalted to a rage of ecstasy, thrice redoubled and surpassing any joy or madness he has ever known. All else is put aside: thoughts of dignity, of personal feeling, even of individual existence are effaced and submerged in the all-filling flood of emotions. Sober mothers and fathers, yes, even staid grandmothers are caught up in the whirl and are blown like leaves in the passion of the tempest. Gray haired professors who seldom smile, and never shout, and who expressed merely a placid satisfaction at the signing of the armistice, are now leaping and throwing hats in maniacal frenzy. Joy, mad, hilarious joy, is the one supreme fact of the universe. Nothing else exists.[92]

In his own dissertation, Allport was not interested in simply echoing the concerns expressed by Floyd and Cabot. The question that he wanted to address was whether there was a way of safeguarding the individual in modern life. Was it possible to devise a set of techniques that would improve administrative efficiency without compromising individuality? Could a person be both a unique individual and an administrative object? By 1920, a number of social workers, psychiatrists, and psychologists believed that it was possible to preserve individuality within a bureaucratic context. In fact, many argued that progress in the area of bureaucratic efficiency could only proceed if greater attention was paid to the individual. "Social progress," Graham Wallas wrote in 1921, "lies on the line of recognized difference."[93] The way forward did not involve any sort of nostalgic return to a preindustrial America; quite the opposite, in fact. Specialists were encouraged to bring the individual human subject within the sphere of scientific discipline. They would undertake a "courageous plunging beneath the surface of things" in order to reveal "the wonderful diversity within each possible social grouping."[94] The rationale behind this approach was empiricist in nature. Science could help safeguard individuality by rendering it legible. Scientists could carefully monitor specified behaviors and then use those observations to establish a network of norms. Behavioral norms could then be converted into graphs, charts, and numbers. Deviations from the norms could be plotted, and in this way individuality could literally be seen. Its visibility made it amenable to administrative consideration.[95] A visible, measurable individuality made it possible for administrators, psychologists, and social workers to fine-tune their policies and interventions right down to the level of the individual.

Allport's interest in preserving and cultivating individuality is apparent throughout his dissertation, but it is especially striking in the final chapter, "The Analysis of Personality in Social Diagnosis." In this chapter, he echoed the concerns of social workers and ethicists such as Richard Cabot and Mary Richmond about the place of individuality in modern society. The position of the socially disadvantaged was a source of special concern for Allport. The well educated had the resources to deal with a "complexly organized society."[96] They could attain a "realization of Self" without any sort of expert intervention. But what of the "population of paupers, defectives, diseased, vicious, and ignorant?" Without special assistance, Allport argued, these individuals "would never attain that realization of Self which the social conscience demands." These "classes of handicapped members" would never realize their fullest potential; their unique talents would be concealed beneath a series of negative group categories.[97]

In her thoughtful discussion of the pioneering psychiatrist Adolf Meyer, historian Ruth Leys drew attention to two important types of individuality that informed the work of many scientists of the 1920s.[98] "Relational individuality" hinged on the statistical relationship between the individual and the group. Within this framework, individuality was "defined in terms of a host of deviations from corresponding norms that are themselves determined by a kind of averaging of those deviations." Relational individuality was thus a measurable, statistical function of a person's deviation from group norms. Although the relational understanding of individuality was pervasive in the 1920s, Leys argued that a kind of "pure" individuality could also be detected in the work of Meyer and a number of his contemporaries. The hallmark of pure individuality was its fundamental uncapturability and indiscipline. Echoing James's views on the transcendental uniqueness of the individual, Meyer argued that there existed within each individual an "irreducible residuum" that "appears to defeat all possibility of comparison and classification."[99]

Increasingly enamored of spiritual categories and premodern religiosity, Allport devoted much of his later career to the ideal of pure individuality. As a graduate student, however, his tests of ascendance–submission and introversion–extroversion advanced the notion of relational individuality and the idea that science could safeguard human difference. During this period Allport was convinced that his tests would transform socially disadvantaged groups into distinct, quantifiable individuals. Instead of dealing with people strictly in relation to sociological categories of "economic status, occupational conditions, educational advantages, [and] domestic relations," administrators would be presented with an "objective" view of the self's own internal economy. The tests would show an individual's "*actual* assets and liabilities and his *potential* assets and liabilities." In making this claim, Allport was not dismissing the importance of sociological information. He maintained that administrators needed both sociological and psychological information to be effective, but his emphasis was clearly in the direction of individual psychology. In the final chapter of his dissertation, he wrote that an assessment of an individual's "assets and liabilities . . . will furnish the most important knowledge which the case worker can possess in determining the direction of social policy."[100]

An "Instrument of Individual Measurement"

Allport's dissertation was clearly embedded in a network of disciplinary and cultural concerns. His psychological categories were those of John Watson, and his ethical rationale was firmly linked to the work of social ethicists Richard Cabot and Mary Richmond. The research methods that Allport used to construct his "instrument of individual measurement" were also grounded in a set of existing disciplinary practices. However, it is important to emphasize the relatively open-ended nature of the research procedures on which Allport drew. As we have already observed, in 1922, personality was not a standardized category of psychological research. A number of scholars were interested in the subject, but they shared little agreement as to the method that this research should use. For example, some researchers used Carl Jung's word association technique to measure traits such as "pugnacity, fear, repulsion, curiosity, self-assertion, tenderness, [and] gregariousness."[101] Other scholars set out to measure personality traits by analyzing samples of handwriting.[102] A third group of investigators used laboratory tests of bodily reactions to examine facets of personality such as "force, initiative, and assurance."[103] Finally, a number of psychologists tried to apply the technology of existing intelligence tests to the study of personality. For example, Pressey and Pressey developed a test of emotional traits using a paper-and-pencil, group-based testing format.[104]

One of the aims of Allport's dissertation was to bring some methodological order to the study of personality. He used a number of different approaches to establish "the validity of certain of the methods employed by previous investigators."[105] The variety and form of those methods are, by contemporary standards, quite remarkable. For example, in one set of experiments, Allport adopted a series of laboratory tests that had first been used in a study of aggressiveness by Moore and Gilliland.[106] One procedure was based on the idea that there was a relationship between a person's ascendance and his or her ability to resist distraction. Following Moore and Gilliland, Allport tested this idea by the use of electric shock. Human participants were periodically given shocks of up to 75 volts while performing mental calculations. The variable of interest was the time it took each participant to perform the calculations. At the outset of the experiment, it was assumed that the calculation time of the participants high in ascendance would be relatively unaffected by the distraction of electric shock. (See insert, Figures 27 and 28.)

Allport also conducted a series of experiments using Jung's word association method and a technique that he termed the *method of represented situations.*[107] The represented-situations method was an amalgam of conceptual and methodological innovations that had been devised in the previous 20 years. From Francis Galton, Allport derived the idea of measuring traits by examining an individual's response to a "miniature" situation. For example, in a preliminary study, Allport presented participants with written descriptions of 10 situations in which the person could assume an active or passive role. Participants were then "directed to feel himself into each situation portrayed, and to tell, spontaneously and truthfully, how he would react."[108] The self-reports were scored by the ratings of three acquaintances of each participant. Allport found the procedure useful but cumbersome. In particular, the long qualitative accounts made scoring difficult. Allport saw a solution to this problem in the multiple-choice procedure of Abraham Myerson.[109] Using this now-ubiquitous technique, participants were asked to respond to a situation not by "subjectively worded replies," but by checking one of several possible answers attached to each question.[110]

The results of Allport's experiments foreshadowed the methodological trajectory of American personality psychology. His laboratory studies of bodily reactions to electric shock were not promising. He concluded that "there is no evidence from the experiments ... that the subject's ability to resist the distraction of staring or of shock can serve as an index to the magnitude of the trait."[111] The procedure that held out the greatest promise was the procedure that most closely resembled the intelligence test: the method of represented situations. Allport concluded that the "evidence of the test is conclusively in favor of the application of the method of represented situations" and that the "device of 'standard response' [multiple choice] is invaluable to such tests, since it aids immeasurably in the interpretation and scoring of replies."[112]

Over the next 5 years, most personality psychologists came to agree with Allport on this methodological point. As Parker noted, by the mid-1920s most personality trait tests used a paper-and-pencil procedure similar to that used in intelligence tests.[113] The success of these tests was based in large part on their versatility and efficiency in administrative contexts. The paper-and-pencil test was relatively cheap; it could be administered simultaneously to large groups of people; and, perhaps most important, it provided "scientifically" validated norms that administrators could use to justify their decisions. The one thing that the tests did not do is pay appropriate homage to the notion of pure individuality central to Allport's growing antimodernist sensibility. The relational tradition of personality research that developed out of the intelligence test did not celebrate or affirm the individual in all of his or her distinctiveness. Individuals were studied only in relation to their standing in a group, and only in relation to their standing on a few administratively defined criteria.[114]

In the years to come, Allport became increasingly aware of the discordance between his spiritual commitment to pure individuality and the research tradition that he had helped initiate. This sense of discordance helped determine the course of his professional interest in personality throughout the 1920s and 1930s. Shortly after his dissertation, Allport began to search for another solution to a question that lay at the heart of his initial interest in personality: Was it possible to have a psychology that would improve administrative efficiency at the same time that it affirmed the dignity and spiritually based distinctiveness of the individual?

DANCING AND PRAYING IN THE "PLASTIC AGE"

While dutifully working to bring the individual into a scientific register, Allport could not help but notice the cultural ferment that was going on around him. In the postwar period, old and new collided as never before, and many young Americans turned their backs on convention. Frederick Lewis Allen observed that a "first class revolt against the accepted American order was certainly taking place during those early years of the Post War Decade."[115] The battle lines for this "revolt" cut a broad swath through the heart of American culture. Long-established assumptions about sexuality, gender, art, religion, manners, and morality were called into question and, in some cases, dramatically repudiated. The past itself became a byword for backwardness and hypocrisy, and young Americans heaped scorn on the world their parents had created. "The older generation had certainly pretty well ruined this world before passing it on to us," John F. Carter remarked to the readers of *Atlantic* in 1920. "Now my generation is disillusioned, and, I think, to a certain extent, brutalized, by the cataclysm which *their* complacent folly engendered. . . . We have been forced to live in an atmosphere of 'tomorrow we die,' and so, naturally, we drank and were merry."[116]

As a graduate student, Allport sensed the spirit of liberation and participated in his fair share of madcap escapades. A trip home to Cleveland in July 1922 was one of the more colorful illustrations of his youthful irreverence, as he cruised the city "on an all night party with my friends of long standing who now own their own cars and hootch." Basking in the era's anarchic spirit, Allport "toured the road houses around Cleveland, finding much liquor and apache dancing." Increasingly alive to new pleasures, Allport also discovered the "sheer undiluted joy" of roller skating: "sweeping on perfect skates around a smooth rink to a good old waltz, vibrating in every muscle and tendon with the music, your tie flapping back against your cheek and over your shoulder."[117] It was a grand time, and Allport experienced a thrill of liberation from the dutiful, carefully structured world of character he had grown up with. "Last night I went to bed at 3am, and it is now 1am of the next night. My hours are most erratic, but I love the lack of restraint."[118] A visit to California found Allport in a similarly carefree mood, cavorting "in a nearby woodsy spot where the moon lit a roofless pavilion, and the young bloods of orange land danced their purposive dance."[119]

Dancing the night away, Allport could see that a new moral order was in the making, but while he embraced the newfound spirit of freedom, he seldom strayed far from the straight and narrow. He counted himself among those "youth who preach unconventionality and give certain carefully planned manifestations of it, but who are at heart bound close and permanently by self-conscious, highly artificial morality."[120] Allport was also indifferent to the era's biting cynicism and religious iconoclasm. Memories of the ancient splendors of Constantinople remained alive amid the "hootch" and "apache dancing," and for all his devil-may-care frolicking, he continued to find more meaning in premodern spirituality than anarchic modernist celebration. Following a pattern begun in Turkey, Allport sought out things ancient and divine, and in Old World beauty he felt a larger spiritual pulse. At Harvard, he decorated his room in a style befitting an Old World romantic:

> The room is a joy. It is as oriental and seductive as I dare make it. I am always tempted to sink into the easy chair with [novelist John] Barrie, and under a soft green light to eat lokum and admire the peacock quill and newly framed Florentine prints. The beautiful head of the boy John the Baptist [Delsarto—of terra cotta fame] beams down upon this letter, sending a sacred benediction from classic Italy.[121]

Allport's antimodern sensibility is also evident in his choice of bookplate. Designed by former Radcliffe student Amelia Brackett, the plate highlights his fascination with premodern exoticism. It was based on photographs of Constantinople taken by Allport, and the text is a quotation from Galsworthy rendered in Kufic script: "When I am here I would be there; When I am there I would be here."[122] (See insert, Figure 29.)

Pursuing his spiritual vision in Boston and beyond, Allport found the premodern even while visiting the ever youthful California. Los Angeles had a side to it that was "Sodom and Godless Gotha," but Allport quickly realized that spirituality flourished amid the sunshine and palm trees. This realization was coupled with an appreciation of the flamboyant character of California's spiritual landscape. Historian Philip Jenkins noted that "even before the Jazz age was under way, southern California was legendary for both cults and the occult," and Allport soon realized that the city's reputation as a center of religious exoticism was well deserved.[123] Within days of arriving, he met a "flagrant, dyed in the wool clairvoyant" who claimed to be imbued with the spirit of a 1,000-year-old Hindu mystic. "She showed me reams of automatic writing, a gazing crystal, slates for independent writing, and answers written by the spirits to her questions." This exotic spiritual fare was quickly followed by a public lecture on psychology and psychoanalysis in the light of "constructive psychology." "When we walked in, the audience (2000 gullible souls) was chanting in unison: *I am a success; I AM a success; I am a SUCCESS!*"

Allport was repelled by these flamboyant displays, and he dryly remarked that "everyone is a psychic out here, or else a 'psychologist.'"[124] Critical of the pop psychology on offer, Allport could not escape the rising tide of interest in all things psychological. His mother persuaded him to give a public lecture on the "subject of personality in popular form" and he spoke on the ethics of personality at a local church.[125] John and Nellie took great pride in these public displays of their son's psychological sophistication, but Allport continued to look for more traditional outlets of his burgeoning spirituality. In California, he was relieved to discover "prominent support of things [more conventionally] artistic and spiritual."[126] He attended a passion play and was moved by the content and the spiritually suggestive surroundings. "The Pilgrimage Play is positively the best set drama I have ever seen, in a notch in the hills—carved by God for this purpose, I do believe. The lighting is superb, and if nothing in the Passion play compelled of itself, the skill of this setting would captivate any mortal spectator."[127] A comfortable apartment and a nearby Episcopalian church gave Allport more opportunities to nourish his soul on things beautiful and sublime. His apartment was "furnished most attractively in velour and velvet, standing lamps of mulberry and gold, long mirrors, gold and blue paneling, mulberry drapes, cream curtains [and] a bath of Roman splendor."[128] The aesthetic splendor fostered divine thoughts, and Allport "rolled out of my luscious bed and ate a ripe fig, an olive, one peach, [and] then sought out morning prayer at St. Stephens nearby."[129]

Combining images of consumption and spiritual contemplation, Allport's experience highlights some of the ironies of American antimodernism. By pursuing premodern beauty might one not succumb to modernist consumerism? Could a reverence of ancient symbols of transcendental salvation be transmuted into a shallow aestheticism of the moment? Could the antimodernist temper inadvertently serve the secularizing tendencies it set out to oppose?[130] Allport sensed these tensions, and he struggled to find a faith that was simple, authentic, and divine. Europe was a useful beacon in this quest, full of "sensitive souls . . . attuned to external beauty." Yet, as he noted in 1920, here too lay the unsettling possibility of artifice and superficiality: "The influence of our European friends is one of a hopeless prostration before the tinseled goddess of 'modern art,' and not a deep-felt kinship with the throbbing drives of life—wonderful mysterious life."[131]

In search of deep, soulful authenticity, Allport found solace in religion, but like many of his antimodernist contemporaries, it was of a carefully constructed and not entirely coherent variety. He continued to have little time for the canons of orthodox Christianity, insisting that "I am even more agnostic than I knew—without an ounce of belief in salvation, heaven, hell, sin or the 'Christian Epic.'" However, Allport still thought himself "unremittingly idealistic and religious." The source of his spiritual solace was his own intuitively conceived notion of premodern beauty. Certain acts and forms had a grace and majesty that transcended the everyday. One could sense their beauty and feel their otherworldly connections. Their sublime attractiveness confirmed a spiritual world while providing a charter for conduct:

> I am convinced that I had too great an access of conscience in my youth, and now I can see no moral issues in anything. Certain acts are unbeautiful to me and are *impossible*, but none are *wrong* in the moral sense. In fact right and wrong have left my personal vocabulary.[132]

Having expunged morality from his own personal lexicon, Allport had effectively created what historian Jackson Lears described as a "surrogate religion of taste," where aesthetic categories of beauty and personality stood in place of the conventional religious categories of conscience, character, soul, and sin.[133] Lears observed that this transformation was well suited to a secular culture of consumption, but in Allport's experience spiritualized taste assumed a more ambiguous form. An appreciation of "true" beauty could be a source of protection against fashion-driven aestheticism and consumerist excess. Echoing the concerns of Progressive leaders such as Jane Adams, Ellen Gates Starr, and *Ladies Home Journal* editor Edward Bok, Allport embraced an ethic of "middle-class simplicity" that sought to balance European-style refinement with American simplicity and hardiness.[134] In a letter to a friend, he explained that the new ethic did "not mean that we should ignore or deride our sophisticated friends from Europe, the cultured world." What was important, Allport believed, was to maintain a focus on a "deeper understanding of happiness":

> Joy in clouds of soot, joy in grimy kiddies, joy in arched bridges or smoke-like winter birches—simple pleasures, are majestic after all— and yet they are not sufficient. There is the call of the "work-bench," the sturdy Carverian doctrine, calloused hands and rugged souls.[135]

Celebrating the simple and the sophisticated, Allport's emerging philosophy of life was a confusing combination of opposites. Science existed alongside a deeply felt spirituality, and a passion for Old World exoticism shared ground with a traditional American suspicion of European refinement. Not always sure of how to stitch these themes together, Allport still hungered for the intense depth of feeling nurtured by revival culture and yearned for the breadth of idealism that belief in God inspired. Two years of graduate school had convinced him of the inadequacy of the older, conventionally religious worldview, but it also underscored the spiritual emptiness of scientific materialism. Unhappy with either alternative, Allport was unwilling to simply drift into the routines of academic life. He felt the need for more study, more beauty and more soul—a tall order that only Europe could supply. "Jobs in New Jersey are being offered me for next year," he wrote in January 1922. "Secretly I am combating a prodigious desire to go to Europe for a year's study in Berlin and Vienna. Two natures are in conflict within me. Let me have your prayers."[136]

THAT WHICH ENDURES: LIFE, LOVE, AND PERSONALITY

Young, sophisticated, and fashionably amoral, Allport's experience reflected a new constellation of American values. In this formation, character and the values that sustained it were boring and increasingly irrelevant. Edward Thurber caught the mood of the age in a 1921 *North American Review* essay in which he likened character talk to a "far off rippling, splashing, like the cadences of water":

> The words carried no distinctness, and yet it was as if they were a continuation of something of which my mind had been a part. We had met and blended and then diverged. The same interests no longer invited us, yet my mental current was floating particles of that contact, and strangely enough, I felt as if those particles were impure; my own stream would have to go until sundown before it could become clear again.[137]

Like Thurber, Allport experienced the discourse of character as a kind of fuzzy echo of a moralistic past that he could verbally reject but never quite escape. As a graduate student, he was alive to the growing importance of image, ambition, and self-presentation. Witty and well-traveled, he could "play for effect all day—with Prof. Ford [and] ... the socially high people at the tea." Staging successful performances as a personality advanced Allport's career, but it could not completely suppress a nagging sense of emptiness and artifice. Indeed, the more performative and self-oriented Allport became, the more he longed for the kind of "authentic" soulful and self-sacrificing self represented by character. "I am never satisfied with the hypocrisy I am filled with," he remarked harshly after one particularly successful social performance. "I can do it, putting on intellectuality and pseudo-intellectuality; and finally I can attain the goal. But what will become of my inner nature?" It was a weighty question, and as a graduate student Allport struggled to find a way of reconciling ambition and authenticity. "[I wish] to live true to myself without even the exterior of the successful poseur!" he exclaimed, but the social and scholarly posturing continued, and try as he might, Allport remained "the being who gets effects and seems to glory in them."[138]

Significant for his professional life, character's demise was also implicated in his personal life. As we have seen, Allport was enamored of beauty, personality, and the joy of the moment. In his romantic relationships, however, as in his scholarly interests, modernist liberation lived alongside a premodern desire for continuity and authenticity. An accomplished dancer, Allport could be dazzled by female beauty, and he enjoyed the company of sophisticated women. "For diversion I have picked an acquaintance with a good looking blonde girl," he wrote in his diary toward the end of his European travels in July 1920. "She has had her education in a French convent and so is interesting. For three nights running we have been to dances together. It certainly is quaint how dances develop for my amusement wherever I go."[139] This sort of romantic reverie continued when Allport returned to the United States, and he felt drawn to women who were imbued with the modernist spirit. "Gordon, I live absolutely in the present," one especially magnetic female personality announced. "Neither past nor future mean anything to me—I want pleasure and I want it now; people I hate, unless they please me *now*." Such unabashed loyalty to pleasure and the present was unnerving, but in the newly emerging "culture of personality," it was also strangely compelling. "She held for me . . . a charm —like nothing else in the world," Allport wrote of his unnamed pleasure-seeking friend, "for she has the gift of radiating energy and personality."[140]

Reared on a diet of self-sacrificing moralism, Allport was not sure what to make of the dramatic disconnection of morality from social appeal. The sweet, young things of the new order proudly proclaimed their allegiance to a selfish ethic of the moment, and yet somehow they were still appealing. "How can one be so supremely selfish and so diabolically fascinating at the same time?"[141] In this, as in so many other questions posed by the newly emerging culture of personality, Allport had no pat answers. However, a fellow graduate student, Ada Gould, was struggling with a similar set of issues, and together they tried to piece together some sort of order amid a confusing panoply of values.

Gould was born on October 13, 1898, in Lincolnville, Maine, to Robert Eugene Gould—an "elevated [train] conductor"—and Jennie Lufkin. After graduating from the Girls' High School in Boston, Gould entered Radcliffe College in September 1916, and she received her B.A. degree magna cum laude in philosophy and psychology in 1920. Fascinated by psychology, she was admitted to the Harvard Psychology Laboratory, where she obtained her M.A. in psychology in 1921. (See insert, Figure 30.)

Attractive, but by no means magnetic, Gould had been a research participant in Allport's dissertation. Appearing under the pseudonym "Miss Penn," Gould was characterized in the dissertation as a "social type, with marked emotions, but by no means introverted; possessed of good Insight and qualities for leadership (high Intelligence and Ascendence)."[142] Well-versed in the language of science and progress, she envisioned a future for herself as an agent of scientific benevolence. "I am definitely devoted to

Child Welfare Work of some sort," she remarked in the fall of 1920, "either with normal children or delinquents."[143] Scientifically minded, Gould retained a spiritual vision, and she found the era's increasingly strident scientific materialism depressing. "I know that science is to be the salvation of Europe as well as of America, but it sounds so brutal and drab to mention wires and fuses in the midst of the reveries of the rich browness [sic] of a mediaeval cathedral, and the scintillating colorfulness of Parisian skies and parks, of arched bridges across the Seine, of Italian lakes."[144]

From Allport's perspective, Gould stood at the median of a spiritual continuum that featured self-seeking iconoclasm at one end and self-sacrificing moralism at the other. She seemed to finesse the tensions that he was himself struggling with, and their similar outlook acted as a powerful emotional elixir. In one tender letter, Allport remarked that Gould combined a "frivolity [and] impishness" with "strengthening constructive help of one voyager for his perplexed companion." Unlike those present-loving personalities who were so strangely compelling, Gould seemed to posses a depth of perspective that grew in the fullness of time. In her outlook, "the past was considered, the present appreciated, and the future pointed with golden colors of true possibility." She had an artistic temperament and could appreciate beauty, yet her aesthetic sense was animated by a spirit of timelessness. For Allport, Gould possessed "more than the exquisite indulgence of an Epicure; there was the *depth* of happiness such as Socrates might approve and Epicure envy."[145]

Gould enjoyed the attention, but in her own heart she experienced a clash of values that was much more acute than Allport realized. The imperatives of personality—self-expression, personal happiness, and living for the moment—resonated strongly with her, and she privately admitted to having an "individualistic nature [that] craves stimulation, intrigue, freedom from feeling ... and a life of pleasure for myself."[146] Such sentiment was not "distasteful," but a wholesale embrace of pleasure seeking, selfism, troubled her deeply. The ideals of self-sacrifice continued to assert themselves, and Gould lamented how "this love of others, this conscience business drives me almost mad at times. I do the [charitable] acts but without the conviction behind them." The charitable self seemed more authentic in discussions with Allport, but Gould sensed that it was not an intrinsic part of her nature: "By myself I sink back into the old intriguing, excitable selfish self, unable to convince my self that charity is worthwhile."[147]

Allport had a sense of Gould's "habitual independence," but he remained largely unaware of the full extent of her dilemma.[148] During the early years of their romance, he idealized her—a tendency of which Gould was herself aware.[149] Mobilizing a spiritually minded, scientifically aware, considerate self, Gould captured Allport's heart, and he showered her with love letters full of mystical imagery. "You have taught me the cause of mankind; you have taught me the glories of the enchanted islands; you have taught me the secret of life—and hence the nature of God."[150] Alive to Allport's antimodernist sensibility, Gould acted as one of his spiritual confidantes throughout his 2 years of graduate school. She sympathized with his complaints about the soul-deadening nature of scientific psychology, and she could relate to his religious aestheticism. With Gould as an audience, Allport poured out his antimodernist soul and gave free rein to a growing mysticism:

> To-day for five minutes I had the rarest experience of the ecstasy of harmonies and beauty. I went alone just at sunset to the lake. The moment when the sun is most soft and generous with suffused light and in the grove by the beautiful water, I simply sank to my knees in religious devotion. . . . For the moment I was alone with nature, and nature both chastised and inspired me in one short space of time.[151]

CONCLUSION

Allport's experience in graduate school marked the formal start of what would become his life's work: the study of personality. Although he would later characterize this period of his life in relatively straightforward terms, both his decision to become a psychologist and his choice of personality as an object of study were embedded in a complex spiritual dilemma. Allport had a sharply felt sense of reverence and mystery, and he wanted to find a way to nurture that spirit and share it with others. At the same time, however, he was an extremely able and ambitious person, and he understood the hold that the scientific idiom was coming to have on discussions of human nature. The challenge he faced as a graduate student was to somehow bring these elements together in a way that was personally and professionally meaningful. It was a difficult task—especially for a student dependent on the approval of advisors—and at times Allport was obliged to resort to outright duplicity. He embedded personality into a behaviorist discourse of stimulus–response without believing the underlying materialist epistemology. Psychologist-as-natural-scientist was a pose for Allport, one that he was willing to adopt, but never fully inhabit.

Professionally uncertain, Allport gravitated to a category that was itself psychologically new and untested: personality. In pursuing his research, however, Allport was careful to follow a theoretical and methodological framework that conformed to existing disciplinary traditions. Psychiatrists and social workers had constructed personality into an objective entity that could be measured, and the limitations of intelligence testing provided a further impetus for personality measurement. In drawing on these disciplinary resources, Allport mapped out a self that reflected the new realities of industrial, urban America. This was a self that could be known, governed, managed; it was a self that could be embraced by employers and officialdom and one to which upwardly mobile individuals could aspire. Paradoxically, this was also a self that promised liberation from standardization and a heightened level of individuality. Individual measurement would transform an intangible value—individuality—into an empirical reality and in the process would free Americans from the sociological straitjacket of group-based categories.

6

A PSYCHOLOGY OF THE SPIRIT: GERMANY AND ENGLAND (1922–1924)

I have never, like so many other experimental psychologists, become scientificated.
—William Stern, 1930[1]

Beauty always makes me mystical.
—Gordon Allport, 1922[2]

Don't be a sponge for absorbing all the Germanic ways.
—Floyd Allport to Gordon Allport, 1924[3]

Allport submitted his dissertation in May 1922. Although he had worked hard on the project, his self-confidence remained shaky and "there were times, however, when I absolutely did not see the fulfillment of my purpose ahead."[4] Academic success and the encouragement of Langfeld could not allay a residuum of self-doubt, and Allport approached the oral defense of his dissertation with a mixture of optimism and dread. "The execution takes place at 4 pm Friday," he noted jokingly to Gould. "The doomed is selfish Thursday night, spending the time in fasting and prayer."[5] Despite his concerns, Allport's ability was never in any doubt, and he "passed off easily [after] an hour and [a] half gruelling [sic] by Langfeld, McDougall, and Ford."[6] The faculty was impressed with his dissertation and his work as a graduate student. Herbert Langfeld described him as "one of the best students we have had in Psychology for some years," and he predicted that Allport "will some day be among the leaders in his profession."[7] Walter Dearborn was equally effusive in his praise, describing Allport as "one of the ablest men I have had in my classes for several years."[8] William McDougall was somewhat more restrained in his assessment, but he also had a high regard for Allport. "I have not seen very much of his work," McDougall wrote pointedly, "but I have formed the impression that he is a very capable and keen student who would do credit to the university."[9] Summing up this chorus of praise, philosopher James Woods, chairman of the Department of Philosophy and Psychology, wrote, "I have a high opinion of [Allport's] character and know of no one of his instructors who is not impressed by his great ability."[10]

A SECOND INTELLECTUAL DAWN

Mindful of his growing scholarly reputation, Allport applied for and received a Sheldon Traveling Fellowship from Harvard.[11] The generous terms of the fellowship allowed him to travel to Europe and support himself quite comfortably for an entire year. He decided to spend his time in Germany, and in September of 1922 he set sail. In a letter to department chair James Woods, Allport indicated that his plan for the Sheldon Fellowship was to develop a course of study around the "psychological problem of the traits of personality and character."[12] Two universities seemed particularly promising in this regard. The "psychoanalytic school of Vienna makes prominent contributions . . . and I believe a semester of study at the university would be eminently worthwhile."[13] Allport also saw scholarly opportunities at the University of Berlin: "Experimental methods for the study of individual differences have been highly developed in the laboratory at Berlin, and a period of work in this laboratory would afford invaluable training in technique." Together, Allport believed, "the two approaches seem to offer unusual opportunities for rounding out the research work which I have been engaged in the Harvard psychological laboratory for the past two years."[14]

Psychology provided Allport with the scholarly rationale for his European foray, but the trip was propelled as much by spiritual uneasiness as it was by professional opportunity. In Germany, Allport hoped to find what the frenetic routines of American scientific life stripped away: reverence, antiquity, spirituality, and charm. "I hate my Cantabrigian [Cambridge, Massachusetts] personality," he noted harshly in a letter to Powers. "My R.C. [Robert College] personality is my favorite." As a graduate student, brief visits with Dodge and Powers helped Allport sustain his romantic, antimodernist self, and he noted happily that "my spirits rose high as soon as I met you and Pete at the McAlpine, and have been soaring ever since." In Europe, Allport was convinced that his spirits would remain high, "for I feel that freedom and energy returning which I experienced when I was abroad before."[15] For her part, Gould was reluctant to see Allport leave, and she feared that a prolonged separation might jeopardize the relationship. However, by 1922 she had come to appreciate the depth of Allport's philosophical convictions, and she understood the essentially spiritual nature of his European foray. On the day he set sail, "[Gould] wished a big wish for me," Allport recalled, "namely that in Europe I should return to my idealism, which was quashed out by two trying years in Cambridge."[16]

For all of his spiritual musings, there was a certain degree of inevitability in Allport's choice of Germany and Austria as the place for his postdoctoral study. Germany was generally regarded as the birthplace of the modern university, and of scientific psychology in particular. American students had begun traveling there in considerable numbers in the late 19th century. Initially the inspiration was primarily scholarly. Laboratory facilities did not exist in the United States at the time, nor did the kind of scientific method that the laboratories fostered—a systematic investigation of details. Josiah Royce summarized the powerful intellectual appeal of the German university in an 1891 paper: "German scholarship was our master and our guide. . . . One went to Germany still a doubter as to the possibility of the theoretic life; one returned an idealist, devoted for the time to pure learning for learning's sake, determined to contribute his Scheflein to the massive store of human knowledge."[17]

In the late 19th century, the scholarly environment that Royce described changed rapidly. American universities were quick to emulate their German counterparts, and by 1895 they offered training that was comparable and, in some cases, superior to that found in Germany. Nevertheless, American students continued to travel to Germany in large numbers in the 1890s. Some were attracted by the relatively inexpensive cost, and others by the prestige that a German degree continued to carry in the United States.[18] According to historian David Leary, German scholarship had become such a "fetish" in the late 19th century that "even a brief stay in Germany, with no real training, could confer a 'distinct advantage in the professional race at home.'"[19]

Whatever the motive, after 1890 few found their study in Germany all that intellectually rewarding.[20] American C. M. Bakewell spoke for many when he remarked in 1894, "there is but one verdict given by the men who come back from Germany these days, and that is that one could get more from his Professors in any of our large universities than he could get from his Professors in a German university."[21] Allport's education at Harvard reflected this perception. As an undergraduate, he developed an appreciation for the "Teutonic foundations" of psychology from the textbooks of James and Titchener and from the lectures of Münsterberg and philosopher Ralph Barton Perry.[22] Unlike the first generation of students, however, Allport did not consider going to Germany for his graduate training. With its greater resources and purportedly higher methodological standards, Harvard provided training that was equal, if not actually superior, to anything offered in Germany. But there was an important academic asset that no North American institution could provide: an aura of Old World erudition. In the 1920s, German psychology still enjoyed a measure of intellectual cachet in America, and psychologists who had studied in Germany were perceived as more urbane and scholarly. The prestige of German training in the 1920s is readily apparent in E. G. Boring's autobiography: "I have never been to Germany. That lack in my education was a matter of some shame and some bitterness before Hitler destroyed German science."[23] To acquire this aura of Old World sophistication, it was not necessary to stay long or engage German thought in any depth. For those who could afford it, a leisurely stroll through the German research institutes, coupled with a generous course of sightseeing and socializing, would be enough to acquire a final layer of academic polish.

Initially, Allport's trip to Europe had an element of frivolity about it. As a postdoctoral student, he later recalled that he was "not prepared" for any sort of "powerful" intellectual development.[24] Germany was a kind of academic "finishing school" for newly minted American Ph.D.s and not a place where basic disciplinary assumptions were challenged.[25] Allport's initial engagement with Germany did not prompt him to revise this view. He traveled first to what many regarded as the center of German psychology: the psychological laboratory at the University of Berlin. Here, Allport attended the lectures of many of Germany's most distinguished psychologists, including Carl Stumpf, Max Wertheimer, Eduard Spranger, Wolfgang Köhler, and Max Dessoir. Seated in a classroom, listening to one of these fine scholars lecture, Allport was at times deeply moved. He reported feeling "like a pilgrim to Mecca when I heard from [Stumpf's] own lips the explanation of the factors involved in experience of consonance and dissonance."[26] "One must be insensible indeed," Allport wrote, "not to appreciate the opportunity of hearing men of such intellectual strength."[27]

Allport was determined to make the most of his opportunity, and he did allow "foreign jargon" to become a problem. He arranged to have a fellow student's notes "transcribed on a typewriter every week" and he then spent "hours together discussing them."[28] Unfortunately for Allport, these sorts of intellectually intense experiences were relatively infrequent. Most of the lectures proved to be rather disappointing in both quantity and quality. Allport complained to Langfeld that "the total amount of lecturing accomplished was not great" because his professors "commenced their readings several weeks late and were frequently ill or indisposed."[29] In the same letter, he commented on the poor quality of the lectures that were delivered. "None of the psychology professors excepting Stumpf attempted to cover any definite ground," he wrote. "The lecture of the day was commonly nothing but a public soliloquy on the part of the professor concerning his temporary prevailing interest."[30]

Presented with a "general lack of system and responsibility," Allport devoted much of his time to events outside the laboratory and lecture hall.[31] "I have not delved too heavily into German psychology," he wrote in December 1922. "Operas, plays, excursions, friendships, and more than a little gentle philandering complete my enjoyable schedule of pursuits."[32]

A Hallowe'en (*sic*) party at the Assistant American Commerical Attache in Berlin was one of the more colorful events on Allport's social calendar. The party was well stocked with "warm punch made of red wine and cinnamon" and "expensive German women" with "free floating libidos" who "flirted and smoked and smoked and flirted."[33] These lighthearted activities did not expand Allport's intellectual horizons, but they were not without consequence. Exposure to the values and possibilities of Weimar Germany posed a further challenge to the Methodist earnestness of his youth. Old prohibitions and pieties now seemed disconcertingly provincial, and long established truths concerning the sinfulness of self-indulgence were open to question. He remarked that "German students shame us with their eagerness and their intellectual discipline, as well as their capacity for unremitting, individual endeavor."[34] Casual conversations with German students also spoke to those feelings of self-doubt that Allport so regularly entertained. He was pleased to discover that the bookish, introverted social type that he seemed to personify had a different social standing in Europe than it did in the United States. "I find that this condition of the mind [introversion] is condoned and approved in Europe," he noted with evident satisfaction. "America penalizes the Introvert with social disfavor and economic failure—Europe rewards it with, at least tolerance, and often with downright acclaim."[35] Allport now felt an increasing sense of "freedom and maturity" and a "feeling of self-confidence." He still had a "simon-pure" commitment to the "ideals of educational service," but he was determined to somehow combine the call to service with an attention to self-fulfillment.[36]

In the ensuing months, Allport continued his "enjoyable schedule" of "gentle philandering," but at a somewhat slower pace.[37] His scholarly interests grew, and by March 1923, what had begun as a lighthearted excursion had developed into a searching inquiry into aspects of German psychology. Unlike previous generations of American students, Allport appears to have obtained a great deal from his foray into Teutonic thought. In his autobiography, he actually reversed the story told by many 19th-century American psychologists by suggesting that it was his graduate study in the United States, not his work in Germany, that was a disappointment. "Graduate years at Harvard were not particularly productive intellectually," he wrote.[38] Germany, in contrast, he described as having a liberating effect that was just as powerful as the Harvard experience had been during his freshman year. He later described the year spent in Germany as a "second intellectual dawn."[39]

The phrase *second intellectual dawn* is so dramatic that one may suspect Allport of engaging in some retrospective embellishment. This would not be out of character for Allport, especially since the issue involved touches on one of his favorite professional concerns: the shortcomings of American psychology. On balance, however, his recollections of Germany are consistent with his experience at the time. His letters to colleagues in the United States reveal him in a state of breathless excitement as he struggled to assimilate and convey all the new ideas he was encountering. In one letter, he remarked that he "could soliloquize all night about the general status of psychology here [in Germany], for I find myself in a new world of thought."[40]

THE PERSONALIST PSYCHOLOGY OF WILLIAM STERN

The person most responsible for leading Allport into this "new world of thought" was William Stern. Stern was a Hamburg-based psychologist who had published extensively in philosophy, differential psychology, applied psychology, forensics, and developmental psychology.[41] The extent and originality of his contributions had put him among the leaders of continental psychology. One historian recently described Stern's laboratory as being comparable in quality to the famous Vienna Institute.[42] Another scholar described Stern as "the most influential psychologist in Germany at that time."[43] Allport first became acquainted with Stern's work in graduate school. He found the German's clever theory and innovative methods impressive, and in his dissertation he described Stern as a pillar of the "great contemporary German school of individual psychology."[44]

Drawn by Stern's reputation, Allport traveled to Hamburg to meet the famous psychologist and to find out more about his approach to personality.[45] In his dissertation, Allport had faulted Stern for failing to respect the distinction between personality as a natural object and personality as a moral ideal. Stern had a "dual interest [that] frequently amounts to a confusing of the psychological and metaphysical problems of personality."[46] Allport had also criticized Stern for his apparent inconsistency. Stern purported to speak to the "total personality," but in Allport's view, the methods of individual psychology led to a different end:

> Stern states that the explicit aim of *differentielle Psychologie* is the creation of a system of principles by which to explain the "unity of individuality"; but he emphasizes the need for first analyzing and measuring the *elemental* reactions before attempting to study them in combinations or functional wholes. In actual fact, the result of this attitude is that personality comes to be considered simply as a *sum-total* of all single reactions and unitary mental states. The study of personality then becomes nothing more than the study of the psychology and correlation of individual differences.[47]

Convinced that Stern was guilty of reductionism, Allport soon discovered that he had been somewhat hasty in his initial assessment. His criticisms of individual psychology had been undertaken with little understanding of the philosophical position on which those investigations were based. It was a point that Stern wasted no time in conveying to the young American. At their first meeting, Stern told Allport that he was a philosopher as well as a psychologist.[48] To fully appreciate the latter, one had to first understand the former. The merits of Stern's position did not become immediately apparent to Allport, but this first meeting did serve to heighten his interest in the Hamburg psychologist. He began to think seriously about leaving Berlin and moving on to Stern's Hamburg Institute.

From a scholarly standpoint, the move made a great deal of sense. With few exceptions, the Berlin psychologists had relatively little interest in Allport's field of study: applied psychology, psychological measurement, and personality. Stern, however, had published extensively in all of these fields. "Professor Stern in Hamburg appeals to me especially," Allport wrote. "He, Professor Lipmann, and Professor Moede [Stern's Hamburg colleagues] seem to be the men who have the greatest sympathy with applied psychology and still a sound groundwork of theory and experimentation."[49] Allport hoped to be able to "spend a few profitable weeks" with these scholars when his "desultory" semester at Berlin ended.[50]

Allport contemplated the move to Hamburg with noticeable relish, for although his Berlin professors had been "courteous," they were all careful to maintain a wide gulf between themselves and their students.[51] Disappointed to discover that the Berlin professors "pay little attention to the students," he felt dismayed by the condescending atmosphere. Academics in Berlin "give the impression of being unsusceptible to regulation by earthly or celestial laws."[52] Stern represented a refreshing departure from this atmosphere of carefully cultivated distance. Friendly, approachable, and intellectually engaging, Stern was somehow able to generate a scholarly aura without that "Herr Professor Doktor von So and So" formality.[53] His fine mind and disarming, agreeable manner appealed strongly to Allport's American sensibilities. Allport told a friend at the time that Stern was the "most approachable of all German pedagogues, and his broad sympathy with all fields of psychological research is what I approve most highly of."[54] Evidently, Stern regarded Allport's scholarly interests and friendly manner with equal favor. The two arranged for Allport to spend the summer semester studying at Stern's institute. In early March 1923, Allport moved to Hamburg, where he began what was to be his most rewarding period of European study.

On arriving in Hamburg, Allport was delighted to discover a city rich in premodern architectural charm. "I am very happy in Hamburg," he remarked, "because it is so beautiful":[55]

> Hamburg is not only the prettiest port city I ever saw, but is, I verily believe, the most interesting and most immaculate city of any kind I ever saw. There are dizzy sections where mediaeval architecture, Hansiatic constructions of all kinds, are absolutely unaltered. I found the 15th cent. [sic] house today where Brahms was born. But there are

parks and avenues and an immense lake in the city which give elegance unending to the Aussicht.[56]

Captivated by the city's medieval ambiance, Allport was also mindful of the sorry state of the Weimar economy. Germany had gone into a precipitous economic decline in the years after World War I. By 1923, the economy was in a truly desperate state. In a letter home, Allport told one friend that he knew several professors "who are forced to live on $1 a month for lodging, food, and university expenses."[57] Stern's financial circumstances were not quite this bleak, but like most Germans, he was struggling. To supplement his meager income, he offered Allport room and board for the duration of his time in Hamburg. It proved to be a highly satisfactory arrangement for Allport, who described Stern as an "admirable host" and a provider of "comforts extraordinary," including a "glorious large room" that contained a "tinkling piano" and one of the most famous photographs in the history of psychology:[58]

> Over my desk is a marvelous photograph of the Psychology Congress which met in Clark Univ. [sic] in 1909. Freud, Jung, Stern, James, Titchener, Holt, Hall, and all the rest of the sacred clan are in it, and beam upon the new pilgrim to Neumann's Institute. I feel quite inspired by the picture and at times feel truly like an adventitious psychologist.[59]

A devoted academic, Stern also provided Allport with a steady stream of weighty tomes and high-powered conversation, much of it involving his own carefully crafted philosophical system. Allport got a great deal out of these conversations, although he did admit to Langfeld that it was sometimes a "trial to live in the same house with such eternal Zweckmaßigkeit [practicality], Selbsbestimmungschaft [self-determination], and equally formidable concepts."[60]

The "formidable" philosophy that Allport endeavored to digest was embedded in the German "mandarin" culture of the late-19th and early-20th century.[61] Mandarin culture comprised a social elite drawn largely from medicine, law, the civil service, and the university. Its principal spokesmen were university professors, particularly professors in the social studies and humanities. These scholars were intellectually diverse, but they shared a number of assumptions, which taken together formed the mandarin worldview. To begin with, the mandarins viewed the empiricism of the Anglo-French Enlightenment with suspicion. What disturbed them was the technological ethos that pervaded Western European science. Anglo-French scholars seemed to equate science and learning with practical manipulation and environmental control. The German mandarins subscribed to an alternative ideal that they expressed through the term *Kultur*, which was usually contrasted with *civilization*. Kultur referred to the organic, "inner" world of art, learning, and morality, whereas civilization was associated with the superficial, mechanical, external world of manners and social nice-ties. Spengler defined Kultur as the "ennoblement of man through the development of his ethical, artistic, and intellectual powers; also the result of the activity of such cultivated men, a characteristic personal style of life; [and] the products of such activity (cultural objects and values)."[62]

The mandarins placed a great deal of emphasis on Kultur, and they regarded it as a distinctly German characteristic. The concept played an important role in German academic discussions throughout the 19th cen-tury, but with the advent of industrialization in the 1880s, discussions of Kultur reached a new level of intensity. For the main representatives of Kultur—the professors—industrialization brought with it a crude utilitar-ianism that threatened to consume the traditional mandarin values, leaving Germany a "soulless" shell.[63] The mandarins responded to this threat with a vigorous critique of positivism, utilitarianism, and a number of other philosophical tendencies that threatened to make the Germans a "people without music."[64]

As historian Anne Harrington noted, much of the mandarin discourse of this period was cast in negative terms.[65] The mandarins were clear about what they rejected, but rather vague when it came to specifying precisely what their commitment to Kultur entailed with respect to scientific work. Harrington's concept of an "enchanted epistemology" provides some clarity on the issues at stake. The term referred to a "Kantian-based refusal to admit that nineteenth-century scientific methodology represents a neces-sary final court of appeal in matters of truth." The more radical forms of this epistemology strove to "transform science into a mystical and intuitive enterprise capable of uniting its insights with those of art and religion."[66]

Stern was a central figure in the German mandarin tradition and an earnest exponent of the "enchanted" epistemology. Like most mandarins, his work was animated by a desire to reach past what he saw as a rather depressing materialism to grab hold of an uplifting idealism that would invest the world with a sense of unity and meaning. In his autobiography, Stern spoke of a "*furor metaphysicus* that . . . burned . . . internally."[67] It was, he explained, a "desire for conviction in ultimate things, for the con-struction of a new world-aspect." The focus of Stern's metaphysical wrath was mechanism. He criticized the mechanical theories of natural science for their "extreme artificiality" and intellectual "paucity." What disturbed him most about mechanism was its "crushing influence" on the spiritual life of the German people. The "all-devouring" scientistic ethos of the age was in large part responsible for the "atomization of the world, life, and civilization" and a loss of "conviction in ultimate things." Society needed a new, all encompassing metaphysic that would give the natural sciences "their due weight and application without [allowing them] to mechanize our whole view of reality."[68]

Staying with the Sterns, Allport was exposed to Kultur as a living entity and not just an intellectual critique. Beauty and soul had free range in the Stern household, and scientific discussions often led to musical enchantment:

> Late last night while I sat reading modern German philosophy, the good Stern's came in, and visited with me a while. Then we had some music. It warmed my soul to see the dear old fellow abandon himself at the piano while playing Schumann for me, as only a Deutscher *can* play Schumann.[69]

PERSONALISM AND PURE INDIVIDUALITY

Threatened by the growing mechanization and urbanization of German life, Stern set out to construct a psychology that would protect individuality. This interest sparked well-known psychometric innovations, such as the intelligence quotient, for which Stern is now widely known.[70] More significantly, however, his focus also fostered a searching examination of precisely what was meant by *individuality*. Stern eventually concluded that there were essentially two kinds of individuality: *relational* and *real*. Relational individuality was defined statistically in terms of deviations from corresponding norms. In contrast, real, or pure, individuality referred to a kind of unique, "spiritual" unity that defied scientific capture.[71] By the time Allport met him in 1923, "real individuality" had become Stern's main intellectual preoccupation. He wanted to show that human experience was characterized by a "synthesizing higher unity. Not a complex of differential forms of psychical phenomena, but a genuine individuality, something indivisibly singular, a personality."[72]

Stern thought that his own metaphysical speculations contributed toward just such a structure. Entitled *Person und Sache*, his philosophy was closely related to the work of "personalist" philosophers Charles Renouvier and Borden Parker Bowne.[73] The central tenet of all of these scholars was that the person is ontologically fundamental and that all philosophical study should proceed in reference to the concept of the *person*. According to Stern and the other personalist philosophers, this meant rejecting the atomistic, deterministic philosophy of associationism and anything else that analyzed away human volition and the unity of the mind. Beguiled by the idea of pure individuality, Stern argued that intellectual inquiry should proceed from the premise of the person, which he understood as "that kind of being or existence which in spite of the plurality of its parts constitutes a real, unique, and intrinsically valuable unity, and as such, in spite of the plurality of the functions of its parts, achieves a unitary, purposive self-activity."[74]

Allport was himself preoccupied with individuality long before he set foot in Stern's home. However, his growing awareness of the European cultural context gave the issue added urgency. In Germany, as in America, the individual seemed to be an endangered species. Order and discipline were supreme values, and although those themes gave rise to a breathtaking range of scientific, artistic, and spiritual accomplishments, the scope for individual expression was exceedingly narrow:

> Only the "over-personalities" such as the *class* and *state* have reality. How easy it is to see how the war and all the hell subsequent were engendered in this over-socialization! Out of pure inertia the [German] people continue to subjugate themselves to system, and the philosophers continue with their ponderous idealism which removes all thought from the funny little individual who in himself has no worth![75]

Alarmed by the cultural priorities of German society, Allport was equally troubled by the reports coming out of Soviet Russia. Dismissing the Communist Party as a "peculiar tyranny," he clung to a faint hope that the regime would not last and that a spirit of individuality would develop. "When the pendulum swings back we may see the *individual* emerge in his unique, colorful, helter-skelter, Russian self."[76]

Energized by this troubling political context, Allport studied Stern's personalism in earnest and found its general tenor "quite appealing." Stern's highly detailed philosophical elaborations of personalism were another matter, however.[77] The dense, neo-Kantian language of personalism seemed excessively abstract, and in a letter to Langfeld, Allport described Stern's three-volume *Person und Sache* as "ponderous" and "unnecessarily involved."[78] Evidently, Allport wanted from his German teachers what had been so readily supplied by his American mentors: a philosophically lean psychology that could be readily applied to practical questions. However, he quickly discovered that the disciplinary structures and scholarly priorities were quite different in Germany from in the United States.[79] Back at Harvard, Allport had come to think of psychology as an independent discipline, and he had learned to frame psychological questions in the language of behaviorism—a framework he jokingly described as America's "sacred creed."[80,81] Research was valuable to the extent that it (a) could be confirmed using the standards of natural science and (b) could make a practical contribution with respect to the prediction and control of the "organism" under study. In Germany, Allport was surprised to discover that far from being independent disciplines, psychology and philosophy were "original Siamese twins."[82] Psychology had its administrative base in philosophy, and most German psychologists felt a strong intellectual affinity with philosophy. In a letter to William Taylor, a puzzled Allport remarked that "no one is half a psychologist in Germany who cannot at the same time hold his own in the debates of the Kant-Gesellschaft and offer a respectable systematic Weltanschauung of his own, which must have body and a power of resistance."[83]

What was especially troubling to Allport about German psychology was not the fact that it had a relationship to philosophy. It was the nature of this relationship that he found disagreeable. In Germany, psychology's intellectual agenda appeared to be set by philosophical systems; in a letter to Langfeld, Allport complained that "psychology is so disciplined by philosophy here that it dares not forget its place, that is after all only a Hilfswissenschaft [assistant science]."[84] One of the most unfortunate by-products of this arrangement in Allport's view was a disconcertingly casual attitude toward the psychological phenomena under study. The German psychologists seemed more interested in establishing a harmony with the precepts of neo-Kantian idealism than in documenting the empirical character of the phenomena under investigation. Allport told Langfeld that it was "amazing to me to see how naively a [German] professor detaches his philosophical and psychological system, even when it is supposed to be empirically founded, from the real genetic facts of the case."[85]

German inattentiveness to empirical "facts" was a source of some frustration, but by the end of his year in Germany, Allport came to accept and to value, up to a point, the philosophically informed work of his German teachers. One event appears to have played a particularly important role in modifying his intellectual orientation. Allport was invited to give a talk to a German seminar. Accepting the offer, he "endeavored to explain my own work [on] personality analysis."[86] Unfortunately for Allport, his German audience did not find his behavioristic formulations especially convincing. In a letter to Ford, Allport recalled that his efforts "succeeded in bringing a crash of destructive criticism upon my head." Speculating that linguistic difficulties may have contributed to his poor showing, Allport conceded that some of the criticism was well deserved. The critique made him realize that his "approach to the problem [of personality] is (in sich) vulnerable."[87]

Over the next several months, Allport did his best to build on the criticisms that had been directed at his dissertation research. One of the first principles that he had to contend with concerned the intellectual division in German scholarship between what Wilhelm Dilthey (1833–1911) called the *Naturwissenschaften* and the *Geisteswissenschaften*. The tradition most familiar to American psychologists was the Naturwissenschaften, as exemplified by the experimental work of Oswald Külpe. Patterned on the natural sciences, research in this tradition drew heavily on laboratory technology and statistics. Its principal aim was to explain mental life by analyzing its component parts and to prove the "dependency of mental phenomena upon certain bodily processes."[88] The other tradition within German psychology was the Geisteswiesschaften, as exemplified by Wilhelm Wundt's Völkerpsychologie, a compendious study of expressive movements, language, and culture.[89] Work in the tradition of the Geisteswissenschaften was patterned on the human sciences of history, anthropology, religious studies, and mythology. The aim of these investigations differed according to the author, but all shared a concern with the cultural, linguistic, and personal context from which mental experience derives its meaning.

A sense of difference between natural science and human science was a recurring theme in Stern's work, perhaps because he was himself an intellectual product of these two traditions, his primary mentors being the famous experimentalist Hermann Ebbinghaus and M. Lazarus (1824–1903), a marginal academic whose work in Völkerpsychologie predated that of Wundt.[90] Stern drew on both of these traditions, although in spirit, his views were closer to the Geisteswissenschaften. He routinely attacked what he regarded as a reverence among his colleagues for the methods and exactitude of the physical sciences. The source of Stern's concern was not with the sciences themselves, but with the tendency to import physically based frames of reference into contexts that he believed were not appropriate. Stern directed particularly heavy fire at psychologies that were based *entirely* on the methods and metaphors derived from the physical sciences. Most of his criticism was focused on "elementaristic psychology": the search for the elements of mind, the manner in which they are constituted, and the way in which they are bound together. Stern criticized elementaristic psychology for its tendency to view mental elements as being "of the same kind (corresponding somewhat to protons or electrons in physics)."[91] He also questioned elementaristic psychology's tendency to explain solely by elements and processes that lie within the mind. The narrow scope and neglect of qualitative difference led him to conclude that "elementaristic psychology is far removed from the realities of psychological experience; in fact, it forces experience into an wholly arbitrary system of assumptions."[92]

In criticizing elementaristic psychology, Stern was not trying to deport psychology's sense of scientific exactitude back to the physical sciences. In his view, elementaristic psychology had, for all its shortcomings, contributed much to the understanding of human psychology. To dismiss these findings and the methods they had generated would be "entirely inadvisable." Stern's goal in attacking elementarism was to partially deflate the ego of what he regarded as an arrogant scientism while creating a space for a new psychology that would be based on "entirely different theoretical assumptions." One of the main focal points for Stern's new psychology was the concept of "wholeness" and the related concepts of "configuration," "structure," and "unity of consciousness." In his view, "anything mental either is itself a whole (i.e., a unity meaningful in itself that is more or less definitely bounded), or belongs to a whole." This straightforward-sounding proposition had important implications for Stern's program of psychological research. Psychologists who respected the "wholes" with which they were dealing would not speak of psychic "elements," nor would they try to explain personality by reference to synthesis of parts. The approach advocated by Stern was to characterize psychic parts as "subordinate 'aspects' of the whole" and to then interpret them "in their relation to the totality."[93]

As in his philosophy, the primary totality in Stern's psychology was the person. He maintained that psychology was "the science of the person" and that the "immediate subject matter of psychology, experience, is therefore to be identified and interpreted in terms of its matrix, the . . . person."[94] The selection of the person as the anchor point of psychology reflected what some would regard as Stern's flattering portrait of human nature. Nowhere is this more in evidence than in his thoughts on motivation. Then-popular theories of motivation, such as psychoanalysis and behaviorism, emphasized determinism and reductionism. Thoughts and actions were largely the products of either instincts or the environment. Higher motives—values, ideals, a sense of duty—were not "real" motives at all. They were rationalizations or delusions that could be traced back to the press of a more fundamental motivational process. Stern was mindful of the contributions of psychoanalysis and behaviorism in his writing on motivation, but his formulation differed from both of these systems. The most significant point of departure was his emphasis on voluntarism. He argued that a significant proportion of human activity could be understood as a manifestation of "the will." The will was a complex and distinctively human feature. It referred to the human capacity to consciously depart from the "steady current" of events and move toward a new goal that was somehow significant to the person's life pattern.[95]

Stern did not view the will as an "unyielding, inimical sovereign" capable of overriding instincts and the environment, nor did he regard it as an illusory cover for the many considerations that inform thought and conduct. The will referred to a real ability in humans, yet it was not independent of instincts or environmental context. Both instincts and the setting of will shaped the parameters within which acts of will could occur. In most cases, however, these parameters were thought to be extraordinarily broad. Humans thus had a wide expanse of life space over which they could exercise personal choice. Stern developed a complex theoretical array to account for this willed action. Human drives, needs, intentions, personal history, and energy were all taken into account.

Allport did not assimilate all of the details of this theory, but he did pick up on a number of its main points of emphasis. In the years to come, one of Stern's themes would stand out as being especially important: the "reenchantment" of the individual. Like most mandarins, Stern saw psychology as a tool for reinvesting the world with a sense of meaning, wonder, and purpose. The position of the individual in modern life was a special concern. Positivist psychology had "dissect[ed] the unity of spiritual life" and in the process had fostered a "dreadful impoverization [sic] of the world picture."[96] Through his "personalistic" philosophy and psychology, Stern hoped to revivify the dignity, purposiveness, and unity that he believed lay at the heart of the human experience.

One of the clearest illustrations of Stern's "reenchantment" project was his work on motivation. This work made a particularly strong impression on Allport, and it was to figure prominently in his later theorizing. Stern maintained that people's actions at birth are governed by a relatively narrow band of basic instincts, but as they mature, their actions are increasingly subject to a host of other considerations: "drives toward speech, thought and knowledge; the drive to portray and create; metaphysical, religious, ethical, political, technological drives and impulses."[97] The contents of these "higher" drives were products of culture, but the drives themselves were biological in nature and thus could not be dismissed as "mere secondary products of the elementary drives."[98] Stern posited a relationship between the higher and lower drives, but its point of emphasis ran counter to the sex-based theories of motivation that were popular in the 1920s. In the personalistic system, the sex drive was not an unchanging primary force that needed to be contained by an array of defenses. For Stern, sexuality was part of a larger matrix of propensities that varied depending on the person in question and their stage in life. Central to Stern's thought in this regard was the notion of motivational development. "Higher" drives developed alongside basic ones, but the two constantly interacted with each other as the person matured. The result was an uplifting of the person's motivational Gestalt: The "activity of emotions and will may be comprehended only by regarding it as a progressive *spiritualizing* of basic vital processes. This signifies an enriching and elevating of those functions which are common to man and animals, by means of strictly human developmental forms."[99]

Professional posture was another aspect of personalist psychology that would find its way into Allport's thought. Stern called for the expansion of the field's intellectual domain, as did many other psychologists of his day. Unlike most of his colleagues, however, particularly those in the United States, Stern tempered his professional enthusiasm with a broad-minded critique of the field's shortcomings. Echoing William James's critique of scientific psychology, Stern repeatedly emphasized the difficulties of rendering something as fluid as the human psyche into the kind of stable scientific categories that lead to accurate predictions: "The very act of creating psychological classifications and definitions makes for a certain arbitrary treatment" and gives it "a peculiar rigidity and fixity that cannot be ascribed to the mind itself."[100] In Stern's view, an honest recognition of these categorical limitations obliged the psychologist to become more intellectually ecumenical, rather than less so. The reality of the psyche would be understood not through the cultivation of an ever more abstract scientistic rigor, but through a wide-ranging sharing of categories among all the discourses that talk about human experience:

The rigidity of classification may be modified through the easier and richer constructions and through shifts in definition. Placing one and the same mental phenomena in varied perspectives is one attempt to get at its diverse meaning; by cultivating a language that grows continually richer in shadings, by creating transitional concepts . . . that which seemed inexpressible is given increasingly appropriate forms.[101]

The shifts in perspective that Stern encouraged were not confined to the points of view conceived in psychological laboratories. Again departing from the increasingly scientistic sensibility of American psychologists, Stern argued that psychologists should both respect and borrow points of view from philosophy, art, and common sense. "Each in its own way can lead to unsurpassable heights of achievement."[102] "In no case," he wrote, "may the scientific psychologist thrust aside indifferently the artistic type of imagination and portrayal because they belong to a different region of life."[103]

LEBENSFORMEN: THE PSYCHOLOGY OF EDUARD SPRANGER

The Hamburg months were a crucial period in Allport's intellectual development. The close relationship he developed with Stern gave him a good working knowledge of personalism, and it also gave him the philosophical resources to appreciate the details of the lectures he had attended at the University of Berlin the previous semester. In the years to come, the Berlin psychologist that Allport drew most heavily on was Eduard Spranger. What captured Allport's attention was Spranger's intellectual focus—the psychology of personality—and the manner in which he construed the topic. In Spranger's thought, Allport encountered a systematic approach to the psychology of personality that was different from anything he had read while studying the subject as a graduate student in the United States.

The principal components of Spranger's psychology of personality were outlined in his 1922 book *Lebensformen*.[104] Much of the book's intellectual foundation was constructed out of the thought of Spranger's mentor, Wilhelm Dilthey. One of its most fundamental Diltheyian themes was the idea of two kinds of psychology, one rooted in tradition of the Naturwissenschaften and the other associated with the Geisteswissenschaften. Like Stern, Spranger believed that psychology could profit from both approaches. His complaint was that the field had developed only one of these traditions—the natural science approach—which he termed the "psychology of elements." Proponents of this approach attempted to "analyze the processes of individual consciousness into their last differentiable components."[105] Spranger did not see any "fault with the attempt to give similar and fundamental phenomena in experience general names," but he did question whether "the province of psychology is thus exhausted."[106] In his view, the psychology of elements was, in fact, a small and relatively insignificant corner of the domain over which psychologists could travel.

The larger and more important dimensions of psychic life could be traversed only by means of methods and metaphors from outside the natural sciences. Subjectivity, the unity of personality, purpose, and culture were all crucial to the psychic economy of the person, yet in Spranger's view they could not be satisfactorily understood by means of elementaristic psychology. "We no longer believe that the higher psychic achievements can be understood through the summation or elaboration of simple psychological elements."[107] The key to unlocking these "higher" psychic functions was to interpret them in relation to a larger whole. Spranger argued that psychologists should remain "on a higher conceptual level, and immediately consider the inner process as a significant whole which has importance because it is part of a total mental situation."[108] The primary "higher" concept of Spranger's system was the *Lebensform* (or *life-form*): a "meaningful life-totality."[109] The Lebensformen were the pattern or Gestalt that was the person. It was formed out of the interaction of all of those aspects that psychologists traditionally explored—feelings, instincts, adaptation, variation—and many they ignored—language, culture, and expression.

The combination of so many different features made the life-form a highly complex structure. It also made the life-form something more than the sum of its parts: "Complex forms contain characteristics which could not be predicted from the original elements."[110] The question that Spranger proposed to consider was how these life-forms could be approached scientifically. Was it possible to develop a scientific discourse about the person without "destroy[ing] the soul's meaningful total?"[111] The problem, he wrote, "is to build up the total structure of the soul from qualitatively different, yet always significantly interrelated mental attitudes."[112] It was this interest in the soul's "structure" and a related concern for maintaining its integrity that led Spranger to the method of the "ideal type," a procedure made famous by Max Weber. The method involved the construction of a typology of the phenomenon under consideration. The investigator would survey relevant information from history, sociology, and literature to piece together an "abstract, pure case." These cases need not be statistically frequent. Spranger thought that it would be "wholly erroneous to believe that any one of these types really exists as described by our wholly one-sided method." The ideal types were not "photographs of real life," but scientific contrivances that served "only to clarify and bring order to the confusion of complex real forms."[113]

In the case of life-forms, Spranger constructed a series of ideal types out of what he regarded as the dominant value directions in Western culture. His investigations led him to conclude that there were six main ideal types of life-forms: the theoretic, economic, aesthetic, social, political, and religious. The labels referred to the principal *meaning*, or *value direction*, that Spranger regarded as dominant within the personality structure. He saw each meaning as a kind of life metaphor that shaped and ordered a person's perceptions. The meaning was a lens that focused on a specified range of objects while tingeing those that it did see in a characteristic hue. The meaning was also a distinctive style or manner that was "immanent" in that it touched on every single facet of an individual's personality. In the case of the economic type, for example, utilitarianism was the dominant principle in the person's life: "He sees everything as a means for self-preservation, an aid in the natural struggle for existence and a possibility to render life pleasant."[114]

For Spranger, the determination of a person's value direction was thus a matter of considerable intellectual importance. The Lebensform or value-direction would shed light on a person's manner of expression, specific life choices, and life story. Spranger likened his approach to personality to the study of music. Personality is like a musical melody, a "formed total in which articulate parts are recognizable." Just as a melody is made up of a variety of motifs—a "characteristic rhythmical sequence of intervals"— Spranger reasoned that personality was composed of sets of life-motifs— characteristic "feelings of significance." The psychologist's job was thus much like that of the musicologist: "Our entire study might be regarded as an endeavor to discover the leitmotifs of life and to examine their repetitions and infinite variations, their harmonies and contrapuntal movements."[115]

Spranger presented his types as value-free descriptions and not normative prescriptions. He maintained that "no value judgments are made in regard to the types."[116] Yet in reading over the value types, it is quite clear where Spranger's sympathy lies. The economic, aesthetic, social, political, and theoretic social types were all presented as narrow and ultimately self-defeating. The most fulfilling type, Spranger implied, was the religious. The superiority of the religious position was a function of the emphasis on values in personality. Spranger argued that people struggled at various points of their life with the question of what they regard as the highest value in their experience. Moments of uncertainty in this regard are experienced as feelings of being "homeless, torn and despairing." In contrast, the person who possesses a confident awareness of a highest value experiences feelings of "salvation and blessedness."[117] The theorist becomes religious when he tries to "fathom the final secret" through cognition. "The social type finds God in infinite love, and the political type in the exhibition of power on a big scale." What distinguished these types from the specifically religious type was the scope of their "pursuit of infinity."[118] The various nonreligious types attempted to grasp the meaning of the world in terms of one specific value direction. The result of this approach was a strong sense of disappointment and loss:

These somewhat circumscribed seekers for God, who try to reach in-finity by progressing in one direction, naturally experience more strongly than others the inadequacy of their narrow outlook to perceive the meaning of life. Though these one-sided people often exhibit a grandiose element, nevertheless they cannot escape the tragedy of a conflict with their limitations which makes them feel a breach in their souls.[119]

In contrast, the religious type pursued God—the "highest personal value experience"—from one of three alternative perspectives.[120] The *immanent mystic* was a universalist; he looked for God in every aspect of life —nature, politics, science, society, art. The *transcendental mystic* did not believe that God could be discovered in any human or natural form. Consequently, he took a negative view of this world in the form of a self-denying asceticism: "He comprehends God or the meaning of the world, through absolute contrast with all special meaning forms of the world."[121] In between these two extremes, Spranger identified a third and more common religious possibility. The *intermediary religious type* was a combination of both religious forms. This type confronted "both affirmatively and neg-atively every region of life."[122] A person whose life was lived in relation to one of these religious value orientations was better able to avoid the con-flict of material limitations that bound the other types. A commitment to the "highest value which surrounds world and soul" led to a "blessed full-ness" that Spranger equated with "God's Grace."[123]

PSYCHOLOGICAL VISIONS AND ANGLO-CATHOLIC DREAMS

Determined to resist the "disenchantment" of human experience, Stern and Spranger stood well outside the scientistic orthodoxies of Amer-ican psychology. Both Germans were voluntarists, both trafficked in meta-physical categories, both used methods that were not sanctioned by natural science, and both valorized the unscientific ideal of pure individuality. Fresh from his lessons in the behaviorist idiom, Allport felt a measure of discomfort with these characteristics, as his letters to Taylor and Langfeld make clear. For all his concerns, however, he felt more at home in the German psychological universe than he ever did in the United States. In Germany, spirituality and personality were topics of manly debate, and Allport had been warmly welcomed by one of the country's biggest psy-chological men: William Stern. The contrast between Stern's soulful ben-ediction and Titchener's imperious repudiation was not lost on Allport, and in a report on the Leipzig Congress of Psychology published in one of the field's foremost periodicals—the *American Journal of Psychology*—he delighted in highlighting German interest in personality and its indiffer-ence to the kind of experimental psychology so revered by Titchener.[124]

"Very little of the classical German psychology remains in active use," he noted with barely concealed glee. "It was characteristic of the Congress that in none of the lectures or discussions was reference made to the name or the teachings of Wundt!"[125] Titchener was the editor of the *American Journal of Psychology*, and Allport knew that his report would infuriate the Wundtian trained experimentalist.[126] "I took the sweetest revenge upon him [Titchener] you can imagine," Allport announced triumphantly to Gould. "I never forgave him for his dig of two years ago, and what a joy it was to announce, embellish, and extol the fact that the central theme of the German Congress this year was PERSONALITY!"[127]

Reveling in the prestige of personality within German psychology, Allport also identified with the spiritual focus on real individuality. Stern and Spranger seemed to be in communion with something deep and soulful, and Allport came to conclude that his own scientifically earnest offerings were shallow by comparison. "Something is lacking, Ada, from those psychographs [in the dissertation]," he remarked emphatically in 1923.

> Even if the analysis is perfect, something is lacking. . . . Who would be so inhuman as to identify Miss PENN [*sic*] with the one original and only Skook [Ada Gould]. No, it is the Personality itself that is lacking! The problem has worried me muchly, and it is this sense of inadequacy that has kept me . . . from working out articles from the old thesis.[128]

This worry was soon translated into action, and in 1924 Allport published a paper entitled "The Study of the Undivided Personality" in *The Journal of Abnormal and Social Psychology*.[129] The influence of Stern and Spranger is discernible throughout Allport's essay. His introduction consisted of a brief, impassioned critique of elementaristic psychology applied to the study of personality. By "analyzing, testing, and correlating most of these [psychometric] investigators [had] become blind to the true nature of the problem before them," he wrote. Instead of developing "an adequate representation . . . of the total personality," Allport argued, personality psychologists had developed a "series of separate measurements which pertain only to isolated, and arbitrarily defined traits."[130] Again echoing the thought of his new German mentors, Allport insisted that the problem with elementaristic personality psychology lay in its conception of the nature of personality. American researchers tended to view personality as the "sum-totality of the individual's traits."[131] Mobilizing the ideal of pure individuality, Allport argued that personality was not the sum of traits, but a "unique quality" that had its "origin in the *form* in which the traits are combined, and in the manner in which they function *together*."[132] In his view, it was this "form" in which personality psychologists should be primarily interested, not individual traits. By considering personality as a life-form, psychologists would arrive at a "really thoroughgoing comprehension" of their subject and would not "lose sight of the forest in their preoccupation with individual trees."[133]

In Germany but a year, Allport had abandoned the relational model of individuality that he had so carefully constructed in his dissertation. It was a dramatic turnabout, but not altogether surprising in view of his spiritual restlessness and antimodernist leanings. As a graduate student, Allport had discovered that the sacraments of scientific psychology were a poor substitute for the sensuous exoticism of Constantinople and the venerable spirituality of Europe. While working on his dissertation, he continued to indulge his religious appetite, and his spiritual meanderings eventually led him to Boston's Church of the Advent and the ornate world of Anglo-Catholic Episcopalianism.

Historians have frequently noted the class consciousness of Anglo-Catholicism, and some have interpreted the Church's growth in the late-19th and early-20th century as a manifestation of upper-class status seeking.[134] The class dimension was pronounced, and the Church counted many of the country's leading citizens among its members. However, as Lears observed, Anglo-Catholicism's appeal reflected a broader and more complex range of ambitions than mere class snobbery.[135] Spiritual frustration with liberal Protestantism spurred many into the pews of Anglo-Catholic churches. Liberal, or "new," theology blurred the distinction between heaven and earth and played down the transcendental character of the Gospel. God was now assumed to be immanent in nature, and as religious historian William Hutchison noted, the faithful were encouraged to "render all spiritual facts and processes, including the nature of God, in moral as opposed to 'magical' terms."[136] This retreat from the supernatural was conducted in the name of reason, and it was designed to keep Protestantism current with the latest advances in science and technology. For these reasons, the new theology enjoyed a wide following, but many Americans continued to yearn for a sense of theological rigor and sublime otherworldliness. Indeed, the industrial era's commodification and routinization of experience intensified desires among some for a religious language and environment that was completely different from the rational banalities of everyday life. "Religion is dying out in our churches," one disgruntled liberal minister complained in 1892, "because it has no lyrical lift, no aroma of poetry, no wings of spiritual imagination, no vital communion with sublime natures."[137]

Anglo-Catholicism sought to provide that "lyrical lift" and revive a transcendental worldview that placed values, meaning, and selfhood beyond human rationality and control. Communion with the divine was achieved by reaffirming a premodern theology and celebrating a medieval religious aesthetic. To underscore the separation of the sacred from the secular, Anglo-Catholics constructed elaborate Gothic churches with "jewelled windows" and an "incense-laden atmosphere."[138] Spectacular, medieval-looking structures sheltered worshippers from modernity's frenzy while generating a sense of human insignificance and the sublime majesty of God. "The first desideratum of a church," the American Anglo-Catholic architect Ralph Cram remarked, was that "so far as man is concerned, . . . he shall be filled with the righteous sense of awe and mystery and devotion."[139] Elaborate sacraments, ornate priestly vestments, and ancient Latin verse served the same transcendental purposes. Sacramentalism was a particularly important aspect of Anglo-Catholicism and a central part of the project to maintain the miraculous in a disenchanted world. The sacraments of baptism, confirmation, the Eucharist, penance, extreme unction, ordination, and matrimony were not simply rituals, but visible signs of the divine. The supernatural element was especially evident in the Eucharist, where consecrated wine and bread were thought to contain the "real objective presence of God."

Disenchanted with "progress," Allport embraced Anglo-Catholicism with an almost sexual intensity. In a letter to Powers, he remarked that he had found an "indescribable release for my spirit in the religion of ritual and sacrament."[140] Mindful of Catholicism's status as the church of the immigrant, Allport was careful to note that he had embraced neither "Papism nor Greekism."[141] The "good old church of England" was the recipient of his "heart and soul," and like many of his contemporaries, he was fascinated by Anglo-Catholicism's medieval aura.[142] While in the United States, he wrote movingly of "the historical continuity of my communion" with the "English branch of the Holy Catholic and Apostolic Church reaching back to the primitive Church founded by Christ himself."[143] Impressed by the "solemn mass" and "stately and historic liturgy," Allport felt the sublime presence all the more while in Europe and England during his postdoctoral fellowship. "Don't you ever long for this flavor of olde [sic] English worship—a blending of 17th century organ notes, 14th century choir stalls, and flickering altar candles which have been in place continually since the sisterhood of St. Radgund back in 1133? I know I shall long for it when I have to leave."[144]

Moved by Anglo-Catholicism's premodern aesthetic, Allport also took the Church's theology seriously, and he found its refusal to accommodate secular trends enormously appealing. Theological rigor brought him back to a spiritually purer time when he was a boy and faith was a priority:

> The church of my boyhood held morning worship at eleven o'clock on Sundays. At one time there were likewise an evening service and a midweek meeting. For a while movies and entertainment kept the evening services alive, but finally these were abandoned. What is more, there was no sense of discipline that compelled attendance at the one remaining service. Fatigue, golf, or weather was a sufficient excuse for

absence. And the services, I noted, grew more secular and apologetic in tone.[145]

Driven in part by boyhood nostalgia, Allport's fascination with Anglo-Catholicism was also a reflection of adult unease with the impersonality and instrumentality of American consumer culture. He felt cut adrift by material progress, and his forays into Unitarianism, Christian Science, and the YMCA provided no anchor points. Unable to find "an acceptable hitching post for my slight spirit and slighter intelligence," Allport had gone to the ancient world of Constantinople and, ultimately, to the venerable theology of Anglo-Catholicism, which he described as the "consummation of a long developing inclination."[146] The ancient sacraments and medieval atmosphere gave him the spiritual mooring he was looking for. Church membership was "not just playing at something," he wrote. "It has a meaning, and for me at least the meaning is deeper than anything else."[147]

Part of that meaning for Allport involved more than the ethics of human dignity; Anglo-Catholicism affirmed the reality of a world beyond the senses. "I remain a mystic," he wrote in 1924, and he glimpsed in High Anglicanism "visions . . . of Reality far beyond the tangible world." The challenge of accounting for these experiences did not trouble him especially, for the sense of intuitive conviction and contentment outweighed any scientific imperative to explain. "I can't explain it; but everything good is associated with it; happiness is inseparable from it . . . [and] neither science nor history can rob me of [it]."[148] For Allport, sacramentalism was a flight path to the divine and an expression of dissent against a culture of disenchantment. No matter what the "intellectual difficulties," he wrote, "I am not greatly troubled, for I know that somehow God reaches me through the Sacrament."[149]

Drawing spiritual strength from a sense of divine assurance, Allport turned again to William James for scholarly backing for his religious choices. In 1923, he began "re-reading to my infinite inspiration James' *Varieties of Religious Experience.*"[150] In the *Varieties*, James spoke at great length of the importance of aesthetic "richness" in spiritual life. Contrasting Protestantism and Catholicism, he described the latter as an "incrusted work of jewelry or architecture . . . majestic in the hierarchic interrelatedness of its parts, with authority descending from stage to stage, and at every stage objects for adjectives of mystery and splendor, derived in the last resort from the Godhead who is the fountain and culmination of the system." In contrast to the ornate splendor of Catholicism, Protestantism appeared to James as a barren, featureless, "almshouse," that "pauperizes the monarchical imagination."[151] James was willing to concede the theological merits of Protestant arguments, but he insisted Catholicism would always remain the more popular faith insofar as its institutional and aesthetic forms allowed for a wider range of spiritual expression.

The strength of these aesthetic sentiments makes it rigorously impossible, it seems to me, that Protestantism, however superior in spiritual profundity it may be to Catholicism, should at the present day succeed in making many converts from the more venerable ecclesiasticism. The latter offers a so much richer pasturage and shade to the fancy, has so many cells with so many different kinds of honey, is so indulgent in its multiform appeals to human nature, that Protestantism will always show to Catholic eyes the almshouse physiognomy.[152]

Emboldened by James's celebration of Catholic aestheticism, Allport pursued formal Church membership, something he had neglected to undertake during the 2 years he had attended church in graduate school. Contacting the chaplain of the Anglican Church in the Monbijou Gardens in Berlin in 1923, he was baptized "after a long season of preparation" and confirmed during a visit of the Bishop of London.[153] It was a moment of great personal significance for Allport, and the "spiritual fellowship" and mystical union he gained from the church were reflected in his professional outlook. As a graduate student, he had drawn heavily on the modernist idiom of behaviorism, and he had constructed personality in the materialist language of habits and reflexes. In Germany, Allport cemented his union with the divine and fed voraciously in the spiritually rich pastures of the Geisteswissenschaften. Feeling spiritually and intellectually well armed, he moved away from his earlier behavioral interpretation of personality and toward the enchanted vision of Stern and Spranger. "I am less of a behaviorist now than a 'mentalist,'" he concluded in September 1923, and he professed little patience with the "superficial postulates of scientists."[154]

THE FRATERNAL SHADOW

The full impact of Allport's new commitment to an enchanted, or pure, model of personality can be seen in his relationship with Floyd Allport. As we have seen, Allport had spent the better part of his graduate career in Floyd's shadow. The elder Allport had provided him with both a dissertation topic and a behaviorist rationale. As a graduate student, Allport does not appear to have been especially troubled by this arrangement. Intellectual life under Floyd's tutelage was productive, and with its behavioristic cast, it was in keeping with the prevailing currents in American psychology. As a postdoctoral fellow, however, Allport began to glimpse some of the shortcomings of his scholarly life up to that point, and he made the first in a series of moves to forge his own intellectual identity.

Emerson once observed that

there is a time in every man's education when he arrives at the conviction that ... imitation is suicide; that he must take himself for better or worse as his portion; and know that though the wide universe is full of good, no kernel nourishing can come to him but through his toil bestowed on that plot of ground which is given to him.[155]

Reading the Geisteswissenschaften while absorbing the Anglo-Catholic spirit, Allport arrived at his moment of personal conviction. He could no longer live with the model of personality he had championed with Floyd, and in his private correspondence, he began to assert his own spiritualized psychology. In a letter to Langfeld, Allport mobilized his German acquisitions to criticize Floyd's recently published book *Social Psychology*.[156] Although he viewed the book with "pardonable fraternal pride" because it contained "less nonsense than most books on the subject," Allport now felt that Floyd was "wrong in his exclusive use of 'trial and error' in learning, and far too sweeping in some of his accounts of the conditioning process."[157] Convinced that "Floyd's astoundingly neat system will not suffice," Allport told Langfeld of his decision to put his recently developed sense of intellectual independence on a more public footing. "The paper I worked out for the Congress [meeting of the British Psychological Association] yesterday is an attack on the position of [Floyd's] chapter on 'Personality,' though it was my position too when I wrote the thesis."[158]

The paper that Allport had written as an "attack" on Floyd's conception of personality was "The Study of the Undivided Personality." As we have seen, the tone and focus of the paper reflected the mandarin ambition to reenchant individuality; American psychologists were encouraged to play down their interest in "isolated and arbitrarily defined traits" and concentrate instead on the "form quality" of the individual.[159] The significance of Allport's paper as a statement of intellectual independence was not lost on Floyd. Allport had sent the paper to his brother in his capacity as coeditor of the *Journal of Abnormal and Social Psychology*. Floyd agreed to publish the paper, but he was quick to comment on the obvious difference of opinion that had developed between him and his younger brother. "You seem to be developing a type of Psychology [*sic*] somewhat different from mine," Floyd wrote.[160] Floyd's subsequent comments reveal the pronounced power differential that existed between the brothers. His comments also highlight some of the difficulties that Gordon Allport had to contend with when trying to establish a professional profile of his own. Floyd clearly recognized his brother's growing independence of mind, and he tried to view the development in a positive light. In his letter, he suggested that a difference of approach "is a good idea so that people will not get us mixed up in reading our various contributions."[161] However, Floyd's magnanimity was undercut by several expressions of a long-established fraternal superiority. Shortly after commenting on his brother's new approach, Floyd paid Gordon a backhanded compliment by suggesting, "it is the next best thing to mine." Further into the letter, Floyd made light of his brother's Germanic interests. He suggested that Allport had created an atmosphere of "'Gestalt' and pretzels" and he cautioned his brother not to become "a sponge for absorbing all the Germanic ways."[162]

Floyd's ill-chosen words were symptomatic of a growing rift between the two brothers. "He [Floyd] just doesn't seem to *feel* anymore," Allport remarked sadly in 1923. "He writes to me as he would to an unknown prof [*sic*], in some distant dinky college."[163] Frustrated by Floyd's condescending attitude, Allport cut his emotional ties to his former mentor. "I truly do not care if I never see my brothers and sisters-in-law again," he remarked angrily in 1924. "My correspondence with them [his brothers] is nothing now and will in all probability become less in years to come."[164] When Allport returned to the United States in 1924, he and Floyd maintained a civil relationship; however, their personal and scholarly contacts were comparatively few in number. Allport did publish one more paper with Floyd in 1928, but the bulk of material was based on work done when Allport was a graduate student.[165]

CAMBRIDGE: 1923–1924

Allport had drunk deeply from the enchanted pools of German psychological thought, and his lavish, carefully edited descriptions of the experience made a favorable impact on his Harvard sponsors. In January 1923, Herbert Langfeld wrote that he had been "much impressed with the manner in which [Allport] is making use of his opportunities [in Germany]. He is meeting the right men, attending the best lectures, and planning very profitable research."[166] Langfeld urged the university to make the most of Allport's intellect and commitment by renewing his Sheldon Fellowship for one more year. "As a psychologist, I feel that it would be a great advantage to our science to give a man of Allport's ability every opportunity to become acquainted with the work of the leading psychologists of the world."[167]

With the support of Langfeld, Allport's Sheldon Fellowship was renewed in March 1923. Taking his former advisor's recommendation, Allport decided to leave Germany and head to Cambridge University.[168] He arrived in Cambridge in the fall of 1923, and he set about exploring the ancient university. However, the excitement of moving to a new location was soon dimmed by some tragic news from home. In September 1923, Allport learned that his father had died. As a boy, he had not been especially close to his father and had thought of John Allport as a "hard man and not especially understanding."[169] Despite the distance between the two, Allport was deeply saddened by the news of his father's death. In December 1923, he wrote that "the autumn for me has been a solemn time, owing to the grief which has come to us."[170]

The beauty and serenity of Cambridge brought Allport a degree of comfort during his time of loss. "Since it is impossible to be with my father,

I am thankful that I have been able to find some measure of re-adjustment in this sacred shade."[171] Spiritually nourishing, Allport quickly realized that from the standpoint of modern psychology, the ancient university had its limitations. Its troubles were those of British psychology as a whole: a highly conservative academic structure and a philosophical resistance to the idea of the human sciences.[172] Many university officials remained wedded to 19th-century notions of the gentleman–scholar. Others resisted the development of psychology on the grounds that it would "insult religion by putting the human soul in a pair of scales."[173] Irrespective of the objection, the end result was the same. By 1920, British psychological laboratories were well back of their German and American counterparts in size, resources, productivity, and importance. As British psychologist Hans Eysenck noted, "altogether psychology at the time was parochial, small-scale, and exceedingly feudal."[174]

The relatively undeveloped state of British psychology did not go unnoticed by Allport. English psychologists lacked the uncompromising drive of the Germans, and Allport complained sharply about the "pampered, handsome English chappies" and their "tea-soaked and buttery" scholarship.[175] The luminaries of British psychology—Frederick Bartlett and Charles Spearman—were pleasant enough, but in contrast to the Germans, they seemed tired and unfocused. Allport described Spearman as a "good old soul—utterly absent minded":

[Spearman]—Oh, Dr. Allport I wrote you a letter the other day to the Imperial Hotel about something very important. But I've forgotten now what it was.

[Allport]—Perhaps the letter will reach me yet.

[Spearman]—Oh no, it was returned to me, but I've forgotten where I put it.[176]

Summarizing his views in a letter to Langfeld, Allport noted that although Cambridge was "obviously the best place in England," it had "little or nothing new" to offer.[177] Novelty aside, professional opportunities were plentiful, and Allport quickly discovered that the language of personality measurement resonated in England just as it did in America. It was a fascination that he could certainly address, but one at odds with his growing commitment to pure individuality. In England, Allport continued to dutifully preach the gospel of the measured self that he had recited in his dissertation, but he derived little satisfaction in the interest his work generated. The language of pure individuality was what stirred his soul, and he now viewed measurement-oriented psychologists and social workers with a mixture of amusement and irritation. After presenting his dissertation research on measuring personality traits at the University of London Psychological Society, Allport spoke derisively of the "large swarms of maidens (old and young) [who] seem to be working on the subject and ready to impose to any extent. . . . The evening lecture on our tests and graphs caused great expression of glee, as it always does, from those studying psychology for its application."[178] (See insert, Figure 31.)

Britain may have had little new to contribute to Allport's psychological education, but it was long in premodern charm, and he used the opportunity to further cultivate his Anglo-Catholic sensibility. While at Cambridge, he toured the city's many churches and chapels and basked in the pronounced Anglican ambiance. "I like it particularly on Sundays here. There is not a particle of activity except church-going. All transportation stops; all shops and restaurants close. Nothing moves. Everywhere is silence but for the incessant chiming of innumerable bells on college chapels and parish churches."[179] Enveloped by the "serenity and dignity" of Cambridge's "sacred shade," Allport's sense of the divine gained further definition. "Cambridge breathes Platonic values," he wrote, "and easily convinces the docile person of the existence of eternal principles, and enables each one to discover for himself what these principles are."[180] Inspired by Cambridge's ancient aura, Allport underwent confirmation in the Church of England at Ely Cathedral, and he delighted in all the medieval trappings that went with the ceremony. "The processional down that mighty Norman Nave was impressive," he remarked, as was the distinguished setting for the tea that followed the service. It was ancient building of "sumptuous, decanal elegance" known as the "Deanery," and Allport reveled in its network of historic associations: "The dean came up to me and said, 'Sir, where you are now taking your tea, once King Edward III and [his] Lady took their tea."[181]

Ever alive to things ancient and divine, Allport was not completely indifferent to the modernist current coursing through European artistic and intellectual communities. While in London, he visited the Tate Gallery, where he "enjoyed fishing for the contentless emotion in some of the ultra-moderns." In art as in life, however, the charms of modernism paled in comparison to the beauty and majesty of time-honored forms. At the Tate, it was the pre-Raphaelite style of Millais that really spoke to his soul. "I persist in preferring the more conventional technique [in art]," he wrote to Gould, "so long as it has reasonable individuality."[182] Allport expressed a similar sentiment with regard to modern poetry. "I like word pictures such as Ausländer's," he remarked, "but I cannot feel content with the whines of subjectivity. I miss the self-restraint of the English romanticists."[183]

"A SACRED LOVE"

In his youth, Allport had identified strongly with his mother and the more "civilized," spiritual femininity she embodied. As a young man, he continued to regard Nellie as a kind of quasi-religious figure who possessed an incalculable depth of saintliness and virtue. In a letter to Gould, Allport described his mother as "lovely and mother-like sitting before the fireplace with her sainted face lit in Rembrandt amber." Nellie's virtue and love moved Allport as no other and formed a mother–son bond that was "unusually sacred": "My love for my mother is one of the very few things in my life that have remained pure and sacred," Allport declared in 1924. "It is very profound, and compels me to devote every ounce of energy to her when she needs it."[184] (See insert, Figure 32.)

Ever attentive to Nellie's needs, Allport took an active interest in his mother's spiritual life. As noted in chapter 2, Nellie had been a devout young woman, but her confrontation with modernity had tempered her religious enthusiasm. As the flamboyant excesses of Free Methodism fell away, her spiritual energies came to be focused on the more liberal ways of the Methodist Episcopal Church. When she and her husband moved to California in 1921, her embrace of liberalism was such that she now found mainstream Methodism too confining. Nellie left the church and joined a quasi-religious group known as Anthroposophy, which was based on the writings of Rudolph Steiner, a German theosophist who argued that divine wisdom was naturally accessible.[185] Nellie's devotion to the new faith soon equaled her earlier Methodist enthusiasm. She pored over Steiner's published work and visited the Anthroposophical Farm at Spring Valley, New York. Allport recalled that his mother took to the movement with "missionary zeal" and that she soon set about cultivating a new spiritual tone for the family.[186] With her sons spread out across the country, Nellie had to be resourceful in her missionary efforts. She would often mail annotated copies of Anthroposophy books and tracts to her children, and by 1942, the year she died, Allport had almost filled a 5-foot shelf with her spiritual material.[187]

Nellie's spiritual enthusiasm was not appreciated by Gould, nor was the doting reverence that Allport had for his mother. Gould criticized Allport for being a "softy" and "passive" in his mother's company, and she intimated that the relationship was marked by a "pathological subservience."[188] Critical of Nellie's spiritual power, Gould struggled to maintain a civil relationship with her, and the effort was not always successful. Allport complained bitterly about Gould's "consistently rude and insulting" behavior toward his mother:

> I cannot endure it. . . . Whatever the provocation yesterday it was not sufficient (nothing could be) to warrant your rudeness. I do not believe of course, that it was intentional on your part. But what I want to emphasize is that I do not believe you have taken yourself in hand. Even "religion" seems to feed rather than to mitigate your "self-centeredness."[189]

Gould continued to resent the "holy" bond that connected mother and son, just as Allport continued to venerate his mother's spiritual energy and selfless purity. Her Anthroposophical enthusiasm was trying at times, and he later remarked that Steiner's "statements are too general, his conclusions too sweeping, and his semantics quite terrible."[190] Unlike his brother Harold, however, who refused "categorically to read any of [Nellie's] marked passages," Allport appreciated the spiritual impulse that propelled his mother's religious forays.[191] He was fired by this impulse himself, and his own search for religious meaning in the 1920s was sustained, at least in part, by his mother's expansive spirituality.

CONCLUSION

In 1922, Allport had traveled to Germany spiritually hungry and intellectually uncertain. When he returned to America in 1924, he had the repose of someone who had met the divine and had his questions answered. The spiritual psychology of Stern and Spranger legitimated his own antimodernist commitments, and their status as the "right men" indicated that mechanistic psychology was not the only route to manly success in the discipline.[192] Armed with a secularized language of the spirit, Allport launched the first salvo of what would eventually develop into an intellectual barrage. His specific target was his brother Floyd, but the larger objective was modernity itself. Inspired by his mandarin mentors, Allport stood against the rationalizing, quantifying, mechanizing processes that were draining human nature of its unity, dignity, and soul. Repudiating much of the work that he had undertaken as a graduate student, Allport took up the challenge of reenchanting personality and safeguarding it from further psychometric dissection. He abandoned the upbeat idiom of positivist science and replaced it with an antimodernist language of limits. Personality could never be measured or known in any comprehensive or authoritative sense, he now insisted. There always remained a "unique character which cannot adequately be represented in any analysis however accurate."[193]

Emboldened by German spiritual psychology, Allport drew further strength from Anglo-Catholicism. The church's premodern forms and rich liturgy possessed a compelling gravity and authenticity, and church membership gave Allport the serenity and groundedness that psychology had been unable to provide. Comfortably enmeshed in an ancient idiom, he heaped scorn on the grandiose predictions and scientific pretensions of American psychologists. Reverence was reserved for things mystical and divine, and as Allport surveyed the ancient majesty of the Church, he again drew strength from William James. James's fascination with the aesthetic richness and beauty of Catholicism matched his own, and it provided him with an intellectual framework large enough to accommodate both his spiritual convictions and his scientific ambition.

7

CONSTRUCTING A CATEGORY: PERSONALITY PSYCHOLOGY AT HARVARD AND DARTMOUTH (1924–1930)

Take heed now; for the Lord hath chosen thee to build a house for the sanctuary; be strong, and do it.

—I Chronicles 28:2–10

I have never essentially wavered from my desire to correlate Psychology and Social Ethics.

—Gordon Allport, 1923[1]

By the fall of 1923, Allport's reputation as an up-and-coming scholar was firmly established. He had demonstrated his ability to Harvard's psychologists and social ethicists, and with one highly productive year of post-doctoral work under his belt, he had shown that he had the initiative and discipline necessary for independent work. It was not especially surprising, therefore, that Allport's name was raised in connection with a Harvard teaching position in October 1923. There was widespread support for All-port among both the psychologists and the social ethicists, with James Ford being Allport's principal advocate. Ford was planning on taking a sabbatical leave in the 1924–1925 academic year and needed a "competent person" to take over his courses.[2] Allport had been one of Ford's top students in the classroom and in the field, and with a PhD and postdoctoral fellowship behind him, he was eminently suitable for the job. In early November 1923, Ford wrote to Allport asking if he would "consider an instructorship in Social Ethics, with possible tutoring as well."[3]

Allport's background made him a logical choice for the job, but his experiences in Turkey and, more recently, in Europe made the prospect of a social ethics appointment less enticing than it might once have appeared. The degradation and despair of Constantinople had stripped squalor of its charm, and the sheer weight of human suffering had weakened the reformist spirit. Graduate work and a further 2 years of postdoctoral study in Europe had done little to rekindle the reforming zeal that had gripped Allport as an undergraduate. "There is no loudness in my idealism," he told Ada in 1923, "*nor is there reform. It is modified from those enthusiasms of years gone by*" (emphasis added).[4] For Allport, urbanism and its problems had become objects of revulsion, and where he had once wanted to engage a downtrodden humanity, Allport now preferred to seek out beauty. In downtown Naples in 1924, for example, he reacted to social decay with the same sort of aesthetic dismay he had first displayed in Constantinople. All around was "life, commotion, and dirty color; . . . a bedlam in the arcade outside where aimless and untidy and distinctly unnecessary humanity presses and quarrels and squirms." Allport could see nothing redeeming in the face of such ugliness: "It is all so hideous," he wrote. "The crush, the lewdness, the dirtiness, [and] the unqualified hopelessness of the Neopolitan [sic] dagoes."[5]

His social idealism tempered, Allport also found it difficult to muster any enthusiasm for a career in American psychology. Disciplinary trends in the United States were at odds with the spiritual psychology he had come to embrace, and he remained current with scientific research in the field only because it was professionally expedient to do so. "When once I stand on my own feet financially I shall cease forever to *pretend* an interest in experimental psychology," he noted harshly.[6] Alienated by the reductionism of U.S. psychology, Allport often felt that American culture as a whole was incompatible with a soulful life. In a letter to Gould, he complained bitterly of the "rank materialistic pressure of our native land," and he admitted that he was "often tempted . . . to deny my native land." At odds with American culture and the materialistic psychology it had produced, Allport took some comfort in sharing his spiritual outlook with Ada Gould. She understood the language of beauty and soul, and she had a critical eye for shallowness and vulgarity. "You characterized us aptly; 'romantic, sentimental, religious idealists,'" Allport wrote to Gould approvingly. "That indeed is our Lebensverfassung [philosophy of life] and thank God for it. We shall have each other to understand this with."[7]

The uncertainty of the future pressed down on Allport, and he found it difficult to envision any sort of professional scenario that would accommodate his own complex brand of antimodernist social science. After a year of what he described as "tormented thrashing," he eventually settled on "educational psychology. Only in this can I resolve my interests and pursue my ideals."[8] Allport remained intrigued by educational psychology, but the social ethics position was not without its professional advantages. Weighing his options, Allport noted that the job would allow him to play one department off the other. "Doubling my departmental work will give me such a good defense," he observed. "One department will say, 'He isn't much of a Social Ethicist, but must be a first-rate psychologist.' T'other will aver: 'He leaves much to be desired as a psychologist, but perhaps is a noteworthy ethicist.'"[9] Such short-term strategic considerations figured prominently in Allport's mind, but the social ethics position also conveniently mirrored his own personal and scholarly duality. A joint psychology and social ethics appointment contained the promise of a combination of the material and spiritual, the modern and premodern, the masculine and the feminine. In his letter to Ford, Allport indicated that he had "never essentially wavered from my desire to correlate psychology and social ethics. It has merely become a practical question as to how this purpose might be accomplished."[10]

Although Allport had envisioned educational psychology as the best institutional home for this project, Ford's proposal provided him with another option. "Your inquiry has suggested the possibility of uniting more immediately than I had hoped the two streams of my interest." Before accepting Ford's offer, however, Allport wanted to clarify the precise nature of his professional project. He wanted to link the exactitude and precision of psychological science with the humanitarian concern and ethical mindedness of social ethics. The most important professional implication of this project in the short term was in the area of courses. Allport did not want to return to Harvard simply as a stand-in for Ford. His 2 years in Europe had convinced him that he had something important to say, and he was anxious to share his insights with students. Allport told Ford that he would be inclined to accept the appointment if "in addition to teaching orthodox social ethics I might give some such new course."[11]

Never one to take major career decisions lightly, Allport approached Ford's offer cautiously. He sensed that there would be more room for intellectual experimentation in social ethics than in psychology, but he also knew that psychology was a more established discipline. In the long run, psychology might well be a better professional bet. Before committing himself to one discipline or the other, Allport decided to seek assurance that an acceptance of Ford's offer "would not be prejudicial to me eventually securing a situation in psychology."[12] By taking a prudent course in his negotiations with Ford, Allport was clearly trying to keep his professional options open. When Ford communicated the Social Ethics Department's interest "in having the two fields [of psychology and social ethics] brought closer together," Allport was convinced. In January 1924 he accepted a 1-year position at Harvard beginning in the fall. His title was Instructor in Social Ethics, and his primary responsibility was to teach Ford's course titled "Social Problems and Social Policy: Treatment and Prevention of Poverty, Defectiveness, and Crime" and a new, untitled course to be based on his own investigations of personality. Understandably pleased by the arrangement, Allport sent off a spirited letter to one of the Department's secretaries: "The die is cast, and . . . you will have to put up with my presence around Emerson Hall again next year. . . . I shall try to be agreeable and not too green."[13]

Allport's enthusiasm was sincere, but the assurances of Ford and the flexibility of the position did not completely quell the antimodernist angst that had troubled him for so long. Before commencing his appointment, he confided to Gould that if it weren't for her, he might not return to the United States at all. "I am worried about the readjustment I shall have to make," he noted anxiously. "If you weren't there to help me through I do believe I'd manage to escape to the Balkans or someplace where I'd feel more at home than in Harvard Square."[14] Allport echoed much the same sentiment in his letters to Powers and Dodge. "I have felt pretty low about leaving Europe and returning to—heaven knows what" he noted sadly. Having to face up to the crass, shallow materialism of America was bad enough, but Allport also found it difficult to contemplate life as a "scientist." He wrote forlornly to Powers of his need to "retire at once with you to orient myself again before plunging into the ridiculousness of my teaching at Harvard, *teaching stuff I don't know anything about, nor believe in*" [italics added].[15]

What sustained Allport through these low moments was a conviction that his psychological work was part of a deeper, spiritually sanctioned good. Duty and service—concepts so central in the vocabulary of character —still exerted a powerful hold on his imagination, and he told Gould that "everything counts somehow, I firmly believe, towards our productive life." Happiness would come through service and looking out onto the future, and Allport decreed that he and Gould would "work and live intensely, in order that we may serve." This was service for a divine cause, but it would be undertaken through a self-consciously modern psychological identity. Its true religious significance would be known only to Allport and Gould: "We are born missionaries, you and I, sweetheart, but no one need ever know what lies closest to our heart. We shall never be obvious or sentimental about it."[16]

A MATTER OF MORALS, A MATTER OF SCIENCE: VISIONS OF SELFHOOD IN THE DEPARTMENT OF SOCIAL ETHICS

From a distance, the department Allport had joined in 1924 was as stable as any other at Harvard. The department was located on the second floor of Emerson Hall, a building that it shared with the Department of Philosophy and Psychology. Unlike most departments, Social Ethics was financially independent of the university administration, largely as a result of the financial backing of Alfred Tredway White, a wealthy New York philanthropist. Beginning in 1903, White kept the department supplied with a "continuous stream of benefactions" that included a $50,000 contribution toward the construction of Emerson Hall and two $100,000 endowment funds dedicated to social ethics.[17] With its generous benefactor and dignified location, social ethics had the look of an established field.

Appearances, of course, can be deceiving, and in 1924 the social ethics department stood as a testament to the truth of this old cliché. The department was financially sound, but it lacked something that was perhaps even more important than money: a clear sense of purpose, a disciplinary vision that could propel it into the future. As we have seen, the department had been founded to advance a religious vision rooted in the 19th-century denominational college. Francis Peabody wanted to use the new methods of scientific investigation to strengthen the moral and religious fiber of American society. At the turn of the century, Peabody's vision did succeed in capturing the imagination of some wealthy philanthropists like White, but as an academic ideal, social ethics was outdated even before the department was formally consecrated in 1906. Scholars in philosophy, psychology, political science, and economics were then embracing notions of objectivity and pure, disinterested research. For this new breed of investigator, social ethics had a "hortatory flavor" that was considered "alien to the cold, dry atmosphere of science."[18]

As America industrialized and new models of selfhood emerged, Peabody's project was rendered increasingly untenable. His replacements—Ford and Foerster—struggled to update the field's raison d'être. However, both men had difficulty finding the language that would both modernize social ethics and keep it distinct from sociology and applied psychology. The department's autonomy seemed to depend on a continued commitment to the language of character. By 1918, the department was in a state of disarray. It had no tenured faculty members, and more alarmingly, perhaps, no clear sense of its own intellectual purpose. Elements of the Peabodian emphasis on character building existed alongside scientifically minded concerns about technique. The field had no distinctive methods, and its course offerings seemed to be duplicating those of other disciplines. The situation was so bad that President Lowell thought seriously about transferring the whole department to the divinity school. White's financial intervention halted Lowell's plans, but the department remained an intellectually troubled place.[19]

The department's fortunes appeared to take a turn for the better in 1920 with the arrival of Richard Clarke Cabot (1868–1939).[20] A physician by training, Cabot had joined the faculty of the Harvard Medical School in 1909 as an instructor of clinical medicine. Promoted to full professor in 1918, he was offered the chair in social ethics the following year. Strong-willed, dynamic, and from a prominent Boston family, Cabot was given the job of rebuilding social ethics. Unfortunately for the department's future, the strategy that Cabot adopted amounted to little more than a vigorous reaffirmation of Peabody's language and program. Like Peabody, Cabot encouraged his colleagues to break down disciplinary boundaries in order to enrich social ethics.[21] At the same time, the new chair reaffirmed the department's historic commitment to moral principles and character. "Conduct, right doing, [and] unselfishness" had the right to "command and subordinate all other human interests," he wrote. "What Emerson called 'the Sovereignty of Ethics' [was] the most vivid interest that the world disclosed."[22]

Cabot regarded his appointment in social ethics as a platform from which to "put ethics on the map" of American society.[23] It was a task to which he attached a great deal of importance. Military service during World War I had convinced him that the country was slipping off its ethical foundation. Cabot directed much of the blame for this state of affairs at the nation's educational system. Schools were teaching people a variety of technical skills, but they were not providing them with the means to judge how those skills should be used. The result, in Cabot's view, was a heightened potential for "another world-disaster, like the Great War," and the creation of a society of "smarter villains and livelier crooks."[24] To forestall this outcome, society needed to vigorously assert its ethical precepts and then inculcate them into the nation's youth. Cabot's courses at Harvard attempted to do both. He "pledged" himself "to the adventure of trying to make men better themselves" by "uprooting habits of haziness, self-centeredness, [and] self-deception" and "building habits of honest thinking."[25] (See insert, Figure 33)

In the short run, Cabot's social stature, charisma, and enthusiasm were enough to revitalize the flagging department. By the time Allport arrived at Emerson Hall in September 1924, however, many of the old identity problems had returned. Moral exhortation lived alongside a language of scientific precision, and a commitment to character building coexisted with the desire to attain greater objectivity in the study of personal and social life.[26] Allport's experience in the department was indicative of the intellectual ambiguity that surrounded the field. Nowhere was this ambiguity more apparent than in the negotiations that surrounded the new course that Allport proposed to Ford.

PERSONALITY IN THE DEPARTMENT OF SOCIAL ETHICS

Allport had made his pedagogical intentions clear right from the outset of his negotiations with the Department of Social Ethics. In addition to covering Ford's course, he wanted to be able to teach his own course that would cover materials from his dissertation and postdoctoral fellowship. The course was tentatively titled The Psychology of Personality and

Social Adjustment; in a letter to Ford, Allport explained that he would "draw from individual psych [*sic*], social psych [*sic*] and psychoanalysis all the data available concerning individual differences in ability, personality, mental and characteral 'types,' [and] the reaction of the individual in the group."[27] These themes were developed more thoroughly in a tentative course description that Allport developed for use in the university calendar.

In the ensuing negotiations, Ford did not express concerns about Allport's plan, but the department's chairman, Cabot, approached the idea cautiously. In February 1924, he wrote to Allport to clarify his concerns. The substance of Cabot's letter centered on the recurring question of social ethics identity. What exactly was social ethics, and how did it differ from the other social sciences? Cabot had little difficulty answering those questions in the abstract. Social ethics was a moral discipline; its purpose was to "make men better themselves" through the use of "objective" social scientific procedures. The identity of social ethics only became a problem for Cabot when it came time to develop a workable administrative structure for the department. Forging a healthy relationship with neighboring disciplines was a particularly vexing problem. On the one hand, Cabot wanted his colleagues to incorporate the research and methods of other departments. He believed that interdisciplinary exchanges of this sort would enhance the department's ethical project. On the other hand, Cabot was mindful of the need to police the divide between his department and related fields. If too much interdisciplinary traffic occurred, the departmental border could disappear altogether: Social ethics would be absorbed into adjacent fields. To survive as a separate discipline and to fulfill its ethical mandate, Cabot believed that social ethics needed to strike a delicate balance between isolationism and inclusivity.

Cabot wrote to Allport with this ideal of balance in mind. Allport's proposal to "correlate" psychology and social ethics met with his approval; however, Cabot was quick to remind his new appointee of the need to anchor the course within the Department of Social Ethics. The title of Allport's course was a matter of particular concern. Cabot noted with some alarm that the "name of [the new course] is a little hard to phrase so as to make it clear that it is a course in Social Ethics and not in Psychology."[28] To prevent any misunderstanding and to buttress the ramparts of a fragile department, he suggested that the course be called Personality and Social Amelioration.[29]

The administrative concerns that prompted Cabot's request were not unfamiliar to Allport, and he readily agreed to change the name of his course. Indeed, Allport signaled his willingness to compromise on this point even before receiving Cabot's letter. In January 1924, he told Ford that his new course could be called "'Individual Psychology and Social Amelioration' or 'The Individual Client.'"[30] The title of the course was of less concern to Allport than the substance. "It doesn't matter to me what the course is christened so long as you allow me to deal with the subject in some such way as I suggest in the announcement."[31]

Allport's course appeared in the 1924–1925 Harvard course catalog under the name Cabot had suggested.[32] The new title helped clarify the disciplinary identity of the course, but not without creating ambiguities of its own. The problem was that the social ethics department already had a course similar to the one Allport proposed. That course was taught by Cabot himself, and it was titled The Study of Character in Difficulties.[33] Cabot was understandably anxious to "make clear the difference which I am confident exists between this course of yours and my own course [on character]."[34] The department chair did not specify what steps he took to highlight this difference, possibly because it was a relatively straightforward exercise. There was an obvious symmetry between his course and that of his young recruit, but beneath the level of broad abstractions, the two courses were markedly different in both method and subject matter.

Cabot's course was firmly rooted in the character-building tradition of the 19th century. Like Peabody, Cabot's primary goal was not to clinically dissect individuality, but to provide it with strength and rectitude. Scientific research in psychology, psychiatry, and sociology could help in this task, and Cabot would occasionally mobilize this literature in his courses. However, his use of this material was notoriously unsystematic; he did not even try to be comprehensive. In the words of one student, his courses lacked "unity, coherence, [and] order.[35] What they had in abundance was moral inspiration. Allport himself commented on his chairman's "remarkably forthright social conscience" and his ability to "stir undergraduates profoundly with his uncompromising teaching of his own Puritan brand of ethics."[36] Cabot's favorite method for generating this ethical enthusiasm was the study of individual lives. He had his social ethics students read numerous biographies of people such as "St. Augustine, St. Francis of Assisi, Tolstoi, Pasteur, Lincoln, Philips Brooks [and] Jesus Christ," whom Cabot believed "exemplif[y] by far the highest type of character that I know anything about."[37] Cabot did not approach these subjects with the critical, irreverent eye of a Lytton Strachey, nor did he try to systematically analyze their mental life. His goal was moral; individual lives were studied because of their inspirational efficacy. Cabot reasoned that students were seldom influenced by explicit appeals to do what was right. What they did respond to was the example set by some of the people around them:

> Admiration itself, together with the understanding to which it leads, is capable of transfusing some of the hero's valor into his admirer. Is it not true in the lives of most of us that we have been helped most by people who said not a word to us about ethics, but who lived their

> lives close enough to us so that, as we watched and admired ... we
> began to feel their motives active in us?[38]

In the final analysis, Cabot's course may be viewed as a continuation of the "moral philosophy" courses that had been a staple in American colleges throughout the 19th century.[39]

Allport's new course differed quite substantially from this venerable tradition. In its organization, his course looked more to natural science than moral philosophy. The loose, freewheeling discussions of moral issues favored by Cabot were eschewed in favor of a carefully paced, methodical survey of the literature pertaining to personality. In March 1923, Allport told Cabot that he planned to "present in a more or less formal way, the general problem of individual differences and the distribution of characters, with current methods for the classification and measurement of traits."[40]

The spirit of science was not confined to the "formal" structure of Allport's course; far from it. Scientific considerations suffused every facet of the new course. The course title was the most obvious, although perhaps unintentional, indication of Allport's scientific sensibility. Cabot had used the term *character* in his course title, but Allport's course featured the term *personality*. For Cabot, the use of the term personality may well have been an administrative convenience. For Allport, however, the term had a definite connotation, and it was linked to a specific professional project. In his 1921 literature review, Allport had carefully outlined "the distinction between personality and character" and argued that it was an "important one for psychologists to observe."[41] The position Allport took on this issue was again linked to the Watsonian behaviorism that had colored several other components of his dissertation. Like Watson, Allport argued that character was an ethical construction. It was "personality evaluated according to prevailing standards of conduct." The term personality was thus psychologically fundamental. It was the individual viewed not as an ethical being, but as an objective "reaction mass."[42] In the spring of 1924, Allport was moving rapidly away from the behaviorism of his dissertation. However, the distinction Watson had made between character and personality retained its place in Allport's thinking. He remained convinced that personality was the appropriate site of scientific investigation.

Over the years, Allport's colleagues came to agree with him. By 1940, universities across the United States were offering courses on personality, while courses on character quietly disappeared.[43] On the surface, the transition may seem relatively straightforward: The hortatory moralizing of the likes of Cabot was gradually displaced by the objective research of scientists like Allport. A close examination of the period, however, reveals a historical picture of much greater complexity. Allport provided a glimpse of one corner of this canvas in an early letter to Ford. His goal was not to develop an "objective" science of personality; he wanted to "correlate" psychology and social ethics.[44] The only question for Allport was the "practical [one] as to how this purpose might be accomplished.[45] Allport's first course on personality contained hints of the solution that he developed over the course of the next 20 years. Moral categories like character were translated into behavioristic terms, such as personality.[46] The change in language paralleled a change in the manner of moral persuasion. Cabot had relied on the example of fine character to fortify his students' ethical sense. Allport put his rhetorical faith in the power of science. He presented an ethical self, but he draped it in the garb of natural science.

The ethical dimension of Allport's course is worth emphasizing if only because of the place Personality and Social Amelioration occupies in the history of psychology. The course is widely recognized as one of the first of its kind in an American university and a milestone in the history of American personality psychology. The credit is well deserved, but in highlighting the novelty of Allport's accomplishment, scholars have generally neglected the continuity of intention between Allport's work on personality and social ethics. Both scholarly programs were ultimately aimed at identifying and cultivating human "goodness."

The ethical dimension of Allport's personality research became increasingly clear as his career unfolded. Between 1924 and 1926, however, a heavy teaching load left him little time to develop his personality interests in any systematic fashion. A year after taking the Social Ethics position, Allport told Taylor that he found "the teaching burden so heavy at Harvard that I have done nothing but get up courses to be given and disposing of the routine."[47] Frustrated by the lack of free time, Allport took stock of his options. Perhaps it was time to leave behind the "strenuous" life of Cambridge, Massachusetts, and try his fortunes somewhere else.[48] The number of teaching requirements in Social Ethics was one issue, and the tentative status of the department was another. Cabot's dynamic personality and interdisciplinary interests had done little to solidify the field's shaky standing within the university. In 1925, the department's future was uncertain at best. Allport had his reservations about social ethics even before joining the department in 1924. He later recalled that the field was "a little soft, a little soupy."[49]

Professional uncertainty had been a recurring theme in Allport's experience since entering graduate school. With its scientistic pretensions, psychology seemed an unwelcoming home for someone in search of soul and authenticity. Social ethics was more spiritually fulfilling, but it lacked the stability and professional cachet of a "science." As a faculty member in the Department of Social Ethics, Allport continued to weigh his professional options and contemplate the possibility of returning to psychology; however, changes in the Department of Psychology at Harvard did little to hasten his return to the disciplinary fold. In 1922, Floyd Allport left for a post at the University of North Carolina, and in 1924, Herbert

Langfeld left Harvard to take a position at Princeton. When Allport returned to Harvard in the fall of 1924, McDougall was still on the faculty, but the principal advocate for psychology at Harvard was E. G. Boring, a Cornell-trained experimental psychologist who had arrived in Cambridge in the fall of 1922. Boring "walked in the shadow" of his mentor Titchener, and he set a torrid pace for his fellow psychologists.[50] "Having a compulsive temperament, I drove ahead on an eighty-hour week with the firm conviction that I might not be so bright as many of my colleagues but that I might make up for this deficiency by working harder."[51] Although Allport was not in the psychology department, he had agreed to teach several sections of experimental psychology to maintain his connection to the field.[52] This link to psychology brought him within Boring's purview, and after the leisurely academic pace of Britain, Boring's frenetic intensity came as a bit of shock. In a letter to Gould, Allport remarked that "Prof. Boring blew in like a Kansas Cyclone into the [psychology] lab today. . . . How things flew! In three minutes he had me at work on the new course, Psych 1, for next year." Although he was impressed by the scholarly energy that swirled around Boring, Allport was unnerved by the strident scientism of Harvard's new standard bearer. "[The new course] is going to be largely experimental, and too steep, I'll wager, for the poor Anfänger [beginner]. I shall like a little of Boring's cyclonism; but not too much of it."[53]

Uncomfortable with Boring's brand of "cyclonic" psychology, Allport felt equally ill at ease in social ethics, and by January 1925 he had seen enough of the Department of Social Ethics to know that he wanted to leave. Cabot tried to persuade him to stay in social ethics with the promise of tenure and regular promotions. By this time, however, Allport was "quite convinced that such a course [of action] would not be wise nor [sic] agreeable."[54] He envisioned a job at a "small and fairly neighborly locality, [in] a progressive but not necessarily prominent university [that was situated in] congenial natural surroundings." In such a setting, Allport believed he could "work effectively."[55] Allport began searching for his ideal position in January 1925. To improve his chances, he made inquiries about putting his relationship with Harvard's Department of Philosophy and Psychology on a more formal footing. In March 1925, the department agreed to a new arrangement with the Department of Social Ethics.[56] In the 1925–1926 academic year, Allport was to teach two sections in psychology in addition to Ford's old course in social ethics. Allport's course in personality was to be renamed Personality: Its Psychological and Social Aspects, and it was to be offered in both departments.[57] In recognition of his contributions to both departments, Allport received the title Instructor in Social Ethics and Psychology.[58]

The new title was no honorific term as far as the Harvard psychologists were concerned. The title signified their confidence in Allport as a scientist and colleague. McDougall held Allport in particularly high esteem. In a letter to Boring, McDougall included Allport's name among a small group of psychologists that "I should be glad to have . . . attached to the department as firmly as possible."[59] If hiring decisions had been left up to the famous British psychologist, Allport may well have received an offer from Harvard. However, Boring was committed to a vision of psychology as an experimental, natural science.[60] Prospective faculty were evaluated with this scientific criterion in mind. In 1925, Boring's disciplinary vision had no place for someone with Allport's interests. Boring told McDougall that he

> should much prefer [the experimentalist Jack] Beebe-Center to . . . Allport, degree or no degree. I still stick by the original conditions of my coming [to Harvard], i.e. that the introd. lab. [sic] course and the quantitative course must be well given. In my view these two half courses are fundamental to our standards. *Allport's interest is on the other side of things psychological* [italics added].[61]

As was often the case in the 1920s, Boring's views ultimately prevailed. Allport was not invited to join the Department of Philosophy and Psychology, and in January 1926 he accepted an offer from the Department of Psychology at Dartmouth College.[62]

DARTMOUTH COLLEGE (1926–1930)

No object seems to demand more insistently that it be regarded as a coherent datum for perception than the single human personality.
—Gordon Allport, 1930[63]

Allport's decision to leave Social Ethics proved to be a timely one. The Department of Social Ethics continued to struggle for the remainder of the decade, and it was abolished altogether in 1931. Doomed though it may have been, Allport's association with the department stood him in good stead. In fact, his connection with the field was one of the main reasons Dartmouth recruited him in the first place. The Dartmouth administration was anxious to diversify its psychology program, which up until the mid-1920s was largely experimental in focus. Social ethics was one of the directions senior administrators wished to pursue. They believed that "this [social ethics focus] was a more profitable field for the liberal college to be working in than the field of experimental psychology."[64] With his background in social ethics and psychology, Allport appeared to be the ideal person to steer Dartmouth psychology toward new intellectual horizons. (See insert, Figure 34.)

Dartmouth's interest in Allport was a sign that his stock as psychologist was on the rise. The terms of his appointment are another indication. He was immediately offered an assistant professorship because the Dartmouth administration surmised that it was "the only basis upon which we can hope to get him."[65] That Allport's star should have risen so fast is somewhat surprising. His publication record was promising but not especially long, and he was not known as a memorable teacher. The growing popularity of personality undoubtedly contributed to his academic worth. Equally important in this regard was Allport's own demeanor. He lacked the flamboyance and showmanship of an "ascendant" personality like Cabot, but following the advice he offered in his test of ascendance–submission, he compensated by making the most of "social intelligence," or tact. It was a virtue that he appears to have had in abundance. The reminiscences of his students and colleagues are almost uniform in their description of his tactful nature. The remarks of Philip Vernon and Jerome Bruner, in this respect, are quite typical. Vernon described Allport as "kindliness personified; urbane, cultured, humorous and above all sincere."[66] Bruner said that Allport was a "reserved" man who "never seemed harassed, [and] was never discourteous."[67] The professional efficacy of so agreeable a manner is made evident in a letter of recommendation that Cabot wrote on Allport's behalf to the officials at Dartmouth. Cabot noted that Allport possessed a "certain lack of self-confidence" and that he was not a "particularly magnetic or effective lecturer." Nevertheless, the social ethicist felt that Allport's positive qualities more than made up for these shortcomings. Allport was an "extraordinarily conscientious, hard-working, and scholarly chap," who was "unusually sympathetic, tactful and sensitive . . . an altogether delightful personality."[68]

FEMINISM, PROFESSIONALISM, AND PERSONALITY: ADA LUFKIN GOULD

Allport took up his duties at Dartmouth in the fall of 1926. Leaving Harvard for the third time, on this occasion he would not be traveling alone; accompanying him on the short trip to Hanover, New Hampshire, was his wife, Ada Gould. The two had met in graduate school, and they had maintained a regular correspondence throughout Allport's 2-year postdoctoral fellowship. They were married on June 30, 1925, and their wedding was a testament to their antimodernist commitments. The setting paid tribute to the beautiful past, and in a three-page description of the wedding written for family and friends, Allport carefully highlighted the church's premodern aesthetic:

> Trinity Church is one of the most historic and beautiful of Boston Churches. It is of the basilica type showing a marked Byzantine influence in its altar. Columns of green marble support a ciborium set with holy scenes in rich mosaic. Peacocks, the eastern symbol of immortality perch at either horn of the arc of its canopy. . . . The church itself is

very large and dark; but not gloomy.... We chose the choir of this lovely church for our wedding.[69]

The calm majesty of the ancients was not lost on the newly married. On a train trip to their honeymoon suite in Maine, the newlyweds came face to face with the new modernist ethic, one that stressed surprise, demonstration, and liberation from convention. "Two couples, newlyweds, burst in [to the train carriage] strewing confetti . . . followed by some thirty odd noisy, shouting, molesting friends," Allport recalled. To the Allports' antimodernist mind, such exuberance was self-indulgent and unseemly. In contrast to this group of demonstrative personalities, Allport proudly reported that he and Ada "conducted ourselves like ten years married, endless dignity, composure and quiet congeniality."[70] (See insert, Figure 35.)

"Dignity" was a recurring theme in the Allport home, and it set the standard for a wide range of personal choices. In clothing, Allport opted for a formal look, and in public he was usually well dressed in a good quality business suit.[71] Some years later, one of his former students recalled Allport's "erect posture and dark suit" in contrast to the "tweedy informality we were more used to."[72] Dignified in appearance, Allport looked for a house that would reflect his antimodernist commitments. "I am very much excited about a house," Allport wrote energetically in the spring of 1925. "It is the essence of my dreams in respect to dignity, age, and beauty."[73] Fascinated by venerable forms, the Allports sought out friends who shared their opposition to the lewd commercialism and superficiality of modern America. Gestalt psychologist Kurt Koffka was just the sort of person that appealed to the Allports' antimodernist sensibilities. Koffka was a visiting professor in the United States in 1926 and 1927, and while staying in Boston with his wife, he met up with Allport for dinner. "I am strongly in favor of Koffka & Mrs. (no #1–3 or #2–4?) [sic]" Allport commented later to Ada. "They are above all civilized":

> The evening was solidly and interestingly packed with literature, politics, and philosophy. The reading they do, and the charm of their manner of carrying it! . . . I like them, and learned that there are no plans after this year. I think I'll start maneuvering, so we may make a corner on *civilized psychologists* [italics added].[74]

Searching for a "civilized" life, the Allports were also professionals, and their life together involved a reconciliation of past and present, masculine and feminine. The challenges were large—especially for Gould. She had been a bright student, and she was well versed in the new idiom of professionalized benevolence. In the early 1920s, she wrote a number of reviews and short essays celebrating the professional importance of personality, the case study method, and scientific knowledge in the practice of social work: "These cases cited," she remarked earnestly, "are just two ac-

Figure 1. Nellie Wise, 1886.

Figure 2. John Allport, circa 1887.

Figure 3. Allport family home and Glenville Hospital, 653 East 105th Street, Cleveland, Ohio, circa 1910. The Allports lived in an apartment above the post office. The hospital was the small brick building to the left of the post office.

Figure 4. The Allport family restaurant. The youth seated at the counter is Gordon Allport.

Figure 5. The new Glenville Hospital, circa 1907. The figure is probably John Allport.

Figure 6. Newspaper article, "Women and Their work."

Figure 7. Mother's Club, Cleveland, Ohio, circa 1905. Nellie Allport is seated on the far left.

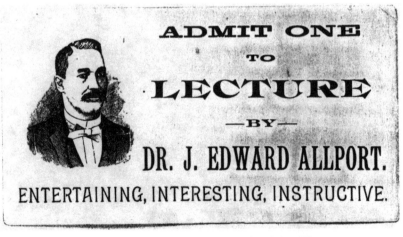

Figure 8. Lecture ticket for a talk by John Allport.

Figure 9. John Allport in Akron, Ohio, circa 1914.

Figure 10. "Feminizing boyhood":
Gordon Allport, Hudson, Ohio, age 5.

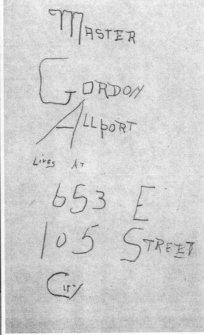

Figure 11. Handwritten note by
Gordon Allport, circa 1905.

Figure 12. The brothers Allport. Left to right: Gordon, Fayette, Floyd, Harold.

Figure 13. Rejecting boy culture: Gordon Allport and an unidentified female friend.

Figure 14. Gordon Allport, 8th grade photo, North Doan School, Cleveland, Ohio. Allport is on the extreme left of the rear row.

Figure 15. "Dear old B": Gordon Allport and B, circa 1912.

Figure 16. Glenville High School, circa 1910.

Figure 17. Bringing "civilization" to Cleveland, *Cleveland Plain Dealer*, 1914.

Figure 18. Allport family, 653 E 105th Street, circa 1912. Rear row standing: Gordon, Floyd, Fayette, Harold. Front row seated: John, Nellie, B, Alexander Wise (Nellie's father).

Figure 19. College days: Gordon Allport, Mildred Burt, and Paul Berryman at Harvard Yard.

Figure 20. The culture of personality. Cover of *Personality Magazine*, May 1922.

Mr. and Mrs. John Edward Allport of Cleveland, Ohio, cheerfully and willingly gave their consent that their four sturdy sons should represent their country on the field of battle. Lieut. Floyd Henry Allport is already "somewhere over there" with the 103rd Field Artillery; Lieut. Fayette Ward Allport is at Camp Sherman, Chillicothe, Ohio; Private Harold Edward Allport is stationed at Fort Benjamin Harrison, Indianapolis, Ind., while the youngest boy, Gordon William Allport of the Reserve Officers' Corps is at Cambridge, Mass.

Figure 21. Allports at war, Autumn 1917. Left to right: John, Floyd, Fayette, Harold, Gordon. Insert Nellie. This photograph was published in *Leslie's Weekly*, and several newspapers used it to promote the American war effort.

Figure 22. Harvard at war. Paul Berryman and Gordon Allport in the Harvard Student Army Training Corps, circa 1918.

Figure 23. Graduation Day, June 1919: Gordon and Floyd Allport.

Figure 24. A modern missionary: Gordon Allport, 1919.

Figure 25. Splendid fellows: Pete Dodge, Gordon Allport, and Ed Powers, 1925.

Figure 26. "Masculine Science": The Society of Experimental Psychology, 1916. Note the cigars. (Courtesy of the Archives of the History of American Psychology, the University of Akron.)

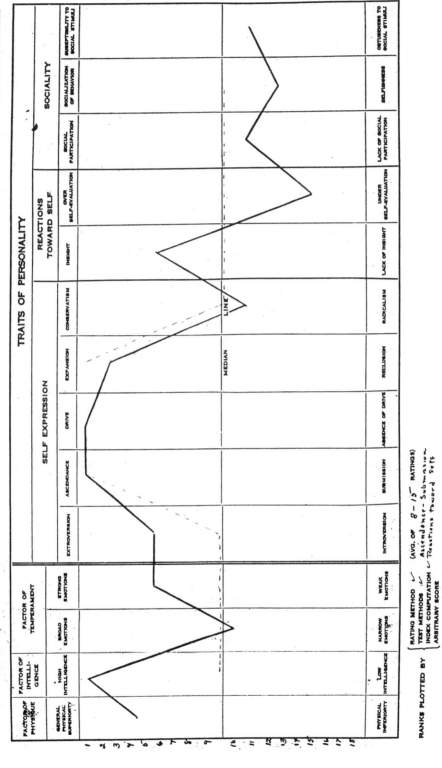

Figure 27. Personality revealed: a psychograph from Allport's dissertation.

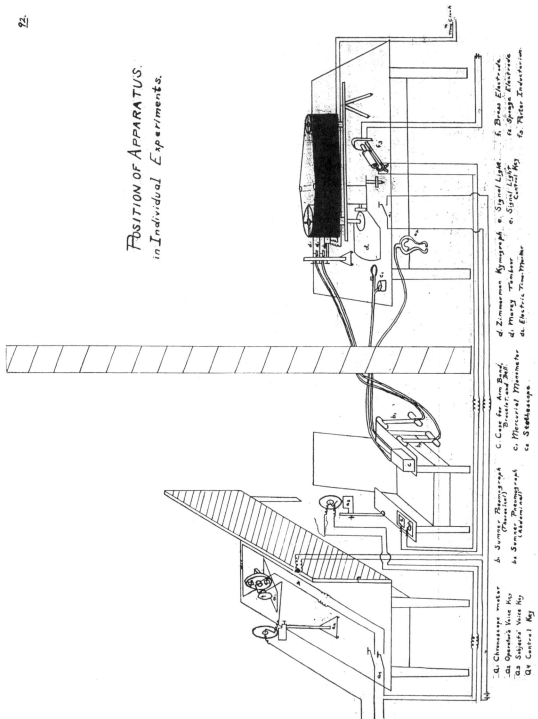

POSITION OF APPARATUS.
in Individual Experiments.

a. Chronoscope motor   b. Sumner Pneumograph   c. Case for Arm Band,   d. Zimmerman Kymograph.   e. Signal Light   f. Brass Electrode
a₁ Operator's Voice Key   (Thoracic)   Bracelet, and Bell.   d₁ Marey Tambour   e₁ Signal Light   f₂ Sponge Electrode
a₂ Subject's Voice Key   b₁ Sumner Pneumograph   c₁ Mercurial Manometer   d₂ Electric Time-Marker   Control Key   f₃ Ritter Inductorium
a₃ Control Key   (Abdominal)   c₂ Stethoscope

Figure 28. In search of the self: Alport's apparatus for testing personality traits.

Figure 29. The antimodernist spirit: Allport's bookplate.

Figure 30. Female personality: Ada Gould, 1920.

THE UNIVERSITY OF LONDON PSYCHOLOGICAL SOCIETY

Summer Term, 1924

The next meeting will be held on Wednesday evening, May 21st, at 8.0.p.m. in the Debating Hall of the University of London Union, Malet Street, W.C.1.

Dr.G.W.ALLPORT (Harvard)
will read a paper on

METHODS FOR TESTING THE TRAITS OF PERSONALITY.

Summary:-
    Traits should be defined as dynamic or prepotent trends of behaviour which result from the integration of numerous specific adjustment habits, and which express the character-istic modes of the individual's response to his surroundings.

    Traits like all habits may be considered susceptible of measurement. Several suggestive tests have already been evolved. Rating scales are at present a necessary supple-ment to the tests.

A Schedule of Personality

The Factor of Physique
     Factor of Intelligence
     Factor of Temperament.

Traits of Personality
     Self Expression.
               1. Extroversion
               2. Ascendance
               3. Drive
               4. Expansion
               5. Conservatism
     Reactions toward Self.
               6. Insight
               7. Self-evaluation
     Sociality.
               8. Social Participation
               9. Socialization of Interests
              10. Susceptibility to Social Stimuli.

Discussion and Refreshments.

Members are cordially invited to introduce their friends.

Applications for Membership (Annual Subscription 2/6) and all enquiries about the Society should be made to your College Representatives for the Session .... 1923-24.

                    University College (H.D.J.White (President)
                                       (F.Akroyd
          U.U.Hospital Medical School: Miss E.S.Morris.
               Kings College : G.L.F.Martin (Secretary)
               Bedford College: Miss G.R.Steed (Treasurer).

Figure 31. Promoting personality: Allport's address to the University of London Psychological Society.

Figure 32. A sacred love: Gordon and Nellie Allport, Munich, Germany, 1924.

Figure 33. Professing character: Richard Clarke Cabot.

Figure 34. A professor of personality: Gordon Allport, circa 1930.

Figure 35. Dignified souls: Pete Dodge, Gordon Allport, Ada Allport, and Amelia Brackett on Allport's wedding day, June 30, 1925.

Figure 36. The call to personality: Ada Gould, 1922. Gould is wearing a silk shawl that Gordon Allport gave her.

Figure 37. A Harvard personality: Gordon Allport, circa 1930.

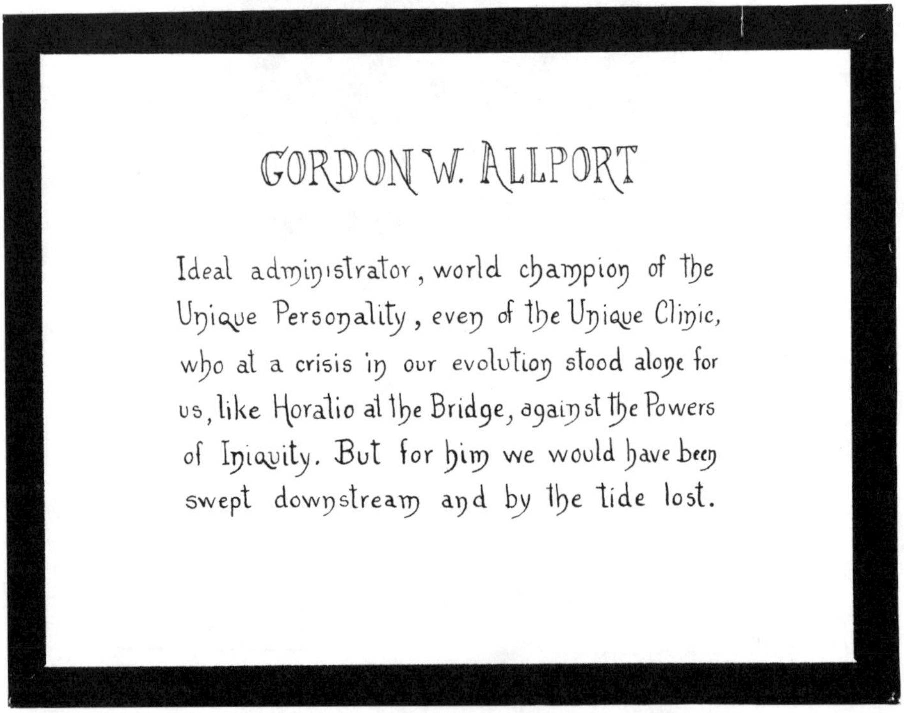

GORDON W. ALLPORT

Ideal administrator, world champion of the Unique Personality, even of the Unique Clinic, who at a crisis in our evolution stood alone for us, like Horatio at the Bridge, against the Powers of Iniquity. But for him we would have been swept downstream and by the tide lost.

Figure 38. Certificate of appreciation given to Allport in recognition of his support of the Harvard Psychological Clinic.

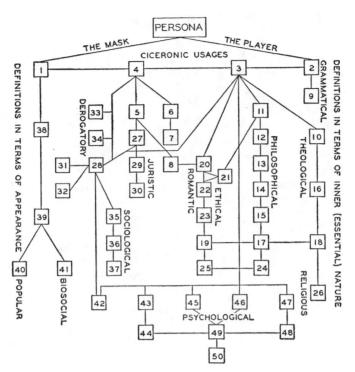

Figure 39. Plotting the self: The discursive path to psychological personality. From *Personality: A Psychological Interpretation, 1st edition*, by G. W. Allport © 1941. Reprinted with permission of Brooks/Cole, an imprint of the Wadsworth Group, a division of Thomson Learning. Fax 800 730-2215.

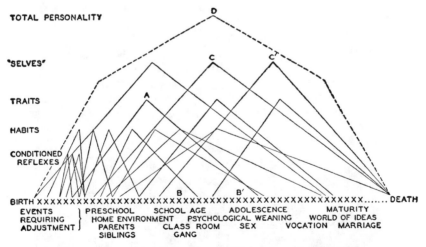

Figure 40. The transcendent self: Allport's "total personality." From *Personality: A Psychological Interpretation, 1st edition*, by G. W. Allport © 1941. Reprinted with permission of Brooks/Cole, an imprint of the Wadsworth Group, a division of Thomson Learning. Fax 800 730-2215.

Figure 41. Nellie Allport, Hollywood, California.

Figure 42. Allport's study, 24 Arlington Street, Boston, circa 1935.

Figure 43. A biological being: Robert and Gordon Allport, Hanover, New Hampshire, March 1928.

Figure 44. Seekers of personality: Gordon and Ada Allport, Laguna Beach, California, March 1937.

Figure 45. Gordon, Robert and Ada Allport, June 1929.

Figure 46. "A real boy": Robert Allport, 1935.

Figure 47. Harold Allport, 1935.

Figure 48. "The man of the hour": Gordon Allport, Camden Hills State Park, Maine, August 1937.

tual instances where a knowledge of the psychology of personality was purposively used as a foundation and method of treatment."[75]

An exemplar of the new model of professional, scientific social work, Gould is also an illustration of the gendered limitations of the personality ideal. Like many social workers, Gould was attracted by the emancipatory potential of personality. The category invoked ideals of individuality, freedom of expression, and liberation from outdated social codes. Unlike character, which had strong associations with manhood, personality had a refreshing aura of gender neutrality.[76] Both genders had personalities, which implied that both genders had ambitions, dignity, and the right to be viewed as an individual personality over and above one's social status as a man or woman.

Gould's fascination with personality began in high school through the influence of Alice Cook, her history teacher. Cook was "disciplined and principled," and she was unconcerned by those "who were still befuddled with ideas of Victorian gentility and who scorned any career more assertive than needle point in the garden."[77] Inspired by an "unvarying" faith in the "sanctity of the individual personality," Cook posed a "new and humanistic ideal for women," and she encouraged her female students to think of themselves as "modern, present-minded, humanistic, [and] effective."[78] Gould learned the lesson well, and as a young woman she felt an "intense desire for power and influence, and a life of pleasure and success."[79] However, Gould also realized, as Cook had done, that the "sanctity of personality" did not completely transcend the social significance of gender. Male and female values and social spheres still existed, and rather than try and transcend these dichotomies, Cook urged Gould to work creatively with them. "She [Cook] could do a 'man's job' in a woman's way," Gould wrote admiringly:

> There is little distinction for a woman to do a "man's job" in a man's way; a mere colorless duplication. But to bring to teaching or to administrative work as Miss Cook did the gifts of womanhood should be one ideal of the modern woman: the sympathetic fairness of the mother, the fine feminine appreciation of and respect for the conflicting intimacies of human nature, and faith in the moral worth of character. She achieved not only the man's ideal of "success" but the woman's ideal, a creative life.[80]

As a single woman working in a traditional female occupation, Cook had been able to finesse the tension between personality and femininity. As Gould contemplated the professional and personal opportunities that lay before her in the early 1920s, a balance seemed increasingly elusive. Committed to the emancipatory ideals of personality, she was professionally ambitious and for a time was unwilling to allow traditional expectations of female duty to stand in her way. "Until I was 21 it was always myself first, my ambitions first sacrifice everything as scrupulously as possible to that."[81] The prospect of marriage prompted Gould to rethink her earlier commitments. Marriage seemed incompatible with single-minded self-expression, and as a woman it seemed especially challenging. Was it possible to be an active, independent, self-affirming personality and a loyal, supportive wife? In the early 1920s, Gould was unsure, but the more she reflected on the question, the more she came to subordinate her dreams to those of her prospective husband. (See insert, Figure 36.)

In a series of letters to Allport, Gould struggled to find a way to bridge the ideals of personality and marital happiness. Still haunted by a "want-to-do-something feeling," Gould continued to take great pride in her professional identity.[82] After receiving an internship at the Boston Psychopathic Hospital, she felt "so glad that I am going to live for a few months in so stimulating a setting." The new position inspired dreams of a professional future, and she noted enthusiastically that "Professor L. is quite sure it will lead to a much finer position."[83] As her romance with Allport progressed, however, Gould sensed that her ambitions might collide with his. Unable to imagine a scenario in which her interests would take precedence over his, she took some comfort in the idea of male and female difference. "There are many vital things of life which a man must face alone," she remarked. "He is a pilgrim in many moral ventures, but others may be his inspiration: he alone must reach out his hand and accomplish." With men cast in the more active role of "pilgrim," Gould could envision herself as a loyal helpmate. "Gordon, there is nothing I desire more in the world than to be your inspiration," she wrote.[84] "Every particle of knowledge or wisdom that I gather this year is for you. So long as I can push on wisely and know that I can gather chips for your intellectual wood pile I'm willing to say 'career be dashed.'"[85] Surrender to a more conventional domestic ideal brought its own kind of liberation as Gould no longer had to struggle with conflicting ideals. "My life seems much less messy now that I have something beyond my own self-centered desires to work for." Happy with her decision, Gould's only regret now was not sacrificing enough, and she complained to Allport that "I do feel thwarted at times in not being able to assist you just as I would."[86]

Allport listened sympathetically to Gould's soul-searching, and he had some appreciation of the dilemma she faced. He spoke encouragingly about her career and occasionally chastised her for not telling him more about her professional accomplishments. "I insist upon regarding you as 'able' (ugly word)," he remarked in 1924. "All year you have refrained from telling me much about your work or anything about your successes. Honey, I know your reticence and your sound knowledge of values, why not give yourself credit!" Professionally supportive and personally consistent, Allport did not want his own scholarly fascination with personality to somehow impede the development of an actual personality. "*Never, never, never,* feel under any obligation to me," he told Gould. "If I interfere with your plans or your quests don't hesitate to put me off. I dread to be an imposter [*sic*]."[87]

Gould did not view Allport as an "imposter," and in a note to herself written in 1923 she observed that her prospective husband was "most careful of my liberty [and] most cautious about my feelings."[88] Such respect was welcome, but it was not unbounded. Allport was an extraordinarily ambitious and able person, and for all his admonitions to the contrary, Gould sensed that she would have to sacrifice some of her ambitiousness if she wanted to pursue a relationship with someone so successful. Ironically, Allport's nod to personality made Gould's dilemma all the more difficult. His carefully phrased letters held out the promise of mutual self-fulfillment, but long-established patterns of male authority in professional life seemed to foreclose the full expression of this ideal. At times, Allport tried to overcome this obstacle with the promise of scholarly collaboration. He encouraged Gould to continue developing her scholarly skills "so that sometime we may jointly produce a *Manual of Psychology for Social Workers* [*sic*]."[89] These dreams were enticing, but Gould still found herself grappling with a discomforting ambiguity whereby the possibility of female personality was acknowledged in theory but largely subordinated in practice. Aware of the disjuncture, she sometimes yearned for a clearer and more conventional expression of male authority and female submission: "If Gordon had swept me off my feet that conflict [love vs. power] would have been destroyed forever I think, I would have accepted fate," she remarked in 1923. Straightforward assertions of male authority were not forthcoming, however, and as her life with Allport unfolded in the 1920s and 1930s Gould was frequently buffeted by the contradictory expectations of personality and feminine domesticity.

THE "ACTUAL" NATURE OF PERSONALITY

Allport's cautious maneuvering at Harvard and Dartmouth belied the growing scholarly interest in the category he championed. The once obscure term was coming into psychological vogue, and beginning in 1923, the American Psychological Association (APA) began to hold special sessions on the "study of personality" at its annual meetings. These sessions grew into APA "roundtable" conferences, and in 1925 Herbert Langfeld observed that a roundtable conference on personality that year was "well attended and enthusiastically endorsed."[90]

The academic interest in personality was clearly evident, but there was little agreement about how the topic should be studied and even less consensus over the question of what personality consisted of. During his brief tenure at Dartmouth, Allport tried to bring a measure of clarity to this rapidly growing and increasingly fractious field. In a 1927 paper titled "Concepts of Trait and Personality," he took aim at the pervasive sense of confusion within the field of personality psychology, and he paid particularly close attention to the terms character and personality.[91] In the United States, Allport noted, the terms were often used interchangeably to refer to a "characteristic mode of human behavior."[92] Among those researchers who distinguished between character and personality, there existed a variety of contradictory definitions. Morton Prince defined character as the manifest, or outer, personality, whereas "personality is the sum total of all the biological innate dispositions, impulses, tendencies, appetites, and instincts of the individual and of all the acquired dispositions and tendencies."[93] A. A. Roback adopted a similar inner–outer framework to distinguish character from personality, except he reversed the order. Roback spoke of personality as the "external manifestations ... such as charm, bearing, carriage, and presence." He contrasted the psychic surface of personality with character: the "deeper or inner" aspects of the self that "[cover] the volitional and inhibitory phases of behaviour."[94]

Anxious to secure a scholarly niche for personality within the stridently scientific discipline of psychology, Allport viewed this multiplicity of definitions with alarm. Imprecise terminology "retards the interpretation of reliabilities," he argued, "[and] is generally prejudicial to advance in the field."[95] Temporarily abandoning his fascination with German spiritual psychology, Allport redeployed the behaviorist distinction "between personality *devaluated* and personality *evaluated*, that is, between personality and character."[96] It was a message born out of his own close proximity to the idiom of experimental psychology. His recent Harvard experience had underscored the growing power of scientific rhetoric and the importance of institutional support. One way of gaining this support was to constitute the object of study along preexisting methodological and discursive lines. Because mainstream American psychology was defined largely in relation to the ostensibly value-neutral science of physics, the verbal categories of personality psychology had to be presented as being analogous to the categories of nature.[97] Allport was well aware of the discursive demands of his disciplinary context, and in his theoretical papers he described personality as a natural object with an "actual nature" that could be approached by "experiment and theory."[98]

In calling for the abandonment of character, Allport was giving voice to a positivist trend that was well under way. Although a number of psychologists continued to insist on the importance of character as a scholarly topic, by the late 1920s the category's moral connotation was a matter of general consensus. Psychologist A. A. Roback's observations in his 1927 book *The Psychology of Character* typified the prevailing view: "[T]he most general use of the word 'character' in everyday life is invariably colored with moral predicates." What was particularly important for psychologists like Roback was not the moral vocabulary of character, but the scholarly conclusions that strident positivists derived from this context. Roback noted that the scientific legitimacy of character was "spoilt by [the] ethical atmosphere. . . . Just because it was born and bred in an ethical milieu, the psychologist would be apt to disown it as spurious."[99] Roback was clearly frustrated by psychology's growing aversion to explicitly ethical categories, and his difficulty in advancing character as a research category was duly noted by Allport. Allport read *The Psychology of Character* before it went to press, and in the book's preface Roback expressed his "indebtedness to Dr. G. W. Allport of Dartmouth College" for his "numerous critical suggestions." Ever sensitive to the idiom of American natural science, Allport was convinced that the personality psychologists needed to distance themselves from talk of character if they were to prosper. One of the advantages of personality was that it was not encumbered by the same moral baggage. Allport noted that the term "personality, like Mesopotamia, is a blessed word; it induces in both the writer and in the reader a sweet sense of stability, security, and modernity."[100] Personality's "sweet modernity" made it the logical choice for the new science, and as historian James Parker noted, by the late 1920s most psychologists had stopped using the term character.[101]

Personality was clearly the preferred category for the scientific minded. To understand its appeal for the antimodernist Allport, however, it is important to attend to the ambiguity that is implicit in his description of the term. In the previously quoted passage, Allport describes personality as a category that is both "blessed" and "modern." The juxtaposition of the two terms was not a linguistic eccentricity on Allport's part. In the 1920s, personality had a modern ring that lent itself to the sort of scientific projects that Allport had developed in his dissertation. At the same time, however, the concept had been colonized by ethicists and social workers in search of new categories with which to reach an increasingly skeptical public.[102] The ethical cargo loaded onto personality varied, however; for most writers the term signified a unique and intrinsically valuable essence within each individual. For example, philosopher Felix Adler defined personality as "that quality in every man which makes him worth while [*sic*], aside from the uses to which he may be put by his fellows."[103] Much the same view was expressed by school superintendent Thomas McCormack, who described personality as the

> final stage of the ethical, the aesthetic, and the intellectual development of the human animal. It is the human zoological individual at its maximum intensity, at its ethical, aesthetic, and intellectual flower, as representing the highest form of life possible for the individual in question.[104]

Allport was well aware of personality's double meaning. In the concluding chapter of his dissertation, he cited the work of Mary Richmond, who used personality in a manner similar to that of Adler and McCormack.[105] "Only an instinctive reverence for personality," she wrote, "and a warm interest in people as people can win for the social case worker [change] in the direction of higher and better wants and saner social relations."[106] In his scholarly work at Dartmouth and, later, at Harvard, Allport traded off personality's flexibility. In his formal scientific presentations, he usually distanced himself from any overt ethical interest by deploying the behavioristic definition of personality. On other occasions, however, he criticized psychologists for approaching personality from an exclusively materialistic standpoint. For example, in a critical review of Percival Symonds's *Diagnosing Personality and Conduct*, Allport drew an unfavorable comparison between the "exact" formulations of modern American psychology and the ethical conception of personality expressed by Goethe:

> When Goethe gave it as his opinion that personality is the supreme joy of the children of the earth, he could not have foreseen the joyless dissection of his romantic ideal one hundred years hence. There is certainly nothing poetical, metaphysical, or even humanistic in the modern psychological approaches to personality which are so conveniently surveyed in this volume.[107]

Allport expressed much the same sentiment in his assessment of psychiatrist Karl Menninger's book *The Human Mind*. "What I like best about it," he told Menninger, "is that it is so damned *civilized*. It is the humanism that is so much needed in both our fields."[108]

The ambiguity in Allport's use of personality reflected the duality that lay at the center of his professional vision. As he indicated in his letter to James Ford, Allport wanted to "correlate" psychology and social ethics into a new professional identity of "personality psychologist."[109] To do so, however, he needed to cultivate a light step when it came to ethical issues. If he placed too strong an emphasis on precision, objectivity, and materialism, the ethical component of personality psychology might well be lost. Yet, Allport knew the professional risk that attended any sustained talk of sensitivity, humanity, and idealism in matters of personality. For Allport, the most logical way forward was to subtly exploit the fuzziness of the term personality. He oscillated between the scientific and ethical meanings of the term without ever clearly stating that he was doing so.

TRAIT THEORY

Allport's belief that personality had an "actual nature" led to a search for the basic material or "existential unit of personality."[110] In the mid-1920s, there was little agreement as to the nature of these units or, indeed, as to whether personality units existed at all. Critics observed that personality inventories often measured a variety of attributes, including intelligence, physique, and temperament. Others drew parallels between traits and the discredited faculty psychology, thereby suggesting that the former existed in name only. Percival Symonds, a personality psychologist at Teachers College, Columbia University, expressed a widely shared incredulity as to the existence of traits: "When I read over a list of traits such as intelligence, neatness, humor, beauty, refinement . . . vulgarity, I am wondering if there is any one thing that corresponds to those names."[111] Symonds thought not. He encouraged personality and character researchers to "come down out of the sky" and think less in terms of "traits" and "more in terms of habits of conduct, or specific reactions to well defined situations."[112]

Symonds's counsel amounted to an avoidance of the question of the nature of personality. Validity of the test measure—the degree to which a test actually measured what it was supposed to be measuring—was pushed to the one side. Symonds proposed reliability—consistency across tests— as the new goal for personality psychologists: "Would not progress be more rapid if we attempted to construct reliable tests, regardless of the specific thing they measure?"[113] The suggestion seemed counterintuitive, but Symonds reasoned that it was the practical approach for personality psychologists to take. Once psychologists had developed a series of reliable tests, he thought that it would be relatively easy to determine just what it was that the test measured. Evidently, most personality psychologists agreed. In 1932, A. A. Roback, author of the authoritative *Bibliography of Character and Personality*, described the field as being in the midst of an "era of measurement."[114] In Roback's view, trait tests represented an "avalanche which bids fair to sweep away from the foreground nearly all interests in American psychology, to the exclusion of personality measurement."[115]

Allport shared the concern expressed by Symonds over the elusive nature of personality traits. In his 1927 paper on traits and personality, he noted that "inventories of 'traits' at present include a reckless array of noncomparable factors."[116] Unlike Symonds, however, Allport saw no intellectual deliverance in the construction of reliable tests. He admitted that the procedure might identify the existence of certain general tendencies across a broad spectrum of people, but Allport expressed serious reservations about the type of program Symonds proposed. When pursued with too much vigor, Allport argued that the test approach actually retarded the development of personality psychology. To begin with, testing shifted the attention of the researcher from the individual human subject to a general dimension shared by a number of subjects. Next, testing fostered a tendency to think of personality dimensions as discrete entities, something analogous to the 19th-century faculties. Testing also worked toward the fragmentation of personality. Little thought was given to the way personality functioned as a whole or to how the tested dimensions related to other aspects of an individual's personality. Finally, Allport argued that testing amounted to a primitive "sum-total" or "omnibus" theory of personality that equated personality with a person's score on a series of tests.[117]

To avoid the fragmented, simplistic conclusions of the standard paper-and-pencil group personality test, Allport maintained that researchers must confront, head-on, the "problem as to what constitutes the existential unit of personality."[118] "The truth of the matter is that neither measurement nor inventories of 'attitudes' and the like can be intelligible until the substantives themselves are clearly understood," he wrote.[119] Allport did not think that this task involved a skyward ascent to a nebulous realm, as Symonds had suggested. Conceptual clarity and a close attention to the scholarly literature could deliver into the hands of personality psychologists the real "unit or element that is the carrier of the distinctive behavior of a man."[120]

In Allport's view, that unit was the *trait*, a term familiar to most American psychologists. It had been used interchangeably with a number of other colloquial terms, such as *tendency*, *disposition*, and *characteristic*. Most psychologists used the word in a biological sense, although as one historian recently pointed out, in the 1920s it was not uncommon for behaviorists to occasionally refer to traits.[121] Allport's use of the term was more in keeping with the conventional biological sense of the term. Traits were the "biophysical" units of personality.[122] They had a "genuine" existence, which meant that they could be established on "neurological grounds."[123] Allport conceived of the trait as a kind of higher order habit, although it was much more generalized. Traits organized habits into characteristic patterns and styles of execution—"great systems of interdependent habits."[124] In addition to this organizing role, Allport argued that traits had a volitional character. "The stimulus is not the crucial determinant in behavior that expresses personality; the trait itself is decisive."[125] Unlike the faculties of old, Allport argued that traits were not distinct entities within personality. They had a fluid, overlapping quality that made them "fundamentally and uniquely dependent on the 'form-quality' of the total personality."[126]

The manner in which traits changed became a major theme in Allport's later work. During the 1920s and early 1930s, however, Allport was more concerned about establishing the existence of traits than he was in exploring their formation and subsequent development. Widespread acceptance of trait theory would provide personality psychologists with a distinctive object of investigation while granting them a measure of respectability. Allport also hoped that trait theory would open up the field methodologically and intellectually. In his view, psychologists who took his version of trait theory to heart would diversify their approaches to personality. Statistical data gathered from large groups would be enhanced by qualitative studies of individual participants.

TRAIT THEORY AND THE REENCHANTMENT OF THE SELF

Allport's efforts to forge a more precise, scientific language of selfhood occurred at the same time that religious discourse was in full retreat. Industrialization, urbanization, commercialization, and scholarly developments in the arts and sciences had been undermining religious authority for decades, and by the mid-1920s many observers had come to feel that religion was the worldview of an earlier, more innocent era. One contemporary commentator noted that there had been "an undeniable weakening of loyalty to the church and an undeniable vagueness as to what it had to offer."[127] John Dewey thought it "hardly possible to overstate [religion's] decline as a vitally integrative and directive force in men's thought and sentiments."[128] The new, secular mood was perhaps best summarized by theologian Reinhold Niebuhr, who spoke of a "psychology of defeat" that had "gripped the forces of religion."[129]

The decline of traditional religious frames of reference was a source of concern for Allport, who was a devoted Episcopalian, but what was perhaps even more alarming was the rapid erosion of all discourse that situated the human subject in a context of higher concern. Behaviorism, psychoanalysis, and gland psychology were among the most corrosive agents in this regard. During the 1920s, a number of commentators argued that these psychologies were constituting a new human subject, grounded not in a spiritual discourse of character, individual uniqueness, and moral striving, but in a deterministic language of conditioned responses, instincts, and physiological process. Psychologist A. A. Roback observed that "psychological textbooks teem with nihilistic theories and analogies." Psychologists were "whittling away mephistophelically our principles, standards and values."[130] Roback's views were echoed by psychologist–theologian George Albert Coe.[131] Coe noted that a new, "high-strung humanity" had emerged that was "awake on some sides of its mind if not on others; it is highly organized, industrially focalized, scientifically managed, psychologically analyzed; it is rich in things, but it is distracted and ethically upset." In Coe's view, the source of that upset was a sense of "disillusionment . . . with respect to the genuine worth of all our motives and all our straining and striving and organizing."[132]

As a champion of the new science of personality, Allport was in the paradoxical position of being both a part of this process of disenchantment and an opponent of it. He clearly believed in the social benefit of bringing personality within the sphere of scientific discipline. Yet the totalizing implications of this process—the eradication of human agency, the loss of individuality, the heightening of instrumentality—was a source of great concern. It is within this context of ambivalence that Allport's trait theory needs to be viewed. Was it possible to subject personality to scientific scrutiny and discipline without subverting all those alleged qualities—individuality, volition, purpose—that set people apart from the natural world? Allport's search for traits was an affirmative response to this question. By searching for the traits of personality, Allport was working within the naturalistic frameworks of biology and chemistry. Traits were the "real" carriers of personality. They existed on a neurological level, and their existence could be established empirically and statistically. The crucial issue for Allport was the properties to be assigned to these real entities. Traits were "dynamic," at least partially "unique," and integrated into a "common path" by a "subjective scale of values."[133] The demonstration of their existence did not enable the scientist to predict or control any given person, because a person's behavior was a function of the pattern of traits, not the individual traits themselves. What the empirical demonstration of traits did provide, at least for Allport, was a scientific foundation for his own religiously derived sense of self. Traits provided a biological warrant for affirming an enchanted view of the person as individually unique, at least partially self-determining, and integrated by purposeful striving.

The strategic value of this biological confirmation is difficult to overemphasize. In the 1920s, American social science was hostage to a powerful scientism that took the methods and categories of the natural sciences as the ultimate arbiters of truth. The intellectual vitality of psychological categories depended on their ability to pass this natural science muster.[134] Allport was highly aware of the importance of couching "higher" psychological categories in the frameworks of natural science. However, his attempt to ground the principles of uniqueness, self-determination, and purposeful striving in biology was not undertaken in a spirit of calculation. Allport himself was at least partially invested in a scientistic ontology. He had been socialized into accepting a vision of psychology as a natural science while an undergraduate. Some years later, he noted in private correspondence that his "own point of origin . . . is the late 19th Century Psychology. I feel myself, as it were, stemming from the 'reaction experiment' and similar seed pods."[135] Allport's Anglo-Catholic commitment to the language of spirit had tempered his enthusiasm for positivistic psychology, but its systems of intelligibility and the explanatory metaphors it generated continued to command a measure of allegiance.

Allport's encounter with the Geisteswissenschaften of Stern and Spranger is a case in point. Allport greatly admired the theoretical creativity of Stern and Spranger, and he agreed with the basic tenets of their model of personality. Yet there was something speculative about their approach that disturbed him. The scholars of the Geisteswissenschaften were too wrapped up in the process of theory development; too little attention had been paid to the search for evidence that would confirm the theory. For Allport, as for most other American-trained psychologists, at least a part of that evidence had to come in the form of statistics and rigorously controlled experimental procedures. Those facets of personality not susceptible to methodological rigor of this sort should be confirmed under some other equally exacting set of standards. Allport expressed his reservations about German psychology in a letter to a colleague written shortly after his return from the 1932 International Congress of Psychology. He noted that "testing and behaviorism were slighted" but added, "I do not hold in contempt the bulk of American work, as most of our German friends seem to do." In fact, Allport thought that there was much to admire in American methodological precision. "In general one felt the superiority of American methods," he remarked. "Our standards are really more exacting than the Germans, although their clever insights and broad theory remain ahead." It was only a matter of time, in Allport's estimation, before American psychologists would "outstep them all."[136]

THE "INTUITIVE" METHOD

The other component of Allport's professional project in the 1920s was methodological. Convinced as he was of the need to view the "carriers" of personality within the frameworks of natural science, Allport was equally convinced of the inadequacy of the existing methods of exploring personality as a whole. The dominant method was the paper-and-pencil test, which was based on the metaphor of "dismemberment."[137] Allport did not dispute the benefits that had accrued from this approach, but he did warn against the dangers that attended extensive testing. Personality measures sometimes "usurped the [psychologist's] field of attention" to the point where "a part of the person had come to supplant the whole." Testing had also fostered a neglect of issues of "unity and congruence" in personality. Psychologists knew little about the "integrating forces which knit the traits and attributes together into an internally congruous pattern." The consequence of neglecting these issues was, in Allport's view, a psychology of personality that had almost nothing to say about any given individual personality: "Expressed bluntly, psychology has not been interested in [single cases] although it is into concrete personalities ... that human nature is naturally divided, not into intelligence, reaction time, and introversion spread along abscissas."[138]

What Allport wanted to devise was a methodological framework that would capture the scientifically grounded individuality of the person. His first systematic thoughts on the subject were laid out in his 1929 paper "The Study of Personality by the Intuitive Method: An Experiment in Teaching From *The Locomotive God*."[139] Allport argued that the Geisteswissenschaften contained a method that would round out the psychometric procedures that had been so exhaustively applied in the United States. *Verstehen*, usually translated as "understanding," was the German term for this method. Quoting Spranger, Allport described Verstehen as "the mental process of grasping events as fraught with meaning."[140] Verstehen was thought to be an active process, so Allport followed the lead of psychologist Christian Ruckmick by translating it into the term *intuituitionism*. This new, intuitive method did not draw on mystical or innate knowledge, nor did it presume any telepathic powers. Intuition in this context was simply the attempt to understand a particular person in his or her cultural setting. The process of understanding was thought to involve something more than tabulating lists of traits. Allport argued that "arbitrary schedules for listing attributes of personality have a diabolical propensity for losing the personality itself."[141] To really understand a personality, one needed to determine the patterns into which the traits were organized. Again citing Spranger, Allport suggested that this organization proceeded with reference to the "major purposes of life": "It is the understanding of the values which the individual is seeking which alone provides intelligibility for the items on the schedule of traits."[142]

Spranger proposed to understand personality through his six value types (see chapter 6). Allport appropriated the notion of understanding and applied it in a more general sense. The intuitive method was a refined form of the commonsense manner of apprehending personality. It was analogous to the artistry displayed in a particularly incisive biography. The biographer does not usually "explain" the subject in terms of basic elements of personality. Rather, understanding is the customary goal—an understanding constructed out of a series of interpretations of the subject in relation to the purposes toward which he or she was working and the context of his or her thoughts and actions. Psychiatric and psychological categories, such as ascendance–submission and introversion–extroversion, could be used, as could ideal types, but in Allport's view the intuitive method did not necessarily involve either procedure. An approach to personality warranted the term intuitive if it (a) scrutinized the unities of the individual personality and (b) emphasized the active role played by the mind of the personality psychologist. Thus, a psychologist using the intuitive method would seek out a subject's value system from a range of clues: diaries, clinical interviews, expressive movement, and so forth. This was not a machinelike process, but was something uniquely human. "Associations are not like the cards in a filing cabinet, speedily produced under sensory stimulation and arranged swiftly into a mosaic of 'meaning.'"[143] Understanding personality was a nonmechanical procedure of holistic perception. Until psychologists realized this, Allport argued, they were likely to remain poor "judges of personality in the concrete" and relatively unsuccessful in "personnel work."[144]

MARKETING A METHOD

In calling on American psychologists to adopt the intuitive method, Allport was sounding a defiant note. American psychologists had a well-known "distrust of clouds"—methods that they thought departed from the rigorous procedures of physical science.[145] Critical though he was of psychometric procedures, Allport's project was not as subversive as it initially sounded. His intention in mobilizing the intuitive method was not to supplant the conventional procedures of psychometric psychology, but to complement them. The intuitive method could address important questions of personality left unexamined by existing procedures:

> A concrete personality presents problems of both genesis (causation) and meaning (interpretation). Though not always sharply separable in practice, the first of these problems requires the current "explanatory" technique, the latter, an "intuition" which focuses upon the unities of its subject. A combination of these attitudes is essential.[146]

Allport's criticism of American personality psychology was thus accompanied by a conciliatory promise of further expansion. Psychometrics could proceed as before; all that was needed was an interpretive balance to its quantitative emphasis. Strategically, this conciliatory posture was quite apt. It is far easier to expand the range of existing methods than it is to eradicate them altogether. Allport had a certain savvy with respect to intellectual salesmanship. He was probably mindful of the advantages to be gained from cultivating an image of moderate. At the same time, however, Allport was genuinely committed to the spirit of what he was proposing. In his view, psychometrics had contributed as much to the study of personality as had the Geisteswissenschaften. A "full-bodied" psychology of personality would emerge when the two came together.

The precise manner in which the two were to be brought together was an issue that Allport struggled with for the remainder of his career. *The Study of Personality by the Intuitive Method* contained a hint of some of the frustrations to come. In this work, Allport illustrated some of the principles of the intuitive method by referring to *The Locomotive God*, the autobiography of William Leonard, an English professor at the University of Wisconsin. Leonard was a self-described neurotic who had been in therapy with a number of specialists over the years, including the Harvard psychiatrist Morton Prince and psychologist W. S. Taylor. Leonard's autobiography was at once a description of his condition and a chronicle of the numerous therapeutic engagements that he had sought out. Psychology, psychoanalysis, reminiscences, and everyday understanding were all mobilized in an attempt to make sense of his own condition. Allport liked the book because of the vivid way it communicated a sense of a whole personality: "There is always a homogenous impression of the personality as a whole; successive pages give not merely added data, but clarify the impression of the personality which from the beginning is felt as a unity."[147] Allport went on to suggest that Leonard's book could be profitably used as a textbook in undergraduate courses on personality, and he listed a number of benefits that had accrued from his own use of the book in this fashion. In so doing, Allport made a valuable contribution to the pedagogy of personality psychology. What he did not do is provide his readers with a coherent framework for mobilizing the intuitive method themselves. He failed to provide any programmatic statements about the method, and he neglected to further the interpretations set forth by Leonard. Psychologists curious to know more about the intuitive method could not turn to Allport for an example of the "state of the art." They were directed to turn to Leonard's work.

On this point, the usually shrewd Allport made a serious tactical error. In the 1920s and 1930s, psychologists had a large appetite for new methods, largely because these procedures contributed to the authority of the field. Methods involving large arrays of numbers, charts, and machines invested the discipline with an aura of scientific respectability. This was an important consideration because psychologists were not the only ones claiming expertise in matters of human subjectivity. Psychics and mystics claimed part of this domain, as did other academic disciplines. To keep the competition at bay, psychology needed to maintain a well-stocked arsenal of rhetorical procedures capable of clearly differentiating expert psychological knowledge from the "quackery" of psychicalism and common sense.[148] The problem with Allport's proposal for the adoption of the intuitive method lay in his failure to speak to this issue of professional authority.[149] No special procedures were proposed; there were no new statistics and no new machines. Allport was apparently convinced that logical argument would be enough to sell the method to American personality psychology. If he had thought otherwise, he probably would not have selected *The Locomotive God* as his exemplar. The book did illustrate some of the principles of the Geisteswissenschaften that Allport was trying to promote, but as the work of a layman (albeit a psychologically sophisticated one), it was a poor vehicle for promoting a new psychological method. Leonard's work made extensive use of psychology and psychoanalysis, but it conferred no special authority onto the practitioners themselves. The book actually weakened the distinction between psychologists and everybody else by implicitly suggesting that psychological expertise was within the province of any articulate, well-educated person. In the book's introduction for instance, Leonard claimed that his highly detailed self-scrutiny enabled him to "know more intimately than Freud" that the "child is father of the man and that men are but children of a larger growth."[150] In a context of intense competition and professional pressure, this effacing of expert authority made the intuitive method a poor bet.

In the 1930s, few American personality psychologists were prepared to make such a wager. The intuitive method proposed by Allport does not appear to have had any appreciable impact on the field. If anything, the trend within the field was toward an even greater use of psychometric procedures. One historian recently calculated that 74% of all research papers published on personality between 1934 and 1936 used an intelligence test format. In sharp contrast, only 36% of personality papers used the intelligence test format from 1924 to 1926.[151] The psychometric tenor of the field is clearly evident in the correspondence between Allport and University of Wyoming psychologist June Downey. Like Allport, Downey had developed a popular paper-and-pencil test, but she was also interested in graphology, creativity, and theories of personality.[152] When surveying personality psychology in the United States, what impressed her was not the rich discourse around these issues but the "narrowness and dogmatism of so many American psychologists." Great "sins are committed in the name of objectivity," she told Allport:

> It seems to me when I mingled with the graduate students at one of our large midwest universities that they were actually writing their doctor's dissertations by formula and that it was considered doubtful propriety to do any thinking. They were using their statistics without any understanding whatever of psychological concepts.[153]

Allport might have been able to influence this psychometric trend had he developed the intuitive method in a manner that would allow psychologists to safeguard their professional domain. However, substantial shifts in this trend were unlikely, irrespective of the distinctiveness of the method that Allport proposed, because issues of professional authority were not the only force sustaining test technology. Broad issues of culture were also involved. What historian Joanne Brown called the "rhetorical force of numbers" in American culture was of particular importance.[154] Brown noted that scientific investigations that use banks of numbers have had a peculiar resonance in the United States since the 19th century. French psychologist Alfred Binet commented on this tendency at the turn of the century: "The Americans, who love to do things big, often publish experiments made on hundreds and even thousands of persons. They believe that the conclusive value of a work is proportional to the number of observations made."[155] The faith in numbers that Binet noted in 1903 was, if anything, even more pronounced by the time Allport began formulating his criticism in the late 1920s and early 1930s. By then, hundreds of highly detailed, statistically based school surveys and intelligence tests had consolidated into a powerful tradition capable of fending off all but the most sustained criticism. The metaphors of medicine and engineering that sustained the initial development of psychological tests fossilized into standard categories through which psychologists perceived their various domains of study.[156] In this context, scales that purported to measure aspects of personality were invested with considerable scientific plausibility.

CONCLUSION

In her thoughtful discussion of William James's *Principles of Psychology*, historian Deborah Coon drew attention to James's notion of the self and early Christian notions of the soul. Positioning the *Principles* within a larger context of secularization, Coon argued that the notion of *self* helped James construct a naturalistic psychology while allowing him to "retain the most important of the ethical and metaphysical concerns that those positivistic goals demanded he leave out."[157] In the 1920s, Allport came to use personality in a similar bridge-building fashion. The terms *soul* and *character* both suffered from associations with religion and a discredited Victorian moral code. Personality seemed to reflect the temper of the times, and more important for Allport, it was able to house a wide range of cultural and scientific cargo. The term unified psychology's contradictory promise: Through personality one could glimpse both a self that could be measured and manipulated and an enchanted, uncapturable self of hidden potential and unlimited horizons.

Allport's early experience in social ethics and psychology reflected the cultural and academic ambiguities of personality. Obliged to satisfy both staunch positivists, such as Boring, and humanitarian character builders, such as Cabot, Allport constructed a delicate discourse of correlation that subtly blended science and ethics. Mindful of the increasingly scientistic temper of the times, he chose his categories and institutional commitments carefully, and he correctly sensed the rhetorical advantages of being an ethically minded scientist rather than a scientifically minded ethicist.

8

THE POLITICS OF MODERATION: PERSONALITY PSYCHOLOGY AT HARVARD (1930–1936)

> It seems that the middle of the road is not only the safest but also the most correct path to follow.
>
> —Gordon Allport, 1929[1]

> For my thoughts are not your thoughts,
> nor are your ways my ways says the Lord.
> For as the heavens are higher than the earth,
> so are my ways higher than your ways
> and my thoughts higher than your thoughts.
>
> —Isaiah 55:8–9

By the early 1930s, Allport had established himself as one of the leading authorities in the burgeoning new field of personality. In addition to regular contact with most of the eminent scholars in the area, he was invited to join the editorial board of the *Psychological Bulletin*[2] and to comment on the entries pertaining to personality in the *Dictionary of Psychology*.[3] Allport's success stemmed in part from the thoroughness of his work. His review of personality was exhaustive and authoritative, and his test of ascendance–submission was well respected and widely used.

Equally important to Allport's rise was his rhetorical style. The significance of Allport's rhetorical style has been partially obscured by his various works of self-presentation. In his autobiography, Allport explicitly denied any persuasive intent. Rather, he was a courageous "maverick" untroubled by "rebukes or professional slights."[4] Personality psychology was the undiluted product of this courageous self. It reflected only his own internal convictions; the intended market for his knowledge products did not shape their production. For instance, when describing his first book on personality, Allport claimed that he "did not write the book for any particular audience. I wrote it simply because I felt I had to define the new field of the psychology of personality as I saw it."[5] Allport took a similar

163

tack in a 1962 biographical reminiscence. He described himself as a forth-right theorist who minced no words. "Over the succeeding years I have *not* cared what my colleagues thought, and that's been fortunate. I have definitely been a maverick, a minority deviant in modern psychology. But, I couldn't care less! It doesn't trouble me."[6]

Allport was not a hostage to any intellectual orthodoxy, nor was he a straight-talking, tactless individualist. On the contrary, he was keenly aware of the social and intellectual contexts in which he was moving, and beginning with his first publication, he carefully crafted his articles to maximize their appeal. His preferred approach was the rhetoric of moderation. Usually this involved Allport positioning himself between the theoretically interesting but scientifically suspect Geisteswissenschaften, on the one hand, and the scientifically rigorous but intellectually impoverished psychometric tradition, on the other. Drawing out the strengths and weaknesses of each approach, he cast himself in the role of sober moderate.

The persuasive appeal of Allport's rhetoric becomes apparent when it is projected against the intellectual backdrop of American psychology in the 1920s. Psychology was enjoying unprecedented popularity, largely as a result of the public's fascination with mental testing and psychoanalysis.[7] Despite this success, the field was badly fragmented along several different lines. Structuralist psychologists defined the field strictly in terms of consciousness, whereas behaviorists ruled out consciousness altogether. Mental testing had fostered personality testing and the newly emerging category of clinical psychology. These developments were all viewed with dismay by some older, laboratory-based psychologists who believed that the field's scientific integrity would be sullied by applied concerns.[8] The propriety of various forms of investigative practice was another point of tension, especially in newly emerging fields such as personality psychology. As we have seen, personality could be conceived of in terms of general dimensions and approached through the psychometric testing of groups, or it could be approached qualitatively in the form of case studies using handwriting analysis and interpretation in relation to ideal types. Finally, a number of theoretical differences divided psychologists within Allport's own broad field of social psychology. Floyd Allport identified seven approaches to social psychology in his 1927 interpretation of the field: the social forces school, social mind theories, the social laws approach, the cultural approach, innate individual causation, socialization theories, and the behavior approach.[9]

RETURNING TO HARVARD: A MODERATE COMES HOME

In this context of division, the discourse of moderation could be extremely powerful. Moderation represented a way through theoretical impasse; it could be a pleasing synthesis of opposites. On a broad political level, moderation was a way of presenting a unified disciplinary front at a time when psychology was concerned about its public profile. On a micropolitical level, moderation could be a soothing balm in a department torn by theoretical difference. The appeal of the moderate stance that Allport cultivated for himself is clearly evident in the circumstances surrounding his return to Harvard in September 1930. Allport was brought in to fill the vacancy created by the departure of British psychologist William McDougall. Controversial from the start, McDougall's philosophical orientation, aristocratic ways, and combative style had won him few friends in the United States, and he was never fully accepted at Harvard.[10] One historian remarked that "his name became almost synonymous with theories and practices regarded by most American psychologists as remnants of exploded but still dangerous superstitions."[11] McDougall had hoped to win converts to his approach, but he quickly discovered that most graduate students were unwilling to even consider his ideas. In his autobiography, he recalled that he had

> not foreseen that the numerous graduate students were drawn to Harvard in the main from other colleges and universities; and, with very few exceptions, they had been taught some form of mechanistic psychology, with the consequence that they looked at upon me and my outlandish theories with suspicion."[12]

Anxious for a change, McDougall jumped at the opportunity to leave Harvard. According to one account, when McDougall received a letter from the president of the newly formed Duke University asking him to recommend a psychology chairman, he replied, "I accept."[13]

Ironically, Allport was one of the few American psychologists to view McDougall's work sympathetically. Study in Germany had made him receptive to the purposive character of McDougall's psychology, and when the second edition of McDougall's *The Group Mind* appeared in 1928, Allport wrote a favorable review.[14] "Professor McDougall's views remain substantially unrefuted," Allport noted, "and probably to a large extent are prophetic of the collective psychology of the future."[15] This support was greatly appreciated by the beleaguered McDougall, who described Allport's review as "Galen to my soul": "The social psychologists of this country write for the most part in a lingo which means nothing at all to me and it is a relief to find that my lingo is not utterly unintelligible to you."[16]

McDougall may have been an unpopular figure in American psychology, but he was still a prolific writer with an international reputation. Indeed, in 1928, psychologist A. A. Roback described McDougall as "undoubtedly the foremost psychologist in the English speaking countries today."[17] Allport was a young scholar of considerable promise, but he was clearly not in the same league as McDougall. His arrival and McDougall's departure may have bode well for the future of psychology at Harvard, but for the moment the transition did little to improve the department's standing.

The disparity in the prestige of the two scholars had not gone unnoticed by senior officials at Harvard. Psychology's principal advocate at Harvard, E. G. Boring, was especially mindful of the department's diminished profile. When McDougall's position became available, Boring spread the word across North America and Europe. He hoped to secure a prominent scholar in order to maintain and ultimately improve the standing of Harvard psychology. Boring's search was complicated by Harvard's rather dated administrative organization. Unlike most American universities, Harvard included philosophy and psychology within the same academic department. This arrangement was not especially significant in the day-to-day operations of each discipline, and the psychologists proceeded to operate as a de facto department.[18] In matters of policy, resource allocation, and hiring, however, the departmental organization became a matter of great consequence. The philosophers held the balance of power in the department, having three full professorships against psychology's one. Furthermore, the chair of the department was always a philosopher. The philosophers regarded themselves as a broad-minded group, but their decisions with respect to psychology had an unavoidable degree of professional self-interest. They wanted to further psychology at Harvard, but only if it could further philosophy at the same time.

The interests of philosophy and psychology clashed violently over the question of McDougall's replacement. In 1928, a hiring committee at Harvard offered the position to Karl Lashley, who equaled McDougall in professional eminence. However, to the chagrin of the faculty at Harvard, he declined. The philosophers then wanted to offer the job to the Gestalt psychologist Wolfgang Köhler, whose theoretical interests would have blended well with their own. Boring was strongly opposed to this move, and he successfully vetoed it. In a letter to the chairman, he wrote that "American psychologists who felt that Harvard had made a mistake with both Münsterberg and McDougall would feel that it again erred."[19] The committee considered a number of other "star" candidates, including Kurt Koffka, Karl Bühler, Charles Spearman, and Knight Dunlap, but they could not come to any agreement. Age of the candidates was a concern for some committee members, and the candidates' philosophy of science was an issue for others.

Nationality was also a factor. The previous two full professors in psychology at Harvard had been Europeans—Münsterberg and McDougall—and neither one had proved entirely satisfactory. Boring argued that Harvard needed a "stable, long continuing, American nucleus, before . . . we can then add European comets."[20] Finding a stable and eminent American nucleus was easier said than done. Speaking for the committee, Boring eventually concluded that "it rather looks as if Harvard would have to give up trying for the great."[21] Harvard president Lowell concurred, and in 1927 he partially resolved the problem by promoting Boring into the full professorship that had been occupied by McDougall. The move still left the department understaffed, so the committee continued its search with its sights set somewhat lower. After a round of further consultations they began "thinking seriously of Gordon Allport as assistant professor."[22]

Allport's emergence as a candidate was based partly on his area of expertise. The departure of McDougall had imbalanced the department. The biological dimensions of psychology were well represented, but social psychology—which included personality—lacked effective representation. The department needed a strong voice to represent what was a rapidly developing field. Allport was not yet an international figure, but his teaching and research record made him a good prospect in this regard. Boring was probably not exaggerating when he conveyed to Allport "the confidence which everyone shares with me in your future, [and] the great relief about our future that I should feel could you be added to our staff."[23]

Allport's prospects at Harvard were undoubtedly enhanced by the collegial relationships he had built up with various members of the department over the years. The seeds of most of these relationships had been planted in the early 1920s, when Allport was a graduate student and junior faculty member in social ethics. After his move to Dartmouth, Allport maintained his Harvard connections by returning to Cambridge, Massachusetts, every summer to teach in the summer school. By 1929, he was well acquainted with all the faculty members in psychology at Harvard. Once again, Allport's congenial personality appears to have stood him in good stead. He established good relations with McDougall and the strong-willed Boring. As before, Allport's consideration of "social intelligence" appears to have been the basis on which these relationships developed. McDougall described Allport as "industrious, agreeable, [and] open-minded."[24] Boring spoke of the "personal good will" he felt toward Allport and of the personality psychologist's habit of "*fitting in as you always do with any total situation that is found to exist*" [italics added].[25]

The mood among the Harvard psychologists, especially Boring, invested Allport's "moderate" personality with special significance. Boring envisioned the department not as a collection of individual scholars, but as a team of scientists unified around a clearly defined set of administrative, pedagogical, and intellectual principles.[26] In his autobiography, Boring admitted that he was "obsessed with the idea that we ought somehow to weld our psychologists, all of them Harvard individualists, together into an understanding unity."[27] Some sense of the degree of Boring's obsession may be gleaned from the initiatives he introduced in the 1920s. One of his first ideas to be implemented was the introduction of a comprehensive, 2-year, 200-lecture systematic course on psychology conceived along team-teaching lines. A faculty member would teach units closest to his area of expertise, and all members of the staff would attend each others' lectures. Another outgrowth of Boring's desire for unity were the "laboratory luncheons." Boring enticed faculty members and graduate students to come together every lunch hour with the promise of free coffee. By the early 1930s, he recalled that "most of us came together [for lunch] nearly every day."[28]

Collegiality was thus an extraordinarily important virtue for any prospective Harvard faculty member. Evidently, Allport's particular brand of collegiality was a relatively rare commodity in the academic world of the 1920s and 1930s. Boring complained at length of the difficulty of finding scholars who combined a first-rate intellect with broad-minded sympathies. He thought that intellect contributed to creativity and leadership in a field but that it often bred arrogance and a contempt for opposing points of view. In a departmental context, the frequent result was a destructive discord and divisiveness. Conversely, broad-mindedness fostered collegiality and departmental unity, but it, too, had a downside. It seemed to promote an indecisiveness that was paralyzing to intellectual creativity. Instead of leading, the broad-minded scholar was content to follow. The result in this case was a weakened department. Boring explained the dilemma in a letter to Harry Murray, the head of Harvard's Psychological Clinic: "Fundamentally the point is that you get distinction, scholarship, and good research from an inexhaustible drive, generally an ego drive, and you get disunity, controversy, tuquoques, and argumenta ad hominen from the same drive if ever you try to put those multiplicities into the unity."[29]

In Allport, Boring saw someone capable of fostering unity and distinction. It would seem that the rest of the department agreed. Boring told Allport that "the Department has been unanimous . . . in wishing to bring you back here in psychology."[30] Allport was unofficially offered the Harvard position in February 1929 on the understanding that he would start in September of that year. It was an attractive offer: A return to Harvard would free up more time for research, and it would boost his professional standing. It would also mean a return to the more cosmopolitan environs of Cambridge. Dartmouth had proved to be "all we hoped for in point of beauty, congeniality, and leisure." Yet it had an almost exclusively Yankee character about it that Allport found rather boring. "There is a most overwhelming normalcy here," he wrote to his friend W. S. Taylor. "I miss the eccentrics, deviates, and Jews which spice the student body at Harvard."[31]

There was one other advantage to the Harvard offer that Allport never mentioned in his letter to Taylor. A psychology appointment at Harvard would elevate his standing in relation to his one-time mentor and longtime competitor, Floyd Allport. As we have seen, Allport occupied a position subordinate to Floyd for most of his life, and he continued to do so throughout the mid-1920s. As late as 1928, Allport was telling correspondents that he had "published several articles of no great importance, and [was] not to be confused with my more eminent brother, F. H. Allport of Syracuse University."[32] For Gordon, Boring's offer represented a way of bridging the gap in status that still separated him from his brother. The appointment had a particular significance in this respect since it was, in a certain sense, Floyd's old job that was on offer. Floyd had taught social psychology at Harvard from 1919 to 1922.[33] He became expendable when McDougall arrived in 1920, and after a short stay at the University of North Carolina, he moved on to Syracuse University, where he spent the rest of his career. The records of Floyd's appointment at Harvard are regrettably sketchy, but it does appear that his departure was hastened by his rather brusque manner. In a letter to Langfeld written shortly before Floyd's departure from Harvard, Boring reported that President Lowell was "violently set against [Floyd] Allport."[34]

Evidently, Lowell's dim view of Floyd Allport did not change with the passage of time. Floyd's name was not raised in connection with McDougall's old position, despite the fact that he was one of the foremost young social psychologists in the nation. It is not clear whether Floyd was troubled by this omission; however, he appears to have been irritated by the news that his younger brother was being considered for the job. In a moment of indiscretion, Gordon had told Floyd of his negotiations with Boring. Shortly afterward, Floyd met up with Boring at an academic conference in New York. Instead of waiting for an opportune moment to inquire discretely about how the negotiations were progressing, Floyd "hailed" Boring "in a large group of psychologists" and asked, "What's all this I hear about my brother going to Harvard?"[35] Not surprisingly, Allport was embarrassed by this public airing of delicate contract negotiations, and in a letter to Boring he expressed "regret [for] my brother's indiscretion."[36]

For all its personal and professional appeal, a Harvard appointment was not without its drawbacks. To begin with, the university's antiquated disciplinary organization made for an uncertain future with respect to tenure. In 1930, the university had only one tenured position in psychology —and that position had already been filled by the relatively young Boring. If Allport was looking for the long-term security of a tenured appointment, Harvard was not a good bet. Another consideration that crossed Allport's mind was the rather "strenuous" academic atmosphere of the famous Cambridge institution.[37] Despite the relative decline of Harvard psychology since Münsterberg's death in 1916, the department was still regarded as one of the standard bearers of American psychology.[38] To hold his own in this hallowed institution, Allport would have to exert himself to a much greater degree than he would at Dartmouth. "They [Harvard psychologists] are all very hard workers," Allport remarked in a letter to Ada. "I suspect my brain is as good as theirs; but I am not used to such effective application to research."[39]

Scholarly commitment and ability were essential ingredients for the up-and-coming Harvard scholar, but as the example of McDougall made clear, it was also important to cultivate some entrepreneurial savvy. Success involved keeping theoretical categories current and becoming something of an academic personality, as one of Allport's undergraduate psychology instructors Edwin Holt remarked in a 1918 letter:

> From the side of the young instructor the system operates thus; —he is eager to "get on," and so he must become as soon as possible "well-known." He therefore reads immature papers at Christmas meetings of his scientific society, scrambles old notes and threadbare formulae together into a "textbook," palavers with everybody who has the slightest academic influence, and turns himself generally into a personal publicity bureau. All this he substitutes outright for anything resembling the sober and honest pursuit of truth, and for all save the most perfunctory attention to the instruction and guidance of his students. . . . Agreeably to the present level of American intelligence, the young man who has advertised himself most loudly is called upon to the first academic vacancy that occurs. On receiving the call he hastily brushes his hair, waits upon his college president, and blandly presents a cut-throat proposition; of which the impudence is more or less swamped in unctuous verbiage.[40]

Holt added that scholars were routinely using these "familiar hold-up maneuvers" and "a variety of similarly unworthy tricks."[41] Not wishing to participate in these activities, Holt left Harvard for a part-time position at Princeton. The new location and the passage of time did little to diminish his distaste for Harvard's high-stakes academic gamesmanship. In a 1930 letter to Allport, Holt described a Harvard appointment as a "rash venture (to which nothing on earth would tempt me)."[42] Allport was certainly aware of the stratagems that a Harvard appointment would entail, but he was not deterred by these requirements. Indeed, in his correspondence with Boring, Allport exercised the tactical sense that he would need if he were to succeed at his alma mater. In his initial response to Boring, he declined the Harvard offer, citing prior commitments to students at Dartmouth and concerns about salary.[43] However, Allport did indicate his willingness to move the following year at a higher salary. "It would give me great satisfaction to work with you all," he told Boring, "and to cooperate in every way possible with the projects you have initiated for the development of the department."[44] Allport craftily added that Harvard was not the only university interested in his services. "A couple of rather florid offers have come to me within the last few days from the west. The total situation has caused us to deliberate rather intensely."[45]

Allport's stratagem had the desired effect. Not wanting to lose out on a bright young prospect, Boring agreed to Allport's terms. The arrangement was finalized in May 1929, and Allport agreed to commence his duties at Harvard in September 1930. Any doubts that Allport may have had concerning the reception he would receive at Harvard were likely allayed by the enthusiasm with which Boring greeted the news of his decision to return. "I am tremendously happy over this appointment," Boring wrote. "It will give us in 1930 a real department . . . [that] may show some unity as the result of our personal intimacies and discussions within the group."[46]

Over the next few months, the two men maintained a detailed correspondence concerning prospective courses and departmental organization. These issues served as a preliminary test of the efficacy of "personal intimacies" in maintaining departmental unity. Graduate research in social psychology was a notable case in point. The terms of Allport's appointment invested him with authority in the field of social psychology. Boring wrote that "we think of you as coming to uphold social psychology at Harvard [and] as advising us in the courses that ought to be given."[47]

What was not stated in the terms of Allport's appointment was the range of his authority. Allport was especially anxious to know if his social psychology students had to conform to the methodological conventions of experimental psychology. Did every psychology dissertation have to involve experimental procedures and statistical analysis? One might have surmised that the experimentally minded Boring would probably have answered this question in the affirmative. Allport was certainly prepared for this response. He broached the subject tentatively, toward the end of an otherwise uncontroversial letter:

> I have often wondered what attitude prevails regarding a non-experimental doctoral thesis in psychology. I should agree immediately that every problem that can possibly be approached experimentally should be so approached. Now, a number of genuine problems cannot be made accessible to the laboratory method. . . . My question is simply this, should such problems be accepted for a thesis in the department?[48]

Allport need not have been quite so diplomatic with respect to the merits of experimentalism. Boring had assumed from the start that Allport would be interested in supervising nonexperimental investigations. He wrote that he had "taken it for granted that the majority of dissertations that were completed under your primary direction would not be experimental."[49] Allport's tactfully phrased suggestion to the contrary had come as a complete surprise: "Your thought that we might accept only experimental dissertations in social psychology is a leaning over backwards that causes mild astonishment in me."[50]

Boring may have been astonished by Allport's suggestion, but he was also pleased, for it confirmed his earlier assessment as to the amiability of his new recruit. Allport's query made it apparent that he was anxious to approach departmental issues in a spirit of sustained compromise. He clearly wanted to develop what he regarded as appropriate intellectual procedures, but not at the expense of strained relations with the rest of the department. This was just the sort of message that Boring wanted to hear, for he feared that a new social psychologist might bring to the department a hostility to experimentalism that would probably result in an unproductive disunity. With the arrival of such a person, he wrote, "the staff would be split into cliques, each group feeling superior to the other."[51] Allport's conciliatory letters contained no hints of struggle or divisiveness. Boring could have anticipated only due consideration and reasoned difference, and in the years that followed, this was primarily what he got. (See insert, Figure 37)

A "FEMININE" SCIENCE IN A "MASCULINE" SPACE

Allport's appointment at Harvard was an undeniably impressive accomplishment, but it did not completely allay the suspicion that personality was still too fuzzy and sentimental for a "real man of science." As historian Evelyn Fox Keller noted, modern science has been heavily influenced by an identification with masculinity. "For the founding fathers of modern science, the reliance on the language of gender was explicit: They sought a philosophy that deserved to be called 'masculine,' that could be distinguished from its ineffective predecessors by its 'virile' power, its capacity to bind Nature to man's service and make her his slave."[52] As modern science evolved, Keller argued, the language of science and masculinity became intertwined to the point where scientific thought was unquestionably male. To think like a scientist was to think like a man: objective, detached, with an emphasis on "hard" facts. In contrast, unscientific thought was female: emotional, irrational, with an emphasis on sentimentality, intuition, and feeling.

In the psychology department at Harvard, the link between science and masculinity was especially strong. Boring had created a laboratory culture that was reminiscent of the clubby Society of Experimental Psychologists run by his mentor, Edward Titchener. Former Harvard graduate student Jerome Bruner recalled that "the third floor of Emerson [Hall in the 1930s] was as much a club as a workplace." Students were expected to live a "monkish life" of the "eighty hour work week" centered on the laboratory. "We all routinely trotted back to 'the lab' after dinner," Bruner added, "junior faculty included." This cloistered space resounded with a distinctively masculine idiom. Graduate students ate at what they described as the "enlisted men's mess," where they gloried in the rough-and-tumble of "noisy, quarrelsome . . . sandlot seminars." The topics of discussion revolved around animals, bodies, and brains—physical categories consistent with the muscular science of the day. As Bruner recalled, "perception, memory, learning, motivation, neuropsychology, and animal behavior . . . were the specialties of the 'main' department."[53]

The pressure to conform to "manly" ideals was palpable, and as Allport discovered, those found wanting in masculinity became objects of ridicule. In the 1940s, G. C. Homans recalled performing skits at departmental functions where he portrayed Allport "as a bit of an old woman. . . . 'Remember,' I would tell the graduate students, 'Gordon Allport is *not* your mother.'"[54] Such incidents were extreme, but they reflected a pervasive culture of masculinity that shaped the nature of psychological debate at Harvard. Boring's advice to Allport on the subject and method of psychology is a case in point. In one exchange replete with masculine suggestiveness, Boring urged Allport to "avoid ego-psychology" and "*join my club with me*" [italics added]. He told his younger colleague that to deal with language, intuition, and meaning—categories long associated with femininity—was to "drive fast in a fog." The best approach, in Boring's view, was to reduce psychological categories to "conditioned reflexes." "When there is doubt or disagreement, reduce all cases to animal subjects. An animal is an 'other one.' An animal uses only language where the meanings are explicit and known to E [the experimenter]. Generally E has complete control since he has established the meanings of the communicatory terms by conditioning."[55]

Allport was well aware of Harvard Psychology's masculine swagger and gentlemen's club atmosphere. He had confronted this masculine ethic as a graduate student, but emboldened by his German experience, he continued to search for a language and method of selfhood that reflected his own soulful, more feminine worldview.

GRAPHOLOGY

In search of knowledge that was both soulful and scientific, Allport developed a keen interest in graphology. As historian Tamara Thornton noted, graphology—the study of personality or character through handwriting—enjoyed a huge following in the United States in the three decades leading up to World War II.[56] In 1929, a journalist observed that "everyone seems to be interested in [graphology]," a sentiment echoed 6 years later by a graphologist who described handwriting analysis as a "great American fad."[57] Much of the popular fascination with graphology was inspired by the same fear of homogenizing modernity that animated Allport's interest in psychology. The dramatic growth of industrialization and urbanization in the late 19th and early 20th century threatened to rob Americans of their individuality and autonomy. In this increasingly impersonal context, handwriting emerged as a potent symbol of individual uniqueness and personal freedom. According to Thornton, "graphology was uniquely poised to redefine and soothe the troubled selves of early twentieth-century America."[58]

Most American psychologists viewed graphology with suspicion, if not outright scorn. Graphology was considered in the same light as palmistry and phrenology and was therefore unworthy of serious scholarly attention. The topic was largely ignored by psychologists, who confidently cited a single 1919 study by University of Wisconsin psychologists Clark Hull and Robert Montgomery that purported to disprove graphology experimentally. Although psychologists were undoubtedly correct in decrying the excesses of popular graphology, their hostility to handwriting analysis was not a strictly empirical matter. By the 1920s, the practice of graphology had become a predominantly female pursuit, and the majority of members in the American Graphological Society were women. This feminization rendered graphology problematic in a discipline increasingly enamored of the masculine culture of laboratory science.

Reluctant to engage a predominantly female field, Americans psychologists were also largely indifferent to graphology's principal cultural ambition: the preservation and celebration of the unique individual. As noted in chapter 5, scientific psychologists were devoted to "relational individuality"—the measurement of deviations from established norms—and they took a dim view of the solace and inspiration that graphology and other forms of popular psychology provided. Writing in 1926, psychologist Max Freyd spoke critically of "borderline investigators" pedaling a fraudulent "short cut to health, happiness and success."[59] Similar criticisms were heard throughout the 1920s and 1930s, and although these commentaries did little to dampen public enthusiasm, scholarly interest in graphology was effectively curtailed. As A. A. Roback noted in 1939, "[T]he psychologist who espouses the cause of graphology undoubtedly gives hostages to his reputation."[60]

Allport was well aware of the academic prejudice against graphology, and he approached the topic cautiously. "The prevailing attitude toward graphology among American psychologists is one of skepticism and distrust," he noted in 1933. "As a consequence of this point of view very few psychologists in this country have studied its methods or claims seriously." Aware of the risk, but intrigued by the topic, Allport set out to study graphology in all its complexity. His interest in the topic dated back to graduate school—if not before. As a graduate student he read American psychologist June Downey's 1919 book *Graphology and the Psychology of Handwriting*.[61] The topic intrigued him, but like many American psychologists, he was skeptical of the grandiose claims made by popular graphologists. While reading Downey—who was quite measured in her approach to the topic—he sarcastically remarked that he hoped to "discover what demon in my personality produces such hellish script!"[62] Wary of graphology's pseudoscientific reputation within American psychology, the method was not included in his 1922 dissertation on personality traits. However, his postdoctoral study in Germany prompted him to take a closer look at graphology as a topic of serious, scholarly investigation. As historian Trudy Dehue noted, in Germany and the Netherlands graphology gained a measure of academic respectability through its association with the Geisteswissenschaften.[63] Widely respected psychologists such as Ludwig Klages argued that graphology was a holistic method that preserved the individual integrity of personality while revealing its underlying essence, or "real self." As Allport noted, "continental psychologists . . . see in graphic movement the quintessence of expression. It is a 'crystallized' form of gesture, an intricate but accessible prism which reflects many, if not all, of the inner consistencies of personality."[64]

Convinced that graphology represented a way of mastering personality while preserving its spiritual core, Allport promoted the method in American psychology. As a faculty member at Dartmouth and later at Harvard, he endeavored to persuade his skeptical American colleagues that there was more to graphology than outrageous claims and mail-order gimmicks. His first monograph, *Studies in Expressive Movement*, contained a long discussion of graphology, much of which was based on Edwin Powers's master's thesis, which Allport had supervised at Dartmouth College.[65] Insisting that American critics of graphology were ill-informed, Allport carefully explained the distinction between "scientific" graphology and the crass claims of its popular cousin. "Modern graphology," he argued, had evolved from a simplistic matching of "particular signs or details of script . . . to specific traits, abilities or interests." In contrast to the "superficial" method of the field's pioneers, contemporary graphologists tried to "compare the script as a whole and the personality as a whole" using "intuitive impressions of the total form-quality of the script."[66]

To illustrate this idea and bolster graphology's scientific legitimacy, Allport collaborated on a series of experiments to test graphology's ability to ascertain the "form-quality," or pattern of personality. In one experiment, his old Robert College friend Edwin Powers—who was now working on a master's degree—asked 17 professional graphologists to match samples of handwriting with 250-word character sketches that had been undertaken independently by a group of three psychologists. The same experiment was also conducted on a sample of undergraduates and college faculty, and the results were then compared with graphologists' ability to correctly match the handwriting to the character sketch. The results of this experiment and others like it pointed to the existence of a "form-quality" in the writing, but they did not provide the unambiguous support that professional graphologists might have hoped for. "By our criteria," Allport noted, [graphological judgments] are still nearer to chance than to perfection."[67]

Although the results of Allport's experiments undermined the flamboyant claims of popular graphology, they did confirm the existence of an "'inner' personality . . . an essentially stable and constant individual style."[68] It was this individual, holistic self that he wanted to affirm and know, but unfortunately for Allport, such a concern was lost on most of his colleagues. Largely ignorant of the Geisteswissenschaften and suspicious of publicity-seeking charlatans, American psychologists ignored *Studies in Expressive Movement* and its German-inspired fascination with intuitive methods and the form-quality of personality. Sensing the futility of the struggle, Allport gradually abandoned his public campaign to promote graphology within psychology, but his enthusiasm for the topic remained strong. As historian Nicole Barenbaum noted, he continued to promote graphology behind the scenes.[69] His work on graphology remained a point of pride throughout his career, and when asked, some years later, to describe his most significant contribution to psychology, handwriting was among the topics he mentioned:

> I'm not sure which one thing I would point to as a significant contri-
> bution, but I feel that perhaps my early work on expressive behavior
> was somewhat overlooked. I, myself, dropped active research in the
> field, but I still feel that it would be important for us to understand
> how such factors as facial expression, posture, gait, gestures, and *hand-
> writing* can reveal the innermost parts of the personality [italics
> added].[70]

THE EXPERIMENTAL METHOD AND THE STUDY OF VALUES

Aware of psychology's muscular culture, as a junior faculty member, Allport endeavored to give the study of personality a more hard-nosed look. In a 1933 article titled "The Study of Personality by the Experimental Method," he asserted his manly credentials as an experimental psychologist while attempting to preserve the possibility of a more feminine-style, qual-itative psychology.[71] In that paper, Allport presented the experimental method as the royal road to truth in questions of personality. He did argue that "no single method will reveal personality in its entirety," and he main-tained that personality could be illuminated by such notoriously unscien-tific means as "intuition" and by the study of "case-histories and diaries, ratings, biographies, correspondence . . . expressive behavior, drama and fiction."[72] However, Allport insisted that these qualitative approaches amounted to a compromise with the subject matter and were to be used sparingly, only when experimentation proved impossible. "When experi-ment is clearly applicable, and when it can be skillfully employed, it is undoubtedly a method to be preferred above all others."[73]

The problem with Allport's decision to grant imperial status to the experimental method was largely epistemological. One could not salute his proposed hierarchy of methods without simultaneously acknowledging a natural science model of knowledge construction, in which facts are formulated into hypotheses and then tested for their truth. Allport acknowledged as much in his paper. "No matter how entrancing an hypothesis concerning personality may be," he wrote, "it must either submit to some concrete test and be verified, or else it must sooner or later depart to the land of solipsistic fantasies."[74] The problematic aspect of this reasoning becomes clear when one considers the kind of issues that Allport hoped to address: purpose, value, meaning, unity. Could all of these issues be construed in terms of hypothesis testing? Were all of these issues matters of fact that could be "seen" by scientists under experimental conditions or were some matters of interpretation, as Spranger and Dilthey had suggested? Toward the end of the paper, Allport did say that the experimental method "should not be expected to solve every problem nor to make the final pronouncement upon every issue," but the logic of his paper belied this cautionary note.[75] His tough talk about tests made it seem as if everything important that was said about personality was subject to testing in a manner not dissimilar from that of any natural object. Why, then, should anyone wish to bother with substandard methods like understanding? If testing was the criterion of worth in personality psychology, then it was better to spend time refining test technology than to pursue arcane methods that could only deliver a mediocre intellectual return.

The psychometric implications of Allport's argument were borne out in his own work. After he arrived at Harvard, Allport walked a cautious line, carefully blending German ideas with American research methods. Still critical of the American preoccupation with mental testing, he found it impossible to resist what Roback had described as the "tidal wave" of quantification and measurement that had washed over the American personality. With one psychometric test already under his belt, Allport added a second in 1931 when he published *A Study of Values: A Scale for Measuring the Dominant Interests in Personality* with Philip Vernon, a Cambridge PhD who had come to the United States in 1929 on a Rockefeller Fellowship.[76]

The theoretical dimension of the study of values involved a further development of the themes Allport had raised in his paper on the "intuitive method." How was personality to be conceived? What were the best methods for studying personality? What kind of knowledge should a science of the person aim at? In *A Study of Values*, Allport did not depart in any notable way from the theoretical framework he had sketched out earlier. The traditional psychometric approach to personality psychology was criticized for failing to speak to what Allport regarded as the real nature of personality. Measuring traits gave an "incomplete and frequently misleading picture," he wrote. It neglected the "really significant levels of personality," and it failed to explain the relationship between single factors and the "total personality in which they are set."[77] In his paper on the intuitive method, Allport had suggested that the shortcomings of psychometric psychology could be partially offset by adding "understanding" to the discipline's existing repertoire of methods. In *A Study of Values*, he made what was, by American standards, a far less radical proposal.

Allport began by arguing that the position set forth by Symonds, among others (which was to ignore issues of validity in test construction and concentrate only on reliability), was misleading. In his view, the emphasis on reliability seemed to invite a faddish jumping from category to category and test to test. It was hard to imagine how any sustained theory of personality could emerge from such a procedure. Progress in the scientific sense of consolidating and building on existing work could only begin in earnest when scholars "founded" their work on a "definitive set of methodological and theoretical postulates."[78] The theory that Allport proposed to draw on was that of Spranger and the Geisteswissenschaften, but the method was largely in the tradition of American psychometric testing. Allport argued that the psychometric tendency to divide personality into meaningless dimensions could be overcome by shifting the focus from trait measurement to the study of values. The advantage of values stemmed from the position they occupied within personality: Traits were the basic units of personality, but values occupied a higher level. They were the framework into which the traits were organized and from which they derived their meaning. Knowledge of these frameworks was an important step toward knowledge of the personality as a whole.

Spranger had argued that a person's life form, or "real individuality," could be apprehended only by means of understanding. A devoted student of the Geisteswissenschaften, Allport was keenly aware of the limitations of quantitative approaches to personality. However, he was also convinced that Spranger had been too hasty in his dismissal of quantitative scales. In *A Study of Values*, Allport developed a scale to measure the six ideal types conceived by Spranger. What distinguished Allport's scale from other personality measures was its use of relational dimensions—Spranger's value types—to affirm individual uniqueness. This was accomplished by shifting the point of comparison from the group to the individual. Instead of measuring how a person scores on a dimension relative to other individuals, *A Study of Values* asked participants to rank the values in relation to his or her own personality. The resulting profile thus provided a measure of individuality across common dimensions, but because of its self-referencing quality, the test was "strictly personal and individual":

> Your score cannot be compared with anyone else's because the test reflects relative strengths of those values within your own personality. Conceivably, a person whose aesthetic value was the lowest of his six might still be more aesthetic than a person whose highest value was aesthetic because he might have a lot of values or express a lot of value energy.[79]

A psychometric tool to affirm real individuality, the test of values also performed important practical functions. It made a useful teaching aid in psychology courses, and it could help the vocational counselor get a better sense of his client's interests. The test also found its way into a variety of applied settings, including some that Allport had not anticipated. Episcopal bishop Richard Loring began using it in marriage counseling. Years later, Allport recalled that Loring would "counsel no couples nor prepare them for marriage unless they took the test."[80] Personality psychologists took up the test with considerable vigor. Two years after its appearance, Allport and his student Hadley Cantril summarized the findings of seven psychologists who had made academic use of A *Study of Values*.[81]

That the thought of so vigorous a critic of psychometrics as Spranger should itself be converted into a psychometric format was an irony not lost on Allport. In a footnote he pointed out that he and Vernon did not "claim Professor Spranger's patronage. They fear that their work might strike him as a species of the *Amerikanismus* that he has frequently deplored."[82] Allport expressed a similar concern in a 1932 letter to Spranger: "I am quite familiar with your criticism of test methods," he wrote. "Yet I hope that the caution and care with which our test is devised will strike you as an improvement upon previous superficial and ill-considered methods."[83] Spranger was flattered by the attention, and in a brief letter to Allport written 3 years later, he expressed his "gratitude and admiration" of The *Study of Values*. In his public remarks, however, Spranger continued to voice his concerns about the mechanization of subjectivity that psychometrics represented: "For the individual is viewed here in the end as something measurable and graspable in numbers, not as a structured principle of the soul."[84]

Regardless of Spranger's views, Allport's enthusiasm for the *Study* remained relatively constant. Years later, he often pointed with evident satisfaction to the numerous uses of the study, its "astonishing vitality," and its high degree of validity and reliability.[85] However, there was one aspect of A *Study of Values* that did trouble him—its influence on American perceptions of German personality theory. Allport was concerned about American views of German thought and had been since returning from Germany in 1924. The major problem, in his view, was not that American psychologists had a negative view of German psychology, but rather that they did not seem to have any informed opinion. In the United States, the discipline was almost exclusively American in its outlook. The unfortunate outcome was a psychology of rather limited intellectual yield. A 1932 review of Percival Symonds's book *Diagnosing Personality and Conduct* provides a useful summary of Allport's views on the cultural shortsightedness of American psychology. Among other criticisms, Allport argued that the book was "exceedingly limited in scope" because it was "markedly national in its outlook."[86] It contained more than 900 references, but only 5% were to the German sources that Allport found "more sustained, more varied, and more profound" than their American counterparts.[87]

One of the goals Allport set for himself was to combat intellectual ethnocentrism of the sort displayed by Symonds and many other American psychologists. At Harvard, he worked toward this end by requiring his students to develop a "searching acquaintance" with his interpretation of continental, especially German, thought.[88] He told one student that "I regard an acquaintance with German research and theory so far as it concerns personality, quite indispensable to an investigator."[89] A *Study of Values* was a reflection of Allport's belief in the benefits of German theory and an implicit invitation to other American psychologists to explore the pastures of continental thought.[90] What disturbed Allport about the *Study* was the manner in which it was read by his colleagues. Instead of regarding it as a stimulus for further exploration of continental thought, many American personality psychologists appear to have read it as a statement of scientific conquest. All that was good in Dilthey, Spranger, and numerous other German scholars had been translated and distilled down into one neat psychometric package. The irritation this caused Allport is apparent in a later paper, when he wrote dejectedly that "the entire Geisteswissenschaft is known in this country chiefly through an absurd little pencil-and-paper test leading to the inevitable profile."[91]

RELUCTANT PERSONALISM: THE AMBIGUITY OF ALLPORT'S PROFESSIONAL PROJECT

By 1935, a deep ambiguity had emerged in Allport's personality psychology. He clearly believed that American psychometric psychology was incapable of speaking to every issue of importance within the field of personality. Progress in the area of personality required "understanding": a preferably direct, hermeneutic engagement with a concrete personality. Yet as a personality researcher, Allport seemed unwilling to take this step—at least in print. His one published "application" of the intuitive method— *The Locomotive God*—consisted of a brief comment on the possibilities of someone else's analysis, and his two principal research efforts at this time did not involve the intuitive method at all. (The test of ascendance–submission and the study of values were both psychometric tests.) By casting his lot with tests rather than understanding, Allport effectively undermined much of his own criticism. In particular, A *Study of Values* drew attention not to the shortcomings of psychometrics, but to its versatility. The test thus helped pave the way for the psychometric colonization of even more elements of personality.

CASE STUDIES: PROFESSIONAL DILEMMAS AND PERSONAL CONCERNS

Allport's half-hearted advocacy on behalf of the Geisteswissenschaften was a further reflection of the depth of indecision that suffused his approach to personality psychology. Was personality a natural object to be calculated and measured, or was it a unique, soulful quality to be admired and appreciated, but never known in any comprehensive or controllable way? Allport was still unsure of how to answer this question, and his thinking on the topic was further complicated by his feelings of professional inferiority. He continued to experience each public performance as a "strain," and despite disclaimers to the contrary, he continued to worry about his standing vis-à-vis his colleagues.[92] One of the more telling illustrations of Allport's self-consciousness concerned his contribution to the *History of Psychology in Autobiography*.[93] Allport wrote to Boring about his thoughts on the series and his place in it. "Probably because of my ego-involvement (plus an objective interest in how a psychological life history should be written), I have read word for word the whole collection." Allport's willingness to plow diligently through an entire volume of biographical information about other psychologists may be taken as an indication of his thoroughness as a scholar, but it also represents a measure of the depth of his concern about his public profile. His anxiety in this regard is particularly evident toward the end of the letter, when Allport compares his self-portrayal to the others: "I think Carl Rogers comes through most clearly—no doubt because of his long practice in disclosing himself to his clients. By comparison I find myself rigid and prosaic."[94]

One of the outcomes of the tension between Allport's spiritual commitment to "pure individuality" and his considerable self-consciousness was an ambivalent embrace of the Geisteswissenschaften. On the one hand, the reverence for the person that informed the work of Stern and Spranger appealed strongly to so personally minded a psychologist. On the other hand, the Geisteswissenschaft also brought with it a demand for detailed case studies—a kind of intellectual performance that had one distinct disadvantage for a self-conscious person like Allport. Case studies provided little in the way of methodological and statistical armor. The psychologist had to rely primarily on the strength of his literary skill and the depth of his clinical insight. The mystique of science could be invoked by the use of technical jargon, but generally the personal nature of the enterprise lessened the degree to which the project could be carried along by the authority of science. The relative absence of a scientific apparatus gave the case study an unsettling transparency with regard to the investigator. A poor performance could not be shielded by banks of statistics and graphs. In the case study, the investigator's forms of expression, points of emphasis, and analytic ability were on display for all to see.

The kind of performance demanded by a case study created a dilemma for Allport. He was clearly attracted to personal forms of knowledge, but in order to proceed with such a program he had to involve himself in a much greater degree of intellectual risk than was the case with psychometrically oriented personality psychology. The case study method would require him to put his reputation for being a "master of the science of personality traits" to the test in an unambiguous way.[95] Allport was well aware of the professional risk involved in applying his theoretical knowledge to a specific case. "Psychologists are on safe ground so long as they talk in abstractions about personality-in-general" he wrote. "Their real test comes when they attempt to explain . . . a single concrete life."[96] In the 1930s, Allport was inspired enough to take that test, and he began collecting materials on two individuals—Jenny Masterson and Marion Taylor—with a view to writing psychological case studies.[97] As Barenbaum noted, Allport also held seminars on life histories and helped devise a list of "rules and criteria for the writing of scientific case studies."[98] Despite his ongoing interest in case study methodology, Allport was more comfortable with the *idea* of the case study than its actual implementation. Throughout his career, he only ever published one case study—*Letters From Jenny*—a book that did not appear until 1965, 2 years before his death.[99] Even in this book, however, Allport seems uncomfortable with the transparency of the project. "In reflecting on the case of Jenny," he remarked in the book's preface, "I find myself wishing that I could take refuge in vague generalizations."[100]

CODES OF PROPRIETY: INSTITUTIONAL PRESSURES AND METHODOLOGICAL POSITIONS

The ambiguity that ran through Allport's work in the 1930s was as much an institutional issue as it was a personal matter. In the 1930s, Harvard psychology was itself characterized by a deep ambiguity over issues of method and subject matter. Ostensibly, Harvard was committed to maintaining two kinds of psychology—natural science–based psychology and a philosophically oriented, qualitative psychology. Boring's early letters to Allport clearly specified his support for just this sort of arrangement, but when Allport arrived back at Harvard in September 1930, he quickly discovered that among most of the faculty and students, support for qualitative psychology was grudging, at best, despite his determined efforts at rebranding personality as an experimental category. The "real" methods of psychology involved experimentation and measurement, and the "real" subject matter of psychology consisted of manly topics that could fit into an experimental format. Allport's own student Jerome Bruner recalled that the "dominant tone at Harvard did not come from the Allport-Murray wing, but from 'experimental psychology.'"[101]

Allport was thus obliged to function in a departmental context that placed relatively little value on the integrity of the category that he wished to cultivate—personality—or on the method that he wished to consider—understanding. Three years after his return to Harvard, Allport accurately surmised, "I am the departmental mystic."[102] These circumstances invited one of three forms of engagement. Allport could have simply abandoned the "phenomenological attitude" by accepting Boring's offer of "club" membership. The respect of Boring and the boisterous crowd in the "enlisted men's mess" may have appealed to Allport, but a straightforward abandonment of the phenomenological attitude was out of the question. A sudden embrace of logical positivism would have amounted to a repudiation of 10 years of work and a significant reconstruction of his "enchanted" worldview. Instead of capitulation, Allport could have cultivated a position of splendid isolation at Harvard. Laboratory luncheons and departmental colloquia could have been avoided; intellectual and emotional support could have been supplied by like-minded colleagues at other institutions. However, intellectual and emotional support were not the only issues for a young academic to consider. Job security and promotions also entered into the equation. Like most academics, Allport was anxious to get tenured, and he hoped one day to win a promotion to full professor. Professional success of this sort requires the recognition and respect of colleagues at the institution in question. A policy of isolation does little to encourage either one of these perceptions.

The difficulties inherent in both these positions led Allport to a third option. It was more complicated than the other two, but it was potentially more rewarding. Allport attempted to introduce into the intellectual worldview of logical positivism the categories and assumptions of phenomenology. "I should like a conceptual system that would admit both the evidence of experience and an hypothesis in behavioral terms."[103] The advantages of this approach were professional and personal. It enabled Allport to cultivate a sense of affinity with his more positivistically minded colleagues at Harvard without abandoning those categories and approaches to which he attached so much significance.

Henry Murray and the Harvard Psychological Clinic

The institutional pressures shaping Allport's professional posture come more fully into view when considered in relation to Henry Murray. Murray was Allport's principal intellectual ally in the psychology department at Harvard. A physician from a prominent New England family, his research interests centered largely on clinical psychology, Jungian theory, and personality psychology. He approached all of these subjects with an infectious measure of creativity and energy. Students at the graduate and undergraduate level flocked to his classes. An article in the *Harvard Crimson* summarized the views of many students when they described Murray as "one of the best lecturers, stimulating to work with, a coming man."[104] Despite—or perhaps because of—his popularity with students, Murray's departmental colleagues remained unsure of his value. An issue of concern to both Allport and Boring was Murray's rhetorical style. Unlike Allport, Murray lacked—or at least chose not to exercise—discretion in academic matters. A devoted Jungian, he would speak and in some cases write about his views on American psychology in a forthright, almost mocking manner that infuriated his colleagues in mainstream psychology.[105] His 1935 article "Psychology and the University" was in this respect quite typical. Murray argued that psychology was too devoted to esoteric intellectual puzzles and methods to be of much help in understanding people. "Academic psychology has contributed practically nothing to the knowledge of human nature" he wrote.[106] Murray included all the subdisciplines of psychology in his attack, but he targeted personality psychology for special criticism:

> There has arisen a heterogeneous group of workers bent on attacking personality—and a real attack it has proved to be. Armed with questionnaires, rating scales, pop-guns, mazes, peg-boards and numberless other mechanical contraptions, the testers have borne down on their subjects—so heavily, in fact, that the souls of their subjects have been forced to shelter. Hence, when one comes to examine the final results, arrived at by the most approved statistical methods, one discovers nothing of importance.[107]

Caustic and far-reaching, Murray's comments about ends and means were quite unlike the diplomatically phrased critiques of personality psychology that Allport had published. Murray's article also possessed a witty, ad hominem dimension that Allport seldom exercised. Murray suggested that personality psychology was made up largely of insensitive, unimaginative pedants. "One is somewhat disquieted by the once-born, unripe confidence, the peculiar callousness of these testers—men who talk as though they had never been sensitized by a moving grief or joy."[108]

Comments like these may have endeared Murray to like-minded students, but they garnered him little support in a psychology department whose dominant tone was set by orthodox experimentalists.[109] Murray's relative isolation became a matter of grave concern in 1936 to 1937, when his Harvard contract came up for renewal.[110] It was his third 3-year contract; the previous two had been renewed with relatively little fuss. In 1936, however, circumstances were not what they had been 3 years earlier. To begin with, the university had a new president: James B. Conant had taken over from A. Lawrence Lowell in 1933. Conant wanted to implement an ambitious program to modernize many of Harvard's administrative structures and policies. One of his first changes was the introduction of new standards for determining faculty promotion. The "personal intimacies" that Boring had spoken of in his letter to Allport would no longer be the principal criterion. Productivity, as measured by research publications and success in obtaining outside funding, was the new benchmark. Conant's program for change included special provisions for psychology. Unlike his predecessor, Conant had a keen interest in the discipline. Boring recalled the new president telling him that "the day of the physical sciences was passing and the day of psychology dawning."[111] Conant wanted to ensure that Harvard was a big part of the new psychological age. At the suggestion of Boring, he separated philosophy and psychology into two departments. He then appointed an ad hoc committee to find "the best psychologist in the world to elect to a chair at Harvard."[112] The committee selected Karl Lashley, and with the generous funds made available by Conant, they were able to lure him to Cambridge from the University of Chicago.

With these moves, the intellectual tenor within the psychology department underwent a significant shift. Productivity became much more of an issue than it had before, and perhaps more important, the nature of that productivity was called into question. What exactly was good scholarship in psychology? Whose standards were to be used in evaluating contributions in fields as diverse as personality psychology, abnormal psychology, psychophysics, and neuropsychology? The "best psychologist in the world" had clear answers to these questions and a coterie of people to support him. In Lashley's view, psychological science involved experimentation, strictly controlled procedures, and statistical analysis. Research that fell outside this tradition could be insightful, even helpful, but it was not scientific and thus should not be included in the Department of Psychology.

Lashley applied his scientific standards with oppressive consistency. Allport and even the psychophysically minded Boring were both judged wanting in scientific rigor. In a letter to Allport, Boring quipped that "Lashley thinks of me as just a better kind of philosophizing psychologist than most of the verbalists."[113] It was at this point that the strategic advantages of Allport's moderate position were most fully realized: The psychometric components of his work had conferred to him a scientific charter. Allport's scientific status was formally recognized in 1937, when he was notified by James McKeen Cattell that he was "among the 250 who have been added to the list of 1000 leading American workers in science."[114] Lashley might complain about "verbalizing" tendencies in Allport's work, but he would have to use an extraordinarily narrow definition of science to dismiss Allport altogether. Allport's standing as a scientist put him in a position to comment critically on existing forms of scientific practice and, in the case of Murray, to defend scholars who departed from the prevailing standards of scientific orthodoxy.

Allport needed all the scientific capital he had accumulated in order to safeguard Murray and the Harvard Psychological Clinic. In Lashley's view, Murray represented an egregious breach of scientific protocol. Murray's presence in a scientific department was simply intolerable—he would have to go. Lashley's stated objections centered on the kind of psychology Murray was undertaking in the clinic: psychoanalytically informed case studies and theoretical discussions. In Lashley's view, both were of dubious scientific value. Psychoanalytic case studies lacked scientific precision, which for Lashley involved "statistical tests for reliability." Theoretical papers had value in certain fields, under certain circumstances, but Lashley saw little that was credible in Murray's work. "In the field of abnormal psychology we already have some tons of conflicting theoretical papers," Lashley wrote, "and I cannot find that Murray has made any significant addition to these." In a letter to President Conant, Lashley concluded that Murray was a representative of the "older humanistic and philosophical psychology" and therefore constituted an impediment to the "attempt to evolve a more exact science through an objective and biological approach."[115]

With a background in chemistry, President Conant felt an affinity for Lashley and his intellectual project.[116] He took Lashley's criticisms seriously enough to organize a special committee consisting of Allport, Boring, Lashley, and three others from outside the department to look into Murray's relationship to the university. Allport quickly developed into Murray's main defender.[117] He solicited letters of support for Murray from psychologists around the country in addition to writing a series of carefully argued letters of support himself. The vigor with which Allport defended Murray was not based on an uncritical enthusiasm for Murray as a person, nor on his work as a personality psychologist. Murray's indifference to professional opinion offended Allport's scholarly sensibilities, as did the clinician's "rather brusque opposition to academic psychology."[118] Nevertheless, Allport had a sufficiently high regard for Murray's intellectual abilities, clinical contributions, and pedagogical skills that he was prepared to look past these shortcomings. What he saw was a psychologist who possessed an originality and interdisciplinary reach that was unrivaled at Harvard. "I should be utterly desolate if you were to leave," Allport told Murray. "Where else is the human mind adequately represented? Certainly not in the department of psychology at Harvard."[119] Allport told Boring that he regarded the clinic "as the most significant work in the sense of pathfinding and originality that our department has yet produced." As an interdisciplinary institute, Murray's clinic was the "most successful single achievement . . . among American institutions"[120] and a "much needed antidote to the prevailing barbarism of mental tests and statistical psychology."[121]

Allport's confidence in Murray was genuine, but his support for Murray's clinic was not without a degree of self-interest. Murray's dismissal from Harvard for conducting what Lashley regarded as "bad science" would have had an immediate, highly negative impact on Allport's own scholarly investigations. "Unscientific" avenues that interested Allport—understanding, case studies, and personal documents—may well have been closed off. Moreover, if Murray were ousted, Allport could have found himself on the receiving end of another Lashley-led campaign to purify the department of unscientific thought. At a minimum, Allport's academic standing at Harvard would have been severely weakened. Presumably, the consequences would have been seen in a diminished ability to secure promotions, research space, and graduate students.

If Allport wished to continue his present scholarly course, he needed some signal from the administration that the humanistic tradition at Harvard would not be abolished. For Allport, the handling of Murray's contract was part of that signal. A renewal of the contract would indicate a renewal of Harvard's commitment to humanistic approaches to psychology. Murray's dismissal would not necessarily mean the end of humanistic psychology at Harvard, but it would serve as an invitation for Allport to at least consider the possibility of leaving Harvard for friendlier intellectual climes. This prospect held little appeal for Allport, but it was, he recognized, inevitable if the scholarly winds at Harvard were to take a decidedly biological turn. The danger from Lashley was real enough for Allport to actually begin looking for another academic position. He did not have to look far. President Wallace Atwood of Clark University placed an attractive offer in front of Allport, attractive enough for him to travel to Worcester, Massachusetts, for direct negotiations. Atwood offered Allport the chairmanship of psychology and a large say in filling several new faculty positions. The president also promised to shift the bulk of the department's resources from physiological psychology toward personality and developmental psychology. In view of the intellectual climate at Harvard, Atwood's offer had a certain appeal. Allport told Boring that the new position would give him a "sense of freedom from suspicion [and] old-fogeyism" at the same time that it gave him a "relatively cloistered life where being even chairman would presumably be lighter than the present administrative strain at Harvard."[122]

Had President Conant decided to steer Harvard psychology in the biological direction that Lashley suggested, Allport would have almost certainly accepted Atwood's generous offer. However, Conant decided to follow the advice of Allport, rather than Lashley, on the question of what constituted good psychology. Allport was given assurances through Boring that the humanistic tradition at Harvard would be maintained for some time to come. As an up-and-coming representative of that tradition, Allport was also assured that his own future at Harvard would be a promising one if he were to stay. He had been promoted to associate professor in September 1936, and Boring told him, "you are clearly slated to go right through the upper levels at Harvard, the only argument being as to whether you will go as fast as you might wish."[123] Buoyed by these assurances, Allport decided to reject the Clark offer before a decision about Murray's future had been reached. "The final deciding factor," he told Boring, "was your letter . . . in which you tell me of the President's interest in keeping a balanced Department. This official attitude satisfies me whatever ultimate decision is reached."[124] Any doubts Allport may have retained about the president's commitment to "balance" in psychology were dispelled a few weeks later, when Murray's contract was renewed. Later that year, Allport's position was further strengthened when he joined Lashley and Boring as a tenured member of the faculty.[125] (See insert, Figure 38.)

Murray's contract negotiations intensified previously existing divisions in the department. When Conant made his final decision in favor of Murray, Boring did his best to try and bridge the department's two main intellectual communities. In September 1937, Boring announced that he would "continue lunching in the Laboratory this winter" and hoped that the rest of the department would join him. "The group that lunches together gets to understand each other very well indeed," he wrote in a letter to Allport. "If they disagree on psychological matters, they generally know why. They talk over lab affairs and generally stand together, because they have reasoned things out."[126] Boring was particularly anxious to have Allport dine with him. "That would make the Department unitary," he explained, "and [it] would make the luncheon group include the whole."[127]

Allport understood the intellectual and institutional significance of Boring's luncheons, and in previous years he had attended regularly. However, the often bitter negotiations surrounding Murray's appointment had shaken whatever faith Allport had in Boring's commitment to unity. The department seemed to be moving in precisely the opposite direction, and in the years to come, he began to wonder whether a formal division of the psychology department might not be the best thing for all concerned. In the short term, however, Allport handled the issue with characteristic prudence. In response to Boring's invitation, he graciously noted that "the laboratory lunch appeals to me personally as much on principle,"[128] but he told Boring that he would not be able to attend regularly because his "habits of work are somewhat contrary": "I transact much of my professional (student and inter-departmental) business at lunch," he noted tersely.[129] Allport may have been telling the truth about his "habits of work," but his unwillingness to try and change these habits speaks of an indifference to Boring's unificationist project.

CONCLUSION

In 1920s and 1930s America, personality was a language of mediation. Combining past and present, masculine and feminine, sacred and secular, the category's vast ambiguity provided welcome shelter for the uncertainties of the new and self-consciously modern age. As a young student, Allport took personal comfort in personality's palatial uncertainty, and as his career unfolded he discovered the professional utility of ambiguous scientific language. As a personality psychologist, Allport learned that his identity allowed him to be many things to many different audiences. To some, the language of personality signaled science, the body, measurement, and all that was modern and right about academic psychology. To others, personality spoke of time-honored truths, personal freedom, spirituality, and a respect for individual human dignity and subjectivity. By carefully balancing these themes in his writing and reflecting them in his personal interactions with fellow psychologists, Allport emerged as the candidate of choice for one of the most prestigious appointments in all of American psychology: a tenure-track professorship at Harvard.

Embodying the contradictions of personality, Allport struggled to build a coherent academic structure out of the unstable discursive material he had embraced. His antimodernist commitments pointed to a spiritual conclusion: Personality could not be calculated or measured in any scientific sense. The meaning and significance of personality could only be glimpsed through an all-too-human process of intuitive understanding. The challenge for Allport was how to reconcile his antimodernist ambition with the professional imperatives of a discipline enamored of the imagery of measurement, mechanism, modernity, and control. Too strident an embrace of German-inspired spiritual psychology would alienate his peers and undermine his credibility. However, by continuing his psychometric work and by extending its focus into the study of values, Allport ran the risk of expediting the same process that he wanted to oppose: the dismemberment and disenchantment of the self. As an untenured faculty member at Harvard, Allport found it difficult to reconcile all the conflicting elements at play. Bouncing between intuition and measurement, and modern and premodern, he remained as professionally undefinable as the category he championed. It was a loose and philosophically unstable position, but it served him well professionally and enabled him to effectively bridge the scholarly antagonisms that plagued psychology both at Harvard and across the discipline as a whole.

9

PERSONALITY AND SOCIAL CRISIS
(1937–1938)

Why is it that in our times, when Western culture is sadly disorganized,
our personalities are not correspondingly disorganized?

—Gordon Allport, 1937[1]

He gives power to the faint,
and strengthens the powerless.
Even youths will faint and be weary,
and the young will fall exhausted;
but those who wait for the LORD
shall renew their strength,
they shall mount up with wings like eagles,
they shall run and not be weary,
they shall walk and not faint.

—Isaiah 40:29–31

Allport's professional success as a personality psychologist occurred
against the backdrop of great economic and political turbulence. The year
1937 was the seventh year of a severe depression that had crippled the
nation's economy. Between 1929 and 1933, a total of 100,000 businesses
failed, corporate profits fell from $10 billion to $1 billion, and the gross
national product was cut in half. By 1933, a total of 13 million workers
were unemployed, and millions more were underemployed, taking whatever
occasional work they could find.[2] President Roosevelt's New Deal of 1933
brought some measure of relief, but not nearly enough to restore pre-
Depression levels of employment. In 1937, the country was still experiencing great economic hardship.

Most ordinary Americans had reacted to economic downturn with
resignation. There were no mass uprisings and, given the gravity of the
situation, relatively few protests. Most people simply tried to ride out the
hard times as best they could. One of the most notable exceptions to this
trend was the intellectual community. The famous literary critic Edmund
Wilson expressed the sentiment of many writers and academics when he
wrote that "these years were not depressing but stimulating. One couldn't
help being exhilarated at the collapse of that stupid, gigantic fraud. It gave
us a sense of freedom; and it gave us a sense of power to find ourselves
carrying on while the bankers, for a change, were taking a beating."[3]

Wilson and many like-minded intellectuals were not content to simply wait for things to get better, so they took to searching for the causes of the Depression and for a workable solution. This search brought them within sight of many of the incongruities of the capitalist system, such as widespread hunger despite an adequate supply of food and mass unemployment despite an abundance of natural resources and technology. By the end of 1932, these sorts of contradictions and the ineffectual responses of the politicians led most intellectuals to a sense of disillusionment with the status quo and a greater willingness to experiment with radical philosophies and political action. The journalist and social critic Lincoln Steffens wrote in 1932 that "we liberals, the world over have had our day, we and our liberal principles, practices and promises." The future, Steffens added, lay with a different social philosophy: "[A]ll roads in our day lead to Moscow."[4]

By the mid-1930s, many psychologists had come to agree with Steffens's analysis. The economic downturn had been hard on psychology, especially on its younger members. Most had come out of graduate programs in the late 1920s or early 1930s only to find themselves unemployed or, if they were lucky, with temporary work.[5] Some saw in radical politics a solution to their own employment problems. For others, the turn to radicalism had a significance far deeper than their own personal employment status. The Depression signaled the final and conclusive breakdown of a society whose material advancements had far outstripped its cultural and psychological resources. The only way forward was to follow the reasoning of John Dewey, who wrote that "substantial bettering of social relations waits upon the growth of a scientific social psychology."[6] To get America out of its economic and social logjam, psychologists needed to apply themselves vigorously to social questions. Because conventional political parties seemed unwilling to consider the idea of using social science to any great length, many psychologists felt that their efforts would be better spent working with the radical parties. Among those psychologists who gravitated toward left-wing parties were Edward Tolman, David Krech, Goodwin Watson, George Hartmann, and Ross Stagner.[7]

The Depression may have radicalized many younger psychologists, but for most of the older, established figures, it served only to confirm suspicions born in the 1920s that psychology was expanding too rapidly into areas that had not yet been properly investigated. The solution to the unemployment problem posed by the Depression was not to lobby for the expansion of psychological services, as the radicals proposed. The field's future would be better served by raising academic standards in psychology in order to cut the production of PhD candidates. Although the APA assembled a committee in 1932 for this purpose, no changes were actually implemented. Nevertheless, most older members of the profession continued to resist the explicit connection between psychology and politics that the younger members were trying to make.

SCIENCE, POLITICS, AND PERSONALITY

Allport joined the liberal trend to the left, and he voted for Norman Thomas, the Socialist Party presidential candidate in the 1932 and the 1936 presidential elections.[8] However, his experience in Weimar Germany had made him wary of political discourse that placed the interest of the state above that of the person. His politics was a soft socialism, and unlike many of his left-leaning colleagues, he saw no romance in the Soviet experiment, which he dismissed for its "oversimplified Marxist dogma."[9]

While reassessing the American political landscape, Allport also took stock of his own scholarly project. In the early 1920s, he had envisioned personality as a discourse of correlation that would link psychology and ethics, mind and body, science and religion, theory and application. As the 1920s unfolded, Allport continued to trade off the ambiguity of personality, but in his published work he actively repudiated any correlational intent. Distinguishing research from application and facts from values, Allport insisted that personality was a pure, scientific category that operated above the crush of daily circumstance: It would be a "mistake . . . to confuse *research* in personality with the *ulterior* interests of character education, social reform, and industrial exploitation" [italics added].[10]

Enamored of the posture of the natural scientist and mindful of the scientific fragility of his own field of research, Allport crafted his early writings to distance personality from social work, character, and anything else that hinted of Victorian moralism and the female reform tradition. He insisted that personality psychologists were impartial gatherers of facts and that their business was to inform people about what the psychological world *is*. Matters of value—what the psychological world *ought* to be like—were the province of other professions, such as social ethics, theology and, possibly, politics. Allport summarized his official position in a 1926 book review of Knight Dunlap's *Social Psychology*. Dunlap had called for a "marshaling of facts and principles of scientific psychology into new formations, directed towards a scientific purpose, namely, their application to social problems."[11] It was an ambition that closely resembled Allport's own private intention of "correlating psychology and social ethics," but in print, he insisted on policing the divide between "factual" science and normative discourse:

> Now, some day, but probably not until the issue is publicly raised, social psychologists will realize that they are not, qua psychologists, entitled to dictate the protocols of social reform. . . . Social psychology is not a normative science; it is descriptive or explanatory . . . but it cannot without extending its boundaries to include social ethics tell what social conduct *ought* to be.[12]

The march of events during the Depression prompted Allport to reassess his scholarly commitments and to rethink the distinctions that he had defended so hawkishly. By the end of the 1930s, he not only supported the active participation of psychology in social reform initiatives but had become one of applied psychology's leading spokespersons. His more notable efforts in this regard included a 1935 study, *The Psychology of Radio*,[13] and his work to establish the Society for the Psychological Study of Social Issues (SPSSI)—a scholarly organization designed to lend scientific support for "all progressive action that promises to aid in the preservation and creation of human values."[14] Allport's commitment to applied psychology was undeniable, but his approach to personality remained largely unaffected by the upheavals of the Depression. He carefully compartmentalized his politically informed, applied work in social psychology with his study of personality. "In my thinking there is a sharp distinction between personality and social psychology," he argued. Personality referred to the "biophysical or biopsychical structure," and social psychology was "everything else."[15]

Insisting on the separation of the personal and the social, Allport watched uneasily as many of his colleagues reexamined their commitment to an ethos that had pervaded the discipline from the beginning: individualism. Historically, American psychologists had structured their investigations around the assumptions of the utilitarian individualism that had long dominated American culture.[16] Within this ideological framework, a sharp dichotomy was drawn between the individual and society. The individual was of primary importance and was seen as a self-determining agent whose position in the community was almost entirely a function of his or her ability to withstand the "emery wheel of competition."[17] For the utilitarian individualists, society existed only as an abstraction. It was the term given to individuals living or working together for some particular purpose. It had no organic life of its own and did not, therefore, exist independently of the individuals who formed it.[18]

Allport's brother Floyd was perhaps the most outspoken exponent of utilitarian individualism in American psychology. Beginning in 1919 and continuing throughout the 1920s, Floyd repeatedly criticized social scientists who had committed what he called the "fallacy of the group."[19] The fallacy involved assigning explanatory significance to group membership. This was a mistake, in Floyd's view, because "the group is not an elementary fact."[20] Groups were simply amalgams of individuals who were temporarily acting in a similar, but by no means identical, fashion. "Nationality, Free-Masonry, Catholicism, and the like are not group minds expressed in the individual members of these bodies," Floyd wrote. "They are sets of ideals, thoughts, and habits repeated in each individual mind and existing only in those minds."[21] Floyd thus urged social scientists to look past the group when theorizing and focus instead on the "true locus of cause and effect, namely, the behavior mechanism of the individual."[22] Borrowing an old adage, he suggested that if psychologists were to "take care of the individuals, the groups will take care of themselves."[23]

Floyd's counsel had a certain plausibility in the relatively stable economic conditions of the 1920s. However, the uncertainties generated by the Great Depression and the rise of Nazism prompted a number of psychologists to reevaluate the utilitarian individualism on which their theories rested. Many came to the conclusion that the premise of the self-directing, self-sustaining individual could no longer be maintained in an economic and geopolitical context of such palpably social dimensions. The rapid industrialization and urbanization of American society had rendered the 19th-century model of individualism obsolete. A new outlook was needed, one that was attuned to the ever increasing complexities of modern American life. Of those psychologists who arrived at this conclusion, a few turned to communism for answers, but most embraced some version of the liberalism of John Dewey (1859–1952).[24] Dewey's proposal was not to abolish the historic American reverence for the individual; the value of individual was, in fact, the central plank in his social and intellectual program. His main goal, he wrote in 1935, was "the liberation of individuals so that realization of their capacities may be the law of their life."[25] What distinguished Dewey's individualism from the more familiar utilitarian individualism was the link he drew between culture, equality, and individual freedom. Dewey argued that a society of vigorous, free-thinking individuals was not an inevitable by-product of human nature. It was, in fact, the "product of definite social relationships and publicly acknowledged functions."[26] Dewey's position made the free-thinking individual a product, as opposed to a cause, of a vigorous, healthy society. His analysis drew attention to the plasticity of human nature and the close relationship between culture and personality.

Dewey's ideas had their biggest impact in psychology by way of anthropology. In the late 1920s and early 1930s, detailed investigations of tribal societies by anthropologists such as Ruth Benedict, Margaret Mead, and Bronislaw Malinowski instantiated Dewey's views about the cultural embeddedness of human nature.[27] For instance, Margaret Mead argued that her famous South Sea studies showed that "cultural rhythms are stronger and more compelling than the physiological rhythms which they overlay and distort [and] that the failure to satisfy an artificial, culturally stimulated need . . . may produce more unhappiness and frustration . . . than the most rigorous cultural curtailment of the physiological demands of sex or hunger."[28] Mead's study and others like it were often called studies in "culture and personality," and in the mid to late 1930s, they attracted a great deal of interest among psychologists.[29] Their investigations encouraged American psychologists to reverse the scholarly priorities proposed by Floyd Allport: Psychologists interested in human nature should begin their inquiries with a consideration of the social and economic conditions in which individuals must function. Then, and only then, would they be in a position to offer satisfactory explanations of the thought and behavior of particular individuals.

Ross Stagner's work is a good example of the kind of socially sensitive, Deweyan psychology that was inspired by the Depression. A personality psychologist with a PhD from the University of Wisconsin, Stagner received his degree in 1932 and, like many Depression-era graduates, had a difficult time securing a teaching position.[30] "My situation in 1934 was desperate," Stagner recalled. "After earning a Ph.D. . . . I had one year of postdoctoral fellowship and one year of virtually complete unemployment."[31] Stagner's financial situation improved in 1935, when he obtained a full-time academic appointment at the University of Akron. Two years later, he published the book that was for a short time the primary alternative to Allport's own personality text: the *Psychology of Personality*.[32] Like most studies on personality, Stagner's book focused on the individual. Sociological statements of a general nature—"mass production lowers workers to the status of machines"—had "no real place in the psychology of personality," he wrote. The "object of our study is a single human being."[33]

Stagner may have been individualistic, but it was in a Deweyan rather than a utilitarian sense. For Stagner, the individual personality was embedded in a cultural milieu and could only be understood through reference to the cultural context. "Personality is a social product," he wrote. The "ideas, attitudes, traits, desires, motives and urges of the individual are intimately related to and perhaps completely determined by the social environment in which he develops."[34] In keeping with this argument, Stagner devoted approximately half of his text to the "social determinants" of personality. His text included chapters on the family, play and recreation relationships, economic considerations, and social values. Stagner also included a chapter on the cultural relativity of human nature by Abraham Maslow (1908–1970).[35] Like Stagner, Maslow took a Deweyan position with respect to the individual. He argued that it was necessary and useful to make a distinction between the individual and society. Unfortunately for Maslow, what had begun as a "heuristic necessity" had since "degenerated into a sharp dichotomy."[36] Psychologists made a sharp separation between the individual and society and were thus unable to see a person "in his true light as essentially a social, cultural creature."[37] For psychology to progress, Maslow argued, "it must be understood very clearly that the individual is always a member of a cultural group, and that he shares with this cultural group its ways of perceiving, its modes of behaving, its affective reactions, its ethical reactions and all its habitual ways of reacting."[38]

The cultural approach to personality proposed by Stagner and Maslow represented a significant departure from the model that Allport had been outlining since the early 1920s—a fact not lost on Allport himself. Skimming through Stagner's book at the 1937 APA meeting, Allport observed that it was "*entirely* different" from his own approach.[39] Although Allport had never denied the existence of a significant relationship between personality and culture, he had always insisted that personality had a substantive existence of its own and could therefore be profitably studied independently of culture. In his 1930 review of the personality literature, he had actually suggested that cultural treatments of personality were misdirected: "By making the cultural group the principal avenue, and by exploring the avenue rather than the destination, the sociologist is in reality diverting attention from personality to its mere cultural setting."[40]

Mindful of the political and economic upheavals of the 1930s, Allport remained wary of any formulation that appeared to minimize personal freedom and individual distinctiveness. In his mind, the brutality of fascism and the inhumanity of the Depression pointed to the need to reaffirm the emancipation of the individual and the incalculable value of each person. It was with these concerns in mind that Allport published what is arguably his most famous book, *Personality: A Psychological Interpretation.*[41] An artful combination of scientific ambition and antimodernist angst, the book boldly asserted the themes of personal freedom, transcendence, and uniqueness that Allport had been stressing since the early 1920s. In the preface, Allport wrote that "the beginnings of this book lay in certain researches I undertook seventeen years ago. Ever since that time it has been in the process of development and completion."[42] The link between Allport's earlier work and his orientation in *Personality* was particularly apparent on the issue of culture. In the preface of *Personality*, Allport was again quick to admit that "personality is fashioned to a large extent through the impact of culture upon the individual."[43] However, he continued to insist that personality could be meaningfully studied apart from specific social contexts. In the book's preface, he stated that the "interest of psychology is not in the factors *shaping* personality," but "rather in personality *itself* as a developing structure."[44] Allport chose to conclude *Personality* on a similar note. In a famous passage, he wrote:

> Thus there are many ways to study man psychologically. Yet to study him most fully is to take him as an individual. He is more than a bundle of habits; more than . . . a citizen of the state, and more than a mere incident in the gigantic movements of mankind. He transcends them all. The individual, striving ever for his own integrity, has existed under many forms of social life—forms as varied as the nomadic, feudal, and capitalistic. He struggles on even under oppression always hoping and planning for a more perfect democracy where the dignity and growth of each personality will be prized above all else."[45]

The layout of *Personality* was consistent with this notion of a timeless, cultureless spirit or personality. Allport devoted more than 100 pages to an analysis of the "structure of personality." Culture, economics, politics, and the various other social factors that Stagner had devoted so much attention to were not considered at all.

Disavowing the reductionistic excesses of positivist psychology, Allport was quite willing to turn the rhetorical conventions of natural science to his advantage. In explaining the validity of his psychological conception of personality, he carefully translated his discussion into a flowchart of meanings consisting of 50 boxes and cross-connecting lines. As sociologist Bruno Latour noted, scientists make frequent use of charts and graphs in an effort to fortify their claims.[46] Allport's flowchart lent scientific credence to his narrative. The chart transformed a literary review of meaning into a scientific object that could be scrutinized. Moreover, the flowchart provided a kind of scientific confirmation of Allport's claim to authority over personality. Sociological, juristic, popular, and theological conceptions of the topic were portrayed as precursors or sideshows to the ultimate psychological understanding. (See insert, Figure 39.)

In the politically charged climate of the 1930s, Allport's disregard of the social seemed to signal either political conservatism or social ignorance. In his review of *Personality*, Ross Stagner commented sharply on Allport's apparent indifference to the social: "One searches the book in vain for explicit treatment of particular kinds of attitudes and values, for the relation of the individual to social progress, [and] for the evidence of impact of culture change on personality organization."[47] Unable to find the social context he was looking for, Stagner posed the question that undoubtedly occurred to many of Allport's politically active readers. Was Allport "living in the 'ivory tower' of academic monasticism?"[48] As a fellow member of SPSSI, Stagner was well aware of Allport's political progressivism and "alert interest in social problems," but his familiarity with Allport's politics made the "transcendent personality" all the more confusing. "Certainly he could have gotten evidence," Stagner argued, "and to spare, of the effects of culture disorganization upon stability of personal values and attitudes."[49]

A tireless researcher, Allport could have easily obtained the evidence to establish a link between culture and personality. At issue for Allport was not the availability of evidence, but the importance of the ideal he was defending: "real individuality." In the 1920s, he had argued that industrialization and natural science were subverting the real essence of human nature and putting in its place a depressing, threadbare silhouette. In the 1930s, Allport viewed the development of a socially oriented model of personality with similar concern. An excessive emphasis on the cultural context of personality seemed to undermine the integrity of individuality. In the hands of the culturalists, the human subject seemed to dissolve into a matrix of sociological categories. "It is characteristic of all sociological definitions of personality that they deny to it the attribute of agency," Allport complained. "In one way or another personality is always considered a reflection of, or dependent upon the social ground."[50]

PSYCHOANALYSIS, MASCULINITY, AND THE
REENCHANTMENT OF PERSONALITY

The economic upheavals of the Depression did not alter Allport's sense of an individuality imperiled by industrialization, on the one hand, and natural and social science, on the other. In *Personality*, he again echoed the "enchanted" epistemology of his German mentors, insisting that the deterministic discourses of the biological sciences had "destroyed [human-kind's] essential nature [by] drawing the blood and peeling the flesh from human personality, leaving only . . . a skeleton framework of mind."[51] The task that Allport set for himself was to help "reenchant" the human qualities that had been degraded by reductionistically minded psychologists and sociologists—individuality, values, idealism, and freedom.

Dismissing the "culture and personality" school out of hand, Allport undertook a more sustained critique of another prominent theory of disenchantment: psychoanalysis. Freudian theory was first introduced into the United States in 1909. Initially it attracted little public attention, but in the 1920s popular versions of psychoanalysis became highly fashionable. As historian Donald Napoli noted, "millions of people began sprinkling their conversations with 'repression,' 'libido,' 'Oedipus complex,' and the other exciting terms of the psychoanalytic lexicon."[52] Crude versions of psychoanalysis were even packaged for mass consumption. Sears Roebuck listed *Ten Thousand Dreams Interpreted* and *Sex Problems Solved* in its mail order catalog, and in 1924 Freud made his first of two appearances on the cover of *Time* magazine.[53] Taken as a group, American psychologists did not share the public's enthusiasm for psychoanalysis. Within the field of personality, however, considerable weight was attached to psychoanalytic theories of motivation.[54] Allport was not exaggerating when he remarked in 1939, "I came on the scene when many people thought that psychoanalysis held the one and only key to the study of personality."[55]

Part of the appeal of psychoanalysis lay in its ability to calm middle-class anxieties about the growing industrialization and commercialization of American life. As historian Joel Pfister noted, the growth of monopoly capitalism undermined the notion of character and the ethic of the self-made man. "Discourses of 'depth,'" Pfister explained, "provided a class of white-collar professionals and managers with a compensatory belief in and often sexy fascination with its own 'psychological' significance and individualism, a 'depth' that corporate authority seemingly could not standardize, control, or own."[56] As we have seen, Allport's cultivation of a spiritualized personality was inspired by a similar fear of standardization, but instead of viewing psychoanalysis as a way of rescuing individuality, he saw Freudian theory as another manifestation of modernist reductionism.

The antimodernist character of Allport's critique of psychoanalysis is important to emphasize. Americans psychologists have frequently attacked psychoanalysis since the introduction of Freudian theory in the early 20th century. As historian Gail Hornstein noted, most psychological critics have objected to psychoanalysis on methodological grounds.[57] Freudian theory was criticized for its lack of objectivity, its reliance on introspective reports and interpretation, and its emphasis on initiation rites and secret knowledge. Psychologist Knight Dunlap put the matter forthrightly in 1920: "Psychoanalysis attempts to creep in wearing the uniform of science, and to strangle it from the inside."[58]

Like Dunlap, Allport made his share of methodological criticisms, but he took his intellectual bearings more from German spiritual psychology than American experimental psychology. Most of the mandarin psychologists that Allport met viewed Freud as an agent of disenchantment who was "reducing man to the animal level, [while] ignoring his character as an intellectual and spiritual being."[59] From the perspective of the Geisteswissenschaften, psychoanalysis was problematic not because it lacked devotion to natural science, but because it was, if anything, too close to the natural sciences in outlook. Psychologist Max Dessoir certainly left Allport in no doubt on this point. In a letter to William Taylor written in 1922, Allport described a course he was taking with Dessoir, "Parapsychologie und Psychoanalyse," as an "interesting exposition and destruction of the Freudian formulae."[60] However, in a comment that reveals the degree to which he had previously dissected psychoanalysis, Allport added that Dessoir's course "cannot add much, I believe, to our own criticisms of Freud." In the same letter, Allport outlined the conclusion to which that those criticisms had led him:

> Is it not true that some of the fundamental contributions of Freud are as original and significant as the ideas of any one man can ever be in science? Is it not true also that no psychologist who has balance would hesitate to condemn the silly Freudian superstructure? Freud in Vienna is now the old story of a famous man in his own town. He is hooted and hooted. Everyone here laughs at him, and he has no recognition except in a narrow circle of orthodox admirers. Freud would be far better off should he migrate to America.[61]

Allport continued his antimodernist attack on psychoanalysis in his private correspondence throughout the 1920s and 1930s, and he took particular exception to the psychoanalytic notion that the bulk of human thought and action could be ultimately linked to the desire to reduce sexual tension.[62] In another letter to Taylor, Allport maintained that

> specific sex tensions seem to me to be frightfully segmental, and relatively unrelated to personality. . . . There are those who defecate daily, some twice and some thrice a day. But what has this segmental response to do with personality or with sublimation? The same, I think for sex.[63]

Despite his long-standing opposition to psychoanalytic theory and his subsequent renown as an "anti-Freudian," Allport did not undertake any sustained public criticism of Freud until *Personality* was published in 1937. Freud was not cited in his 1921 literature review, "Personality and Character," nor was he considered in the 1930 review of personality that Allport coauthored with Philip Vernon. This seemingly curious neglect may have been a strategic move on Allport's part to subvert the credibility of psychoanalysis by denying it standing within the "scientific" field of personality. Regardless of the source of his earlier neglect, by 1937 Allport clearly felt the need to come out swinging against psychoanalysis. "The bulk of all literature on the psychology of personality is written from this one [Freudian] point of view," he noted in a footnote in *Personality*. "It is time that the story be told in more eclectic terms!"[64] Allport's account of personality was eclectic, but his treatment of psychoanalysis was, in the opinion of some reviewers, excessively harsh. The reviewer for the *Psychoanalytic Review* thought that Allport had "caricatured [psychoanalysis] so crudely that even our 'common sense' wonders."[65] It was a charge with which Allport may well have agreed: In a footnote he described his discussion of Freud as "tardy" and "incomplete."[66] In Allport's estimation, however, the destructive hold that psychoanalysis was coming to have on the American notion of personality more than justified his harsh, cursory treatment.

Convinced that psychoanalysis was a discourse of disenchantment, Allport's opposition to Freudian theory was also fueled by the model of maleness it seemed to endorse. The Freudian emphasis on sexuality, aggression, and powerful instinctual energy lent credence to the emerging model of "passionate manhood" that was gaining ground throughout America.[67] At the heart of this vision was the idea that the essence of maleness lay in a primitive, barbarous, animalistic core of sexual and aggressive impulses. Social and personal problems were said to be rooted in a stifling modernity that had cut men off from their instinctual selves, leaving them weak, effeminate, and "overcivilized." The term "masculinity" came to symbolize this new understanding of manhood, and the fictional character Tarzan was its ultimate cultural expression. The "Lord of the Apes" lacked manners, thoughtfulness, and self-restraint—qualities long associated with manly character—but he had the characteristics that American men now recognized as the markers of a "real man": aggressiveness, physicality, and powerful male sexuality.[68]

As a boy, Allport had struggled to deal with this new masculine ethic, and as a man he continued to feel alienated by its valorization of the primitive, the physical, and the sexual. Inasmuch as Freudian theory represented the intellectual affirmation of these values, Allport felt obliged not only to critique psychoanalysis but also to offer up his own theory that would put manhood back on a spiritual and moral foundation. Attacking all discourses of depth, Allport remarked on their reductionistic reliance on a selfish, instinctual, masculine, ego:

> Scratch ever so lightly the coating of hypocrisy, of social varnish, and the cave-man stands revealed. The one important instinct is the desire for power, for "masculinity," and though overlaid with sweet sounding protests of sympathy and altruism, this root desire is biologically prepotent and ultimate. *Every man is inescapably a Machtmensch [powerful man]; his most coveted experience is the enhancement of his self-esteem, and his most ineradicable trait is vanity* [italics added].[69]

Openly contemptuous of this veneration of masculinity, Allport did not deny the idea of instinctual energy and selfish drives. In his chapter on motivation titled "The Functional Autonomy of Motives," he drew on older vocabularies of manhood to reassert the idea that the instinctual masculine self underwent a transformation through childhood and into adolescence.[70] "Socialization is not simply a varnish laid over personality, but involves, at least much of the time, a genuine transmutation of interests from the egoistic to the altruistic," he wrote.[71] The original motivational matrix of "instincts, wishes, or needs" develop into new and increasingly complex patterns as the person matures, and over time, these patterns assume a dynamic character all their own. The tie to the original instinct or need that gave rise to a course of action is broken. The new motive thus becomes "functionally independent" of "antecedent systems."[72]

Functional autonomy challenged the masculine ethic by severing the connection between instinctual impulse and adult thought and action. In a chapter entitled "The Mature Personality," Allport advanced his critique a step further by reworking the ideal of manly character into a psychological vision of human nature in its most advanced form. In Allport's view, there were "three differentiating characteristics . . . whereby to distinguish a fully developed personality from one that is still unripe": the "extension of the self, . . . self-objectification, . . . and a unifying philosophy of life."[73] The language of manly character resonated throughout Allport's discussion of these characteristics. As noted in chapter 2, the self suggested by character was that of the "true Christian gentleman, pure, upright, intelligent, strong, and brave, possessing a sense of duty, having benevolence, moral courage, personal integrity, and the 'highest kinship of the soul,' devoting service to mankind, being attentive to the 'highest and most harmonious development of one's powers,' to achieve a 'complete and consistent whole.'"[74] The method for generating this self rested on the notion of sacrifice. Selfhood was a product of submission to the discipline of higher ideals of religion, duty, honor, and integrity. Allport's "mature personality" was similar to character in both its points of emphasis and its method of self-development. In keeping with the character ideal, the "mature personality" was an active citizen, deeply concerned with social and religious causes. Unlike the "garrulous Bohemian, egotistical, self-pitying, and prating of self-expression," the mature personality was a "man of confident dignity" who could "lose himself in work, in contemplation, . . . and in loyalty to others."[75] Like character, Allport's model also reflected a reverence of the golden mean and a religiously derived seriousness of purpose. The mature personality had a well-developed "sense of proportion" and a "sensitive and intricate balance."[76] He could "pursue his course diligently" in the knowledge that he "has a place in the scheme of things according to the dispensations of a Divine Intelligence [sic]."[77]

Repudiating psychoanalytic reductionism, Allport again drew on the power of scientific representation to fortify his point. In a chapter titled "Basic Aspects of Growth," personality was portrayed in a pyramidlike hierarchical schematic, with conditioned reflexes at the base and a "total personality" at the apex. The illustration helped transform the abstract principle of functional autonomy into a visible scientific process. In Allport's figure, the total personality was informed by previous events and motivational sources, but it was also potentially independent of those factors. Early experience contributed to later development, but at the highest point was a "supreme, all-inclusive integration" that propelled the individual beyond the limiting confines of biological and environmental influences.[78] (See insert, Figure 40.)

Although the mature personality was suffused with values of character, like most nostalgic invocations it contained a number of modern themes.[79] To begin, Allport encouraged an exploratory attitude to one's individuality and an openness to experience. The mature personality would live a "creative pattern of life" rather than a "static and stupid conventionality."[80] In another departure from character, Allport encouraged people to monitor their conduct not strictly in relation to a higher moral code, but also in relation to a set of psychologically derived norms. Termed "insight," Allport defined this property as the "relation of what a man thinks he is to what others (especially the psychologist) think he is."[81] To be high in insight was to move ever closer to the ideal of maturity. A final point of difference concerns Allport's characterlike directive to embrace a higher moral code. Social historians have observed that 19th-century discussions of the self "presupposed an agreed moral code." The ideals to which one should surrender were thus not in dispute; for the proponents of character, the issue was not "moral relativism but weakness of will."[82] For Allport, however, moral relativism was a presupposition. While insisting on the necessity of self-sacrifice to higher ideals, Allport left the exact content of these ideals unspecified.

Allport's professional career had been launched amid profound spiritual uncertainty. As a young man, he hungered for the authentic, the romantic, and the mystical, but he threw himself into a discipline that celebrated the contrived exactitude of the laboratory. Never entirely comfortable with the disjuncture between these two worlds, Allport had exploited the ambiguities of personality in an attempt to forge an existentially workable and coherent vision. As his academic career prospered, Allport continued to view psychology as a poor substitute for premodern spiritual forms. In search of spiritual fulfillment, he and Ada attended the Episcopal church regularly and he worked hard to demonstrate the relevance of traditional spirituality in modern America. At Dartmouth, Allport delivered periodic lectures on topics of religious importance. In a 1928 lecture titled "What Psychology Has to Say About Prayer," he argued that traditional religious practices could easily be maintained alongside the naturalistic explanations of science. Prayer was beneficial insofar as it "assists in the integration of personality"; provides a "means of getting back into the mode of behavior which agrees with this life plan"; and "cleans house, by releasing repressions."[84]

Allport continued to champion the cause of traditional spirituality after moving to Harvard. He often referred individuals with psychological difficulties to religious counselors on the assumption that "religious discipline and activity with a religious orientation many times prove to be the best of all therapy for depressive personalities."[85] Convinced of the value of the religious life, Allport served as a consultant for the Episcopal Theological School and was an invited speaker at the school's matriculation dinner.[86] In 1932, Allport began preaching an annual sermon at Harvard's Appleton Chapel. Although his sermons were always structured around a passage of scripture, his message reflected his struggle for a more soulful psychology. Intellectual arrogance was a recurring theme, and although he never explicitly mentioned it, the strident positivism of Boring and Lashley was an unmistakable target. "Students and teachers, and research investigators as well, often sit securely on some one branch of the tree of knowledge and feel entirely content," he remarked in a 1936 sermon:

> They declare that their vision is quite sufficient, whereas, of course, it is impossible for them to see themselves and their meager attainments with perspective in the scheme of which they are only a part. . . . Sophomoric arrogance takes many forms, dogmatism and ridicule of others, scorn for one's opponents, and conceit in one's meager attainments and in the fragmentary theories one has evolved.[87]

Critical of the shallow materialism that pervaded American science, Allport looked on his own psychological work in spiritual terms. On the wall of his study at home hung a "large and dramatic depiction of the crucifixion of Christ," and it was from the Lord that Allport took direction in his scholarly work.[88] He saw *Personality* in religious terms and was convinced that the book had been inspired by God. In a 1937 letter to Ada, he insisted that "it isn't my book, never have I felt possessive of it. I believe I was *appointed by Providence to add a bit of push backward to the rising tide of barbarism and ignorance in psychology*" [italics added].[89] Allport communicated a similar message of divine inspiration to his mother. *Personality* was dedicated to Nellie, but this was not intended simply as a straightforward statement of affection. The dedication was also an affirmation of Nellie's religious vision and an expression of continuity between her spiritual vocabulary and the more technical sounding, scientific language of personality. After receiving an inscribed copy of *Personality*, Nellie noted that "the technical points will not be as clear as they would be if I could have studied there . . . however, as you say, I may be able to read 'between the lines.'"[90] (See insert, Figure 41)

PSYCHOLOGICAL RELIGIOUSNESS

Empirically informed and spiritually ambitious, Allport's psychology of personality does not fit neatly into the narratives of selfhood that historians of psychology have been inclined to tell. In most accounts, Allport is usually positioned as part of a broad movement away from the "transcendental self" of Cartesian philosophy. This was a self that stood apart from the ebb and flow of ordinary social life; as James Holstein and Jaber Gubrium have noted, it was "disembodied, separated, and distinguished from the corporeal body upon which it otherwise philosophically mused and cast judgement."[91] William James is usually credited with having played a decisive role in repudiating this notion of a transcendental self. According to Bernard Meltzer, John Petras, and Larry Reynolds, "a significant advance made by James was the removal of the concept of self from the purely metaphysical realm to the view of at least some aspect of it as derived from interaction processes in the social environment."[92] Within this larger narrative, Allport is cast as a latter-day Jamesian and a particularly enthusiastic practitioner of radical empiricism. According to Katherine Pandora, Allport was a "prodigal progeny" of James who shared the famous philosopher's sense of the social sciences as an "advantageous place from which to commence the search for natural knowledge."[93]

Historians are correct to link Allport's psychology of personality to the radical empiricist tradition, but the transcendental, antimodernist implications of this tradition are seldom considered. High and Woodward's thoughtful discussion of the parallels between James and Allport is a case in point: The authors portray Allport as someone anxious to "return the study of the person to real-life experiences—to common sense made rigorous."[94] There is ample evidence to support this claim, but Allport's vision of "real-life experience" had a distinctive spiritual dimension. Personality was an enchanted being beyond society, biology, language, and the banal humdrum of the everyday. It was a self of mystery, dignity, and soul that science could affirm but never really know in any meaningful or practical sense. Traditional religious categories were the only viable route toward this sacred space, yet even here language and iconography ultimately failed.

In placing transcendence at the heart of personality, Allport put forth a message replete with religious suggestiveness. In his vision, personality went beyond both the frameworks of the natural and social sciences and common sense. Exactly where that "beyond" lay, Allport did not specify, but in a culture as steeped in the religious idiom as prewar America, the meaning was clear. The individual had a spiritual existence that was connected to, yet somehow apart from, the material and social world. For Allport, this particular uncapturable sense of personality was what was really important and fundamental; by attending to the transcendental, one could attain things long associated with religion: personal fulfillment, compassionate understanding, and an increased appreciation that one "has a place in the scheme of things according to the dispensations of a Divine Intelligence."[95]

In retaining a hold on the transcendent, Allport's psychology of personality may be viewed as illustration of what historian Robert Fuller described as "psychological religiousness."[96] This term refers to psychological thought that links individual subjectivity to an extrasensory "more" beyond the material world. The nature of this "more" need not be religious in a traditional theological sense, and indeed, the rhetorical power of psychological religiousness lies in its ostensibly secular idiom. The discourse provides the spiritually hungry but theologically skeptical with a way of "embracing the categories of secular culture without capitulating to them."[97] As Fuller pointed out, Allport made no specific allowance for a distinctive form of religious consciousness in his formal psychological theorizing, but his goal of reconnecting the self to a spirit of mystery and incalculability is clear in his own Anglo-Catholic commitment and in his unrelenting celebration of the uncapturable divinity of personality. The individual personality is "more than a bundle of habits," Allport wrote in *Personality*, and "more too than a representative of the species. He is more than a citizen of the state, and more than a mere incident in the gigantic movements of mankind. He transcends them all."[98]

This spiritual ambitiousness constitutes one of the strongest links between Allport and what historian Eugene Taylor described as a distinctly "Jamesian tradition in psychology."[99] Like James, Allport was convinced of the reality of a world beyond the senses and of the need for an up-to-date language that could enchant our vision without doing violence to our intellect. In the discourse of personality, Allport found a way of traversing the divide between scientific control and spiritual freedom. Its extraordinary plasticity could accommodate bureaucratic demands for a knowable, measured self while preserving the idea that the ultimate measure of personhood lay in a deeper, metaphysical order of reality. (See insert, Figure 42.)

PERSONALITY AND THE FAMILY

Devoted to the task of building a new field, in the late 1920s and 30s Allport was also faced with the challenge of raising a new family. On June 29, 1927, Ada gave birth to a son—Robert Bradlee Allport. Attentive to the joys of the spirit, Allport found the raw biology of childbirth distasteful. "Don't ever give birth," he warned his friend Edwin Powers. "It is incredibly horrible." The basics of baby care were just as unappealing, and Allport quipped that his new son was "absurdly vegetative, and guzzles like a piglet, gurgles, slobbers and belches in a way that convinces me of his ordinariness."[100] Despite this rude confrontation with human biology, the new parents delighted in their child, and in keeping with a pattern established by such prominent scholars as Charlotte Buhler, Jean Piaget, and William and Clara Stern, they carefully recorded Robert's psychological and physical development in a daily diary. Within days of his birth, the new parents had "twenty pages of records."[101] These observations formed the basis of a kind of personality inventory that the new parents undertook of their son when he was 4 months old. The young Robert was described as being well-adjusted, active, adaptable, mischievous, and linguistically adept. These characteristics were periodically compared with Robert's school records as he grew up, and in *Personality* the data appeared under the pseudonym "the case of Andrew." Commenting on Andrew, Allport reported with evident satisfaction that "early observed differences tend to persist."[102] (See insert, Figure 43.)

Family life may have provided Allport with a living psychological laboratory, but it also brought new personal challenges. The contradictions of personality that Ada had struggled with during her courtship continued to haunt her as a mother and married woman. After her marriage and the birth of her son, Ada did pursue some professional projects of her own. In 1925, she taught courses on child psychology and general psychology at a junior college in Boston, and in 1933 she accepted a 6-month position as a psychologist for the New England Home for Little Wanderers. From 1935 to 1937, she worked part-time as a psychologist at the Massachusetts Child Guidance Clinic in the Boston Dispensary. Although absorbing, this work was always secondary to her principal role of "helping [her husband] to happiness" as wife, mother, and helpmate.[103] Ada took an active interest in Allport's work, and she read drafts and helped gather research materials. In a letter to psychologist Leonard Carmichael, she remarked that it was her "duty conjugal to keep my husband en rapport with the belles-lettres of the profession."[104]

Although Ada enjoyed these scholarly pursuits, her work with Allport generated its share of tension. At issue was the question of scholarly influence and identity. Allport worked closely with his wife on *Personality*, and he appreciated her input and assistance. "I feel better to have you working along with me," he told Ada while preparing the manuscript, "for I see most clearly that intensive concentration and cooperation will be needed if this thing is ever to be finished."[105] Although Allport welcomed Ada's help, he was anxious to maintain creative control and unwilling to construct his work in terms that would have afforded Ada an authorial role. She was his "constant and loyal collaborator . . . from start to finish," but not a joint author.[106] Scholarly control was a bottom line for Allport, and he told Ada that he "insist[ed] upon . . . privacy and independence in [his] work."[107] Unhappy with the situation, Ada resigned herself to what she perceived to be typical male insecurity in the face of concerted and well-meaning female influence. "Like any man set on his way," Ada remarked in a letter to Boring, "he [Allport] feared the 'control' of his wife."[108]

Never entirely satisfied with her role as scholarly helpmate, Ada found the more conventional domestic duties a chore. She approached motherhood warily, and she bristled at efforts to be socialized into the role. As an expectant mother, she found other people's babies a bore, and the excited baby banter of friends and family was equally tedious: "For an expectant mother I'm unusually disinterested in the babies across the way," she remarked. "There is, of course, bound to be a vast amount of talk round and about baby this summer," she wrote to Allport shortly before giving birth. "Apparently such an occasion offers an outlet for the yarns of any woman who ever had or knew a baby. You must keep me composed under it."[109] As a new mother, Ada succeeded in maintaining her composure, but she hated the domestic tasks of cooking and cleaning. A live-in maid provided some relief, but hired help could not speak to a nagging sense of unfulfilled ambition. In a letter to a friend written some years later, she spoke admiringly of a "self-less candor that I should like to achieve before I die. As I look things over though I don't believe its possible for anyone unless he has salted away certain concrete worldly achievements—I do not mean necessarily a profession but something here and now in this work-a-day world so that everything doesn't back up into the soul."[110]

Unfortunately for Ada, motherhood did not provide much in the way of compensatory rewards, and her relationship with her son was not close. She and Robert battled over efforts to "sissify" him, and moments of warmth between mother and son were rare. Allport was often cast in the role of mediator in this conflict, and it was to his father that Robert looked for emotional support and affection. Known as "Pappy" within the family (after the cartoon series L'il Abner), Allport was a tender father. Robert recalled that he and his father "had a bedtime ritual where we would sit on a window seat and he would sing good night to everything we saw out the window ending with the moon if it were visible."[111] Allport also delighted in sharing his appetite for the exotic with his son. Robert fondly recalled frequent trips to offbeat, out-of-the-way ethnic restaurants in Boston. "My favorite was a small basement place in Chinatown called the Dragon Grotto where we always had subgum chow mein, beef chop suey, pork strips, white rice, sesame candy, and tea for three all for $1.05 total!"[112] These enjoyable outings helped cement a lasting feeling of goodwill between father and son, and Robert later recalled that his father was the "kindest man [he] ever knew."[113] (See insert, Figure 44.)

In keeping with the spirit of his own personality psychology, Allport did not endeavor to build or shape his son according to some predetermined ideal. Respect for his son's individual uniqueness was an operative principle, and at times this respect was severely tested. Although father and son were on generally good terms, Robert Allport had not inherited his father's more feminine-style sensibility. He was, as Allport's friend Edwin Powers noted, a "real boy" interested in "baseball, cycling, hiking, and all kinds of exciting adventures which the normal American boy is fond of."[114] Allport did his best to engage in his son's boyish interests, but as often as not these efforts ended in failure. "The thing that I regretted the most about my parents (but particularly my father)," Robert recalled, "was their unawareness and/or disinterest in my boyish concerns and a rather unbelievable ineptitude in the issues that I was most interested in." From chess, to poker, to pets—Allport never quite got it right, a fact that disappointed the young Robert:

> The most meaningful moment for me ... occurred Christmas Day 1939. . . . I was at that time into printing and I had a small time printing press, but my wish for Xmas was an upgrade. I thought it not possible i.e. too expensive. But to my surprise GWA [Allport] had bought an old second-hand press which was just what I wanted. When he showed it to me, I broke down and cried and hugged him. The problem was it was mechanically defective and never worked right. This is the quintessential example of my relationship with my father.[115] (See insert, Figure 45.)

The psychological divide between father and son was brought into sharp relief on a family trip to California in 1939. While in Los Angeles, the family stayed with Allport's eldest brother, Harold, and his wife, Claribel. Harold was known in the family for his masculine, directive ways, and Robert could see that his uncle represented a different type of manhood from that of his own father. Unlike Gordon, Harold was a handy man who enjoyed outdoor pursuits, and he had a reputation as a dedicated fisherman. Frustrated by his father's disinterest in conventional masculine pastimes, Robert was impressed by his uncle's lifestyle, and he was pleased when he was invited to go fishing. Harold's dominant character seemed to grow over the course of the visit, and at every turn his masculine presence made an impression on the young Robert. Before the fishing trip, Harold took his nephew to a sporting goods store to buy some fishing tackle. Instead of simply paying for the purchase, Harold asked for a discount from the clerk and was given 10 percent off. "I was sort of impressed with that," Robert later recalled. "It was the first time I had ever seen bargaining in action."[116] Able in outdoor pursuits and forceful in commerce, Harold seemed to make a point of keeping his younger brother a bit off balance when it came to the "real world" (as opposed to the academic and misguidedly liberal Eastern way). During a trip downtown with his father and uncle, Robert recalled the "three of us walking down the street [when] out of nothing my uncle said, 'you see that guy walking across the street? . . . he wears women's under wear. As a twelve year old I pricked up my ears in interest and my father said something like, 'oh, he's a transvestite.'" It was a brief exchange, but Robert remembered feeling "quite keenly, that there was something behind [Harold's] comment that was meant to put [my father] on the defensive."[117] (See insert, Figures 46 and 47.)

As the visit continued, Harold's masculinity gained even more definition in his nephew's eyes. Harold showed Robert the service revolver that he had used in the trenches in World War I, and the two then visited Harold's cabin in Malibu.[118] For his part, Allport could only observe his son's interest in the manly world Harold embodied. "Soon I suppose the big fishing will start," Allport wrote in a letter to Ada. "Already discussion, plans, and prospects show a degree of *expertise* that is beyond me." In the presence of his manly brother, Allport seemed to be in out of his depth, and he noted that "the affiliation of the two is perfect, and Bobby no less than [Harold's dog] Fritz worships the master [Harold]."[119]

In the presence of Harold, Allport felt a sense of inadequacy as a father, but his concerns were not shared by his son. Although Robert was intrigued by some of his uncle's manly possessions and pastimes, he quickly discovered that Harold's masculine hobbies were accompanied by some rather unappealing and stereotypically masculine traits. Unlike his friendly, unobtrusive father, Harold was "stern and authoritarian" with a "take charge, no nonsense" style that was directed at anyone who crossed his path.[120] "I remember one time," Robert recalled,

> Harold . . . took us out for a drive, and when he got back, there was a wad of gum stuck on his fender. . . . He took good care of the car, and he interrogated me in a very prosecutorial way [as to] whether I had anything to do with it. I denied [it], but I could see that I was

guilty until proven innocent and he was about to descend on me. He was very stern.[121]

Harold's stern ways offset whatever manly cachet he had built up, and by the end of the vacation Robert felt no special fatherly or masculine bond toward his uncle. "I would not have traded [my father] for Harold by any stretch of the imagination," Robert later recalled.[122] Although loyal to his father, Robert continued to experience a sharp sense of difference, and for his part Allport complained about his son's "banditry, war-whoops, and irresponsibility."[123] Exasperated by the challenges of fatherhood, he struggled to find a way to reach his son. "It seems to take more energy than either of us possess [sic] to combat his [Robert's] chaotic and heathen propensities," he noted in a letter to Ada.[124] Unable to fully engage Robert's boyish world, Allport often left his son to his own devices, and within the home individual self-expression was a more dominant value than family togetherness. While at home, Robert spent much of his time in his own room, and he spent "every summer from age five to age fourteen" in a summer camp or with relatives. For high school, Robert was enrolled in Tabor Academy, a private boarding school. Secure in this highly individualized family structure, Robert could not recall ever feeling "lonesome for my parents or worried that I was abandoned or in danger. . . . To me it was the way the world was."[125] From his perspective, Allport was not quite as stoic about the family divide, and in one low moment he told Ada, "Bobby could have had a far more suitable father."[126]

The boyish Robert remained at odds with his parents' notions of dignity and deportment throughout his adolescence, but his pranks and rebelliousness were never taken to an extreme. Among his more egregious acts were running away from home for a day at age 12 (he returned in the early evening) and taking the family car for a joy ride at age 16. For all their relative innocence, Allport was troubled by these transgressions, but his reaction was typically mild. "I expected rather severe retribution [for taking the family car]," Robert recalled. "But after questioning me and not getting a response to, 'Did I think I had done anything wrong' (which I did), he dropped the matter without one word of censure or any negative consequence."[127] Casting his mind back over his entire youth, Robert could recall but a single occasion of severe discipline:

> On one rare occasion I was flogged with a belt on the bare back. I can't even remember the precipitating incident, it was mostly done because of an accumulation of many, many lesser transgressions. I think I felt it was justified and I did not resent it or hold it against him, although in pre-adolescent character I histrionically presented my welted back to my mother, who had been pretending to be busy at her desk in the next room, and mumbled something like "remember this."[128]

The complexities of family life posed some significant personal challenges for Allport, but they did not deflect him from his "divinely" inspired mission or alter the substance of his theory. If anything, the challenges of fatherhood were a confirmation of his life's work. The pronounced differences between father and son—exasperating though they may have been —seemed to confirm individuality as "the supreme characteristic of human nature."[129] A similar message could be discerned in Ada's frustration with the role of faculty wife, but the ideals of personality and the cultural expectations surrounding female domesticity could not be assimilated into any preexisting theoretical structure. To Allport's credit, he did his best to accommodate Ada's concerns. Unfortunately, no easy solution was on offer, and as Allport's career flourished, Ada continued to experience an undercurrent of resentment with ideals that pulled her in opposite directions.

A PRESIDENTIAL PERSONALITY

The complexities of Allport's personal life were in contrast to the triumphal progression of his scholarly career. At Harvard, Allport had an outstanding reputation among the undergraduates, and he was described in the student newspaper as the "best all around man in the Department, fine lecturer and tutor, very popular, coming man."[130] With the publication of *Personality*, Allport's reputation within psychology was to become just as lofty. At the 1937 American Psychological Association (APA) meeting, Allport discussed the financial and intellectual prospects of *Personality* with Ross Stagner—a friendly rival and, as mentioned earlier, author of *Psychology of Personality*. Stagner generously predicted great things for Allport's book, but he was convinced that his own socially oriented approach was a better reflection of the economically turbulent times and would consequently be a better seller. "His [Stagner's] opinion," Allport noted, "is that he'll take the cash and I the credit."[131] As things unfolded, both books sold well, but Stagner was correct when he suggested that Allport would garner a greater share of the glory for helping to codify the new field.[132] A delegate at the 1937 APA meeting declared that Allport was the "man of the hour" —a sentiment that was echoed at every corner of the conference hall. "Just standing still brings a score of people up at a gallop," Allport recalled, and old colleagues now looked on him with an ever deepening admiration.[133] "Poppa [Herbert] Langfeld has been unusually attentive to me now that I have 'arrived' and purrs softly when we are together."[134] Langfeld's "purring" was reflected in the lavish chorus of praise with which *Personality* was greeted.[135] A. A. Roback described *Personality* as "the most valuable textbook" yet published, a sentiment echoed by Harry Hollingworth, who described it as a "mine of instruction for the serious student."[136] Much of the appeal of Allport's book lay in its combination of scientific order and humanistic possibility. For psychologists troubled by the "loose thinking, faulty definition, and narrow interpretation" of personality research, Allport offered "a precise, well-integrated, [and] coherent defense of the individual as a proper subject for scientific study." For the more humanistically minded reader, Allport offered an enchanted self that transcended the vulgar determinisms of biology and sociology. Harold Lasswell described the book as "something of a return to the urbanity and scope to the genteel tradition. . . . [Allport] brings to the study of personality a broad and even-tempered culture."[137] (See insert, Figure 48.)

In weaving a vision of personality, Allport had walked a fine line between science and spirituality, freedom and control. The ambiguity of personality sheltered conflicting tendencies within Allport and, indeed, within American culture as a whole. As the 1930s wound down, Allport continued to benefit from personality's ability to obscure the contradictions and tensions within American psychology. In 1937, he was selected to occupy the prestigious post of chairman of Harvard's psychology department. Boring had been chair of psychology since the discipline's break from philosophy in 1934, but he believed that the administration of "power" was a job for "younger men," and he quickly set about looking for someone to replace him.[138] In Allport, he believed he had found the person with just the right combination of intellect, humility, and self-assuredness. "He [Allport] seems to me less inferior than the four of us," Boring wrote in a letter to Henry Murray. "When you blow him up, he comes back serene and not resentful. For this reason he will at last make the perfect Chairman."[139]

Allport accepted the chairmanship, although he did not relish the prospect of power. He told Boring that the chairmanship "should be understood to be a rotational matter" and that he was awaiting "my appointment as chairman much as Anne Boleyn awaited the axe."[140] Allport may not have actively pursued power, but as the champion of a fashionable new category at the nation's foremost university, he soon found himself at the center of disciplinary administration. In 1936, he was elected to a 3-year term on the Council of Directors of the APA.[141] This event was an important milestone for Allport, for the council was an elite group within the 2,700 member association. It was responsible for determining APA policy on a broad range of issues pertaining to membership, scientific standards, and professional orientation.[142] Already burdened by a heavy administrative load at Harvard, Allport complained about the council's long meetings, and he jokingly suggested that "the Holy Roman Empire has nothing on the APA for organization." For all his complaints, however, Allport rapidly emerged as one of the council's most influential voices. "Amazing to me," he wrote Ada after a marathon 15-hour council meeting, "I found my views almost always carrying—on every issue."[143]

Word of Allport's influence quickly spread, and several national organizations approached him to be their chair. "Somehow I give the impression of being level-headed and an administrator of ability," he noted modestly, "whereas, I'm not really."[144] Refusing most of these offers, Allport added to his list of administrative responsibilities in 1938 when he accepted the editorship of the *Journal of Abnormal and Social Psychology*—a position once held by Floyd Allport.[145] To round out this impressive string of accomplishments, Allport was elected president of the APA in 1938. At age 42, he was not the youngest psychologist to have ever held the office; that honor belonged to John B. Watson. Allport's election, however, was unusual in three important respects. First, he was considerably younger than the presidents who had preceded him. John Dashiell (1888–1975, elected 1938), Edward Tolman (1886–1959, elected 1937), Clark Hull (1884–1952, elected 1936), and Albert Poffenberger (1885–1977, elected 1935) were all in their 50s when elected president. The second feature that made Allport's election distinctive was his scholarly background. He was the first person clearly identified with the field of personality to be elected APA president. Since 1925, his predecessors had all been drawn from the discipline's old guard of natural science-oriented, experimental psychologists. In fact, all but one (Thurstone) had been members of the Society of Experimental Psychologists, an exclusive organization of laboratory psychologists led by Boring.[146] The final distinguishing feature of Allport's presidency was his term of office. His predecessors had all been elected after serving a 3-year term on the APA council. Allport's election broke with this tradition. In an unprecedented move, he was elected president before his term on the council had expired.[147]

PERSONALITY AND THE FUTURE OF PSYCHOLOGY

Allport's election to the office of APA president was propelled in large part by the centrifugal forces at work within the field. In the 1920s and 1930s, psychology was developing in a number of seemingly antagonistic directions. One of the sharpest points of tension concerned the scope of psychology. Was the discipline strictly a university-based, laboratory science, or did it also encompass applied work in such fields as counseling and mental testing? Psychologists were also divided on epistemological grounds. Was psychology a natural science based on laboratory methods, or was it a human science based, at least in part, on interpretive methods and case studies? A final source of division centered on the discipline's professional orientation. For most of its history, the APA had been run along the lines of a private men's club. A small and highly exclusive, experimentally oriented male elite took steps to maintain a relatively circumscribed vision of the discipline by keeping outsiders—unemployed psychologists, women, Jews, and applied psychologists—at a distance. During the Depression, these groups put pressure on the APA to transform itself from a club into an association that would truly represent the interests of all psychologists. Many began to drift away and form their own organizations, such as SPSSI, the Psychologists League, and the American Association for Applied Psychology.[148] Divisions in the field also generated new, applied psychology-oriented publications such as the *Journal of Consulting Psychology* (founded in 1937).

For most of the interwar period, the experimentally minded old guard on the APA council attempted to contain these centrifugal pressures by consolidating their control of the Association. Full membership in the association was restricted to psychologists with "publications beyond the dissertation."[149] A new class of junior membership—the "associate"—was created for individuals engaged in some form of psychological work but lacking the scholarly credentials necessary for full membership. The council also considered changing the requirements for a PhD in psychology. In 1932, the council appointed a Committee on Standard Requirements for the PhD in Psychology.[150] To deal with the growing divisions among the various groups of psychologists, the council authorized a new policy of affiliation. Competing interest groups could now be affiliated with the APA without endorsing each other's policies.[151]

The council's policies were successful in the short run, but by the end of the decade, tension along the discipline's various fracture lines became so severe that many began to question the future of professional psychology. In 1938, former APA president Knight Dunlap predicted the "impending dismemberment of psychology,"[152] and Allport was himself convinced that a "violent re-alignment of psychology is under way":

> The simultaneous growth of sectional and special interest societies is a proof. These two lines of division are of course antithetical. . . . They both arise from the heterogeneous and unwieldy character of the A.P.A. where the four winds of heaven fail to meet. There is really little in common between social psychology, brain waves, rats and psychophysics.[153]

This talk of dismemberment prompted the APA council to undertake a series of steps designed to bridge the many differences that crisscrossed the field. A new Committee on Scientific and Professional Ethics was constituted in recognition of the increasing importance of "clinical and practical problems."[154] The association also became more active politically: The APA authorized a report on the discrimination encountered by women psychologists; it voted to move the International Congress away from Nazi Austria; and it issued a statement supporting academic freedom. The most significant change, however, was in the association's leadership. Allport's election in 1938 marked the beginning of a new era in the history of the APA and American scientific psychology as a whole. From 1939 onward, the association became increasingly aware of issues of professional development, application, and scholarly diversity.

CONCLUSION

In the 1920s, Allport had been haunted by an antimodernist vision of the American self losing its soul. He was convinced that Americans were unwittingly exchanging their spiritual freedom and individual dignity for scientific progress and economic security. His science of personality reflected this spiritual concern, but as the 1930s unfolded, Allport's formulations were challenged by a new and altogether darker set of circumstances. The economic upheavals of the Depression and dramatic rise of fascism brought the individual's relationship to society into sharp relief. Long-cherished ideals of the vigorous American self triumphing over adversity seemed less relevant; catastrophic new circumstances seemed to demand vigorous new theory to cope with changing conditions.

As a well-connected Harvard psychologist, Allport was in a position to distance himself from the crushing uncertainties that bore down on many Americans during this period. To his credit, Allport reached well beyond the hallowed gates of Harvard Yard and played a leading role in developing a more politically and socially informed psychology. For all his political and disciplinary activism, however, Allport's outlook retained its essentially antimodernist hue. Indeed, his principal scholarly motivation throughout the Depression was that which had first inspired him to go into psychology: the disenchantment of the self and the subsequent weakening of individual dignity, uniqueness, and soul. His magnum opus, *Personality*, bore only the faintest trace of the economic upheavals around him, and throughout the decade Allport continued to view discussions of "culture and personality" as just another discourse of disenchantment.

Facing the present with an eye on the past, Allport's psychology of personality drew heavily on an older vocabulary of manly character. Both his theory of motivation and his model of maturity stressed the triumph of civilized character over instinctual savagery. Implicit in this theory was a refutation of the masculine ethic that had been ascending since the 1920s. Its values of savagery, primitivism, sexuality, and display were all noticeably absent from Allport's vision of a "fully developed personality," and although he drew on the ostensibly gender-neutral language of personality, his reference to a "man of confident dignity" gave his discussion a manly specificity.[155]

Personality was a huge success, and much of its appeal lay in the same clever blending of cultural tensions that had propelled Allport's career since his return from Germany. The book packaged a scientific message of discipline and control with a spiritual message of freedom and distinctiveness. Artfully sidestepping the philosophical problems posed by this arrangement, Allport prospered in his role as one of personality's grand masters. The chairmanship at Harvard was soon followed by the presidency of the APA—personal accomplishments that also symbolized the consolidation of personality as an official category of scientific research.

10

CONCLUSION

In 1938, Allport described the "discovery of personality" as one of the "outstanding events in [the] psychology of the present century."[1] If sheer volume is the measure of scholarly significance, it would be difficult to challenge his observation. Between 1920 and 1940, American psychologists became fascinated with personality, and the once obscure category grew into an "avalanche" of "astonishing proportions" with its own textbooks, journals, and courses.[2] Strategically located and rhetorically gifted, Allport emerged as the "patron saint" of the new science and his vision of personality as a natural object—an objective "psychophysical system" —was widely embraced. What went largely unnoticed at the time, and what I have emphasized in this book, is the rich interplay between the scientific language Allport deployed and the American culture in which he was embedded. Weaving together the personal and the professional, I have argued against what historian Roger Smith described as the "still dominant natural-scientific view that scientific language shuts out normative meaning."[3] Using Allport's own experience, I have drawn attention to some of the ways in which the science of personality was implicated in a broad cultural transformation in the language of American selfhood.

PSYCHOLOGY AND THE "CULTURE OF PERSONALITY"

At the most general level, personality psychology was, at least in part, a scientific reflection of the shift from the self-sacrificing language of character to the self-affirming idiom of personality. Throughout the period under study, Allport repeatedly attacked all talk of character and any other psychological language that hinted of old-fashioned moralism. His project was a self-conscious refutation of the character-building tradition, and it drew much of its impetus from a personal desire to escape from a morally stifling past. In search of a less constricted future, Allport embraced the category that had entered the vocabulary of so many other Americans—personality. The category was conceived as a culture-free object of science, but his early scientific representation of personality closely paralleled the new priorities of American culture. Ascendence—submission and introversion–extroversion did not gauge the moral self: They were the morally lean reference points for life in an industrial age.

Implicated in a larger discursive transformation, Allport's career as a personality psychologist also highlights the cultural plasticity of psychology and the complexity of the discipline's relationship with the larger culture. From the outset of his professional life, Allport's relationship with psychology was an uneasy one. He had been extensively schooled in the language of natural science, and he had at least partially assimilated its spirit of certitude and precision. Learned and self-consciously modern, Allport still retained an antimodernist hunger for depth, soul, and authenticity, and he looked on America's brash materialism with suspicion. Viewing psychology as both a cause of spiritual decline and a possible source of new meaning, Allport worked to direct science toward an antimodernist end. His ambition was to breathe new life into some old values and restore a spirit of depth, dignity, and divine otherworldliness to an American self that was buffeted by the superficial appeals of commercial culture.

Personality was an ideal vehicle for the complex integration of opposites that Allport's project entailed. He needed a language large enough to house the modern and premodern, the material and the spiritual, the masculine and the feminine, and science and sentiment. Personality possessed this capacity and more; in his textbook Allport noted that "scarcely any word is more versatile."[4] Throughout his early career, Allport played on the category's unique combination of modernist cachet and historical depth, and he always insisted that he was, first and foremost, a personality psychologist. "All of my work has focused on personality theory," he remarked near the end of his career, "particularly on the structure and motivation of the personality."[5] For Allport, personality was a convenient shorthand for all that was new and fashionably up-to-date. It represented a fresh way of thinking about the self, one that was "objective," "professional," "realistic" and "honest." Alluring to the modern ear, personality also carried a heavy philosophical and theological cargo, and Allport drew on this rich network of historical meanings while purporting to clearly demarcate science from culture. German romanticism was especially influential in this regard, and Allport discovered that he could use the language of personality to transport selfhood to an older space of sublime values and spiritual worth.

The journey was not entirely unsuccessful, but it came with an ironic price. By promoting the idea of a devalued self—a self that exists independently of moral frameworks—Allport unintentionally reinforced a tendency that lay at the heart of the new culture of personality: a detachment of the self from social and cultural contexts. The personality ideal made the individual self "the ultimate locus of salvation."[6] Personal fulfillment involved an efficient mobilization of the self's own resources; social and ethical considerations were of secondary importance. Although Allport occasionally warned his readers about the dangers of "self-seeking and vanity," most of his scholarly time was spent celebrating the capabilities and prowess of the individual self.[7] To "study [a person] most fully is to take him as an individual," he wrote.[8] In Allport's hands, this position implied that selfhood could, and perhaps should, be considered in relation to its own internal properties, rather than in relation to a cultural or moral milieu. By 1937, Allport thus found himself advocating a position that was largely identical to the emerging personality ideal. In both cases, the isolated individual was the proper object of scrutiny and the source of fulfillment.

Although Allport's participation in the culture of personality may have been unwitting, the moral thrust of his psychology was by no means idiosyncratic. Despite their century-long valorization of objectivity, American psychologists have frequently traversed the divide between scientific description and moral prescription. Indeed, a number of historians have persuasively argued that morality is one of the discipline's driving concerns. According to Graham Richards, American psychology has been animated by an "enduring moral project" for most of its history. Its mandate has been to provide a "culturally authoritative foundation for conventional morality in a society which is constitutionally pluralistic in terms of religion and ideology."[9]

Allport's 20-year engagement with personality represents an illuminating illustration of American psychology's moral project at work. Like many of his colleagues in the 1920s, he was convinced that the solution to America's ethical dilemma lay not in history, culture, or religion, but in science, particularly psychology. Psychometric methods, experiments, and case studies could cut through layers of prejudice and distortion that had long governed matters of conduct. The appeal of this program lay in psychology's ability to shift the basis of ethical authority from society to human nature itself. Instead of haggling over arbitrarily defined social creeds, psychologists could use their methods to scrutinize the "actual nature of personality."[10] An objective understanding of human nature would serve as the foundation of a new moral code. Such a code would be ethical, as historian Nikolas Rose explained, "because it has a basis not on an external truth—be it divine right or collective good—but one essential to the person over whom it is exercised."[11]

ALLPORT AND THE HISTORY OF PERSONALITY PSYCHOLOGY

In telling the story of personality's principal advocate, I have sailed against a strong historiographic current.[12] Biographical studies are viewed suspiciously in history-of-science circles, and a number of scholars have questioned the value of life studies of scientists for anything other than knowledge of the particulars of the specific life in question. Richard Lewontin captured the prevailing spirit when he warned of biography's potential to obscure important issues: "By concentrating on the individual creators of ideas or fashions, one may easily fail to ask what social circumstances engendered the problematic in the first place."[13] This message has been echoed by a number of prominent historians of psychology. In his illuminating study of psychological categories, Kurt Danziger cautioned against any attempt to approach scientific language through biographical study: "The history of categories as elements in discursive formations obviously cannot be written in terms of the history of individual personages."[14] In writing this book, my ambition has been not to refute these observations, but to temper them. A close reading of an individual life can complement a wide-ranging investigation of scientific language and practice. As historian of science Thomas Hankins noted, "if biography is honest we can learn a great deal about the way in which science works, and we can also be protected from too-hasty generalizations."[15]

Personality psychology has been the subject of its fair share of generalizations, and through a close study of Allport's experience, I have suggested that some of them are in need of reexamination. One historical convention that has been rendered particularly problematic is the view of Allport as a solitary creator of the field of personality. This view is quite common, especially among psychologists, and in contemporary textbooks on personality it is not unusual to read accounts of Allport having "singlehandedly created the field of American personality psychology."[16] In this book, I have endeavored to go beyond the antiquated "great man" historiography of the textbooks and toward a more dynamic and socially embedded model of scientific development. Instead of celebrating Allport's individual genius, my intention has been to describe the network of circumstances that lent amplitude to his voice and made his scholarly program plausible. What should be clear by now is not Allport's intellectual isolation, but his connection to a rich network of social relationships and discursive practices. His psychology of personality reflected developments in social work, psychiatry, behaviorist psychology, and intelligence testing, and those fields, in turn, were informed by the broad discursive shifts in the language of American selfhood.

In going beyond the view of Allport as a solitary inventor, I have also sought to problematize the portrayal of the field as an exclusively modernist project. In most historical accounts, personality psychology is thought to have grown as a result of the confluence of bureaucratic need and methodological convention. According to Todd Sloan, personality theory has served the purposes of therapeutic intervention and "prediction based on assessment of individual differences."[17] From this perspective, Victorian notions of selfhood are said to be largely absent from personality psychology. According to Danziger, "personality [psychology] never had anything in common with traditional concepts of the person as a social agent."[18] Although there is much to recommend this position, Allport's experience suggests that it is somewhat overdrawn. Victorian notions of selfhood continued to inform some of the most important discussions of personality in psychology long after the category of character had been largely abandoned by psychologists.

By positioning the science of personality alongside the culture of character, it becomes possible to invest important theoretical developments in the field with a sense of cultural purpose. The relationship between personality psychology and psychoanalysis is a notable case in point. A number of historians have commented on the threat that "depth" psychology posed to empiricist psychology in the interwar period.[19] Danziger argued that personality was a useful tool in a broad empiricist campaign to domesticate psychoanalysis and subordinate its tenets to the scientific methodology of academic psychology. It is a compelling argument, but if Allport's experience is any guide, it would be a mistake to view psychology's opposition to psychoanalysis strictly in terms of safeguarding professional turf or defending a particularly methodology. Throughout his career, Allport's opposition to psychoanalysis was more spiritual than professional. In keeping with the views of Stern, Spranger, and other German mandarins, he rejected psychoanalysis not because it was unscientific, but because it asserted a vision of human experience that was, if anything, too scientific. Like behaviorism, psychoanalysis was a discourse of disenchantment that rested on evolutionary assumptions of sexual drive and biological adaptation. In the psychoanalytic universe there was no place for the sublime, the dignified, or the enchanted. The higher reaches of humanity were subordinate to a crude, base core of animalistic energy that no amount of refinement could ever fully domesticate. Personality provided Allport with a disciplinary platform to counter this vision. The category enabled him to use the discourse of science to subvert the most starkly scientific aspects of psychoanalytic theory and thereby safeguard a higher vision of the self.

Allport's scholarly refutation of psychoanalysis is but one example of a broad antimodernist temper that colored virtually every aspect of his psychological thinking. His antimodernism, like that of many of his contemporaries, was a sophisticated discourse of accommodation that sought to position the new alongside the old and the spiritual alongside the material. One of the scholarly by-products of this sensibility was a profound ambivalence concerning the purpose of personality psychology and the ways it should be studied. Allport was fascinated by the possibility of knowing personality, but as we have seen, he was also anxious to protect personality from prying modernist eyes and controlling ambitions. Unable to escape the gravity of his antimodernist commitments, Allport found himself in the paradoxical position of advancing a science whose purpose was to both know and not know. The field's mission was to bring the individual within a scientific register while demonstrating personality's essential freedom and uniqueness. The tensions inherent in these contradictory ambitions created the methodological peculiarities for which Allport is famous. As Oliver John and Richard Robins have observed, Allport was both "father and critic of the five-factor model"—an "empirically derived classification of personality traits, based on the intercorrelations among trait ratings across individuals."[20] He was a champion of the vision of an empirically known, measured self, and his empirical work and text helped cement the idea that personality could be brought within a psychometric register. Yet, Allport mocked the same quantitative methods that he himself put into practice while venerating an intuitive, qualitative approach to personality that he seldom implemented. As former Allport student Bertram Cohler observed, he appeared to "mistrust the very person-centered approach that he championed."[21]

For many psychologists, Allport's greatest weakness was his ambiguous embrace of scientific orthodoxy. His former student Robert Holt summed up the views of many psychologists when he complained that the "artist [in Allport] has probably dimmed the vision of the scientist."[22] One of the great ironies of Allport's career is that this alleged weakness was also the source of his considerable power within the field. The strength of his moderate position lay in his ability to address two important problems confronting American psychology in the 1920s and 1930s. The first is what may be termed the irony of objectivity. As noted in chapter 7, psychology has fought a long-running battle with common sense. To bolster their authority, psychologists adopted a variety of technical procedures designed to increase their objectivity. These procedures were effective, but as historian Mitchell Ash noted, the technical methods that validated psychological knowledge in the real world were also responsible for fueling "public doubt about the applicability of such 'objective' knowledge in the real world."[23] Psychology thus found itself in the awkward position of relying on a practice that put its own authority into question.

Allport's success as a psychologist was based in part on his efforts to address this issue of professional authority. His psychology of personality attempted to suspend popular suspicion of scientific psychology without any serious disruption to its established methods. The tactic that Allport advocated involved a subtle loosening of psychology's scientific strictures. He did not "demand [an] abolition of controls and a return to mysticism," nor would he "forget the rules . . . [he had] learned in the laboratory."[24] The discipline would continue to use experimental methods, and it would continue to cultivate a spirit of natural scientific rigor. What would change would be the degree to which these methods were practiced. Allport proposed a "more liberal conception of science and methods" in which natural science would be brought together with "common sense."[25] By bringing these two together under the rubric of personality, Allport thought it possible to overcome the "irony of objectivity" that had handicapped the discipline. In *Personality*, he argued that psychologists could "strike a balance between the excessively rigid and perfectionistic standards (that accomplish nothing but a sterilization of research, limiting it to worthless fragments of behavior having no essential bearing upon personality) and loose standards that permit wanton assertions and extravagant claims to go without check or proof."[26]

In the 1930s, most psychologists found Allport's arguments unpersuasive. Nevertheless, the issues of professional adequacy to which he spoke and the verve and balanced tone with which he expressed them struck a chord in the field. Psychologists felt obliged to respond to his challenge, if only to refute the thrust of his "liberal" critique.[27] The attention helped propel Allport to the forefront of the discipline and to the office of the American Psychological Association (APA) presidency.

Allport's remarkable professional success was aided by his ability to speak to a second problem that confronted psychologists in the 1930s: the question of identity. Was the field's identity grounded in the laboratory or the clinic? Was the field's raison d'etre scientific knowledge or social improvement? No clear consensus had emerged on either of these questions, and in the absence of agreement, a number of psychologists concluded that the field was on the verge of dismemberment. In this context of fragmentation, Allport's ambiguous identity as a personality psychologist emerged as an important professional resource. The language of personality gave him the flexibility to bridge the various fracture lines that crisscrossed the field. At Harvard, he was the link between the psychodynamic psychology of Murray and the operationalism of Boring, Stevens, and Lashley. Within the APA, Allport helped bridge the gap that separated the young social activists of Society for the Psychological Study of Social Issues and the older, politically conservative members of the APA council.

THE CULTURAL POLITICS OF PERSONALITY

William James bequeathed a complex legacy for the discipline that he helped establish, and Allport's legacy for personality psychology is no less involved. The search he began in graduate school for a "complete and sensitive instrument of individual measurement for personality" continues unabated, and indeed, many psychologists now feel that the psychometric dream has been realized.[28] According to personality psychologist John Digman, "the hope that the method of factor analysis would bring a clarity to the domain of personality ... seems close to realization."[29] Digman is hardly alone in his views, but the psychometric legacy that Allport bequeathed to the profession continues to share ground with a less technical and more biographically informed spirit. Personality psychology's preoccupation with statistics and methodology is routinely criticized, and many psychologists continue to sense, as Allport did in the 1930s, that field is being driven more by its allegiance to scientific method than by its commitment to the subject matter. In their entry on personality in the *Annual Review of Psychology*, David Magnusson and Bertril Törestad noted that "too much research is now evaluated with reference to the technical sophistication of the methods and statistics, rather than with reference to the strength with which it answers relevant questions."[30]

It is easy to detect the echo of Allport in the furious methodological debates that characterize modern personality psychology. However, as I indicated at the outset of this book, my intention has not been to identify a particular conception or method of personality as the more historically correct. Instead, I have examined the cultural, political, and spiritual issues at stake in the ostensibly neutral scientific language of selfhood. As we have seen, personality was never a simple, neutral category; it carried a rich cargo of cultural connotations. Its appeal for Allport and for many Americans lay in its ability to integrate and obscure contradictory desires for a self that was cataloged and controlled at the same moment that it was unique and free. This ambition was born out of the confrontation with modernity, but as Allport's career illustrates, it was a goal that was never fully realized. The psychometric, "relational" model of personality remained at odds with the idea of "real" personality that was utterly distinct and special. Unable to completely connect the language of measurement to a world of meaning, Allport often turned to a premodern discourse of religious reverence. The rich liturgy and ancient forms of Anglo-Catholicism spoke to the feelings of "weightlessness" that modernity had generated, and it provided him with a welcome sense of depth and authenticity.

As historian Jackson Lears noted, the existential implications of life in a scientifically driven, corporate culture remain part of the unfinished business of our time. "Yearnings for the authentic, the natural, [and] the real pervade contemporary American culture" and live alongside strident desires for measurement, control, and exactitude.[31] Allport's experience provides no easy answer to the disenchantment of our own age, but his work does invite us to think more carefully about the kind of cultural work performed by the language of psychology.

NOTES

CHAPTER 1: INTRODUCTION

1. G. Allport, 1938/1960a, p. 5.
2. Vernon, 1933, p. 157.
3. Cabot's remarks are quoted in the "informal discussion" section of Jarrett, 1919, p. 593.
4. Boring, 1920; Fernberger, 1928.
5. James, 1890/1983, p. 358; Prince, 1905/1978.
6. Rugg, 1921, p. 90.
7. Roback, 1932–33, p. 215.
8. Danziger, 1990, pp. 156–173.
9. Cantril, 1938, p. 107.
10. Eysenck, 1990, p. 3.
11. G. Allport, 1921, 1922.
12. G. Allport, 1937.
13. Schafer, Berg, & McCandless, 1951.
14. Cited in Susman, 1979, p. 219.
15. Macleod, 1983. Character's role in Victorian political thinking is considered in Collini, 1985.
16. Smiles, 1875, p. 1.
17. The etymology of personality is discussed in Williams, 1976, pp. 194–197.
18. Anonymous, Glenville High School Yearbook, 1915, Cleveland, Ohio.
19. Fox, 1993, p. 647.
20. For a brief overview of psychological meanings of personality, see R. Smith, 1997, pp. 599–606.
21. Randall, 1912.
22. For a good discussion of critical historiography in psychology, see Harris, 1997. See also Rose, 1996. In Rose's view, "critical history disturbs and fragments, it reveals the fragility of that which seems solid, the contingency of that which seemed necessary, the mundane and quotidian roots of that which claims lofty nobility" (p. 41).
23. For a good discussion of the scientific uses of personality, see Danziger, 1997.
24. Farr, 1989, p. 26.
25. Danziger, 1997.
26. Bederman, 1995, p. 7.
27. Danziger, 1997, p. 8.
28. G. Richards, 1995, p. 15.
29. Danziger, 1997.
30. Ibid., p. 15.
31. Rose, 1996, p. 54.
32. See Romanyshyn, 1971.
33. Danziger, 1997, p. 140.
34. To date, there is no book-length biography on Allport. A book billed as a biography appeared shortly after his death, but this work is more of a summary

of Allport's ideas than a historical discussion. See Ghougassian, 1972. For a helpful discussion of Allport's early career, see Pandora, 1997.

35. See Craik, Hogan, & Wolfe, 1993.
36. Pandora, 1997, p. 2.
37. Ibid., p. 177. In her conclusion, Pandora argued that Allport was doing for psychology what

> Franklin Roosevelt had asked the nation to do. . . . In an era when the nation's leaders had pledged that "the pattern of an outworn tradition" would be cast off to initiate a "New Deal" for the American people, these three psychologists [Gordon Allport, Gardner Murphy, and Lois Murphy] critiqued science and society in a similar spirit. (p. 177)

CHAPTER 2: "FINE CHARACTER AND SPLENDID IDEALS": ALLPORT'S EARLY YEARS (1897–1915)

1. Nellie Wise Allport, diary entry, September 3, 1896, Allport Family Papers (AF).
2. Nellie Wise Allport, diary entry, 1896, quoted in G. Allport, 1944, p. 14.
3. G. Allport, 1967.
4. G. Allport, 1952.
5. Nellie Wise Allport, diary entry, 1897.
6. For a good discussion of character in the 19th century, see Susman, 1979. Character is also discussed in Bledstein, 1976; Coben, 1991; and Szasz, 1981.
7. Smiles, 1853, p. 363.
8. Quoted in Szasz, 1981, p. 146.
9. Character was a heavily gendered category, and it was usually related to the ideal of manhood. For an insightful discussion of character's gendered dimensions, see Lunbeck, 1994.
10. Roosevelt, 1913, p. 527.
11. Smiles, 1853, p. 364.
12. Cunningham, 1992, p. 8.
13. Quoted in Hill, 1985, p. 29. For Methodists, notions of a natural female spirituality found additional support in the historical example of the movement's founder, John Wesley. Wesley had drawn special attention to the role played by his mother Susanna Annesley Wesley in his own religious formation. Subsequent generations of Methodists followed his lead by extolling the virtues of motherhood in general and the "Mother of Methodism" in particular. Susanna Wesley was portrayed as the embodiment of female virtue, the model on which every Methodist woman should base her life: "Every Christian wife and mother throughout Methodism should make the life and character of Susanna Wesley a constant study, and the good effect would be manifest upon the discipline of our families, the welfare of our children, and the piety of our Churches." See J. Potts, 1891, p. 255.
14. Cross, 1950.
15. G. Allport, 1952.
16. See Dieter, 1980, pp. 51–52.
17. Bledstein, 1976, p. 146.

18. G. Allport, 1944, p. 8, Gordon W. Allport Papers, Harvard University Archives (GWAP). Unpublished archival materials, courtesy of the Harvard University Archives.

19. The phrase "boiling hot religion" is associated with Francis Ashbury, one of the founders of American Methodism. See Hatch, 1994, p. 181.

20. G. Allport, 1944, pp. 8, 28.

21. Nellie Wise Allport to Gordon Allport(?), June 1, 1922, AF.

22. G. Allport, 1952.

23. Ibid.

24. G. Allport, 1944, p. 7.

25. J. Allport, 1919, p. 3.

26. Ibid., p. 4.

27. John Allport to Bessie Avent, July 29, 1907, AF. Bessie Avent was John's sister.

28. J. Allport, 1919, pp. 9, 10.

29. Ibid., p. 13.

30. Ibid., p. 15.

31. In an autobiographical statement, John Allport (1919) recalled that "this next move [to Cleveland] was not in any sense a product of my uneasy nature, but a desire to educate our sons or at least give them the advantages due them" (p. 15).

32. Ibid., p. 17. In an interview, Allport (1952) recalled that many of his father's rural patients had no money and would often pay their bills in farm produce: "After the person got well, he [John Allport] would say 'Well, when are you going to kill this pig?'"

33. J. Allport, 1919, p. 17.

34. For a discussion of Cleveland's development as an industrial center, see Barton, 1975.

35. Ibid., p. 12.

36. See Gordon Allport, "Personal experience with racial and religious attitudes," n.d., GWAP.

37. G. Allport, 1944, p. 7.

38. Szasz, 1981.

39. Abbot, 1910.

40. Warner, 1964, p. 61.

41. Steffens, 1905, p. 302.

42. Starr, 1982.

43. J. Allport, 1919, p. 18.

44. G. Allport, 1952.

45. John Allport to Bessie Avent, July 29, 1907, AF.

46. Methodist Memorial Hospital to A. G. Burry, February 20, 1917. This letter is taken from a scrapbook kept by John Allport that documents his work in the field of hospital construction, AF.

47. Horatio Alger is discussed in Cawalti, 1965, pp. 101–123.

48. J. Allport, 1919, p. 4.

49. Bertha Young to Gordon Allport, March 11, 1947, AF. In this letter, Young described her experience as the mother of a patient of John Allport in 1918–1919. The elder Allport's messages of support were especially important to

her, and she noted that "I wrote these words down and have passed many copies to friends." Young enclosed a copy for Gordon Allport that contained 21 hopeful messages and sayings, none of which are especially original: "Have unbounded faith in recovery coupled with every sensible and intelligent thing that might operate for good."

50. J. Allport, 1919, p. 16.
51. Ibid., p. 17.
52. Freedman, 1996, p. xii.
53. For a general discussion of 19th-century women's voluntary associations, see Hill, 1985. Nellie Allport was elected president of the Portage County WCTU in 1900. A local newspaper account of her election indicated that she had been a member of the WCTU for 10 years and that she was "very popular." The exact date and name of the newspaper are not indicated on the clipping. See "New President Portage County WCTU," AF.
54. A note about the meeting of the Mother's Club appeared in a local newspaper on February 15, 1906, AF. The meeting of the Hudson Home Circle was mentioned in an unnamed local newspaper in October 1906, AF.
55. G. Allport, 1952.
56. Ibid.
57. J. Allport, 1919, p. 5.
58. Cited in Rotundo, 1993, p. 255.
59. J. Allport, 1919, p. 3.
60. Ibid., p. 9.
61. Rotundo, 1993, p. 51.
62. G. Allport, 1952.
63. Ibid.
64. Gordon Allport to Harold, Floyd, and Fay Allport, July 29, 1947, AF.
65. G. Allport, 1952.
66. B to Gordon and Ada Allport, July 24, 1927, AF.
67. Personal reflection on B, undated manuscript. The events described in the passage suggest that it was probably written sometime in late 1917–1918.
68. Rotundo, 1993, p. 265.
69. Cited in Bederman, 1995, p. 99.
70. Cited in Rotundo, 1993, p. 268.
71. G. Allport, 1952.
72. "Bring Latin up to date at Glenville," *Cleveland Plain Dealer*, 1914, AF. The exact date of this item does not appear on the newspaper cutting.
73. H. H. Cully to John Allport, June 17, 1915, AF.
74. Gordon Allport, "Personal experience with racial and religious attitudes" n.d. GWAP.
75. F. Allport, 1917, p. 6.
76. G. Allport, 1952.
77. Ibid.
78. Ibid.
79. Wiebe, 1967, p. 44.
80. James, 1907/1955, p. 22. James described a clash between the "tender-minded" and "tough-minded." The former were "rationalistic (going by prin-

ciples), intellectualistic, idealistic, optimistic, religious, free-willist, monistic, dogmatical," whereas the latter were "empiricist (going by facts), sensation-alistic, materialistic, pessimistic, irreligious, fatalistic, pluralistic, [and] scep-tical" (p. 22).

CHAPTER 3: A NEW WORLD: HARVARD (1915–1919)

1. Quoted in *Signal*, 1987, p. 7.
2. Bledstein, 1976, p. 129.
3. Eliot, 1906.
4. Veysey, 1965, p. 90.
5. Brooks, 1908, p. 612.
6. Lowell's 1909 inaugural address is reprinted in Lowell, 1934.
7. "The Duty of Scholarship" is reprinted in Lowell, 1934.
8. Ibid.
9. G. Allport, 1967, p. 5.
10. Malcolm Cowley to Ardys Allport, May 21, 1976, Allport Family Papers (AF).
11. Allport's undergraduate scrapbook is available in the Harvard University Archives. Unpublished archival materials, courtesy of the Harvard University Archives.
12. See Morison, 1965, pp. 400–438.
13. Reed, 1936.
14. G. Allport, 1952.
15. Allport's friendship with Paul Berryman led to one of all Allport's most famous books: *Letters From Jenny*. The book consisted of an analysis of 301 letters written during the years 1926 to 1937 from a middle-aged widow named "Jenny" to "Glenn," the college roommate of her son "Ross." His-torian David Winter (1993) has established that Allport was Glenn and that his Harvard roommate Paul Berryman was Ross.
16. Gordon Allport, "Harvard's Best Tradition," October, 1917, Gordon W. All-port Papers, Harvard University Archives (GWAP). Allport's undergraduate essay is discussed by Winter, 1996.
17. Glenville High School Yearbook, 1915, AF.
18. A record of Allport's course of study and extracurricular activities can be found in his undergraduate scrapbook in GWAP.
19. Hamlin, 1913, p. 547.
20. For an insightful history of social ethics at Harvard, see D. Potts, 1965. See also Ford, 1930. In his article, Ford reported that the name "Social Ethics" had been suggested by William James.
21. D. Potts, 1965, p. 97.
22. Ford, 1923, pp. 1, 2.
23. Ford's comments are taken from a 1920 pamphlet entitled *Harvard University Social Service*. A copy of this pamphlet is available in PBHP.
24. G. Allport, 1952.
25. The impact of industrialization on American life is discussed in Wiebe, 1967.

26. Kunzel, 1988.
27. Lubove, 1965, p. 20.
28. According to the prominent social theorist Mary Richmond (1922), case-work provided the social worker with a "clearer understanding of the numberless ways in which bad social conditions affect the lives of individuals." Record keeping also served as an "indispensable guide to future action in [*sic*] behalf of the person recorded."
29. Ibid., pp. 149, 151.
30. Todd, 1920.
31. Quoted in Gutman, 1973, p. 541.
32. Susman, 1979, p. 217.
33. Cited in ibid., p. 220.
34. Ibid.
35. Fisher, 1922, May.
36. Croly, 1909, p. 432.
37. Bourne, 1913, p. 294.
38. G. Allport, 1944, p. 23.
39. Nellie Allport summarized her thoughts on James and Griggs in an unpublished notebook entitled "Synopsis of Books Studied in 1904," AF.
40. Griggs, 1899/1908.
41. Nellie Allport, "Synopsis of Books Studied in 1904," AF.
42. Griggs, 1899/1908, p. 59.
43. Ibid., p. 62.
44. Ibid., p. 51.
45. Richmond, 1922, p. 90.
46. For a good discussion of the place of personality in Protestant theology, see King, 1989.
47. Richmond, 1922, pp. 93–94.
48. Ibid., pp. 93–94.
49. G. Allport, 1919, p. 108.
50. G. Allport, 1967.
51. Ibid., p. 6.
52. G. Allport, 1952. For an illuminating discussion of Münsterberg's career, see Hale, 1980.
53. Kuklick, 1977, p. 436.
54. Cited in Kuklick, 1977, p. 186.
55. Knight Dunlap quoted in O'Donnell, 1985, p. 226.
56. Münsterberg, 1914.
57. Ibid., pp. 11, 12, 306.
58. Ibid., p. 15. For a good discussion of the German interest in purposeful psychology, see Ringer, 1969.
59. Münsterberg, 1914, pp. 287, 313.
60. Ibid., pp. 292, 11.
61. Ibid., pp. 40, 46, 37.
62. Bakan, 1966, p. 12.
63. Quoted in Lears, 1981, pp. 138–139.
64. Münsterberg, 1914, p. 214.

65. Ibid., p. 214.
66. Stern, 1917, p. 187.
67. G. Allport, 1962b.
68. Ibid., p. 2.
69. G. Allport, 1967, p. 6.
70. Cited in Hale, 1980, p. 57.
71. G. Allport, 1962b. Allport paid private tribute to Münsterberg while visiting Danzig—the birthplace of the renowned psychologist—in 1923.

    > I wish I could find Münsterberg's birthplace in town, I should pay it a devoted pilgrimage. The eminent native son is not yet recognized, however, I shall have to revere in silence and seclusion, until someone discovers the birthplace and tags it for future psychologists who stray. Gordon Allport to Ada Gould, February 27, 1923, AF.

72. G. Allport, 1967, p. 6.
73. F. Allport, 1917, p. 6.
74. For a brief overview of Floyd Allport's career, see Post, 1980.
75. Langfeld & F. Allport, 1916.
76. F. Allport, 1919b.
77. G. Allport, 1952.
78. G. Allport, 1967, p. 6.
79. F. Allport, 1974, p. 6.
80. F. Allport, 1919a, pp. 299, 300.
81. Ibid., p. 300.
82. G. Allport, 1967, p. 5.
83. Quoted in R. L. Moore, 1986, p. 108.
84. G. Allport, n.d., p. 5.
85. Lears, 1981.
86. Cited in Lears, 1981, p. 42.
87. G. Allport, n.d., p. 5.
88. Allport's undergraduate scrapbook is available in GWAP.
89. Ibid. The fanfare surrounding Sunday's visit is evident in the headline of one of the articles: "Excited crowd storms Sunday gospel shed. 30,000 fight to hear evangelist preach to students."
90. Gordon Allport to Edwin Powers, March 20, 1923, AF.
91. G. Allport, n.d., pp. 6–7. This article may be viewed as the religious counterpart to the "professional" autobiography Allport published in the *History of Psychology in Autobiography*. On the first page, Allport describes the booklet as the "story of my religious development." The booklet was published by the Boston-based Church of the Advent.
92. Ibid., p. 6. Floyd Allport did not share his younger brother's spiritual sensibility. In his autobiography (1974), Floyd remarked, "I must have reacted differently from Gordon to what I felt to be the rather heavy religious influence in our early life" (p. 3). As a graduate student, Floyd was a committed materialist, and in the 1920s and 1930s he became highly critical of organized religion in general and Christianity in particular. For example, in a *Harper's* essay he described the term "Christian" as a "slogan of an intolerable slavery of the spirit" (F. Allport, 1930, p. 365).

93. Fuller, 1986.
94. Quoted in Fuller, 1986, p. 25.
95. Pandora, 1997, p. 21; High & Woodward, 1980, p. 67.
96. Leary, 1990, p. 120.
97. For two exceptions to this trend, see Fuller, 1986, and Taylor, 1992. Scholarly inattention to the religious sources of James's influence in psychology is a reflection of a broader neglect of the discipline's spiritual past. For some reflections on the importance of religion in the development of psychology, see P. Homans, 1982; Nicholson, 1994; and Vandenberg, 1993. Psychology's insecurity with respect to spiritual issues is discussed in Coon, 1992.
98. G. Stanley Hall to Joseph Jastrow, February 9, 1920. Cited in Coon, 1992, p. 147.
99. James, 1907/1955, p. 24.
100. Ibid., p. 26.
101. Ibid., p. 33.
102. Ibid., p. 46.
103. Ibid., pp. 61–62.
104. James, 1909/1977, p. 142.
105. Ibid., p. 26.
106. James, 1904/1984, p. 178.
107. James, 1897, p. 261.
108. James, 1911, p. 109.
109. James 1909/1977, p. 131.
110. Quoted in James, 1902/1982b, p. 512.
111. For a good discussion of the theology and practices of Methodism, see McCulloh & Smith, 1964.
112. Kuklick, 1977, p. 439.
113. Ibid., p. 441.
114. Ibid., p. 441.
115. Ibid., p. 437.
116. Ibid., p. 445.
117. Gordon Allport to Nellie Allport, February 8, 1917, AF.
118. F. Allport, 1974.
119. Floyd's poem contains 14 stanzas and was written in France in 1918. A copy of Floyd's poem can be found in AF.
120. G. Allport, 1967, p. 6.
121. Allport's 10-page reminiscence was titled "November Eleventh 1918."
122. G. Allport, 1967, p. 5.

CHAPTER 4: THE MISSIONARY LIFE: ROBERT COLLEGE, CONSTANTINOPLE (1919–1920)

1. Unknown author quoted in G. Allport, 1919, November 7, p. 67.
2. James, 1902/1982b, p. 515.
3. Calvin Coolidge, commencement address, June 19, 1919, Allport Family Papers (AF).

4. G. Allport, 1967, p. 7.
5. Gordon Allport to Nellie Allport, February 8, 1917, AF.
6. Floyd received the Croix de Guerre (a French citation for bravery).
7. G. Allport, 1952.
8. Harvard Mission Committee to G. E. Higgins, June 2, 1919, PBHP.
9. Undated statement by the Harvard Mission, Gordon W. Allport Papers, Harvard University Archives (GWAP). Unpublished archival materials, courtesy of the Harvard University Archives.
10. G. Allport, 1919, August 22, p. 7.
11. G. Allport, 1919, August 22, p. 9.
12. G. Allport, 1919, September 14, p. 42.
13. G. Allport, 1919, September 20, p. 46.
14. Clarke, 1900, p. 19.
15. Gates, 1940, p. 288.
16. Cited in Greenwood, 1965, p. 16.
17. Gordon Allport to Walter Tibbetts, January 14, 1920, PBHP.
18. For an interesting discussion of changes in the American missionary temper, see Hutchinson, 1974.
19. "Philips Brooks House and its Activities," *Harvard Alumni Bulletin*, February 15, 1917, PBHP.
20. Cited in Greenwood, 1965, p. 62.
21. Arthur Beane to Miriam Carpenter, July 15, 1919, PBHP. Beane was the treasurer of the Harvard Mission Fund.
22. Gordon Allport to Powers Hapgood, September 28, 1919, PBHP.
23. Gordon Allport to Walter Tibbetts, December 14, 1919, PBHP.
24. G. Allport, 1919, August 25, p. 11.
25. G. Allport, 1920, Feb. 17, p. 119.
26. G. Allport, 1919, August 25, p. 12.
27. G. Allport, 1919, September 14, p. 43.
28. Ibid., p. 43.
29. Edwin Powers was born in New York in 1896 and graduated from Williams College in 1918. Harold (Pete) Dodge was born in Oriskany, New York, in 1896 and graduated from Hamilton College in 1918. For more information on Dodge see his obituary, "Peter Dodge, 1965."
30. G. Allport, 1919, September 14, p. 41.
31. G. Allport, 1919, September 16, p. 44.
32. G. Allport, 1920, January 19, p. 105.
33. G. Allport, 1920, January 22, p. 107.
34. G. Allport, 1920, June 16, p. 162.
35. J. Richards, 1987, p. 92. The danger of imposing modern sexual categories on historical figures has also been noted by historian Estelle Freedman. Writing on the career of prison superintendent Miriam Van Waters, Freedman (1996) noted that the "discovery that Van Waters had a deeply romantic relationship with one of her benefactors, but did not identify as a lesbian, forced me to think about the limits of the sexual categories that have been read into the past" (p. xii).
36. J. Richards, 1987, p. 93.

37. G. Allport, 1919, September 1, p. 25.
38. Gordon Allport to Harold Allport, December 9, 1919, AF.
39. G. Allport, 1920, January 23, p. 108.
40. Allport's reference to Henry Goddard's infamous study "The Kallikak Family" is notable. Eugenic theory is often thought to have been incompatible with Christianity, but as historian Leila Zenderland (1998) has persuasively demonstrated, many religious leaders were attracted to eugenic doctrines. The Kallikak study was particularly popular "precisely because of its blend of new eugenic theories and traditional Christian morality" (p. 522).
41. G. Allport, 1920, January 23, p. 108.
42. Gordon Allport to Walter Tibbetts, December 14, 1919, PBHP.
43. Gordon Allport to Albert Staub, March 15, 1931, GWAP.
44. George Huntington to Leolin Keeney, May 28, 1920, PBHP. Celeb Gates to Walter Tibbitts, March 1, 1921, PBHP.
45. G. Allport, 1920, January 23, p. 137.
46. Ibid.
47. See Lears, 1981.
48. G. Allport, 1920, June 16, p. 162.
49. G. Allport, 1920, June 16, p. 163.
50. G. Allport, 1920, June 21, p. 168.
51. G. Allport, 1920, July 2, p. 171.
52. Ibid.
53. G. Allport, 1920, July 8, p. 180.
54. G. Allport, 1919, November 7, p. 67.
55. Katz, 1979.
56. G. Allport, 1920. Undated between dated entries of April 18 and April 27, 1920, p. 135.
57. Ibid.
58. Gordon Allport to Robert Foerster, May 6, 1920, Department of Social Ethics Papers, Harvard University Archives (DSEP).
59. Ibid.
60. Robert Foerster to Floyd Allport, June 2, 1920, DSEP.
61. G. Allport, 1920, May 7, p. 140.
62. Ibid.
63. Floyd Allport to Robert Foerster, June 3, 1920, DSEP.
64. Fayette Allport had a successful career in the American diplomatic corps. Between 1920 and 1923 he worked as a clerk to the U.S. Trade Commissioner, first in Vienna and then in Warsaw. He was made the assistant Trade Commissioner in Vienna in 1923, and the following year he was appointed Trade Commissioner to Germany. Fayette left the diplomatic corps in the 1930s and accepted a position as European manager of the Motion Picture Association of America.
65. William James quoted in Gay, 1988, p. 211.
66. Holt, 1915.
67. Allport's undergraduate transcript is in his academic file at the Registrar's Office of Harvard University.
68. G. Allport, G.W. *Allport Recalls a Visit to Sigmund Freud, July 1920*, Unpublished manuscript, GWAP.

69. E. B. Holt, 1915, p. v.
70. G. Allport, 1967, p. 7.
71. G. Allport, 1920, July 28, p. 197.
72. Gordon Allport, G.W. *Allport Recalls a Visit*, GWAP.
73. E. B. Holt, 1915, p. v.
74. Gordon Allport, G.W. *Allport Recalls a Visit*, GWAP.
75. Ibid.
76. G. Allport, 1967, p. 8.
77. Ibid., p. 8.
78. Ibid., p. 8.
79. Ibid., p. 8.
80. See Elms, 1993, and Morey, 1987.
81. The phrase "habits of the heart" was first used by Alexis de Tocqueville when describing the mores of American society. See Bellah, Madsen, Sullivan, Swidler, & Tipton, 1985.
82. Freud's disparaging remarks about Americans are quoted in Gay, 1988, p. 570.
83. G. Allport, 1967, p. 8.
84. G. Allport, 1920, July 28, p. 197.
85. Ibid.
86. Ibid.
87. G. Allport, 1967, p. 8.
88. Ibid., p. 8.
89. Lears, 1981.

CHAPTER 5: A SCIENCE OF PERSONALITY: GRADUATE SCHOOL (1920–1922)

1. F. Allport & G. Allport, 1921, p. 37.
2. G. Allport, 1920, August, p. 213.
3. Eksteins, 1989, p. 211.
4. G. Allport, 1920, August, p. 213.
5. G. Allport, September 11–17, 1920, p. 244.
6. Ibid., pp. 241, 242.
7. Ibid., pp. 241, 242.
8. Most published works on social ethics and the related field of social work stressed the importance of psychological research. Mary Richmond's (1917) remarks are, in this respect, quite typical: "From the physician and psychologist social work has more to learn than from either lawyer or historian, inasmuch as science, unlike law or history, can throw direct light on the social needs and possibilities of the case worker's clients" (p. 62).
9. Gordon Allport to Edwin Powers, November 15, 1920, Allport Family Papers (AF).
10. Ibid.
11. Gordon Allport to Edwin Powers, January 12, 1921; Gordon Allport to Edwin Powers, January 31, 1922, AF.

12. Gordon Allport to Ada Gould, June 16, 1921, AF.
13. Ibid.
14. See O'Donnell, 1985.
15. Kuklick, 1977, p. 437.
16. Ibid., p. 413.
17. Ibid., p. 565.
18. For a good discussion of the research ideal, see Veysey, 1965.
19. Lipset & Riesman, 1975, p. 153.
20. Cited in ibid., p. 153.
21. Cattell's work in psychology is discussed in Sokal, 1987a.
22. Kuklick, 1977.
23. F. Allport, 1974, p. 6.
24. For an overview of McDougall's career, see Hearnshaw, 1964, pp. 185–195.
25. McDougall, 1921, p. v.
26. McDougall, 1930a, p. 203.
27. McDougall, 1927, p. 105.
28. McDougall, 1930a, p. 213.
29. Allport took McDougall's "seminary" in social psychology during the 1921–1922 academic year. A copy of his graduate transcript can be found in his undergraduate scrapbook in Gordon W. Allport Papers, Harvard University Archives (GWAP). Unpublished archival materials, courtesy of the Harvard University Archives.
30. G. Allport, 1967, p. 12.
31. Gordon Allport to Ada Gould, December 5, 1921, AF.
32. Bartlett, 1958, p. 617; Pratt, 1958, p. 321.
33. Gordon Allport to Ada Gould, September 26, 1921, AF.
34. Gordon Allport to Ada Gould, December 10, 1920, AF.
35. Gordon Allport to Ada Gould, October 1, 1921, AF.
36. G. Allport, 1952.
37. Rosanoff, 1920, p. 281.
38. See Danziger, 1997, pp. 124–126.
39. Lunbeck, 1994, p. 69.
40. Barenbaum, 2000a.
41. Burgess, 1923, p. 680.
42. Quoted in Barenbaum, 2000a, p. 476.
43. Pound, 1923, p. 915.
44. Freund, 1917, p. 7.
45. Cited in Moddelmog, 1998, p. 340.
46. Watson's career is discussed in Buckley, 1989.
47. Watson's famous essay, *Psychology As the Behaviorist Views It*, is reprinted in Dennis, 1948, p. 465.
48. J. Watson, 1919, p. 9.
49. Ibid., pp. 10, 417.
50. Samelson, 1985, p. 35.
51. G. Allport, 1922. During this period, the term *genetic* was used to refer to issues that contemporary psychologists would label *developmental*.
52. Floyd Allport (1974) discussed his early interest in Münsterberg's "causal psychology" in his autobiography.

> I remember walking in the corridor of Emerson Hall [at Harvard] and reflecting upon the complexities of the psychological facts which had been gained up to that time regarding memory, problem solving, perceiving, and the like. I was wondering what the underlying basis of all this could possibly be in the nervous system, cortex, or the whole physiology of the organism. . . . It seemed for me a question of the profoundest significance. It was the problem of psychology *par excellence*, capable of opening new vistas. (p. 7)

53. F. Allport, 1919a.
54. See Post, 1980.
55. G. Allport, 1922, p. 10.
56. Ibid., pp. 11, 20.
57. Ibid., pp. 24, 29, 30, 34.
58. Ibid., pp. 30, 38.
59. Furumoto, 1998. The androcentric character of early American psychology is also discussed in Minton, 2000.
60. Shakow, 1976, p. 19.
61. For an excellent reading of the gendered character of the Society, see Furumoto, 1988.
62. Quoted in ibid., p. 94.
63. E. C. Sanford, 1904, quoted in ibid., p. 104.
64. Gordon Allport to Ada Gould, April 9, 1921, AF.
65. G. Allport, 1962a.
66. For more on women's relationship to academic psychology during this period, see Furumoto, 1998, and Milar, 2000. For a detailed study of female alienation from academic psychology in the 1910s, see Freedman's 1996 biography of Miriam Van Waters.
67. Gordon Allport to Ada Gould, April 9, 1921, AF.
68. G. Allport, 1967, p. 8.
69. Gordon Allport to Ada Gould, September 2, 1921, AF.
70. Gordon Allport to Ada Gould, September 14, 1921, AF.
71. For a thorough discussion of the field of intelligence testing, see Fancher, 1985.
72. James McKeen Cattell's 1922 remarks are quoted in Samelson, 1977, p. 275.
73. Freeman, 1926, p. 13.
74. Samelson, 1977.
75. Danziger, 1990, pp. 101–117.
76. Spaulding, 1921, p. 106.
77. Fernald, 1920, p. 7.
78. G. Watson, 1925, p. 1. For a detailed discussion of Watson's career, see Nicholson, 1997a.
79. Rugg, 1921, p. 85.
80. Ibid., p. 85.
81. G. Allport, 1922.
82. Ibid., p. 61.
83. Ibid., p. 61.
84. Carl Jung cited in ibid, p. 57.
85. Susman, 1979, p. 217.
86. G. Allport, 1922. In the published version of the test, Allport 1928a elab-

orated on its "vocational" implications in considerable detail. "The present test," he wrote, "though designed primarily for college students, may serve as part of a scale by which to determine fitness for appointments or training" (p. 134).

87. G. Allport, 1920, p. 242.
88. Cabot, 1919, p. viii.
89. Richard Cabot, cited in G. Allport, 1922, p. 338.
90. See Michaels, 1989.
91. Wiebe, 1967.
92. F. Allport, 1919b, p. 4.
93. Wallas, 1921, p. 98.
94. Richmond, 1922, p. 155.
95. For an influential discussion of how the social sciences render individuality visible, see Foucault, 1979, pp. 170–194.
96. G. Allport, 1922, p. 336.
97. Ibid., p. 337.
98. Leys, 1991.
99. Ibid., p. 9.
100. G. Allport, 1922, p. 339.
101. H. T. Moore, 1916, p. 228.
102. Downey, 1920.
103. H. T. Moore & Gilliland, 1921, p. 97.
104. Pressey & Pressey, 1919.
105. G. Allport, 1922, abstract.
106. H. T. Moore & Gilliland, 1921.
107. G. Allport, 1922, p. 103.
108. Ibid., pp. 104–105.
109. Myerson, 1919.
110. G. Allport, 1922, p. 106.
111. Ibid., p. 291.
112. Ibid., p. 126.
113. Parker, 1991.
114. Danziger, 1990, pp. 156–178.
115. Allen, 1931/1964, p. 73.
116. Quoted in Fass, 1977, p. 18.
117. Gordon Allport to Ada Gould, September 14, 1921, AF.
118. Gordon Allport to Ada Gould, June 27, 1922, AF.
119. Gordon Allport to Ada Gould, August 1, 1922, AF.
120. Gordon Allport to Edwin Powers, November 15, 1920, AF.
121. Gordon Allport to Edwin Powers, October 13, 1921, AF.
122. Allport's bookplate is courtesy of AF.
123. Five years after Allport's visit to Los Angeles, journalist H. L. Mencken noted dismissively that "osteopaths, chiropractors and other such quacks had long marked and occupied it [Los Angeles]. It swarmed with swamis, spiritualists, Christian Scientists, crystal-gazers, and the allied necromancers" (quoted in Jenkins, 2000, p. 90).
124. Gordon Allport to Ada Gould, August 1, 1922, AF.

125. Gordon Allport to Ada Gould, August 4, 1922, AF.
126. Gordon Allport to Ada Gould, July 29, 1922, AF.
127. Gordon Allport to Ada Gould, July 24, 1922, AF.
128. Gordon Allport to Ada Gould, July 23, 1922, AF.
129. Gordon Allport to Ada Gould, July 24, 1922, AF.
130. See Lears, 1981.
131. Gordon Allport to Ada Gould, December 10, 1920, AF.
132. Gordon Allport to Edwin Powers, September 12, 1922, AF.
133. Lears, 1981, p. 192.
134. See Shi, 1985.
135. Gordon Allport to Ada Gould, December 10, 1920, AF.
136. Gordon Allport to Edwin Powers, January 31, 1922, AF.
137. Thurber, 1921, pp. 664–665.
138. Gordon Allport to Ada Gould, June 16, 1921, AF.
139. G. Allport, 1920, July 28, AF.
140. Gordon Allport to Ada Gould, n.d. This letter is addressed to "chum girl" and was written sometime in the fall of 1920. AF.
141. Ibid.
142. G. Allport, 1922, p. 325. For a discussion of the identity of "Miss Penn" see Gordon Allport to Ada Gould, April 6, 1923, AF.
143. Ada Gould to Gordon Allport, n.d. This letter is addressed to "Dear Boy," and was written sometime in the fall of 1920. AF.
144. Ada Gould to Gordon Allport, December 9, 1920, AF.
145. Gordon Allport to Ada Gould, n.d. This letter is addressed to "chum girl" and was written sometime in the fall of 1920. AF.
146. Gould, personal reflection, June 4, 1923.
147. Ibid.
148. Gordon Allport to Ada Gould, August 8, 1922.
149. Ibid.
150. Gordon Allport to Ada Gould, December 4, 1920, AF.
151. Gordon Allport to Ada Gould, August 10, 1921, AF.

CHAPTER 6: A PSYCHOLOGY OF THE SPIRIT: GERMANY AND ENGLAND (1923–1924)

1. Stern, 1930, p. 340.
2. Gordon Allport to Edwin Powers, December 29, 1922, Allport Family Papers (AF).
3. Floyd Allport to Gordon Allport, March 14, 1924, AF.
4. Gordon Allport to John and Nellie Allport, May 27, 1922, AF.
5. Gordon Allport to Ada Gould, n.d. The events described in this letter suggest that it was written sometime in May 1922.
6. Gordon Allport to John and Nellie Allport, May 27, 1922, AF.
7. Herbert Langfeld to LeBaron Briggs, Dean of the Faculty of Arts and Sciences, February 23, 1922, Committee on General Scholarships and the

Sheldon Fund Papers, Harvard University Archives (CGSP). Unpublished archival materials, courtesy of Harvard University Archives.

8. Walter Dearborn to LeBaron Briggs, Dean of the Faculty of Arts and Sciences, February 23, 1922, CGSP.

9. William McDougall to LeBaron Briggs, Dean of the Faculty of Arts and Sciences, February 23, 1922, CGSP.

10. James Woods to LeBaron Briggs, Dean of the Faculty of Arts and Sciences, February 23, 1922, CGSP.

11. G. Allport, 1967.

12. Gordon Allport to James Woods, February 23, 1922, CGSP.

13. Ibid.

14. Ibid.

15. Gordon Allport to Edwin Powers, September 12, 1922, AF.

16. Gordon Allport to Ada Gould, March 28, 1923, AF.

17. Cited in Veysey, 1965, p. 130.

18. The appeal of German universities is discussed at length in Veysey, 1965.

19. Leary, 1987, p. 319.

20. O'Donnell, 1985. According to O'Donnell, most American students acquired a method in Germany and not "a fresh set of ideas" (p. 26). Some obtained even less. Psychologist Lightner Witmer said that the only thing he got out of his study in Germany in the 1890s was a PhD (p. 35).

21. Cited in Veysey, 1965, p. 131.

22. G. Allport, 1967, p. 9.

23. Boring, 1952, p. 39.

24. G. Allport, 1967, p. 10.

25. Gordon Allport, My Encounters With Personality Theory, unpublished manuscript, Gordon W. Allport Papers, Harvard University Archives (GWAP).

26. Gordon Allport circular letter, n.d., AF. Although the letter is undated, the events described in this letter indicate that it was probably written in December 1922.

27. Ibid.

28. Gordon Allport to Ada Gould, December 3, 1922, AF.

29. Gordon Allport to Hebert Langfeld, March 27, 1923, AF.

30. Ibid.

31. Ibid.

32. Gordon Allport to W. S. Taylor, December 18, 1922, William S. Taylor Papers, Archives of the History of American Psychology, University of Akron (WSTP). Allport met William Sentman Taylor during graduate school at Harvard. Taylor was a philosophy student working on a dissertation titled Belief and Behavior. He graduated in 1921, at which point he undertook further study in psychiatry and clinical psychology under F. L Wells at the Boston Psychopathic Hospital. The details of his friendship with Allport are vague, but the two seem to have shared a number of interests, including a marked dislike of psychoanalysis (see chapter 8). For biographical information on Taylor, see his biographical file in WSTP.

33. Gordon Allport to Ada Gould, November 1, 1922, AF.

34. Gordon Allport to W. S. Taylor, December 18, 1922, WSTP.

35. Ibid.
36. Gordon Allport to Ada Gould, n.d. The first page of the letter is missing. The second page begins with the phrase "sympathy in this period," and it was probably written in November 1922.
37. Allport did not elaborate on precisely what he meant by "gentle philandering," and his other letters to Taylor, Langfeld, and Powers are not especially helpful in this regard. The bulk of his correspondence from this period consists of observations on German culture and discussions of current trends in psychology. Apart from the oblique reference to "philandering," there is no mention of any romantic interest.
38. G. Allport, 1967, p. 9.
39. Ibid., p. 9.
40. Gordon Allport to W. S. Taylor, March 21, 1923, WSTP.
41. Historically, English-speaking scholars have not shown much interest in Stern. Over the past 30 years, his career and thought have been the focus of only a handful of articles, a surprisingly small number for so eminent a figure. For a brief review of Stern's career, see Hardesty, 1976; Kreppner, 1992; and Lamiell & Deutsch, 2000, who edited an entire issue of the journal *Theory & Psychology* on Stern and his work.
42. Kreppner, 1992, p. 541.
43. Misiak & Sexton, 1966, p. 108.
44. G. Allport, 1922, p. 9.
45. Gordon Allport to Herbert Langfeld, January 2, 1923, CGSP.
46. G. Allport, 1922, p. 16
47. Ibid., p. 9.
48. G. Allport, 1952.
49. Gordon Allport circular letter, n.d., AF.
50. Gordon Allport to Herbert Langfeld, March 27, 1923, AF.
51. Gordon Allport circular letter, n.d., AF.
52. Ibid.
53. Ibid.
54. Gordon Allport to W. S. Taylor, December 18, 1922, WSTP.
55. Gordon Allport to Ada Gould, April 27, 1923, AF
56. Gordon Allport to Edwin Powers, March 20, 1923, AF.
57. Gordon Allport to W. S. Taylor, December 18, 1922, WSTP.
58. Gordon Allport to W. S. Taylor, March 21, 1923, WSTP.
59. Gordon Allport to Ada Gould, March 18, 1923, AF.
60. Gordon Allport to Herbert Langfeld, March 27, 1923, AF.
61. For an insightful discussion of German mandarin culture, see Ringer, 1969, p. 5.
62. Cited in ibid., p. 89.
63. Ibid., p. 3.
64. Mathias Meier, 1921, cited in ibid., p. 382.
65. Harrington, 1991, p. 432.
66. Ibid., p. 433.
67. Stern, 1930, p. 345.
68. Ibid., pp. 339, 343, 345, 351, 352.

69. Gordon Allport to Ada Gould, n.d. This letter begins with the phrase "This morning I hunted out" and was writen sometime in the spring of 1923.
70. See Fancher, 1985.
71. Stern, 1930, p. 347.
72. Ibid., p. 348.
73. For a brief overview of personalism, see Brightman, 1950.
74. William Stern, *Person und Sache*, quoted in Knudson, 1927, p. 27.
75. Gordon Allport to Ada Gould, April 6, 1923.
76. Ibid.
77. Gordon Allport to Herbert Langfeld, March 27, 1923, AF.
78. Ibid.
79. The relationship between psychology and philosophy in Germany is discussed in Danziger, 1979. See also Ash, 1981.
80. Gordon Allport to Ada Gould, Nov, 9, 1922, AF.
81. The relationship between psychology and philosophy at Harvard is discussed in chapter 8.
82. Gordon Allport to W. S. Taylor, March 21, 1923, WSTP.
83. Ibid. Goodwin Watson 1934 noticed the same close relationship between psychology and philosophy during his postdoctoral year in Germany. In a later paper, he used a quotation from Wolfgang Köhler to illustrate the difference between the American and the German approach to philosophy: "The successful psychologist in Germany becomes a philosopher; in America he becomes a college administrator" (p. 765).
84. Gordon Allport to Herbert Langfeld, March 27, 1923, AF. In his autobiography, Stern noted that "psychology is essentially an auxiliary, not a foundational science for the study and practice of individuality." See Stern, 1930, p. 349.
85. Ibid.
86. Gordon Allport to James Ford, November 20, 1923, Department of Social Ethics Papers, Harvard University Archives (DSEP).
87. Ibid.
88. Külpe, 1895, p. 6.
89. See Danziger, 1983.
90. Ibid.
91. Stern, 1938, p. 13. Stern's early work on personality was not translated into English. The discussion of his personality theory is based on his 1938 text *General Psychology*. Although not accurate in every detail, this book can be considered representative of the major points of emphasis in Stern's personality theory of the early 1920s.
92. Ibid., p. 14.
93. Ibid., p. 14.
94. Ibid., p. viii.
95. Ibid., p. 401.
96. Stern, 1930, pp. 343, 347.
97. Stern, 1938, p. 382.
98. Ibid., p. 383.
99. Ibid., p. 374.

100. Ibid., p. 11.
101. Ibid., p. 12.
102. Ibid., p. 5.
103. Ibid., p. 6.
104. *Lebensformen* was first published in 1914 and was translated by Paul Pigors under the title *Types of Men: The Psychology and Ethics of Personality* (1928). The discussion of Spranger's work is based on this English translation.
105. Ibid., p. 8.
106. Ibid., p. 10.
107. Ibid., p. ix.
108. Ibid., p. 10.
109. Ibid., p. ix.
110. Ibid., p. 10.
111. Ibid., p. 11.
112. Ibid., p. 29.
113. Ibid., p. x.
114. Ibid., pp. 132–133.
115. Ibid., p. 392.
116. Ibid., p. 105.
117. Ibid., p. 212.
118. Ibid., p. 215.
119. Ibid., p. 215.
120. Ibid., p. 211.
121. Ibid., p. 216.
122. Ibid., p. 218.
123. Ibid., p. 218.
124. G. Allport, 1923.
125. G. Allport, 1923, p. 615.
126. Titchener coedited the *American Journal of Psychology* with G. Stanley Hall and E. C. Sanford from 1895 to 1921, and he was the sole editor from 1921 to 1925. See Tweney, 1987, pp. 38–39.
127. Gordon Allport to Ada Gould, May 31, 1923. Allport expressed a similar sentiment in a letter to Herbert Langfeld: "If Professor Titchener's Spring conference could have been amalgamated for once with the German congress he would have wept bitter tears to find that his conception of psychology belongs not to Germany's contemporary thought but to its archives." See Gordon Allport to Herbert Langfeld, May 3, 1923, AF.
128. Gordon Allport to Ada Gould, April 6, 1923, AF.
129. G. Allport, 1924.
130. Ibid., p. 132.
131. Ibid., p. 133.
132. Ibid., p. 133.
133. Ibid., pp. 132, 140.
134. See Baltzell, 1979.
135. Lears, 1981.
136. Hutchison, 1992, p. 98.
137. Quoted in Lears, 1981, p. 194.

138. These quotations come from Katherine Coolidge's 1899 poem *In the Cathedral*, quoted in Lears, 1981, p. 194.

139. Quoted in Lears, 1981, p. 206.

140. Gordon Allport to Edwin Powers, March 20, 1923, AF.

141. Ibid. In his religious autobiography, Allport (n.d.) recalled his boyhood thoughts on Catholicism: "But surely the Catholic Church was situated yonder across the railroad tracks and was distinguished chiefly for its outlandish ceremonies and for the queer looking immigrants who attended them" (p. 2).

142. Gordon Allport to Edwin Powers, March 20, 1923, AF.

143. G. Allport, n.d., p. 5.

144. Gordon Allport to Ada Gould, February 10, 1924, AF.

145. G. Allport, n.d., p. 12.

146. Gordon Allport to Edwin Powers, March 20, 1923, AF.

147. Gordon Allport to Ada Gould, February 25, 1924, AF.

148. Gordon Allport to Ada Gould, n.d., AF. This letter is undated, but the contents indicate that it was written sometime between February and April, 1924.

149. G. Allport, n.d., p. 14.

150. Gordon Allport to Edwin Powers, March 20, 1923, AF.

151. James, 1902/1982b, p. 460.

152. Ibid., p. 461.

153. Gordon Allport to Edwin Powers, March 20, 1923, AF.

154. Gordon Allport to Edwin Powers, September 23, 1923.

155. Quoted in James, 1903/1982a, p. 111.

156. F. Allport, 1924a.

157. Gordon Allport to Herbert Langfeld, February 24, 1924, AF.

158. Gordon Allport to Herbert Langfeld, February 24, 1924, AF. Allport expressed much the same sentiment to Gould: "I am convinced that Floyd's astoundingly neat system will not suffice." See Gordon Allport to Ada Gould, June 7, 1924, AF.

159. G. Allport, 1924, pp. 132, 133.

160. Floyd Allport to Gordon Allport, March 14, 1924, AF.

161. Ibid.

162. Ibid.

163. Gordon Allport to Ada Gould, December 4, 1923, AF.

164. Gordon Allport to Ada Gould, April 24, 1924, AF.

165. In his autobiography, Allport 1967 tactfully attributed the small number of collaborative studies with Floyd to theoretical differences. "[Floyd's psychology] was too behavioristic and too psychoanalytic for my taste. While our later works on political and social attitudes and on prejudice were similar in orientation, his theories became more positivistic, more monistic, and in a sense more interdisciplinary than my own" (p. 12).

166. Herbert Langfeld to LeBaron Briggs, Dean of the Faculty of Arts and Sciences, January 31, 1923, CGSP.

167. Ibid.

168. Gordon Allport to Herbert Langfeld, February 24, 1924, AF.

169. G. Allport, 1952.
170. Gordon Allport to Edwin Powers, December 2, 1923, AF.
171. Ibid.
172. Hearnshaw, 1964.
173. Ibid., p. 171.
174. Eysenck, 1990, p. 53. Carl Jung was also struck by the "feudal" character of British psychology. Jung 1933 recalled attending a joint meeting of the Aristotelian Society, the Mind Association, and the British Psychological Society in 1914 "at which a symposium was held on the question: Are individual minds contained in God or are they not? Should anyone in England dispute the scientific standing of these societies, he would not receive a very cordial hearing, for their membership includes the outstanding minds of the country. And perhaps I was the only person in the audience who listened with surprise to arguments that had the ring of the thirteenth century" (p. 180).
175. Gordon Allport to Ada Gould, February 4, 1924, AF.
176. Gordon Allport to Ada Gould, May 21, 1924, AF.
177. Gordon Allport to Herbert Langfeld, February 24, 1924, AF.
178. Gordon Allport to Ada Gould, May 21, 1924, AF.
179. Gordon Allport to Edwin Powers, December 2, 1923, AF.
180. Ibid.
181. Gordon Allport to Ada Gould, December 4, 1923, AF.
182. Gordon Allport to Ada Gould, July 6, 1924, AF.
183. Gordon Allport to Ada Gould, June 23, 1924, AF.
184. Gordon Allport to Ada Gould, April 24, 1924, AF.
185. Ahlstrom, 1972, p. 1042.
186. G. Allport, 1944, p. 31.
187. Ibid.
188. Gordon Allport to Ada Gould, April 24, 1924, AF.
189. Gordon Allport to Ada Gould, December 29, 1924, AF.
190. G. Allport, 1944, p. 31.
191. Ibid., p. 31.
192. Herbert Langfeld to LeBaron Briggs, Dean of the Faculty of Arts and Sciences, January 31, 1923, CGSP.
193. G. Allport, 1924, p. 133.

CHAPTER 7: CONSTRUCTING A CATEGORY: PERSONALITY PSYCHOLOGY AT HARVARD AND DARTMOUTH (1924–1930)

1. Gordon Allport to James Ford, November 11, 1923, Department of Social Ethics Papers, Harvard University Archives (DSEP). Unpublished archival materials, courtesy of the Harvard University Archives.
2. James Ford to Gordon Allport, November 2, 1923, DSEP.
3. Ibid.
4. Gordon Allport to Ada Gould, March 26, 1923, Allport Family Papers (AF).

5. Gordon Allport to Ada Gould, April 4, 1924, AF.
6. Gordon Allport to Ada Gould, February 22, 1924, AF.
7. Ibid.
8. Gordon Allport to Ada Gould, n.d., April 1923.
9. Gordon Allport to Ada Gould, December 17, 1923, AF.
10. Gordon Allport to James Ford, November, 20, 1923, DSEP.
11. Ibid.
12. Ibid.
13. Gordon Allport to Miss Carrol, February 14, 1924, DSEP.
14. Gordon Allport to Ada Gould, June 7, 1924, AF.
15. Gordon Allport to Edwin Powers, July 10, 1924, AF.
16. Gordon Allport to Ada Gould, March 1, 1924, AF.
17. D. Potts, 1965, p. 115.
18. Ibid., p. 115.
19. Ibid.
20. For biographical information on Cabot, see Cabot, 1926a. Cabot's career as a physician is discussed in Cannon, 1952, and O'Brien, 1985. For Allport's thoughts on Cabot, see G. Allport, 1966/1968a.
21. D. Potts, 1965.
22. Cabot, 1926a, pp. 123, 124.
23. Ibid., p. 94.
24. Ibid., p. 91.
25. Ibid. pp. 99, 104.
26. In his autobiography, psychologist Ernest Hilgard spoke of the uncertainty that surrounded the Department of Social Ethics. "Before deciding on how to proceed with my study in psychology, I went to Harvard as a guest of Ross McFarland. . . . I also met Gordon Allport, then a young staff member in a new program in social ethics, associated with the physician Richard Cabot, but I did not seriously think of entering upon that unconventional venture." See Hilgard, 1974, p. 134.
27. Gordon Allport to James Ford, November 20, 1923, DSEP.
28. Richard Cabot to Gordon Allport, February 23, 1924, DSEP.
29. Ibid.
30. Gordon Allport to James Ford, January 21, 1924, DSEP.
31. Ibid.
32. Allport's course was listed under the Department of Social Ethics in the *Harvard University Catalogue, 1924–1925*. A complete set of the university's course catalogues is available in the Harvard University Archives.
33. Richard Cabot to Gordon Allport, February 23, 1924, DSEP.
34. Ibid.
35. Cited in D. Potts, 1965, p. 122.
36. G. Allport, 1967, p. 11.
37. Richard Cabot, quoted in G. Allport, 1966/1968b, p. 374.
38. Cabot, 1926a, p. 105.
39. See Veysey, 1965.
40. Gordon Allport to Richard Cabot, March 14, 1924, DSEP.
41. G. Allport, 1921, p. 443.

42. Ibid.
43. Parker, 1991.
44. Gordon Allport to James Ford, November 20, 1923, DSEP.
45. Ibid.
46. G. Allport, 1921, p. 452.
47. Gordon Allport to W. S. Taylor, September 18, 1925, William S. Taylor Papers, Archives of the History of American Psychology, University of Akron (WSTP).
48. Ibid.
49. G. Allport, 1952.
50. Boring, 1967, p. 315.
51. Boring, 1952, p. 43.
52. G. Allport, 1967, p. 12.
53. Gordon Allport to Ada Gould, September 3, 1924, AF.
54. Gordon Allport to W. S. Taylor, January 11, 1925, WSTP.
55. Ibid.
56. For the details of Allport's 1925–1926 appointment, see Richard Cabot to Clifford Moore, March 26, 1925, DSEP.
57. See the *Harvard University Catalogue, 1925–1926*, Harvard University Archives.
58. Richard Cabot to Clifford Moore, March 26, 1925, DSEP.
59. William McDougall to E. G. Boring, July 18, 1925, Edwin G. Boring Papers, Harvard University Archives (EGSP).
60. For a thoughtful discussion of Boring's approach to psychology, see O'Donnell, 1979.
61. E. G. Boring to William McDougall, July 22, 1925, EGBP. Boring had a high regard for Allport as a scholar, but like his mentor, Edward Titchener, he had little interest in the more applied side of psychology. However, when asked to provide a list of the top young scholars in the fields of social and personality psychology, Boring ranked Allport first: "[Gordon Allport] is perfectly splendid in ability and personality. His interest is in social psychology and the psychology of personality." See E. G. Boring to Ray Wheeler, December 18, 1926, EGBP.
62. Gordon Allport to Ernest Hopkins, President, Dartmouth College, January 11, 1926, Department of Psychology Papers, Dartmouth College Archives (DPPDC).
63. G. Allport, 1930c, p. 127.
64. Unnamed correspondent to the Dean, Dartmouth College, November 9, 1925, DPPDC.
65. Ibid.
66. Vernon, 1968, p. 103.
67. Bruner, 1968, p. 282.
68. Richard Cabot to Charles Stone, October 26, 1925, Gordon W. Allport Papers, Harvard University Archives (GWAP).
69. G. Allport, 1925.
70. Ibid.
71. Robert Allport to Ian Nicholson, personal communication, March 12, 2001.

72. Fancher, 1989, p. 2.

73. Gordon Allport to Ada Gould, undated letter. This letter was written on Department of Social Ethics stationery and was probably written in the spring of 1925.

74. Gordon Allport to Ada Allport, n.d. This letter has the inscription "Tuesday Evening, 10:45" and was written during the 1926–1927 academic year. As events unfolded, Allport was unable to bring Koffka to his own corner of "civilization." After leaving Germany permanently, the famous Gestaltist accepted a position at Smith College. At Smith, Koffka had 5 years free of teaching and a salary that made him "one of the highest paid professors in America." For more on Koffka, see Ash, 1998, p. 212.

75. Gould, 1922–1923, p. 407.

76. See Lunbeck, 1994.

77. A. Allport, 1928.

78. Ibid.

79. Ada Gould, personal reflection, June 4, 1923.

80. A. Allport, 1928.

81. Ada Gould, personal reflection, June 4, 1923.

82. Ada Gould to Gordon Allport, n.d. The letter contains the notation "Wednesday evening after the C.R. seminar" and was written between 1921 and 1924.

83. Ada Gould to Gordon Allport, November 8, 1923, AF.

84. Ada Gould to Gordon Allport, n.d. The letter contains the notation "Wednesday evening after the C.R. seminar" and was written between 1922 and 1924.

85. Ada Gould to Gordon Allport, n.d. The letter contains the notation "From my bonny bunk" and was written between 1922 and 1924.

86. Ada Gould to Gordon Allport, October 22, 1924, AF.

87. Gordon Allport to Ada Gould, January 27, n.d. This letter begins with the phrase "Ada my friend" and was probably written in 1922.

88. Ada Gould, personal reflection, June 4, 1923.

89. Gordon Allport to Ada Gould, October 24, 1923, AF.

90. Quoted in Parker, 1991, p. 166.

91. G. Allport, 1927.

92. Hollingworth, 1923, p. 2.

93. Prince, 1921/1973, p. 532.

94. Roback, 1927b, pp. 159, 160.

95. G. Allport, 1927a, p. 284.

96. Ibid., p. 285.

97. Danziger, 1990.

98. G. Allport & Vernon, 1930, p. 716.

99. Roback, 1927b, pp. 6, 7.

100. G. Allport, 1930b, p. 731.

101. Parker, 1991, p. 112.

102. On the use of the term *personality* in liberal Protestant circles, see King, 1989.

103. Adler, 1929, pp. 3–22.

104. McCormack, 1931, p. 44.
105. G. Allport, 1922, p. 337.
106. Richmond, 1923, p. 719.
107. G. Allport, 1932, p. 391.
108. Gordon Allport to Karl Menninger, May 6, 1930, GWAP. See also G. Allport, 1930a.
109. Gordon Allport to James Ford, November 11, 1923, DSEP.
110. G. Allport, 1927a, p. 285.
111. Symonds, 1924, p. 491.
112. Ibid., p. 493.
113. Ibid., p. 492.
114. Roback, 1932–1933, p. 214. See also Roback, 1927a.
115. Ibid., p. 215.
116. G. Allport, 1927a, p. 285.
117. G. Allport, 1930c.
118. G. Allport, 1927a, p. 285.
119. Ibid., p. 284.
120. G. Allport, 1931/1960c, p. 131.
121. Parker, 1991.
122. G. Allport & Vernon, 1930, p. 131.
123. G. Allport, 1928a, p. 118.
124. G. Allport, 1931/1960c, p. 132.
125. Ibid.
126. G. Allport & Vernon, 1930, p. 708.
127. Allen, 1931/1964, p. 164.
128. Dewey, 1930, p. 62.
129. Niebuhr, 1928, p. 2.
130. Roback, 1927b, pp. 554, 555.
131. For a discussion of Coe's early career, see Nicholson, 1994.
132. Coe, 1928, p. 8.
133. G. Allport, 1931/1960c, pp. 125, 133.
134. For a good discussion of the rhetorical power of scientism in 1920s America, see Ross, 1991.
135. Gordon Allport to E. G. Boring, March 23, 1944, GWAP.
136. Gordon Allport to W. S. Taylor, September 24, 1932, Taylor papers.
137. G. Allport, 1930c, p. 124.
138. Ibid., pp. 124, 125.
139. Allport, 1929b, pp. 14–27.
140. Ibid., p. 14.
141. Ibid., p. 16.
142. Ibid., p. 16.
143. Ibid., p. 26.
144. Ibid., p. 19.
145. Ibid., p. 18.
146. Ibid., p. 26.
147. Ibid., p. 21.
148. For a good discussion of the importance of "quackery" in the history of American psychology, see Morawski & Hornstein, 1991.

149. The professional importance of maintaining a demarcation between science and nonscience is considered in Gieryn, 1983.
150. Leonard, 1927, p. 3.
151. Parker, 1991.
152. For a brief discussion of Downey's career, see Parker, 1991.
153. June Downey to Gordon Allport, January 28, 1932, GWAP.
154. Brown, 1991, p. 134.
155. Quoted in ibid., p. 134.
156. Ibid.
157. Coon, 2000, p. 97.

CHAPTER 8: THE POLITICS OF MODERATION: PERSONALITY PSYCHOLOGY AT HARVARD (1930–1936)

1. G. Allport, 1929b, p. 26.
2. G. Allport, 1952.
3. Gordon Allport to H. G. Warren, editor, *Dictionary of Psychology*, September 28, 1932, Gordon W. Allport Papers, Harvard University Press (GWAP). Unnpublished archival materials, courtesy of the Harvard University Archives.
4. G. Allport, 1967, p. 9.
5. Ibid., p. 15.
6. G. Allport, 1962b.
7. Napoli, 1981, especially chapter 3, "The Perils of Popularity," pp. 42–61.
8. For an interesting discussion of the dispute between advocates of pure and applied psychology in the 1920s, see O'Donnell, 1979.
9. F. Allport, 1927.
10. A colorful and rather disturbing illustration of McDougall's low standing among American psychologists was provided by M. Brewster Smith (1989). Smith recalled attending a psychology conference in 1938: "The featured address was given by Knight Dunlap.... I remember Dunlap, a handsome, mesomorphic figure of a man cockily sporting a beret as he talked extempore, saying that he could report from a recent visit to Duke University that McDougall was then in the process of dying of cancer and that 'the sooner he died, the better it would be for psychology.'"
11. Heidbreder, 1973, p. 268.
12. McDougall, 1930a, p. 213.
13. McDougall's departure from Harvard is discussed in Kuklick, 1977, pp. 459–460.
14. In the preface to the fourth edition of *An Outline of Psychology*, McDougall (1928) described the Geisteswissenschaften as being in "close agreement with the teachings of this book": "There are a number of influential contemporary workers in Germany who may be roughly classified as exponents of the Geisteswissenschaftliche Psychologie; the common and distinctive feature of this school (led by Prof. Ed. Spranger) is the repudiation of the mechanical atomistic psychology which has been until recently dominant

in the universities, and their frank recognition of the fact that any psychology that is to be of value to the social sciences ... must at every point take account of the purposive nature of all mental process" (p. xiv).

15. G. Allport, 1929a, p. 126.
16. William McDougall to Gordon Allport, November 15, 1929, Allport Family Papers (AF).
17. Roback, 1928, p. 150.
18. Harvard philosopher Ralph Barton Perry commented on the relationship between philosophy and psychology at Harvard: "At present ... the connections between Philosophy and Psychology are mainly those of administration, counsel, and personal association, and imply little identity in the content of instruction or research (Perry, 1930, p. 217).
19. E. G. Boring to Clarence Lewis, December 7, 1927, Edwin G. Boring Papers, Harvard University Archives (EGBP).
20. E. G. Boring to Lewis Terman, March 27, 1928, EGBP.
21. E. G. Boring to William McDougall, March 3, 1928, EGBP.
22. E. G. Boring to William McDougall, July 16, 1928, EGBP.
23. E. G. Boring to Gordon Allport, February 27, 1929, EGBP.
24. William McDougall to Charles Stone, October 24, 1926, GWAP.
25. E. G. Boring to Gordon Allport, February 27, 1929, EGBP. See also E. G. Boring to Gordon Allport, April 16, 1929, EGBP.
26. For a good discussion of Boring's career, see Rosenzweig, 1970.
27. Boring, 1952, p. 41.
28. Ibid., p. 42.
29. E. G. Boring to Harry Murray, April 14, 1936, EGBP.
30. E. G. Boring to Gordon Allport, February 27, 1929, EGBP.
31. Gordon Allport to W. S. Taylor, October 11, 1926, William S. Taylor Papers, Archives of the History of American Psychology, University of Akron (WSTP). The implicit bigotry of this remark is more a reflection of the predominantly Anglo character of American universities than of any deep seated anti-Semitism on Allport's part. In the 1920s, he regarded Jewish students and scholars as a curiosity, which at that time they were, but he vigorously supported their place in the academy.
32. Gordon Allport to William Leonard, April 5, 1928, GWAP.
33. F. Allport, 1974, p. 6.
34. E. G. Boring to Herbert Langfeld, March 15, 1922, EGBP.
35. E. G. Boring to Gordon Allport, April 16, 1929, EGBP.
36. Gordon Allport to E. G. Boring, April 18, 1929, EGBP.
37. Gordon Allport to W. S. Taylor, September 18, 1925, WSTP.
38. See Kuklick, 1977.
39. Gordon Allport to Ada Allport, undated letter. This letter is address to "my dearest person" on "Friday 5pm." The details in the letter suggest that it was written sometime in the summer of 1928 or 1929.
40. Edwin Holt to A. Lawrence Lowell, January 25, 1918. A. Lawrence Lowell Papers, Harvard University Archives (ALLP).
41. Ibid.
42. Edwin Holt to Gordon Allport, May 18, 1930, AF.

43. Gordon Allport to E. G. Boring, March 5, 1929, EGBP. In a published reminiscence, Ross Stagner (1993) reported a different account of Allport's departure from Dartmouth. A Dartmouth faculty member told Stagner that Allport went to Harvard because he could not get tenure at Dartmouth. At that time, Dartmouth only had one tenured position in psychology. Stagner reported that the position was offered to Edwin Bailor, so Allport then contacted Harvard and arranged to move. Stagner's account of Allport's departure is interesting, but it is not supported by the surviving documentation. To begin with, Allport did not seek out a position at Harvard. The position was offered to him by Boring. Furthermore, in a letter to Boring, Allport indicated that he had been promised a permanent position at Dartmouth. He reported that Dartmouth College President Hopkins "gave me to understand ... that my promotion to full professorship will come about 'sooner than the average,'" which Allport read as meaning "two or three years." It is, of course, possible that Allport was lying to Boring in order to improve the terms of the Harvard offer, but because he declined Boring's offer of an immediate return to Harvard, this seems unlikely.

44. Gordon Allport to E. G. Boring, March 5, 1929, EGBP.

45. Gordon Allport to E. G. Boring, March 8, 1929. This letter was included as a "p.s." in Allport's letter to Boring of March 5.

46. E. G. Boring to Gordon Allport, May 14, 1929, EGBP.

47. E. G. Boring to Gordon Allport, April 16, 1929, EGBP.

48. Gordon Allport to E. G. Boring, February 10, 1930, EGBP.

49. E. G. Boring to Gordon Allport, February 11, 1930, EGBP.

50. Ibid.

51. Ibid.

52. Keller, 1985, p. 7.

53. Bruner, 1983, p. 36. As a graduate student in the 1920s, David Shakow (1976) also detected a palpable hostility to the "feminine" world of language and feelings. Shakow enrolled in E. G. Boring's seminar "The Nature of Control in the Psychological Experiment," and "at the initial session, Boring introduced each member of the seminar.... When he came to me he said, in essence: 'Shakow is now in graduate work, living at the Psychopathic Hospital and interested in psychopathology. Why he is concerned with the problem of control I am not quite sure, but we welcome him anyway.' This benevolently skeptical comment ... illustrates their suspicion that anything smacking of the clinical orientation was contaminated by looseness and verbosity, as opposed to rigorous scientific control" (p. 25).

54. G. C. Homans, 1984, p. 296.

55. E. G. Boring to Gordon Allport, n.d., GWAP. This letter was written in response to a departmental luncheon probably held in December 1935. The extreme mechanism implicit in Boring's remarks had a number of adherents at Harvard in the early 1930s. Allport caught a glimpse of its pervasiveness shortly after he arrived from Dartmouth, at B. F. Skinner's Ph.D. orals. Allport was not on Skinner's committee, but he attended anyway. Skinner (1979) proceeded to outline his views on the explanatory power of behaviorism. He handled the ensuing questions without any great difficultly, but

toward the end of the proceedings, Allport asked him, "What are some of the objections to behaviorism?" At that point, a silence came over the room. Skinner said nothing, and he later admitted that "I could not think of a single [objection]" (p. 75). Skinner's difficulty with so basic a question indicates a great deal about the character of his committee. Evidently, they directed their questions not at the philosophical base of his work, but rather at his conceptual and methodological structure. This suggests that the assumptions about science implicit in Skinner's approach were shared by most of his committee members.

56. Thornton, 1996. I would like to thank Nicole Barenbaum for drawing my attention to Allport's work on graphology. My understanding of this facet of Allport's career has been greatly enhanced by Dr. Barenbaum's scholarship. See Barenbaum, 2000b, 2001.

57. Mullet, 1929, p. 4; Cavanagh, 1935, p. 7, cited in Thornton, 1996, p. 118.

58. Thornton, 1996, p. 132.

59. Cited in Barenbaum, 2001, p. 1.

60. Ibid.

61. Downey, 1919.

62. Gordon Allport to Ada Gould, May 21, 1921, AF.

63. Dehue, 1995.

64. G. Allport & Vernon, 1933, p. 186.

65. Ibid.; Powers, 1930.

66. G. Allport & Vernon, 1933, pp. 188, 189.

67. Ibid., p. 246.

68. Ibid., p. 248.

69. Barenbaum, 2001.

70. Evans & G. Allport, 1971, p. 112.

71. G. Allport, 1933.

72. Ibid., p. 264.

73. Ibid.

74. Ibid., p. 263.

75. Ibid., p. 264.

76. G. Allport & Vernon, 1931. At Cambridge, Vernon conducted his doctoral research on the psychology of music under the supervision of F. C. Bartlett. He received a Rockefeller Fellowship in 1929, and he then spent a year at Yale before traveling to Harvard to work with Allport. The theoretical rationale of the test was developed by Allport, but much of the statistical work was undertaken by Vernon. The collaboration was an arrangement that suited both scholars. Allport was, by his own admission, a poor statistician. In a letter to a prospective research fellow, he noted, "I am not much of a statistician, and prefer myself to use cogitation and *suitable* methods of experimentation to elaborate factor analysis." Gordon Allport to Ross Stagner, November 23, 1932, GWAP. Vernon, however, excelled at the intricacies of statistical procedures. "We blended well," Vernon wrote in his autobiography. Allport "usually wrote up the more theoretical and interpretive aspects, myself the more empirical side" (Vernon, 1978, p. 307).

77. Vernon & G. Allport, 1931, p. 231.

78. Ibid., p. 231.
79. Evans & G. Allport, 1971, p. 85.
80. Cantril & G. Allport, 1933.
81. Gordon Allport to Reverend Donald Kummick, December 5, 1966, GWAP.
82. Vernon & G. Allport, 1931, p. 232.
83. Gordon Allport to Eduard Spranger, February 21, 1932, GWAP.
84. Eduard Spranger to Gordon Allport, March 29, 1935, AF; Eduard Spranger, quoted in Danziger, 1990, p. 231. Allport was well aware of Spranger's opposition to *The Study of Values*—courteous acknowledgements notwithstanding. In a later discussion of *Types of Men* (Spranger, 1928), G. Allport 1937 concluded that Spranger could not be "followed in every respect" because "this school of the Geisteswissenshaften is irreconcilably antagonistic to the contributions of all other branches of psychology, refusing to not only to admit their divergent theories, but also their corrective empiricism" (p. 231).
85. G. Allport, 1967, p. 14.
86. G. Allport, 1932, p. 391.
87. Ibid., p. 391. Allport (1927b) criticized the ethnocentrism of American personality psychology in an earlier review of A. A. Roback's *Bibliography of Character and Personality*. He noted approvingly that "close to 60 per cent of Roback's references are from publications in a foreign language, approximately 50 per cent of the total being in German." Allport then contrasted these figures with Manson's recently published *Bibliography of the Analysis and Measurement of Human Personality*, which devoted "a scant 8 per cent … to foreign contributions." Allport noted that Manson's book was designed "primarily for testers, and American testers do not take kindly to the sophistry and formalism of European characterology, nor, unfortunately, to the nutritious first principles of character study sometimes found in foreign work" (p. 309).
88. Fancher, 1989.
89. Gordon Allport to Ross Stagner, November 23, 1932, GWAP.
90. Allport commented on the role of *A Study of Values* as an introduction to the Geisteswissenschaften in his letter to Spranger: "Whatever defects it may contain, I think it should be regarded as of value at least in bringing to the attention of American psychologists your own work." See Gordon Allport to Eduard Spranger, February 21, 1932, GWAP.
91. G. Allport, 1945/1960b, p. 183.
92. G. Allport, 1967, p. 11. Allport commented on his self-consciousness in his autobiography: "Temperamentally I am a bit of a worrier, and for this reason I prepared my courses with conscientious thoroughness. . . . Ada and I were married in 1925, and for forty years she has had to tolerate the strain that marks all my preparations" (p. 11).
93. Ibid.
94. Gordon Allport to E. G. Boring, June 12, 1967, GWAP.
95. Floyd Allport described his brother as a "master of the science of personality traits" in his autobiography. See F. Allport, 1974, p. 5. Floyd's high opinion of his brother was shared by many in the field. Harry Stack Sullivan de-

scribed Allport as one of the "outstanding authorities" in the "use of the life history method." See Harry Stack Sullivan to Gordon Allport, January 7, 1930, GWAP.

96. G. Allport, 1965, p. x.

97. For a thorough discussion of Allport's work on the case of Marion Taylor, see Barenbaum, 1997.

98. Barenbaum & Winter, in press.

99. G. Allport, 1965.

100. Ibid., p. x. Allport's ambivalent approach to case studies has been noted by a number of scholars. One of the more revealing observations comes from Bertram Cohler, a former student of Allport's. Cohler 1993 noted that All-port "appeared to mistrust the very person-centered approach that he championed.... During the course of my doctoral studies, a group of us became interested in the detailed tracking of particular lives over time and were spending much time examining interview and semistructured test data. When we met with Allport to discuss the issues involved in integrating interview and test results, he cautioned us that 'idiography [sic] was no country for young men.' I regarded this as more than a statement of political realities; it conveyed some of Allport's ambivalence regarding the approach that he had so long championed" (p. 134).

101. Bruner, 1983, p. 36. Allport's intellectual relationship with Murray is discussed later in this chapter.

102. Gordon Allport to E. G. Boring, March, 1936. GWAP.

103. Gordon Allport to E. G. Boring, December 16, 1935(?), GWAP.

104. *Harvard Crimson*, May 1, 1936.

105. E. G. Boring was frequently angered by Murray's sharply worded criticisms of psychology. Murray's paper "Psychology and the University" was a case in point. Murray showed Boring a draft of the paper before he sent if off for publication. "Right away he was down in my office shaking," Murray recalled. "He said, 'If you publish it, you'll be ostracized in the APA all your life.' He advised me never to let anyone see it." Quoted in Anderson, 1988, p. 153.

106. Murray, 1981, pp. 337–351.

107. Ibid., p. 341.

108. Ibid.

109. Bruner, 1983, p. 36.

110. My understanding of the institutional context of Allport's work was greatly enhanced by Rodney Triplet's 1983 dissertation on Henry Murray. See also Robinson, 1992.

111. Boring, 1952, p. 45.

112. Ibid., p. 45.

113. E. G. Boring to Gordon Allport, January 25, 1937, GWAP.

114. James McKeen Cattell to Gordon Allport, September 10, 1937, GWAP.

115. Karl Lashley to James B. Conant, January 6, 1937, GWAP.

116. See Conant, 1970.

117. James B. Conant to Gordon Allport, December 9, 1936, GWAP.

118. Gordon Allport to E. G. Boring, August 4, 1936, GWAP.

119. Gordon Allport to Henry Murray, December 26, 1936, AF.
120. Ibid.
121. Gordon Allport to James Conant, January 5, 1937, GWAP.
122. Gordon Allport to E. G. Boring, January 21, 1937, GWAP.
123. E. G. Boring to Gordon Allport, January 25, 1937, GWAP. Allport was promoted to full professor on September 1, 1942.
124. Gordon Allport to E. G. Boring, January 28, 1937, GWAP.
125. G. Allport, 1967, p. 15.
126. E. G. Boring to Gordon Allport, September 1, 1937, Department of Psychology Papers, Harvard University Archives (DPPHU).
127. Ibid.
128. Gordon Allport to E. G. Boring, September 8, 1937, DPPHU.
129. Ibid.

CHAPTER 9: PERSONALITY AND SOCIAL CRISIS

1. G. Allport, 1937, p. viii.
2. Pells, 1973.
3. Diggans, 1973, p. 110.
4. Quoted in Pells, 1973, p. 53.
5. Finison, 1976.
6. Dewey, 1922, p. 323.
7. For more a detailed discussion of psychologists' radicalism, see Harris, 1998, and Nicholson, 1997a, 1998.
8. Gordon Allport to George Hartmann, June 21, 1940, Gordon W. Allport Papers, Harvard University Archives (GWAP). Unpublished archival materials, courtesy of the Harvard University Archives.
9. G. Allport, 1940a, p. 136.
10. G. Allport, 1932, p. 397.
11. G. Allport, 1926, p. 99.
12. Ibid., p. 99.
13. Cantril & G. Allport, 1935. For an insightful discussion of Allport's work on the psychology of radio, see Pandora, 1998.
14. Finison, 1979, p. 30.
15. Gordon Allport, 1946–1947, quoted in M. B. Smith, 1993, p. 58.
16. For a good discussion of the different varieties of American individualism, see Bellah et al., 1985.
17. Herbert Hoover, 1922, cited in Hofstadter, 1989, p. 386.
18. Bellah et al., 1985.
19. F. Allport, 1919a, p. 297. See also F. Allport, 1924a.
20. F. Allport, 1919a, p. 297. For a critical discussion of Floyd Allport's social psychology, see Danziger, 1992.
21. F. Allport, 1924b, p. 9.
22. Ibid.
23. F. Allport, 1919a, p. 299.
24. The Deweyan character of the SPSSI is discussed in Finison, 1979.

25. Dewey, 1935, p. 56.
26. Dewey, 1930, p. 53.
27. Dewey's book *Human Nature and Conduct* was a standard reference in the prewar works of Benedict, Mead, and Malinowski. For a brief discussion of Dewey's influence on these scholars, see Singer, 1961.
28. Mead, 1939, p. x.
29. For a historical overview of research on culture and personality, see Singer, 1961.
30. For a brief overview of Stagner's career, see Stagner, 1993.
31. Stagner, 1986, p. 36.
32. Stagner, 1937.
33. Ibid., p. viii.
34. Ibid., p. 297.
35. Maslow, 1937.
36. Ibid., pp. 408, 409.
37. Ibid., p. 408.
38. Ibid., p. 409.
39. Gordon Allport to Ada Allport, September 2, 1937, Allport Family Papers (AF).
40. G. Allport & Vernon, 1930, p. 700.
41. G. Allport, 1937.
42. Ibid., p. x.
43. Ibid., p. viii.
44. Ibid., p. viii.
45. Ibid., p. 566.
46. Latour, 1987, p. 48.
47. Stagner, 1938, p. 221.
48. Ibid., p. 221.
49. Ibid., p. 220. Stagner may have also known of the social mindedness that Allport brought to some of his other scholarly projects. For instance, in 1938 Allport was appointed editor of the *Journal of Abnormal and Social Psychology*. On assuming the editorship, he wrote a spirited editorial in which he praised the "liaison" between abnormal and social psychology as a "tour de force" (G. Allport, 1938, p. 6). Social psychology would only be strengthened by the inclusion of a "thorough-going dynamic psychology." Conversely, the study of social psychology would help illuminate the "social etiology in mental disorder." As editor, Allport saw his task as one of "break[ing] down ... the barriers that still exist, by fostering both branches of psychology and by encouraging their interpenetrations."
50. G. Allport, 1937, pp. 37–38.
51. Ibid., p. 549.
52. Napoli, 1981, p. 43.
53. Ibid. See also Fancher, 2000.
54. For example, in the entry on "personality" in the *Encyclopaedia of the Social Sciences*, Freudian psychoanalysis was described as "the most elaborate and far reaching hypotheses on the development of personality which have yet been proposed" (p. 87). See Sapir, 1933, pp. 85–88.

55. Gordon Allport to Samuel Beck, June 5, 1939, GWAP.
56. Pfister, 1997, p. 174.
57. Hornstein, 1992.
58. Quoted in Hornstein, 1992, p. 256.
59. Ringer, 1969, p. 383. In his review of German social science, Ringer noted that he had "encountered only one favorable comment upon Freud's work in the academic literature of this period [1920–1933]."
60. Gordon Allport to W. S. Taylor, December 18, 1922, William S. Taylor Papers, Archives of the History of American Psychology, University of Akron (WSTP).
61. Ibid.
62. See Gordon Allport to W. S. Taylor, September 18, 1925, WSTP.
63. Gordon Allport to W. S. Taylor, February 25, 1933(?), WSTP.
64. G. Allport, 1937, p. 181.
65. Anonymous, 1939, p. 453.
66. G. Allport, 1937, p. 181.
67. See Rotundo, 1993.
68. See Bederman, 1995.
69. G. Allport, 1937, p. 169.
70. Ibid., pp. 190, 191.
71. Ibid., p. 169.
72. Ibid., p. 194.
73. Ibid., p. 213.
74. Susman, 1979, p. 219.
75. G. Allport, 1937, p. 213.
76. Ibid., pp. 223, 224.
77. Ibid., p. 226.
78. Ibid., p. 147.
79. For an intriguing discussion of nostalgia, see Lowenthall, 1985.
80. G. Allport, 1937, p. 218.
81. Ibid., p. 221.
82. Collini, 1985, p. 37.
83. The title for this section comes from the title of a collection of Allport's chapel sermons published posthumously under the editorship of Peter Bertocci (G. Allport, 1978). The phrase "waiting for the Lord" comes from a passage from Isaiah 40:29–31 that Allport used as the basis of one of his chapel sermons.
84. G. Allport, 1928b.
85. Gordon Allport to Mary Foote, March 24, 1939, AF.
86. Henry Washburn to Gordon Allport, November 2, 1932, GWAP.
87. Gordon Allport, unpublished chapel address, March 26, 1936, GWAP.
88. Robert Allport to Ian Nicholson, personal communication, February 20, 2001.
89. Gordon Allport to Ada Allport, September 4, 1937, AF.
90. Nellie Allport to Gordon Allport, November 6, 1937, AF.
91. Holstein & Gubrium, 2000, p. 18.
92. Meltzer, Petras, & Reynolds, 1975, p. 6.
93. Pandora, 1997, pp. 181, 182.

94. High & Woodward, 1980, p. 75.
95. G. Allport, 1937, p. 226.
96. Fuller, 1988, p. 146.
97. Ibid., p. 199.
98. G. Allport, 1937, p. 566.
99. Taylor, 1992, p. 3.
100. Gordon Allport to Edwin Powers and Pete Dodge, July 11, 1927, AF.
101. Ibid.
102. G. Allport, 1937, p. 128.
103. Ada Allport to Peggy MacKaye, February 8, 1937, AF. Margaret MacKaye was a friend of Ada's and wife of James MacKaye, a graduate of Harvard and author and philosopher. She worked as an archivist at Dartmouth College, and in the 1940s she moved to Boston, where she was secretary of the Women's International League for Peace and Freedom.
104. Ada Allport to Leonard Carmichael, October, 19, 1929, CP.
105. Gordon Allport to Ada Allport, February 25, 1937, AF.
106. G. Allport, 1937, p. x.
107. Gordon Allport to Ada Allport, September 1, 1937, AF.
108. Ada Allport to E. G. Boring, February 16, 1937, Edwin G. Boring Papers, Harvard University Archives (EGBP).
109. Ada Allport to Gordon Allport, undated letter marked Tuesday PM, 1927, AF.
110. Ada Allport to Peggy MacKaye, January 31, 1937, AF.
111. Robert Allport to Ian Nicholson, personal communication, April 10, 2001.
112. Robert Allport to Ian Nicholson, personal communication, March 12, 2001.
113. Robert Allport to Ian Nicholson, personal communication, July 20, 2001.
114. Edwin Powers to W. H. Lillard, Director of Admissions, Tabor Academy, May 26, 1941, AF.
115. Robert Allport to Ian Nicholson, personal communication, April 10, 2001.
116. Robert Allport to Ian Nicholson, personal communication, February 20, 2001.
117. Robert Allport to Ian Nicholson, personal communication, December, 23, 2001.
118. Ibid.
119. Gordon Allport to Ada Allport, August 28, 1939, AF.
120. Robert Allport to Ian Nicholson, personal communication, December 20, 2001.
121. Robert Allport to Ian Nicholson, personal communication, February 20, 2001.
122. Robert Allport to Ian Nicholson, personal communication, December 20, 2001.
123. Gordon Allport to Merle Curti, March 21, 1937, Merle Curti Papers, State Historical Society of Wisconsin Archives (MCP).
124. Gordon Allport to Ada Allport, September 14, 1938, AF.
125. Robert Allport to Ian Nicholson, personal communication, April 10, 2001.
126. Gordon Allport to Ada Allport, undated letter, AF. The events described in this letter suggest that it was probably written in August 1937.
127. Robert Allport to Ian Nicholson, personal communication, April 10, 2001.
128. Ibid.

129. G. Allport, 1937, p. 3.
130. "Fields of concentration," 1936, p. 4.
131. Gordon Allport to Ada Allport, September 2, 1937.
132. According to the publisher, Henry Holt, *Personality* sold very well. The editor of the publisher's college department told Allport that "the book continues to go quite well indeed. Almost twice as many copies have been sold since January 1 as were sold prior to that date, and we are continuing to get small reorders and orders for single copies every day." See T. J. Wilson to Gordon Allport, April 8, 1938, GWAP. Stagner's textbook was a steady seller through four editions (1937, 1948, 1961, 1974). For more on Stagner's book, see Craik, 1993.
133. Gordon Allport to Ada Allport, September 1, 1937, AF.
134. Gordon Allport to Ada Allport, September 4, 1937, AF.
135. Gordon Allport to Ada Allport, September 1, 1937.
136. Roback, 1937–1938, p. 243; Hollingworth, 1938, p. 103.
137. Lasswell, 1938, p. 105. Over time, *Personality* assumed canonical status within the field. According to the editors of a recent volume on the history of personality, *Personality* played an important role in "defining and establishing the identity of personality psychology as a distinctive field of scientific inquiry within the United States." See Craik, Hogan, & Wolfe, 1993, p. ix.
138. Boring, 1952, p. 50.
139. E. G. Boring to Henry Murray, April 14, 1938, EGBP.
140. Gordon Allport to E. G. Boring, January 21, 1937; Gordon Allport to E. G. Boring, January 31, 1938, GWAP.
141. See Paterson, 1936.
142. Samelson, 1992.
143. Gordon Allport to Ada Allport, September 1, 1937.
144. Ibid.
145. G. Allport, 1938.
146. See Furumoto, 1988.
147. Samelson, 1992.
148. For an informative discussion of the development of professional societies at this time, see Morawski, 1986.
149. Samelson, 1992, p. 139.
150. Finison, 1976.
151. Samelson, 1992.
152. Knight Dunlap, "The Impending Dismemberment of Psychology," paper presented to the National Institute of Psychology, 1938, quoted in Samelson, 1992, p. 136.
153. Gordon Allport to Stuart Britt, April 8, 1938, GWAP.
154. Fernberger, 1938, p. 281.
155. G. Allport, 1937, p. 213.

CHAPTER 10: CONCLUSION

1. G. Allport, 1938/1960a, p. 5.
2. Roback, 1932–1933, p. 215; G. Allport & Vernon, 1930, p. 677.

3. R. Smith, 1992, p. 224.
4. G. Allport, 1937, p. 25.
5. Evans & G. Allport, 1971, p. 111. Allport's identification as a personality psychologist has not been fully appreciated by subsequent generations of psychologists. For example, in 1997 Herbert Kelman organized a conference at Harvard to mark the centennial of Allport's birth. Instead of honoring Allport's principal scholarly identity—personality—Kelman constructed the conference entirely around "the social psychology of prejudice and intergroup relations" (Ruggiero & Kelman, 1999, p. 405)—fields that Allport always considered of secondary interest. As astonishing as it may seem in the light of Allport's lifelong fascination with personality, the Gordon W. Allport Centennial Symposium did not include a single paper on personality. One can only imagine how Allport himself would have reacted to such a narrow and historically insensitive "tribute."
6. Cushman, 1990, p. 603.
7. G. Allport, 1937, p. 218.
8. Ibid., p. 566.
9. G. Richards, 1995, p. 15.
10. G. Allport & Vernon, 1930, p. 716.
11. Rose, 1992, p. 361.
12. For an excellent discussion of the contemporary state of science biography, see Söderqvist, 1996.
13. Lewontin, 1986, p. 317.
14. Danziger, 1997, p. 13.
15. Hankins, 1979, p. 5.
16. Monte, 1991, p. 637.
17. Sloan, 1997, p. 94.
18. Danziger, 1990, p. 165.
19. For an excellent discussion of psychology's problematic relationship with psychoanalysis, see Hornstein, 1992.
20. John & Robins, 1993, p. 215.
21. Cohler, 1993, p. 134.
22. Holt, 1962, p. 7.
23. Ash, 1992, p. 199.
24. G. Allport, 1937, p. 20.
25. Ibid., p. 20; p. viii.
26. Ibid., p. 399.
27. See Bills, 1938.
28. F. Allport & G. Allport, 1921, pp. 36–37.
29. Digman, 1990, p. 418.
30. Magnusson & Törestad, 1993, p. 435.
31. Lears, 1981, p. 305.

BIBLIOGRAPHY

Abbot, L. (1910). The spirit of democracy. *Outlook, 95,* 741.

Adler, F. (1929). Personality: How to develop it in the family, the school and society. *Essays in honor of John Dewey* (pp. 3–22). New York: Holt.

Ahlstrom, S. (1972). *A religious history of the American people.* New Haven, CT: Yale University Press.

Allen, F. (1964). *Only yesterday: An informal history of the 1920's.* New York: Harper & Row. (Original work published 1931)

Allport, A. (1928). In appreciation of Alice Cook. *Girl's High School Newspaper,* AF.

Allport, F. (1917). *Harvard College Class Reports—Class of 1913—Report II.* Cambridge, MA: Harvard University Press.

Allport, F. (1919a). Behavior and experiment in social psychology. *Journal of Abnormal Psychology, 14,* 297–306.

Allport, F. (1919b). *The social influence: An experimental study of the effect of the group upon individual mental processes.* Unpublished doctoral dissertation, Harvard University.

Allport, F. (1924a). The group fallacy in relation to social science. *American Journal of Sociology, 29,* 688–703.

Allport, F. (1924b). *Social psychology.* Boston: Houghton Mifflin.

Allport, F. (1927). The present status of social psychology. *Journal of Abnormal and Social Psychology, 21,* 372–383.

Allport, F. (1930). The religion of a scientist. *Harper's, 160,* 352–366.

Allport, F. (1974). Floyd H. Allport. In G. Lindzey (Ed.), *A history of psychology in autobiography* (Vol. 6, pp. 3–29). Englewood Cliffs, NJ: Prentice Hall.

Allport, F., & Allport, G. (1921). Personality traits: Their classification and measurement. *Journal of Abnormal & Social Psychology, 16,* 6–40.

Allport, G. (1919). *The journal of Gordon Allport.* Unpublished manuscript.

Allport, G. (1920). *The journal of Gordon Allport.* Unpublished manuscript.

Allport, G. (1921). Personality and character. *Psychological Bulletin, 18,* 441–455.

Allport, G. (1922). *An experimental study of the traits of personality with application to the problems of social diagnosis.* Unpublished doctoral dissertation, Harvard University.

Allport, G. (1923). The Leipzig Congress of Psychology. *American Journal of Psychology, 34,* 612–615.

Allport, G. (1924). The study of the undivided personality. *Journal of Abnormal and Social Psychology, 19,* 132–142.

Allport, G. (1925). *Our wedding.* Unpublished manuscript, AF.

Allport, G. (1926). [Review of the book *Social psychology*]. *Journal of Abnormal and Social Psychology, 21,* 95–100.

Allport, G. (1927a). Concepts of trait and personality. *Psychological Bulletin, 24*, 284–293.

Allport, G. (1927b). [Review of the book *Bibliography of character and personality*]. *Psychological Bulletin, 24*, 309–310.

Allport, G. (1928a). A test for ascendence–submission. *Journal of Abnormal and Social Psychology, 23*, 118–136.

Allport, G. (1928b). *What psychology has to say about prayer.* Unpublished manuscript, Dartmouth College, Hanover, NH.

Allport, G. (1929a). [Review of the book *The group mind*]. *Journal of Abnormal and Social Psychology, 24*, 123–126.

Allport, G. (1929b). The study of personality by the intuitive method: An experiment in teaching from *The Locomotive God. Journal of Abnormal and Social Psychology, 24*, 14–27.

Allport, G. (1930a). Change and decay in the visual memory field. *British Journal of Psychology, 21*, 133–148.

Allport, G. (1930b). [Review of the book *Social psychology*]. *Psychological Bulletin, 27*, 731–733.

Allport, G. (1930c). Some guiding principles in understanding personality. *The Family*, 124–128.

Allport, G. (1932). [Review of the book *Diagnosing personality and conduct*]. *Journal of Social Psychology, 3*, 391–397.

Allport, G. (1933). The study of personality by the experimental method. *Character & Personality, 1*, 259–264.

Allport, G. W. (1937). *Personality: A psychological interpretation.* New York: Holt.

Allport, G. (1938). The Journal of Abnormal and Social Psychology: An editorial. *Journal of Abnormal and Social Psychology, 33*, 3–13.

Allport, G. (1940a). Liberalism and the motives of men. *Frontiers of Democracy, 6*, 136–137.

Allport, G. (1940b). The psychologist's frame of reference. *Psychological Bulletin, 37*, 1–28.

Allport, G. (1944). *The quest of Nellie Wise Allport.* Boston: Author.

Allport, G. (1952). *Interview with Anne Roe.* Unpublished manuscript. Anne Roe Papers, American Philosophical Society Archives.

Allport, G. (1960a). Personality: A problem for science or art? In *Personality and social encounter* (pp. 3–15). Boston: Beacon Press. (Original work published 1938)

Allport, G. W. (1960b). The psychology of participation. *Personality and social encounter* (pp. 181–198). Boston: Beacon Press. (Original work published 1945)

Allport, G. (1960c). What is a trait of personality? In *Personality and social encounter* (pp. 131–135). Boston: Beacon Press. (Original work published 1931)

Allport, G. (1962a). *Interview with Anne Roe.* Unpublished manuscript. Anne Roe Papers, American Philosophical Society Archives.

Allport, G. (1962b). My encounters with personality theory. Unpublished manuscript, GWAP.

Allport, G. (1965). Letters from Jenny. New York: Harcourt, Brace & World.

Allport, G. (1967). Gordon Allport. In E. Boring & G. Lindzey (Eds.), A history of psychology in autobiography (Vol. 5, pp. 3–25). New York: Appleton Century.

Allport, G. (1968a). Dewey's individual & social psychology. In The person in psychology (pp. 326–354). Boston: Beacon Press. (Original work published 1966)

Allport, G. (1968b). The spirit of Richard Clarke Cabot. In The person in psychology (pp. 371–375). Boston: Beacon Press. (Original work published 1966)

Allport, G. (1978). Waiting for the Lord: 33 meditations on God and man (P. Bertocci, Ed.). New York: Macmillan.

Allport, G. (n.d.). The appeal of Anglican Catholicism to an average man. Boston: The Advent Papers.

Allport, G., & Vernon, P. (1930). The field of personality. Psychological Bulletin, 27, 677–730.

Allport, G., & Vernon, P. (1931). A study of values: A scale for measuring the dominant interests in personality. Boston: Houghton Mifflin.

Allport, G. W., & Vernon, P. E. (1933). Studies in expressive movement. New York: Macmillan.

Allport, J. (1919). Biographical statement of John Allport. Unpublished manuscript.

Anderson, J. (1988). Henry A. Murray's early career: A psychobiographical exploration. Journal of Personality, 56, 139–171.

Anonymous (1939). [Review of the book Personality: A psychological interpretation] Psychoanalytic Review, 26, 452–454.

Ash, M. (1981). Academic politics in the history of science: Experimental psychology in Germany, 1879–1941. Central European History, 13, 255–286.

Ash, M. (1992). Cultural contexts and scientific change in psychology: Kurt Lewin in Iowa. American Psychologist, 47, 198–207.

Ash, M. (1998). Gestalt psychology and German culture. New York: Cambridge University Press.

Bakan, D. (1966). Behaviorism and American urbanization. Journal of the History of the Behavioral Sciences, 2, 5–28.

Baltzell, E. D. (1979). Philadelphia gentlemen: The making of a national upper class. Philadelphia: University of Pennsylvania Press.

Barenbaum, N. (2000a). How social was personality? The Allports' "connection" of social and personality psychology. Journal of the History of the Behavioral Sciences, 36, 471–487.

Barenbaum, N. (2000b, August). An "insistence on particulars": Gordon Allport and graphology. Paper presented at the annual meeting of the American Psychological Association, Washington, DC.

Barenbaum, N. (2001, June). "Embryo science," "scientific art," or pseudoscience?

Gordon Allport, A. A. Roback and graphology. Paper presented at the annual meeting of the Cheiron Society, Bloomington, IN.

Bartlett, F. (1958). Herbert Sydney Langfeld. *American Journal of Psychology, 71,* 616–619.

Barton, J. (1975). *Peasants and strangers: Italians, Rumanians, and Slovaks in an American city, 1890–1950.* Cambridge, MA: Harvard University Press.

Bederman, G. (1995). *Manliness & civilization: A cultural history of gender and race in the United States, 1880–1917.* Chicago: University of Chicago Press.

Bellah, R., Madsen, R., Sullivan, W., Swidler, A., & Tipton, S. (1985). *Habits of the heart: Individualism and commitment in American life.* Berkeley: University of California Press.

Bills, A. (1938). Changing views of psychology as science. *Psychological Review, 45,* 377–394.

Bledstein, B. (1976). *The culture of professionalism: The middle class and the development of higher education in America.* New York: Norton.

Boring, E. G. (1920). Statistics of the American Psychological Association in 1920. *Psychological Bulletin, 17,* 271–278.

Boring, E. G. (1952). Edwin Garringues Boring. In E. Boring, H. Langfeld, H. Weiner, & R. Yerkes (Eds.), *History of psychology in autobiography* (pp. 27–52). New York: Russell & Russell.

Bourne, R. (1913). *Youth and life.* New York: Houghton Mifflin.

Brightman, E. S. (1950). Personalism. In V. Ferm (Ed.), *A history of philosophical systems* (pp. 340–352). New York: The Philosophical Library.

Brooks, V. W. (1908). Harvard and American life. *Contemporary Review, 94,* 612.

Brown, J. (1991). Mental measurements and the rhetorical force of numbers. In J. Brown & D. V. Keuren (Eds.), *The estate of social knowledge* (pp. 134–152). Baltimore: Johns Hopkins University Press.

Bruner, J. (1968). Obituary—Gordon Willard Allport. *American Journal of Psychology, 81,* 279–284.

Bruner, J. (1983). *In search of mind: Essays in autobiography.* New York: Harper.

Buckley, K. (1989). *Mechanical man: John Broadus Watson and the beginnings of behaviorism.* New York: Guilford Press.

Burgess, E. W. (1923). The study of the delinquent as a person. *American Journal of Sociology, 28,* 657–680.

Cabot, R. (1919). *Social work: Essays on the meeting-ground of doctor and social worker.* Boston: Houghton-Mifflin.

Cabot, R. C. (1926a). *Adventures on the borderlands of ethics.* New York: Harper & Row.

Cabot, R. (1926b). Richard Cabot. In *The national cyclopaedia of American biography* (pp. 223–224). New York: James White & Company.

Cannon, I. (1952). *On the social frontier of medicine.* Cambridge, MA: Harvard University Press.

Cantril, H. (1938). [Review of the book *Psychology of Personality*]. *Psychological Bulletin, 35,* 107–109.

Cantril, H., & Allport, G. (1933). Recent applications of the study of values. *Journal of Abnormal and Social Psychology, 28,* 259–273.

Cantril, H., & Allport, G. (1935). *The psychology of radio.* New York: Harper.

Cavanagh, B. (1935). *The key to graphology.* Detroit: Cavanagh & Cavanagh.

Cawalti, J. (1965). *Apostles of the self-made man.* Chicago: University of Chicago Press.

Clarke, W. (1900). *A study of Christian missions.* New York: Scribner.

Coben, S. (1991). *Rebellion against Victorianism: The impetus for cultural change in 1920s America.* New York: Oxford University Press.

Coe, G. A. (1928). *The motives of men.* New York: Scribner.

Cohler, B. (1993). Describing lives: Gordon Allport and the "science" of personality. In K. Craik, R. Hogan, & R. Wolfe (Eds.), *Fifty years of personality psychology.* New York: Plenum Press: 131–146.

Collini, S. (1985). The idea of "character" in Victorian political thought. *Transactions of the Royal Historical Society, 35,* 29–50.

Conant, J. (1970). *My several lives: Memoirs of a social inventor.* New York: Harper & Row.

Coon, D. (1992). Testing the limits of sense and science: American experimental psychologists combat spiritualism, 1880–1920. *American Psychologist, 47,* 143–151.

Coon, D. (2000). Salvaging the self in a world without a soul: William James's "The principles of psychology." *History of Psychology, 3,* 83–103.

Craik, K. (1993). The 1937 Allport and Stagner texts in personality psychology. In K. Craik, R. Hogan, & R. Wolfe (Eds.), *Fifty years of personality psychology* (pp. 3–20). New York: Plenum Press.

Craik, K., Hogan, R., & Wolfe, R. (Eds.). (1993). *Fifty years of personality psychology.* New York: Plenum Press.

Croly, H. (1909). *The promise of American life.* New York: Macmillan.

Cross, W. (1950). *The burned-over district: The social and intellectual history of enthusiastic religion in western New York, 1800–1850.* Ithaca, NY: Cornell University Press.

Cunningham, C. (1992). *"A certain and reasoned art": The rise and fall of character education in America.* Unpublished master's thesis, University of Chicago.

Cushman, P. (1990). Why the self is empty: Toward a historically situated psychology. *American Psychologist, 45,* 599–611.

Danziger, K. (1979). The positivist repudiation of Wundt. *Journal of the History of the Behavioral Sciences, 15,* 205–230.

Danziger, K. (1983). Origins and basic principles of Wundt's völkerpsychologie. *British Journal of Social Psychology, 22,* 303–313.

Danziger, K. (1990). *Constructing the subject: historical origins of psychological research.* Cambridge, England: Cambridge University Press.

Danziger, K. (1992). The project of an experimental social psychology: Historical perspectives. *Science in Context, 5,* 309–328.

Danziger, K. (1997). *Naming the mind: How psychology found its language.* London: Sage.

Dehue, T. (1995). *Changing the rules: Psychology in the Netherlands, 1900–1985.* New York: Cambridge University Press.

Dennis, W. (Ed.). (1948). *Readings in the history of psychology.* New York: Appleton-Century-Crofts.

Dewey, J. (1922). *Human nature and conduct: An introduction to social psychology.* New York: Modern Library.

Dewey, J. (1930). *Individualism old and new.* New York: Minton, Balch.

Dewey, J. (1935). *Liberalism & social action.* New York: Capricorn Books.

Dieter, M. (1980). *The holiness revival of the nineteenth century.* Metuchen, NJ: Scarecrow Press.

Diggans, J. (1973). *The American left in the twentieth century.* New York: Harcourt Brace.

Digman, J. (1990). Personality structure: Emergence of the five-factor model. *Annual Review of Psychology, 41,* 417–440.

Downey, J. (1919). *Graphology and the psychology of handwriting.* Baltimore: Warwick and York.

Downey, J. (1920). The adolescent will-profile. *Journal of Educational Psychology, 11,* 157–164.

Eksteins, M. (1989). *Rites of spring: The Great War and the birth of the modern age.* Toronto, Ontario: Lester and Orpen.

Eliot, C. (1906). Address to new students, October 1, 1906. *Harvard Graduates Magazine, 15,* 222.

Elms, A. (1993). Allport's *Personality* and Allport's personality. In K. Craik, R. Hogan, & R. Wolfe (Eds.), *Fifty years of personality psychology* (pp. 39–56). New York: Plenum Press.

Evans, R. I., & Allport, G. W. (1971). *Gordon Allport, the man and his ideas.* New York: Dutton.

Eysenck, H. (1990). *Rebel with a cause: The autobiography of Hans Eysenck.* London: W. H. Allen.

Fancher, R. (1985). *The intelligence men: Makers of the IQ controversy.* New York: Norton.

Fancher, R. (1989). *Gordon W. Allport: A reminiscence.* Unpublished manuscript.

Fancher, R. (2000). Snapshots of Freud in America, 1899–1999. *American Psychologist, 55,* 1025–1028.

Farr, J. (1989). Understanding conceptual change politically, *Political innovation and conceptual change* (pp. 24–49). New York: Cambridge University Press.

Fass, P. (1977). *The damned and the beautiful: American youth in the 1920s*. New York: Oxford University Press.

Fernald, G. (1920). Character vs. intelligence in personality studies. *The Journal of Abnormal Psychology, 15*, 1–10.

Fernberger, S. W. (1928). Statistical analysis of the members and associates of the American Psychological Association in 1928. *Psychological Review, 35*, 447–465.

Fernberger, S. W. (1938). The scientific interests and scientific publications of the American Psychological Association. *Psychological Bulletin, 35*, 261–281.

Fields of concentration: Psychology. (1936, May 1). *The Harvard Crimson*.

Finison, L. J. (1976). Unemployment, politics, and the history of organized psychology. *American Psychologist, 31*, 747–755.

Finison, L. J. (1979). An aspect of the early history of the Society for the Psychological Study of Social Issues: Psychologists and labor. *Journal of the History of the Behavorial Sciences, 15*, 29–37.

Fisher, A. (1922). Introduction. *Personality Magazine*.

Ford, J. (1923). Introduction. In J. Ford (Ed.), *Social problems and social policy* (pp. 1–7). Boston: Ginn.

Ford, J. (1930). Social ethics, 1905–1929. In S. Morison (Ed.), *Development of Harvard University, 1869–1929* (pp. 223–230). Cambridge, MA: Harvard University Press.

Foucault, M. (1979). *Discipline & punish*. New York: Vintage.

Fox, R. (1993). The culture of liberal Protestant progressivism. *Journal of Interdisciplinary history, 23*(3), 639–660.

Freedman, E. (1996). *Maternal justice: Miriam Van Waters and the female reform tradition*. Chicago: University of Chicago Press.

Freeman, F. (1926). *Mental tests*. Boston: Houghton Mifflin.

Freund, E. (1917). *Standards of American legislation*. Chicago: University of Chicago Press.

Fuller, R. C. (1986). *Americans and the unconscious*. Oxford: Oxford University Press.

Fuller, R. (1988). Psychological religiousness: Resisting the tide of disenchantment. *Pastoral Psychology, 36*(3), 146–163.

Furumoto, L. (1988). Shared knowledge: The experimentalists, 1904–1929. In J. Morawski (Ed.), *The rise of experimentation in American psychology* (pp. 94–113). New Haven, CT: Yale University Press.

Furumoto, L. (1998). Gender and the history of psychology. In B. M. Clinchy & J. K. Norem (Eds.), *The gender and psychology reader* (pp. 69–77). New York: New York University Press.

Gates, C. (1940). *Not only me*. Princeton, NJ: Princeton University Press.

Gay, P. (1988). *Freud: A life for our time*. New York: Norton.

Geuter, U. (1992). *The professionalization of psychology in Nazi Germany*. Cambridge, England: Cambridge University Press.

Ghougassian, J. (1972). *Gordon Allport's ontopsychology of the person*. New York: Philosophical Library.

Gieryn, T. (1983). Boundary-work and the demarcation of science from nonscience: Strains and interests in professional ideologies of scientists. *American Sociological Review, 48*, 781–795.

Gould, A. (1922–1923). Psychology in social case work. *Journal of Abnormal and Social Psychology, 17*, 405–409.

Gould, A. (1923–1924). [Review of the book *Case studies one to twenty*]. *Journal of Abnormal and Social Psychology, 18*, 286–289.

Greenwood, K. (1965). *Robert College: The American founders*. Unpublished doctoral dissertation, Johns Hopkins University, Baltimore, MD.

Griggs, E. H. (1908). *The new humanism: Studies in personal and social development*. New York: B.W. Huebsch. (Original work published 1899)

Gutman, H. (1973). Work, culture, and society in industrializing America, 1815–1919. *The American Historical Review, 78*, 531–588.

Hale, M. (1980). *Human science and social order: Hugo Münsterberg and the origins of applied psychology*. Philadelphia: Temple University Press.

Hamlin, W. (1913). Harvard and social service. *Harvard Illustrated Magazine*, 547–549.

Hankins, T. (1979). In defense of biography: The use of biography in the history of science. *History of Science, 17*, 1–16.

Hardesty, F. (1976). Louis William Stern. *Annals of the New York Academy of Sciences, 270*, 31–44.

Harrington, A. (1991). Interwar "German" psychobiology: Between nationalism and the irrational. *Science in Context, 4*, 429–447.

Harris, B. (1997). Repoliticizing the history of psychology. In D. Fox & I. Prilleltensky (Eds.), *Critical psychology* (pp. 21–33). London: Sage.

Harris, B. (1998). The perils of a public intellectual. *Journal of Social Issues, 54*, 79–118.

Hartmann, G. (1939). Value as a unifying concept of the social sciences. *Journal of Social Psychology, 10*, 563–575.

Hatch, N. (1994). The puzzle of American Methodism. *Church History, 63*, 175–189.

Hearnshaw, L. S. (1964). *A short history of British psychology*. New York: Barnes and Noble.

Heidbreder, E. (1973). William McDougall and social psychology. In M. Henle, J. Jaynes, & J. Sullivan (Eds.), *Historical conceptions of psychology* (pp. 267–275). New York: Springer.

High, R., & Woodward, W. (1980). William James and Gordon Allport: Parallels in their maturing conceptions of self and personality. In R. Rieber & K.

Salzinger (Eds.), *Psychology: Theoretical-historical perspectives* (pp. 57–79). New York: Academic Press.

Hilgard, E. (1974). Ernest Ropiequet Hilgard. In G. Lindzey (Ed.), *A history of psychology in autobiography* (Vol. 6, pp. 131–160). Englewood Cliffs, NJ: Prentice Hall.

Hill, P. (1985). *The world their household: The American woman's foreign missionary movement and cultural transformation, 1870–1920.* Ann Arbor: University of Michigan Press.

Hofstadter, R. (1989). *The American political tradition.* New York: Vintage.

Hollingworth, H. L. (1923). *Judging human character.* New York: Appleton.

Hollingworth, H. L. (1938). [Review of the book *Personality: A psychological interpretation*]. *Psychological Bulletin, 35,* 103–107.

Holstein, J., & Gubrium, J. (2000). *The self we live by: Narrative identity in a postmodern world.* New York: Oxford University Press.

Holt, E. B. (1915). *The Freudian wish and its place in ethics.* New York: Holt.

Holt, R. (1962). Individuality and generalization in the psychology of personality. *Journal of Personality, 30,* 377–404.

Homans, G. C. (1984). *Coming to my senses: The autobiography of a sociologist.* New Brunswick, NJ: Transaction Books.

Homans, P. (1982). A personal struggle with religion: Significant fact in the lives and work of the first psychologists. *The Journal of Religion, 62*(2), 128–144.

Hornstein, G. (1992). The return of the repressed: Psychology's problematic relations with psychoanalysis, 1909–1960. *American Psychologist, 47,* 254–263.

Hutchison, W. (1992). *The modernist impulse in American Protestantism.* Durham, NC: Duke University Press.

James, W. (1897). *The will to believe and other essays in popular philosophy.* New York: Longmans, Green.

James, W. (1911). *Memories and studies.* New York: Longmans, Green.

James, W. (1955). *Pragmatism.* New York: Meridian Books. (Original work published 1907)

James, W. (1977). *A pluralistic universe.* Cambridge, MA: Harvard University Press. (Original work published 1909)

James, W. (1982a). Emerson. In F. Burkhardt (Ed.) *Essays in religion and morality* (pp. 109–115). Cambridge, MA: Harvard University Press. (Original work published in 1903)

James, W. (1982b). *The varieties of religious experience.* New York: Penguin. (Original work published 1902)

James, W. (1983). *The principles of psychology.* Cambridge, MA: Harvard University Press. (Original work published 1890)

Jarrett, M. (1919). The psychiatric thread running through all social case work. *Proceedings of the Conference of Social Work, 46,* 587–593.

Jenkins, P. (2000). *Mystics and messiahs: Cults and new religions in American history.* New York: Oxford University Press.

John, O., & Robins, R. (1993). Gordon Allport: Father and critic of the five-factor model. In K. Craik, R. Hogan, & R. Wolfe (Eds.), *Fifty years of personality psychology* (pp. 215–236). New York: Plenum Press.

Jung, C. (1933). *Modern man in search of a soul.* New York: Harvest.

Katz, D. (1979). Floyd H. Allport. *American Psychologist, 34,* 351–353.

Keller, E. F. (1985). *Reflections on gender and science.* New Haven, CT: Yale University Press.

King, W. (1989). An enthusiasm for humanity: The social emphasis in religion and its accommodation in Protestant theology. In M. Lacey (Ed.), *Religion and twentieth-century American intellectual life* (pp. 49–77). New York: Cambridge University Press.

Knudson, A. (1927). *The philosophy of personalism.* New York: Abingdon Press.

Kreppner, K. (1992). William L. Stern, 1871–1938: A neglected founder of developmental psychology. *Developmental Psychology, 28,* 539–547.

Kuklick, B. (1977). *The rise of American philosophy.* New Haven, CT: Yale University Press.

Külpe, O. (1895). *Outlines of psychology.* New York: Macmillan.

Kunzel, R. (1988). The professionalization of benevolence: Evangelicals and social workers in the Florence Crittenton Homes, 1915–1945. *Journal of Social History, 22,* 20–43.

Lamiell, J., & Deutsch, W. (2000). In the light of the star: An introduction to William Stern's critical personalism. *Theory & Psychology, 10,* 715–730.

Langfeld, H., & Allport, F. (1916). *An elementary laboratory course in psychology* (2nd ed.). New York: Houghton Mifflin.

Lasswell, H. (1938). [Review of the book *Personality: A psychological interpretation*]. *Ethics, 49,* 105–107.

Latour, B. (1987). *Science in action.* Cambridge, MA: Harvard University Press.

Lears, T. J. J. (1981). *No place of grace: Antimodernism and the transformation of American culture.* New York: Pantheon Books.

Leary, D. (1987). Telling likely stories: The rhetoric of the new psychology, 1880–1920. *Journal of the History of the Behavioral Sciences, 23,* 315–331.

Leary, D. (1990). William James on the self and personality: Clearing the ground for subsequent theorists, researchers, and practitioners. In M. Johnson & T. Henley (Eds.), *Reflections on* The Principles of Psychology: *William James after a century* (pp. 101–137). Hillsdale, NJ: Erlbaum.

Leonard, W. (1927). *The locomotive god.* New York: Century.

Lewontin, R. C. (1986). [Review of the book *In the name of eugenics*]. *ISIS, 77,* 314–317.

Leys, R. (1991). Types of one: Adolf Meyer's life chart and the representation of individuality. *Representations, 34,* 1–28.

Lipset, S., & Riesman, D. (1975). *Education and politics at Harvard*. New York: McGraw-Hill.

Lowell, A. L. (1934). *At war with academic traditions in America*. Cambridge, MA: Harvard University Press.

Lowenthall, D. (1985). *The past is a foreign country*. New York: Cambridge University Press.

Lubove, R. (1965). *The professional altruist: The emergence of social work as a career, 1890–1930*. Cambridge, MA: Harvard University Press.

Lunbeck, E. (1994). *The psychiatric persuasion: Knowledge, gender, and power in modern America*. Princeton, NJ: Princeton University Press.

Macleod, D. (1983). *Building character in the American boy: The Boy Scouts, YMCA and their forerunners, 1870–1920*. Madison: University of Wisconsin Press.

Magnusson, D., & Törestad, B. (1993). A holistic view of personality: A model revisited. *Annual Review of Psychology, 44*, 427–452.

Maslow, A. (1937). Personality and patterns of culture. In R. Stagner (Ed.), *Psychology of personality* (pp. 408–428). New York: McGraw-Hill.

McCormack, T. (1931). Personality: A study in the history of verbal meanings. *Mental Hygiene, 15*, 34–44.

McDougall, W. (1921). *Is America safe for democracy?* New York: Scribner.

McDougall, W. (1927). *Character and the conduct of life: Practical psychology for everyman*. London: Methuen.

McDougall, W. (1928). *An outline of psychology* (4th ed.). London: Methuen.

McDougall, W. (1930a). William McDougall. In C. Murchison (Ed.), *A history of psychology in autobiography* (Volume 1, pp. 191–223). Worcester, MA: Clark University Press.

McDougall, W. (1930b). The hormic psychology. In C. Murchison (Ed.), *Psychologies of 1930* (pp. 3–36). Worcester, MA: Clark University Press.

Mead, M. (1939). *From the south seas*. New York: Morrow.

Meltzer, B., Petras, J., & Reynolds, L. (1975). *Symbolic interactionism: Genesis, varieties and criticism*. London: Routledge.

Michaels, W. (1989). An American tragedy, or the promise of American life. *Representations, 25*, 71–98.

Milar, K. (2000). The first generation of women psychologists and the psychology of women. *American Psychologist, 55*, 616–619.

Minton, H. L. (2000). Psychology and gender at the turn of the century. *American Psychologist, 55*, 613–615.

Misiak, H., & Sexton, V. (1966). *History of psychology*. New York: Grune & Stratton.

Moddelmog, W. (1998). Disowning "personality": Privacy and subjectivity in *The House of Mirth*. *American Literature, 70*, 337–363.

Monte, C. (1991). *Beneath the mask: An introduction to theories of personality*. Forth Worth, TX: Holt, Rinehart & Winston.

Moore, H. T. (1916). A method of testing the strength of instincts. *American Journal of Psychology, 27*, 227–233.

Moore, H. T., & Gilliland, A. R. (1921). The measurement of aggressiveness. *Journal of Applied Psychology, 5*, 97–118.

Moore, R. L. (1986). *Religious outsiders and the making of Americans.* New York: Oxford University Press.

Moore, T. (1996). *The re-enchantment of everyday life.* New York: HarperCollins.

Morawski, J. (1986). Psychologists for society and societies for psychologists: SPSSI's place among professional organizations. *Journal of Social Issues, 42*(1), 111–126.

Morawski, J., & Hornstein, G. (1991). Quandary of the quacks: The struggle for expert knowledge in American psychology, 1890–1940. In J. Brown & D. V. Keuren (Eds.), *The estate of social knowledge* (pp. 106–133). Baltimore, MD: Johns Hopkins University Press.

Morey, L. (1987). Observations on the meeting between Allport and Freud. *Psychoanalytic Review, 74*, 135–139.

Morison, S. (1965). *Three centuries of Harvard.* Cambridge, MA: Harvard University Press.

McCulloh, G., & Smith, T. (1964). The theology and practices of Methodism, 1876–1919. In E. Bucke (Ed.), *The history of American Methodism* (pp. 592–659). New York: Abingdon Press.

Mullet, M. (1929, May). What your handwriting tells about you. *American,* p. 24.

Münsterberg, H. (1914). *Psychology: General and applied.* New York: Appleton.

Murphy, G., Murphy, L., & Newcomb, T. (1937). *Experimental social psychology: An interpretation of research upon the socialization of the individual.* New York: Harper & Brothers.

Murray, H. (1981). Psychology and the university. In E. Shneidman (Ed.), *Endeavors in psychology: Selections from the personology of Henry A. Murray* (pp. 337–351). New York: Harper & Row.

Myerson, A. (1919). Multiple choice method of studying personality. *Archives of neurology and psychopathology,* 459–470.

Napoli, D. (1981). *Architects of adjustment: The history of the psychological profession in the United States.* Port Washington, NY: Kennikat Press.

Nicholson, I. (1994). Academic professionalization and Protestant reconstruction, 1890–1902: George Albert Coe's psychology of religion. *Journal of the History of the Behavioral Sciences, 30*, 348–368.

Nicholson, I. (1997a). The politics of scientific social reform, 1936–1960: Goodwin Watson & the Society for the Psychological Study of Social Issues. *Journal of the History of the Behavioral Sciences, 33*, 39–60.

Nicholson, I. (1997b). To "correlate psychology and social ethics": Gordon Allport and the first course in American personality psychology. *Journal of Personality, 65*, 733–742.

Nicholson, I. A. M. (1998). The approved bureaucratic torpor: Goodwin Watson, critical psychology, and the dilemmas of expertise. *Journal of Social Issues, 54,* 29–52.

Niebuhr, R. (1928). *Does civilization need religion?* New York: Macmillan.

O'Brien, L. (1985). "A bold plunge into the sea of values": The career of Dr. Richard Cabot. *New England Quarterly, 58,* 533–553.

O'Donnell, J. (1979). The crisis of experimentalism in the 1920s. *American Psychologist, 34*(4), 289–295.

O'Donnell, J. (1985). *The origins of behaviorism: American psychology, 1870–1920.* New York: New York University Press.

Pandora, K. (1997). *Rebels within the ranks: Psychologist's critique of scientific authority and democratic realities in New Deal America.* New York: Cambridge University Press.

Pandora, K. (1998). "Mapping the new mental world created by radio": Media messages, cultural politics, and Cantril and Allport's "The Psychology of Radio." *Journal of Social Issues, 54,* 7–27.

Parker, J. (1991). *In search of the person: The historical development of American personality psychology.* Unpublished doctoral dissertation, York University, Toronto, Ontario.

Paterson, D. (1936). Proceedings of the 44th annual meeting of the American Psychological Association. *Psychological Bulletin, 33,* 677–816.

Pells, R. (1973). *Radical visions & American dreams.* New York: Harper & Row.

Perry, R. B. (1930). Psychology. In S. Morison (Ed.), *Development of Harvard University, 1869–1929* (pp. 216–223). Cambridge, MA: Harvard University Press.

Peter Dodge, veteran, actor and teacher, dies. (1965, February 22). *The Utica Daily Press,* p. 30.

Pfister, J. (1997). Glamorizing the psychological: The politics and performances of modern psychological identities. In J. Pfister & N. Schnog (Eds.), *Inventing the psychological: Toward a cultural history of emotional life in America* (pp. 167–213). New Haven, CT: Yale University Press.

Post, D. (1980). Floyd H. Allport and the launching of modern social psychology. *Journal of the History of the Behavioral Sciences, 16,* 369–376.

Potts, D. (1965). Social ethics at Harvard, 1881–1931: A study in academic activism. In P. Buck (Ed.), *Social sciences at Harvard, 1860–1920* (pp. 91–128). Cambridge, MA: Harvard University Press.

Potts, J. (1891). John Wesley and his Mother. *Canadian Methodist Magazine, 33,* 255.

Pound, R. (1923). Criminal justice and the American city. In J. Ford (Ed.), *Social problems and social policy* (pp. 911–917). Boston: Ginn.

Powers, E. (1930). *Graphic factors in relation to personality: An experimental study.* Unpublished master's thesis, Dartmouth College, Hanover, NH.

Pratt, C. (1958). Herbert Sidney Langfeld. *Psychological Review, 65,* 321–324.

Pressey, S. L., & Pressey, L. L. (1919). Cross-out tests with suggestions as to a group scale of the emotions. *Journal of Applied Psychology, 3,* 138–150.

Prince, M. (1973). *The unconscious.* New York: Arno Press. (Original work published 1921)

Prince, M. (1978). *The dissociation of a personality.* New York: Oxford University Press. (Original work published 1905)

Randall, J. H. (1912). *The culture of personality.* New York: H. M. Caldwell.

Reed, J. (1936). Almost thirty. *New Republic, 86,* 332–333.

Richards, G. (1995). "To know our fellow men to do them good": American psychology's enduring moral project. *History of the Human Sciences, 8,* 1–24.

Richards, J. (1987). "Passing the love of women": Manly love and Victorian society. In J. A. Mangan & J. Walvin (Eds.), *Manliness and morality: Middle class masculinity in Britain and America, 1800–1940* (pp. 92–122). New York: St. Martin's Press.

Richmond, M. (1917). *Social diagnosis.* New York: Russell Sage.

Richmond, M. (1922). *What is social case work?* New York: Russell Sage.

Richmond, M. (1923). Social case work as personality development. In J. Ford (Ed.), *Social problems and social policy* (pp. 715–719). Boston: Ginn.

Ringer, F. (1969). *The decline of the German mandarins: The German academic community, 1890–1933.* Cambridge, MA: Harvard University Press.

Roback, A. A. (1927a). *A bibliography of character and personality.* Cambridge, MA: Sci-Art Publishers.

Roback, A. A. (1927b). *The psychology of character.* New York: Harcourt.

Roback, A. A. (1928). *Popular psychology.* Cambridge, MA: Sci-Art Publishers.

Roback, A. A. (1932–1933). Personality tests—Whither? *Character & Personality, 1,* 214–224.

Roback, A. A. (1937–1938). [Review of the book *Personality: A psychological interpretation*]. *Character & Personality, 6,* 243–249.

Robinson, F. (1992). *Love's story told: A life of Henry A. Murray.* Cambridge, MA: Harvard University Press.

Romanyshyn, R. (1971). Method and meaning in psychology: The method has been the message. *Journal of Phenomenological Psychology, 2*(1), 93–113.

Roosevelt, T. (1913, November 8). Character and civilization. *Outlook, 105,* 527–528.

Rosanoff, A. (1920). A theory of personality based mainly on psychiatric experience. *Psychological Bulletin, 17,* 281–299.

Rose, N. (1992). Engineering the human soul: Analyzing psychological expertise. *Science in Context, 5,* 351–369.

Rose, N. (1996). A critical history of psychology. In N. Rose (Ed.), *Inventing our selves: Psychology, power, and personhood* (pp. 41–66). New York: Cambridge University Press.

Rosenzweig, S. (1970). E. G. Boring and the zeitgeist. *Journal of Psychology, 75,* 59–71.

Ross, D. (1991). *The origins of American social science.* Cambridge, England: Cambridge University Press.

Rotundo, E. A. (1993). *American manhood: Transformations in masculinity from the revolution to the modern era.* New York: Basic Books.

Rugg, H. (1921). Is the rating of human character possible? *Journal of Educational Psychology, 12,* 81–93.

Ruggiero, K., & Kelman, H. (1999). Introduction to prejudice and intergroup relations: Papers in honor of Gordon W. Allport's centennial. *Journal of Social Issue, 55,* 405–414.

Samelson, F. (1977). World War I intelligence testing and the development of psychology. *Journal of the History of the Behavioral Sciences, 13,* 274–282.

Samelson, F. (1985). Organizing for the kingdom of behavior: Academic battles and organizational policies in the twenties. *Journal of the History of the Behavioral Sciences, 21,* 33–47.

Samelson, F. (1992). The APA between the world wars: 1918 to 1941. In R. Evans, V. Sexton, & T. Cadwallader (Eds.), *The American Psychological Association: A historical perspective* (pp. 119–147). Washington, DC: American Psychological Association.

Sapir, E. (1933). Personality. In E. Seligman (Ed.), *Encyclopedia of the social sciences* (pp. 85–88). New York: Macmillan.

Schafer, R., Berg, I., & McCandless, B. (1951). Report on survey of current psychological testing practices. *Supplement to Newsletter, Division of Clinical & Abnormal Psychology, American Psychological Association, 4*(5).

Shakow, D. (1976). Reflections on a do-it-yourself training program in clinical psychology, *Journal of the History of the Behavioral Sciences, 12,* 14–30.

Shi, D. (1985). *The simple life: Plain living and high thinking in American culture.* New York: Oxford University Press.

Singal, D. (1987). Towards a definition of American modernism. *American Quarterly, 39,* 7–26.

Singer, M. (1961). A survey of culture and personality theory and research. In B. Kaplan (Ed.), *Studying personality cross culturally* (pp. 9–90). New York: Harper & Row.

Skinner, B. F. (1979). *The shaping of a behaviorist* (Vol. 2). New York: Knopf.

Sloan, T. (1997). Theories of personality: Ideology and beyond. In D. Fox & I. Prilleltensky, *Critical psychology: An introduction* (pp. 87–103). London: Sage.

Smiles, S. (1853). *Self-help: With illustrations of character, conduct and perseverance.* New York: A. L. Burt.

Smiles, S. (1875). *Character.* London: John Murray.

Smith, M. B. (1989). Comment on "The case of William McDougall." *American Psychologist, 44,* 446.

Smith, M. B. (1993). Allport and Murray on Allport's *Personality*: A confrontation.

In K. Craik, R. Hogan, & R. Wolfe (Eds.), *Fifty years of personality psychology* (pp. 57–65). New York: Plenum Press.

Smith, R. (1992). *Inhibition: History & meaning in the sciences of mind & brain.* Berkeley: University of California Press.

Smith, R. (1997). *History of the human sciences.* New York: Norton.

Söderqvist, T. (1996). Existential projects and existential choice in science: Science biography as an edifying genre. In M. Shortland & R. Yeo (Eds.), *Telling lives in science: Essays on scientific biography* (pp. 45–84). New York: Cambridge University Press.

Sokal, M. (1987a). James McKeen Cattell and mental anthropometry: Nineteenth-century science and reform and the origins of psychological testing. In M. Sokal (Ed.), *Psychological testing and American society* (pp. 21–45). New Brunswick, NJ: Rutgers University Press.

Sokal, M. (Ed.). (1987b). *Psychological testing and American society.* New Brunswick: Rutgers University Press.

Spaulding, E. (1921). The role of personality development in the reconstruction of the delinquent. *Journal of Abnormal and Social Psychology, 16,* 97–114.

Spranger, E. (1928). *Types of men: The psychology and ethics of personality* (P. Pigors, Trans.). Halle, Germany: Max Niemeyer Verlag. (Original work published 1914)

Stagner, R. (1937). *Psychology of personality.* New York: McGraw-Hill.

Stagner, R. (1938). [Review of the book *Personality: A psychological interpretation*]. *Journal of Applied Psychology, 22,* 219–221.

Stagner, R. (1986). Reminiscences about the founding of SPSSI. *Journal of Social Issues, 42*(1), 35–42.

Stagner, R. (1993). Fifty years of the psychology of personality: Reminiscences. In K. Craik, R. Hogan, & R. Wolfe (Eds.), *Fifty years of personality psychology* (pp. 23–38). New York: Plenum Press.

Starr, P. (1982). *The social transformation of American medicine.* New York: Basic Books.

Steffens, L. (1905). Ohio: A tale of two cities. *McClure's, 25,* 293–311.

Stern, W. (1917). Hugo Münsterberg: In memoriam. *Journal of Applied Psychology, 1,* 186–188.

Stern, W. (1930). William Stern. In C. Murchison (Ed.), *A history of psychology in autobiography* (Vol. 1, pp. 335–388). New York: Russell & Russell.

Stern, W. (1938). *General psychology from the personalistic standpoint.* New York: Macmillan.

Susman, W. (1979). "Personality" and the making of twentieth-century culture. In J. Higham & P. Conkin (Eds.), *New directions in American intellectual history* (pp. 212–226). Baltimore: Johns Hopkins University Press.

Symonds, P. (1924). The present status of character measurement. *Journal of Education Research, 15,* 484–498.

Szasz, F. (1981). The stress on "character and service" in Progressive America. *Mid-America, 63,* 145–156.

Taylor, E. (1992). The case for a uniquely American Jamesian tradition in psychology. In M. Donnelly (Ed.), *Reinterpreting the legacy of William James* (pp. 3–28). Washington, DC: American Psychological Association.

Thornton, T. (1996). *Handwriting in America: A cultural history.* New Haven, CT: Yale University Press.

Thurber, E. (1921). Character. *North American Review, 214,* 664–670.

Todd, A. (1920). *The scientific spirit and social work.* New York: Macmillan.

Triplet, R. (1983). *Henry A. Murray and the Harvard Psychological Clinic, 1926–1938.* Unpublished doctoral dissertation, University of New Hampshire, Durham.

Tweney, R. (1987). Programmatic research in experimental psychology: E. B. Titchener's laboratory investigations, 1891–1927. In M. Ash & W. Woodward (Eds.), *Psychology in twentieth-century thought and society* (pp. 35–57). New York: Cambridge University Press.

Vandenberg, B. (1993). Developmental psychology, God and the good. *Theory & Psychology, 3*(2), 191–205.

Vernon, P. (1933). The American and the German methods of approach to the study of temperament and personality. *British Journal of Psychology, 24,* 156–177.

Vernon, P. (1968). Obituary—Gordon Willard Allport. *British Journal of Psychology, 59,* 103.

Vernon, P. (1978). The making of a psychologist. In T. S. Krawlec (Ed.), *The psychologists* (Vol. 3, pp. 303–314). Brandon, VT: Clinical Psychology Publishing.

Vernon, P., & Allport, G. (1931). A test for personal values. *Journal of Abnormal and Social Psychology, 26,* 231–248.

Veysey, L. (1965). *The emergence of the American university.* Chicago: University of Chicago Press.

Wallas, G. (1921). *Our social heritage.* New Haven, CT: Yale University Press.

Warner, H. (1964). *Progressivism in Ohio.* Columbus: Ohio State University Press.

Watson, G. (1925). *The measurement of fair-mindedness.* Unpublished doctoral dissertation, Teachers College, Columbia University, New York.

Watson, G. (1934). Psychology in Germany and Austria. *Psychological Bulletin, 31,* 755–776.

Watson, J. (1919). *Psychology from the standpoint of the behaviorist.* Philadelphia: Lippincott.

Watson, J. (1948). Psychology as the behaviorist views it. In W. Dennis (Ed.), *Readings in the history of psychology.* New York: Appleton-Century-Croft. (Original work published 1913)

Wiebe, R. (1967). *The search for order, 1877–1920.* New York: Hill & Wang.

Williams, R. (1976). *Keywords: A vocabulary of culture and society*. New York: Oxford University Press.

Winter, D. (1993). Gordon Allport and "Letters from Jenny." In K. Craik, R. Hogan, & R. Wolfe (Eds.), *Fifty years of personality psychology* (pp. 147–163). New York: Plenum Press.

Winter, D. (1996). Gordon Allport and legend of "Rinehart." *Journal of Personality, 64*, 263–273.

Woolf, V. (1924). Mr. Bennett and Mrs. Brown.

Zenderland, L. (1998). Biblical biology: American protestant social reformers and the early eugenics movement. *Science in Context, 11*, 511–525.

INDEX

Collegiality, and Harvard psychology department in 1920s, 168
Commercialism, Allport opposes, 220
Commercialization, and psychoanalysis, 199
Communism, 195. *See also* Soviet Union
Conant, James B., 184–185, 186, 187, 188
"Concepts of Trait and Personality" (Allport paper), 150
Constantinople, Allport as missionary in, 56, 57–59, 60, 63–64, 70–71
  and Peter Dodge, 61–62
  nostalgia for, 74
  and reformist spirit, 134
  and religious aestheticism, 64–66
  return to U.S., 66–68
  and scientific psychology, 123
  and spiritual mooring, 125
Consumer culture, Allport on, 125
Cook, Alice, 147
Coolidge, Calvin, 55
Coon, Deborah, 162
Cowley, Malcolm, 31
Cram, Ralph, 124
Critical historiography, 6, 227n.22
Croly, Herbert, 37–38
Cully, H. H., 27
Cultural politics, of personality, 6–8, 225–226
Culture, and personality (Allport), 196–198, 221
Culture of personality, 6, 36–38, 221
  academic, 78–81
  and pleasures of present, 98
"Culture and personality" studies, 195–196, 199, 216
Cunningham, Craig, 15

Danziger, Kurt, 8, 10, 222
Dartmouth College, Allport at, 144–145, 168, 175, 204, 253n.43
Dashiell, John, 214
Dearborn, Walter, 40, 81–82, 103
Dehue, Trudy, 175
Dehumanization, danger of, 88
Depression of 1930s, 191–192, 216
  Deweyan psychology inspired by, 196
  and need to affirm individual, 197
  and reevaluation of individualism, 195
Depth psychology, Allport on, 70

Dessoir, Max, 106, 200
Dewey, John, 155, 192, 196
Diagnosing Personality and Conduct (Symonds), 152, 179–180
Dictionary of Psychology, Allport as commentator for, 163
Differential diagnosis, in casework model of social work, 36
Digman, John, 226
Dilthey, Wilhelm, 114, 118, 177, 180
Diseases of Personality, The (Ribot), 80
Dissociation of Personality, The (Prince), 3
Diversity
  at Harvard, 168
  and social work, 36
Dodge, Pete, 61–62, 104, 136, 235n.29
Downey, June, 161, 174
Drummond, Henry, 14
Dunlap, Knight, 166, 193, 200, 215, 252n.10
Duty, Allport's dedication to, 136
"Duty of Scholarship, The" (Lowell), 30

Ebbinghaus, Hermann, 115
Eddy, Mary Baker, 45
Educational psychology, Allport's interest in, 134–135
Eksteins, Modris, 73
Elective system, at Harvard, 30
Elementarism (elementaristic psychology), 115, 118, 119, 122
Elementaristic personality psychology, 122
Eliot, Charles, 29–30, 51
Emerson, Ralph Waldo, 5
  on intellectual independence, 126–127
  on "Sovereignty of Ethics," 138
Empiricism, James on practice of, 48–49
"Enchanted epistemology," 111, 199
Enlightenment, and German mandarin culture, 110
Episcopal Theological School, Allport as consultant for, 204
Ethical categories
  and double meaning of personality, 151–152
  psychology's aversion to, 151
Ethics, in Allport's personality-study synthesis, 162

as spiritual consciousness, 47

See also Anglo-Catholicism; Free
    Methodism; Methodism; Mission-
    ary vocation; Spirituality; Unitar-
    ianism

Religious aestheticism
    Allport's experience of, 64–66
        and Gould, 100
    and Allport's search for meaning, 71

Religious theorists, and personality, 7

Religious type, of Spranger, 120, 121

Revouvier, Charles, 112

Reynolds, Larry, 205

Rhetorical style
    of Allport, 163–164
    of Murray, 184

Ribot, 80

Richards, Graham, 8, 221

Richards, Jeffrey, 62

Richmond, Mary, 35, 36, 39, 90, 91, 152,
    237n.8

Roback, A. A., 4, 150, 150–151, 153,
    155, 165, 174, 177, 212

Robert College, Constantinople, 58
    Allport as missionary at, 56, 57–59,
        60, 63–64, 70–71
        Cambridge personality contrasted
            with, 104
        and Peter Dodge, 61–62
        nostalgia for, 74
        and religious aestheticism, 64–66
        return to U.S., 66–68

Robins, Richard, 224

Rogers, Carl, 181

Roller skating, 93

Rome, Allport's visit to, 65, 71

Roosevelt, Franklin, 191

Roosevelt, Theodore, 14, 26

Rosanoff, Aaron, 79

Rose, Nikolas, 9, 222

Royce, Josiah, 40, 50, 105

Ruckmick, Christian, 158

St. Sophia, Church of, 65, 71

Samelson, Franz, 81

Samurai, Lowell sees as model, 31

Santayana, George, 29, 50

SATC (Student Army Training Corps),
    51–52, 73

Science (natural)
    Allport on effects of, 198, 199

and Allport as graduate student,
    74–75
and Allport's new Social Ethics course,
    141
in Allport's personality-study synthesis,
    162
and Allport's presentation of ethical
    self, 142
and Allport's psychology, 100, 113,
    126, 156, 224, 225
Allport's questioning of, 50
experimental method of, 157, 176–
    177, 185, 225
vs. Geisteswissenschaften, 114–115,
    118
and German mandarins, 111
Ada Gould on, 99
and 1920s American social science,
    156
vs. normative discourse (Allport), 193
and personality psychology, 9
vs. social ethics, 137
and social work, 35, 36
and Watson's behaviorism, 81

Scientific development, individual vs. so-
    cial model of, 222

"Scientific Spirit and Social Work, The"
    (Todd), 36

Self
    and Allport on personality, 100–101,
        220–221
    disenchantment of, 216
    and James, 162
    19th-century discussions of, 203
    transcendental, 205

Selfhood
    Allport on, 202–203
        cultural or moral milieu separated
            from, 221
    and Allport's work, 6, 82
    and character, 15
    issues in scientific language of, 226
    McDougall on, 78
    and personality, 37, 223
    and personality psychology, 223

Service, Allport's dedication to, 136

Sex Problems Solved (Sears Roebuck mail-
    order book), 199

Sexuality
    and Allport on psychoanalysis, 200
    for Stern, 117

Shakow, David, 83

Urbanization (*continued*)
    and psychology's ambitions, 42
    and shift of values, 28
    social dislocation from, 20

Validity of test measure, 153, 178
Value-direction, and Spranger's ideal
        types, 120
Value(s)
    Allport seeking theory of, 57
    Alllport's study of, 178–179, 180
    and character, 15
    and experimental method, 177
    and Jamesian synthesis, 48
    and moral project of psychology, 8
    and personality psychology (Allport),
        193
Value system, and intuitive method, 158
Varieties of Religious Experience (James),
        125
Vernon, Philip, 145, 177, 179, 201,
        255n.76
    quoted, 3
Verstehen, 158
Volunteerism, benevolent or sentimental,
        35, 36, 53

Wallas, Graham, 89
Ward, Harry F., 46
Warren, Samuel, 80–81
Watson, Goodwin, 87, 192

Watson, John B., 39, 81–82, 83, 91, 141,
    214
Weber, Max, 119
Wertheimer, Max, 106
Wesley, Susanna Annesley, 228n.13
What is Social Case Work? (Richmond),
    39
White, Alfred Tredway, 136–137
Wholeness, in Stern's psychology, 115–
    116
Wiebe, Robert, 28
Will, Stern on, 116
Willard, Frances, 14
Wilson, Edmund, 191
Wise, Mary Ann (grandmother of All-
    port), 16–17
Women
    spirituality attributed to, 15
    See also Femininity
Woods, James, 104
Woodward, Bill, 47, 205
Woolf, Virginia, quoted, 29
Word association technique, 91
World War I, 50–52
    Allport visits battlegrounds of, 73–74
    and Cabot's concern for ethics, 138
    and intelligence testing, 86
Wundt, Wilhelm, 114, 122

Yerkes, Robert, 40
YMCA, and Allport, 34, 125
Youth and Life (Bourne), 38

ABOUT THE AUTHOR

Ian A. M. Nicholson is associate professor of psychology at St. Thomas University in Fredericton, New Brunswick, Canada. A graduate of the History and Theory of Psychology Program at York University, he received the Early Career Award of Division 26 (History of Psychology) of the American Psychological Association and the author of numerous articles on the history of psychology.